Fiscal and Monetary Problems in Developing States

**PRAEGER SPECIAL STUDIES IN
INTERNATIONAL ECONOMICS AND DEVELOPMENT**

Fiscal and Monetary Problems in Developing States

**PROCEEDINGS OF THE
THIRD REHOVOTH CONFERENCE**

Edited by

David Krivine

Published in cooperation with
the Rehovoth Conference on Fiscal and
Monetary Problems in Developing States
by

FREDERICK A. PRAEGER, Publishers
New York · Washington · London

The purpose of the Praeger Special Studies is to make specialized research monographs in U.S. and international economics and politics available to the academic, business, and government communities. For further information, write to the Special Projects Division, Frederick A. Praeger, Publishers, 111 Fourth Avenue, New York, N.Y. 10003.

FREDERICK A. PRAEGER, PUBLISHERS
111 Fourth Avenue, New York, N.Y. 10003, U.S.A.
77–79 Charlotte Street, London W.1, England

Published in the United States of America in 1967
by Frederick A. Praeger, Inc., Publishers

Second printing, 1968

Library of Congress Catalog Card Number: 67–12833

Printed in the United States of America

MESSAGE
TO THE THIRD REHOVOTH CONFERENCE
FROM THE SECRETARY-GENERAL
OF THE UNITED NATIONS

July 21, 1965

My dear Mr. Eban,

On the occasion of the opening of the Third Rehovoth Conference, I wish to convey to you, the organizers and the participants, my best wishes for its success.

In taking as its subject this year the fiscal and monetary problems of developing countries, the Conference will focus the learning and experience of its distinguished members on policies and techniques whose choice and implementation may affect profoundly every aspect of social and economic development.

By placing this discussion into the special context of the Rehovoth "meetings between scientists and statesmen," the conference promises to provide a new approach and new insights in an area where both are greatly needed.

In my Proposals for Action on the United Nations Development Decade, I stated that "the success of the United Nations Development Decade in achieving its objectives will depend in large part on the application of such new approaches. Precisely because they are new, all their implications cannot yet be fully seen."

Through its underlying theme and the broad international range represented by both its agenda and its participants, the Conference places itself in a position to make a continuing contribution to the United Nations Development Decade.

The problems submitted to this year's Conference are, I believe, a fit subject not only for international study and comparison, but also for international action at both the regional and global levels.

I shall look forward with the greatest interest to the results of your proceedings.

Yours sincerely,
U Thant

Editor's Foreword
GETTING OVER THE HUMP
By DAVID KRIVINE

The idea of the Rehovoth Conference was born in July 1959, when Mr. Abba Eban made his inaugural address as President of the Weizmann Institute of Science.

The two most explosive developments of the age, he said, are the revolution in science and technology, and the proliferation of new sovereign States in formerly subject territories. But the two movements are not connected. The scientific transformation has taken place mainly in Europe and North America. The creation of new nations concerns Africa and Asia.

The rich countries, with the aid of automation and cybernetics, are getting richer, the strong countries stronger. The new republics are poor, because they are beginners. And their need has failed to galvanize the scientific world. The most explosive problem of the age is the economic gap between the old and new nations. Science has helped create the gap, by enabling the Western nations to push ahead. Science could mend the gap, by fostering the advance of the other countries too.

Israel stands in the middle, perhaps the only new-born State to have inherited the scientific revolution in full. Mr. Eban saw Israel as a possible meeting place between West and East, between the scientists of the old world and the statesmen of the new.

The Rehovoth Conferences, planned to take place at regular intervals, are staged to provide such an encounter. They have been characterized by a thoroughly down-to-earth approach. Scientists, technologists, agronomists and economists are cross-questioned by men of action from the LDCs (the less developed countries), faced with the need to make critical decisions in their home countries, at a time when great expectations are on the verge of turning into a dangerous disillusionment.

Deliberations have been held about the hold-up, and how to energize the new societies away from poverty and stagnation. The dialogue at successive Rehovoth meetings revolved around two basic formulae. The first is to maximize the mobilization of capital from all possible sources. Mr. Mendès-France spoke at the Third Conference of creating more liquidity in trade; Mr. Horowitz of mobilizing funds in the capital markets of the West, where it is available in abundance;

Dr. Kaldor of securing revenue within the LDCs where dormant assets can be tapped.

The other formula is to make remorselessly utilitarian choices about the use of capital. Fewer machines and more training, according to Professor Galbraith. Less capital-intensive factories and more "intermediate technology," that will help solve homely production problems at small most. And less preoccupation with fundamental scientific research—this last being one of the conclusions reached at the First Rehovoth Conference, in August 1960.

The 1960 conference dealt with *Science in the Advancement of New States*. Science may open new technological possibilities in the future; but LDCs should not invest their rationed supplies of money and talent in this quest. "What they need," Professor W. A. Lewis told the conference, "is rather the application to their problems of what is already known."[1] Professor Shils called it "adaptive research."[2]

Sir John Cockroft explained that, while the world is exploring nuclear physics for new sources of energy, Africa south of the Sahara has immense possibilities of developing hydro-electric power. The Kariba dam, for example, offers a potential output of 8 billion k.w.h. a year, and "further exploitation of the Zambesi and other rivers could develop 100 times the electricity generated by Kariba."[3]

The point is that the LDCs need to concentrate their capital and efforts on the immediate task of speeding up their economic development so that, in the words of Mr. David Ben-Gurion, "all the peoples of the world are not only independent, but more or less on a level in their status and their material and spiritual capacities. Mankind must not continue for long to be divided into rich and poor, progressive and backward. A house so divided cannot endure."[4]

Mr. Paul Hoffman gave figures showing how the gap in living standards is widening. The *per capita* income of a hundred LDCs associated with the U.N. rose from $ 90 in 1950 to slightly over $ 100 in 1959. "Over this same decade, the *per capita* national income in the Netherlands increased by more than $ 300, in the U.K., West Germany and Switzerland by more than $ 400, and in the U.S. by more than $ 500."[5]

---

[1] *Science and the New Nations* (Proceedings of the First Rehovoth Conference), ed. Ruth Gruber (New York: Basic Books, Inc., 1961), p. 24.
[2] *Ibid*, p. 219.
[3] *Ibid*, p. 19.
[4] *Ibid*, p. 4.
[5] *Ibid*, p. 275.

Why have the Western countries progressed so much faster? Professor P. M. S. Blackett cited that between 3000 B.C. and 500 B.C., the most developed parts of the world were the Near and Middle East. For the next two millennia up to 1500 A.D., China and India held the lead. The big advance in Europe and North America has taken place only in the last two centuries.[6]

In order to catch up, the LDCs must start at the bottom of the ladder. Attention must be devoted first and foremost to agriculture, which employs a great majority of the population in developing countries. The subject was taken up at the Second Rehovoth Conference, held in August 1963, on *Rural Planning in Developing Countries*. Professor M. L. Dantwala of India pointed out to this conference that agriculture is expected to play a crucial role in the growth process of industrial and other sectors by providing the food and raw materials, the manpower, the capital (as most of the national income belongs to the farm sector) and the foreign exchange (since agricultural exports are needed to finance the import of machinery and capital goods).[7]

With all that, nascent industries and services can only employ a limited proportion of the rapidly growing populations. According to Professor Gunnar Myrdal, "in most LDCs agriculture for the next few decades will have to absorb the larger part of this increase in the labor force."[8] So planning efforts must be directed toward bettering the productivity of the farmer, while avoiding mechanization where machines merely render labor redundant in the economy as a whole. This practical, unpretentious conclusion brings us back to the First Conference. There is little use in pursuing scientific laurels, "even though science is today part of the regalia of national greatness." The job of the LDCs is to tackle immediate problems by concentrating research on "the application of existing technological knowledge to the climatic, geological or chemical peculiarities of the local situation or the local product."[9]

This policy of austerity refers to the present transitional phase, when LDCs are faced with an imperative necessity: to break out of the strait jacket that cramps progress. Stagnation derives from two key

---

[6] *Ibid*, p. 12.
[7] *Rural Planning in Developing Countries* (Proceedings of the Second Rehovoth Conference), ed. Raanan Weitz, London, 1965, Routledge and Kegan Paul, p. 16.
[8] *Ibid*, p. 286.
[9] *Science and the New Nations, op. cit.*, p. 218–219.

shortages, capital and technical knowledge—and the latter, as Mr. Horowitz indicated, depends likewise on capital outlay. How to mobilize then? This was one of the questions that prompted the choice of subject for the Third Rehovoth Conference held in August 1965. It dealt with *Fiscal and Monetary Problems in Developing States*. The proceedings of this convention are the subject-matter of the present book.

The 1965 Conference was sponsored by the Continuation Committee of the Rehovoth Conferences in cooperation with the Eliezer Kaplan School of Economics and Social Sciences in the Hebrew University of Jerusalem; the Bank of Israel; and the Weizmann Institute of Science. Its organizing Committee was headed by Mr. Abba Eban, at the time Deputy Prime Minister, now Minister for Foreign Affairs of Israel; Mr. David Horowitz, Governor of the Bank of Israel; and Professor Don Patinkin, Dean of the Eliezer Kaplan School of Economics and Social Sciences in the Hebrew University of Jerusalem. Secretary-General of the conference was Dr. Amos Manor.

Proceedings were opened on Monday, August 9, with an address by the Prime Minister of Israel, Mr. Levi Eshkol. Plenary sessions took place on the following two days, after which the conference split into two committees. Committee B dealt with *The Influence of Financial Structure and Monetary Policy on Economic Growth in Developing States*. Committee C dealt with *The Contribution of Fiscal Policy to the Promotion of Economic Growth in Developing States*. Meetings lasted another three days, after which the Final Plenary Session took place on Wednesday, August 18.

Non-Israeli participants totalled 81 persons, from 40 countries and seven international organizations—the U.N., the E.C.A., the Organization of American States, the O.E.C.D., the World Bank and the International Monetary Fund.

CONTENTS

Part III Taxes

Part IV   Foreign Exchange

Contents

Part V   Summary

The Continuation Committee of the Rehovoth Conference wish to express their profound regret at the untimely death on November 30, 1966, of Dr. Amotz Morag, whose paper delivered at the Conference appears as one of the chapters in this book.

LIST OF TABLES

LIST OF FIGURES

Fiscal and Monetary Problems in Developing States

PART I   OBSTACLES

How to accelerate economic growth in the developing countries? There is no evidence that the achievements of the wealthy nations cannot be emulated elsewhere. Their success is unconnected with any particular natural endowments, genetic or other. And today the advancement of science, trade and communications facilitates modernization in all regions of the world.

The developing countries for their part are held up by different and varying obstacles. African countries lack a sufficient cultural base. Latin American countries possess a cultural base but are saddled with a hierarchical social structure that eliminates economic incentives. South Asian countries have a cultural base and a viable social structure but are hampered by excessive population, relative to their resources of land and capital.

The accent in Africa has therefore to be on education, in Latin America on social reform, in South Asia on birth control and the supply of money for investment. While capital is not the only need, it is always necessary, nevertheless, if only to pay for the education and to finance development after the social difficulties are overcome.

Capital formation, and particularly earnings of foreign currency necessary to supply essential imports, are inadequate in the LDCs, partly owing to a deterioration in their terms of trade. This could be offset by reducing tariffs in the West against LDC exports, and by securing more investments from countries that have capital to spare.

Economic planning is recommended as a useful pacemaker, which also ensures that resources are employed in accordance with the best priorities. It is not a substitute for the market economy, but supplements it. In areas dominated by the subsistence economy, planning can speed up the transition to monetization. It also provides a wholesome target for citizens to work for.

Not content with planning, governments ought to go into business and act as an entrepreneur wherever private initiative is lacking. The aim should be to sell each undertaking in due course to private buyers if they are ready to offer a fair market price, and use the money for putting up more ventures.

The "mixed economy" is pragmatic. It does not impose public ownership as a matter of principle, but supplements private enterprise where necessary, in order to maximize development.

1

1

LEARNING FROM THE GROWTH PROCESSES OF THE DEVELOPED STATES

By Simon Kuznets

School of Economics
Harvard University, U.S.A.

1. We identify modern economic growth by some common characteristics displayed over long periods since the late 18th century in a number of countries we consider economically developed—mostly European, some of Europe's offshoots overseas, and Japan. Four major characteristics are specified here. First, these countries have enjoyed a high and sustained rate of aggregate growth. The rates of increase in *per capita* and per worker product—in most countries over 15 per cent per decade—were usually accompanied by a substantial growth of population, reflected a rise in output per unit of input rather than in input per head, and extended over a sufficiently long period (at least half a century) to exercise cumulative effects. Second, these countries displayed a series of rapid shifts in internal economic structure: in industrial structure—away from agriculture and toward industry and services, i.e., industrialization and associated urbanization; in organization of economic enterprise—from small, individual firms to large, impersonal entities; in status of the economically active population—from entrepreneurs and own-account workers to employees, and among the latter from blue- to white-collar occupations; and in distribution of income toward reduction in inequality, perhaps after an initial period of widening inequality. Third, the follower countries in the spread of modern economic growth showed an obvious and increasing dependence upon the earlier pioneers, in learning from them and adopting the ever changing modern technology and, except for the autarkic Communist countries, expanding markedly the relative volumes of foreign trade and foreign capital flows. Finally, the developed countries evinced a variety of non-economic concomitant changes: in demographic processes—birth and death rates, age composition, family structure, and migration within the country; in political structure, with the changing role of the state in provisions for internal economic growth and in external relations with other units at different stages of growth; in scales of values, individual and social, and the priorities accorded

3

to economic relative to other attainments; and finally, in the prevailing views on man and the universe that provided much of the framework for technological and institutional change.

2.   If modern economic growth is identified along the lines suggested, the possibility of learning from it anything relevant to the growth problems of less developed countries rests upon some basic assumptions. The first is that the natural resource endowments, the genetic capacities, and the historical heritage of the presently developed countries are not unique, and that, given the potentials of modern material and social technology, parallels, counterparts or substitutes can be found in most underdeveloped countries. The importance of this assumption for our theme is emphasized by the opposite proposition: that the natural endowments and historical heritage that made economic growth possible in the now developed countries cannot be matched anywhere else. Obviously, in that case, nothing could be learned that would be relevant to the growth problems of the less developed countries.

3.   Because of the inadequacies of our analysis of past growth and the gaps in our knowledge of the natural endowments and historical heritage of the less developed countries, we cannot convert the above assumption into a fully tested conclusion. We must rely on the general weight of evidence and can only note some broad impressions. The first relevant one is the wide diversity displayed by the developed countries, with respect to the growth-determining factors mentioned in the assumption. Thus if by natural resources we mean land, mineral wealth, coast line, climate, and even sheer size of area, and hence of sustainable population, the range in per head endowments of this type is wide—between, say, Switzerland at one end, and the United States at the other, or between Denmark and the U.S.S.R. One cannot be sure of the genetic endowments since it is not clear to what extent they differ among groups in mankind, but one could hardly claim that they are the same in the U.S.S.R. and Australia, or in Japan and Great Britain. As to historical heritage, a broad term that stands for established institutional and social patterns combined with scales of values regarding domestic and international ties, differences were substantial even among the European developed countries; and Japan is again a conspicuous case, having emerged from an historical framework isolated from that of Europe for centuries.

4.   Second, science-based technology, the major source of modern economic growth, has reduced man's dependence on specific, scarce natural resources; has developed methods of controlling some elements

in natural endowments that impede growth; and has facilitated the transfer of useful knowledge from historically conditioned points of origin to the rest of the world. Resources are a function of technology; and modern technology by adding to knowledge has converted many natural elements, previously believed useless, into highly valuable resources. The resulting wider variety of resources increases the probability that some will be found in all countries and reduces the probability that any country will be entirely devoid of resource endowments and therefore incapable of substantial economic growth. Furthermore, much of the development of scientific technology can be likened to the old alchemists' dream of transmutation of elements, i.e., the production of scarce natural resources by transformation of easily and widely available elements of nature—a trend clearly represented by substitution of "synthetic" for "natural" products, greatly accelerated now by the use of atomic energy. For small countries that had to participate intensively in international trade to compensate for the limitations of their internal markets and resources, and for countries located at great distances from the developed areas that are the loci of advanced growth, the technological revolution in transport and communication facilitated the expansion of international trade— just as it facilitated the domestic economic integration of countries with population scattered over large land areas. Finally, the scientific basis of modern material technology had a distinct advantage over the more traditional types of empirical knowledge: its systematic form— independent of personal skills and specific surroundings—could easily be transferred from one area to another. Training in modern physics and engineering, because they are highly systematized, can be acquired more easily, more economically, by more people than the skill of an individual craftsman.

5. Third, as modern economic growth spread from its origin in England to the countries that now account for between one fifth and one quarter of world population, the variety of social adjustment that it generated grew. This expansion of the social component of modern technology, ranging—to list only the economic—from such specific tools as money and exchange controls, credit systems, etc. in public finance to the wide organization of labor and commodity markets, production planning, etc., extended the range in the historical heritage of countries that could enter the process of modern economic growth, and is thus indirect evidence of the diversity of the institutional elements in the historical heritage of the already developed countries. But it also indicates that with the wider variety of social devices now

existing, counterparts and substitutes can probably be found in the heritage of most underdeveloped countries today.

6. The broad arguments presented in paragraphs 3–5 lend support to the assumption in paragraph 2. However, in accepting this assumption, we should specify its meaning further. Since we emphasized the range in the natural endowments and historical heritage of the already developed countries, we implied that this past experience bears some relevance to growth up to a minimum level (of *per capita* or per worker product) at which we would consider a country developed—not to growth to an extremely high level of *per capita* product like that of the United States, which *may* depend on natural endowments or other growth determinants unmatchable in the foreseeable future in most less developed countries. Furthermore, the assumption does not deny that with respect to some determinants, particularly historical heritage, the presently developed countries were better prepared to take advantage of the potentials of modern economic growth than are the less developed countries—an inference that inevitably follows from the facts, and to which we shall return later. On the other hand, the assumption suggests that the completely uncontrollable elements that bar modern economic growth (e.g., the absolute dearth of natural endowments encountered in the Arctic waste land or in the Sahara desert—unproductive as yet) are not a significant condition in most underdeveloped countries—particularly those that sustained large populations even with a pre-modern technology; and that enough of the other elements—the full range of social and ideological adjustments implicit in historical heritage—can be learned, imitated, or substituted for in varying degrees and with varying effort to secure the minimum economic growth suggested at the beginning of this paragraph. It is in this sense of the assumption that we can argue that past economic growth was not associated with antecedents so unique that no relevant lessons can be learned from the growth problems of the less developed countries.

7. But what are these relevant lessons ? They would be specifiable only if analysis of the past revealed some invariance and continuity in the antecedents and concomitants of economic growth, some order in the pattern. In that case we could say that whenever and wherever economic growth occurred, it was under some ever-present conditions that we could then examine as possibly indispensable requisites. Indeed, without this assumption of significant invariance and continuity in the structural (internal and international) aspects of aggregate economic growth of nations, we could not learn anything

relevant to the growth problems of the less developed countries. This assumption, too, is clarified by consideration of its opposite. Assume that the past growth of some fifteen developed countries has been accompanied by fifteen different patterns of change in industrial structure, or in structure of final product—so that even comparability of aggregate rates is jeopardized and must rest upon some artificially imposed common unit. Assume further that these patterns of structure within each country change rapidly over time but with completely diverse sequences. Clearly, unless we can reduce this chaotic diversity of growth experience to some meaningful order by relating them to factors and variables that are common to the various countries, and thus establish some invariance in *relations,* no definite inference of any kind, let alone of relevance to the different universe of less developed countries, is possible. And under the conditions specified, such order probably could not be established, and aggregate growth could be assigned no definite meaning.

8. This assumption of significant invariance and continuity in structure is already implicit in the very definition of modern economic growth—as a process common to a number of countries—experienced by some in the past and possible for others in the future—and identified by the common characteristics suggested in paragraph 1. It is impracticable to survey here these major elements in modern economic growth, as observed in the process in the past and discussed in the rapidly growing literature in the field; we must assume familiarity with at least the empirical findings suggested by the long-term statistical records. Yet it may be useful to illustrate the variety of, and particularly the interconnections among, the common aspects of modern economic growth—under each of the four major heads distinguished in paragraph 1.

9. If the rate of economic growth in terms of *per capita* product is about 15 per cent per decade as a minimum (which means more than doubling in 50 years and more than quadrupling in a century), it must be largely accounted for by the rise in output per unit of 'input—where labor input is measured in manhours (unweighted) and ' capital input is assigned the weight corresponding to the share of property income returns in total product. When measured in this way, input per head of population cannot and did not grow at high rates: manhours per head usually decline in modern economic growth, and growth in capital input per head is reduced by a decline in the aggregate capital-output ratio and the limited weight of the property income share. It is thus generally found that most of the rise in *per*

capita income is due either to improvement in quality of labor, associated with shorter hours, better selection and particularly greater education; and even more to the additional knowledge which is at the base of economies of scale, contributions of education to labor efficiency, and improved organization. The origin of most of the rise in *per capita* product in addition to useful knowledge, embodied largely in human beings through education and partly in modern material capital, is important because of associated impacts on industrial and other aspects of the internal structure of developed economies; because it calls for international ties by which the follower countries can learn, borrow from, and imitate the greater knowledge of the more advanced countries, or if small, participate fully in the use of such knowledge; and because it affects the demographic, political and ideological aspects of human behavior. Thus, there are numerous indispensable links between the origin of high aggregate rates of growth, particularly of *per capita* product, and the other characteristics of modern economic growth distinguished in paragraph 1.

10. A substantial rise in *per capita* income generally calls for structural changes in the composition of final demand, because of the differing income elasticities of demand for various goods—and this, in and of itself, makes for shifts in industrial structure of domestic product. If the increase in *per capita* product is due largely to a rise in efficiency associated with new technological change, there is additional pressure for shifts in internal structure—industrial, labor status, occupations, type of firm—coming from the supply rather than the demand side. For technological progress has an unequal impact on different industries, occupations, types of firms, etc., affecting some more than others, creating new industries and products and leading to obsolescence of old. In fact, there is a significant positive association between the rate of growth of *per capita* product and the rapidity of internal shifts (change per unit of time)—in industrial allocation of product, labor force, and capital; in occupational structure; in status composition of labor force; in distribution by type of firm. In other words, a high rate of growth in *per capita* product can be realized only through marked and rapid shifts in industrial structure and in many if not all other aspects of internal structure of an economy.

11. Of the important consequences that follow, only a few can be noted here. First, if growth begins in a country in which productivity was so low in the past that most labor and capital had to be devoted to output of prime necessities in the agricultural sector, it

requires a marked rise in productivity in this sector to release resources
for other sectors; and, indeed, the records for all the developed
economies show a marked rise in productivity in agriculture—a basic
requirement of modern economic growth which can be met alternatively only in the rare case by imports (i.e., reliance on high
agricultural productivity elsewhere). Second, shifts in industrial
structure usually mean movement of labor and capital out of sectors
whose relative shares in the economy are declining to those that offer
particularly high growth opportunities; and these shifts often involve
different conditions of life and work, requiring adjustments to new
situations and abandonment of long-standing patterns of behavior
that are inconsistent with the new pursuits. Finally, shifts in relative
shares of industries, occupational groups, or types of firms, mean
changes in the relative position of various groups of people—farmers,
handicraftsmen, merchants, manual workers, etc.; and each of these
groups may resist any change that reduces its relative position or
subjects it to pressure to reduce its numbers in response to reduced
economic opportunities. Resistance to change can be a proper check
on economic growth, since it reflects the cost of such growth to some
members of society. But if resistance is great enough to reduce
materially the needed structural shifts, it can reduce the rate of economic growth itself. The implications of these needed shifts and
mobility for the demographic, political and ideological concomitants
of economic growth should be noted, since it is these latter that can
facilitate the movements by minimizing their costs.

12. The increased strengthening of international ties that accompanied modern economic growth has been due partly to the
technological revolution in transport and communication that, for
the first time in human history, placed all nations within reach of
each other; partly to the gradual spread of modern economic growth
from its pioneering beginnings to a series of followers, in which the
latter had to learn from the former; partly to the increasing advantages
of international division of labor created by the differential advance
of the developed countries and, to be sure, frequently imposed by
the latter on other parts of the world that either became colonial
possessions or were forcibly drawn into the network of international
trade. The marked expansion of foreign trade, at rates greater than
those in aggregate product (with few exceptions), is particularly to
be noted. And because, as a general rule, the optimum scale of
production grew, the smaller countries in particular had to rely
increasingly on international trade in order to achieve higher *per*

capita product. There are few exceptions to the propositions that the smaller countries are characterized by larger proportions of foreign trade to domestic product and that the proportions are larger for the *developed* small countries than for the less developed. This rule may apply even to the smaller Communist countries, although here our experience has been too short to permit inferences.

13. The comments in paragraphs 9–12 have already suggested that some demographic, political, and ideological concomitants are closely associated with the changes in the economic institutions and activities involved in the rises of product *per capita* and shifts in economic structure that constitute modern economic growth. And indeed a number of these associations come easily to mind. Every developed country has experienced a decline in death rates, an eventual decline in birth rates, and a marked trend toward small, nucleated families. In every developed country the political structure has shown fair stability, and the government has possessed a minimum amount of power, based on a sense of community, that responded to the continuous conflicts generated by economic growth by attempting to resolve them peacefully and thus minimize obstacles to further growth. In all the developed countries the traditional views have been subjected to substantial modification—which affected scales of values, values and views, views on man, nature and deity, and which represents what is often referred to as Westernization or modernization.

14. The firmness and generality of the aggregative, structural and international aspects of modern economic growth, and of its non-economic concomitants, painted with a broad brush in the paragraphs above, should not be exaggerated. Not all aspects of economic structure change markedly, at least as they are measured. For instance, proportions of gross capital formation to national product do not rise much in the course of growth; the addition of a few percentage points does not constitute a marked shift. And even when the characteristics and association are clearly present, their possible use for policy purposes would require greater specificity than can be given here, and perhaps than present tested knowledge permits. We would have to know the specific parameters of growth, structural change and associated concomitants, tested for invariance and suggesting the range of deviations; we would have to know whether these parameters have changed significantly over time—a kind of typical life circle of growth with empirically distinguishable phases. Above all, it would be highly desirable to have more disaggregated data and analysis

indicating the industries favored in the economic growth of different countries, in response to their specific endowments; the ways in which small countries overcome their disadvantages through foreign trade, and the ways in which large countries move toward greater economic and cultural integration through overhead investments in transportation and education; the products favored as exports, reflecting specific comparative advantage, and the technical properties of these products that made for the export potentials and thus provided a basis for sustained economic growth within the country—given the limited period over which the specific comparative advantage could be expected to be maintained. These and many other questions are treated in the literature; but this is not the place to push the discussion further. We only note that even in its most general terms, a proper understanding of all that is involved in modern economic growth is immensely useful—if only to prevent the adoption of partial views that tend to lead to a wasteful commitment to one or two lines of policy viewed as panaceas promising growth miracles.

15. But even with the most diligent and detailed study of the pattern of growth in the developed countries, the attempt to derive lessons relevant to the problems of the underdeveloped countries would face two types of difficulties; and these must be explicitly considered. First, it is hardly likely that an adequate analysis of past growth experience, covering the full range needed to test the important parameters and relations to be applied to many underdeveloped countries, would emerge in time to be of any use. One may reasonably ask whether a tested theory of growth for many underdeveloped countries today with less than $ 150 *per capita* product (in current prices) and an entirely different heritage, could be formulated in the proximate future on the basis of the economic growth experience of the developed economies of which only one, Japan, had so low an income and so different a past, immediately before industrialization. A possible approach by extrapolating from the limited range of experience to points well outside those covered by the data is subject to a wide margin of error and requires a variety of indirect support— again a matter of time and ingenuity, both in scarce supply.

16. If we agree that a tested theory of economic growth with a relevant range is unlikely in the foreseeable future, one possible alternative remains. With the established knowledge concerning common and recurrent features of modern economic growth as background, it might be most promising for a less developed country to try to learn from the experience of one or a few more developed countries

that provide the most relevant pattern of endowments and original historical heritage. This alternative is particularly important because the range among the less developed countries themselves is wide, and for some the most relevant pattern may be that of another, more advanced country but one that may still not be among the handful of economically developed countries; and also because, as already indicated, even among the latter, natural endowments and original historical heritage vary fairly widely, so that the experience of some may be more relevant than that of others. Indeed, one may argue that the experience of a country that began developing but did not attain enough cumulative growth to bring it into the group of developed countries is in many ways as valuable and relevant as the growth experience of the highly advanced countries. In short, selectivity and flexibility in choice of pattern is a worth-while alternative. It may not be easy, since its feasibility depends upon the existence of analyzed growth records for a variety of countries, both developed and less developed. Yet this is no reason for discarding this alternative as a possible guide both for underdeveloped countries and for scholars concerned with useful lessons for economic growth policy.

17. But this alternative, if pursued, raises the second difficulty, which is an obstacle to the useful application of *any* lesson of the past, *viz.*, the paucity of knowledge concerning the underdeveloped country that would apply the relevant lessons. Clearly, since economic growth uses a country's natural endowments and the population embodying its historical heritage in attaining higher rates of output with whatever desirable greater diversification such higher levels of economic performance permit, the application of any knowledge derived from other countries' experience to the growth problems of a given country requires adequate data on its own natural endowments, institutions, and historical heritage. But many underdeveloped countries do not have this indispensable information. We need not expound on the scarcity of both quantitative and qualitative data on the basic magnitudes in underdeveloped countries, on their natural endowments, and on the institutional components of their historical heritage. One can only note that we have here a vicious circle not unlike that observed in the economic realm, with material poverty leading to scarcity of available surplus and further economic poverty. It is the developed countries that possess a wealth of tested data on their economy, past and present, and on various institutional features, economic and non-economic, of their society; and it is the developed countries that draw upon this information for various policy changes

that facilitate and sustain further growth. The underdeveloped countries, with their scarce resources, possess little tested knowledge about themselves, which might be used to devise more relevant and productive policies than those likely to emerge in a state of relative ignorance. Moreover, this dependence of socially relevant knowledge upon the level of a country's development, while contributing to the explanation of sustained growth once initiated, is a major constraint on the accumulation of enough social knowledge to be useful to the economically less developed societies.

18.   Whatever the explanation of this circle of underdevelopment and undersupply of knowledge, it must be broken in the way all other such circles are—by the intervention of adventurous individuals who act as entrepreneurs in assembling more knowledge, just as in other areas individuals act as entrepreneurs in introducing technological innovations into economic production or social innovations into the old institutions. Obviously in order to draw lessons from the growth experience of economically developed nations relevant to the problems of less developed nations, knowledge of both the former and the latter is required—to provide the specifics to which lessons are to be applied and to select the past patterns that seem most relevant. It would be idle to ask which of these bodies of knowledge is more important; they are both essential, and rational decision must balance the two to optimize relevant learning. One obvious lesson from the experience of presently developed countries is that a steady accumulation of tested knowledge about the society's economic and social performance accompanies economic growth, and is an essential ingredient in the latter—providing the basis for agreement on a wide variety of facts, for consideration of policy alternatives, and for resolution and limitation of conflicts by reference to a widening background of accepted knowledge. Such knowledge applies not only to obvious elements like a country's natural resources—a function of learning by exploration and research (and many natural resources in many presently underdeveloped countries may still be unknown), but also to data on population, economic product and its components, family structure and various other aspects of the size and functioning of a country's society. Whatever one may learn from the experience of the already developed nations will hang suspended without adequate knowledge of and within the underdeveloped countries themselves; and, however great the assistance from outside, the latter can be gained only when a body of organizers and producers of such knowledge is established within these countries, able to draw the most

relevant lessons from the past in application to their present and future.

20. The chapter can be effectively summarized as a discussion of four questions. The first is: Can anything of value be learned from the growth experience of the developed countries that would contribute to the economic growth of the less developed countries? The answer would have to be *no,* if we thought that the developed countries grew either because they were exceptionally lucky (with respect to natural resources), or unusually endowed otherwise (genetically); or that their growth experience was so chaotic that no orderly pattern could be discerned. We answered *yes* because some orderly pattern of growth can be observed in the experience of the developed countries and because such growth did not depend merely on luck or on the dubious distinction of genetic endowment. Economic growth at a fairly high and rapidly rising minimum level is attainable by all societies.

20. The second question is: What precisely can be learned from the growth experience of developed countries? The answer dwelt largely on the recurring connective aspects of modern economic growth: the connection between the high rate of growth in *per capita* product and the rapid shifts in internal structure of the economy; between the former and utilization of science-oriented technology; among the latter, internal mobility, and the capacity of a society to endure shifts in the economically determined status of various groups without a breakdown of political and social unity; between the economic and demographic processes, and between these two and changes in the values governing men's views and patterns of behavior. The answer was general, because a specific answer has meaning only in reference to the conditions and growth problems of a specific country or group of countries.

21. The third question is: What are the conditions required for the application of learning from the past to specific cases? Here the emphasis was on the need for data for a given, less developed country. Such data—on natural resources, population size and structure, aggregate product and its components, dominant institutions, etc.— are essential for the selection of the past experience that is most relevant and for the modifications to be adopted in applying it to the specifically defined situations and growth potentials within the country.

22. The last question, only lightly touched upon, is: Who are the learners? Obviously, the lessons from the past must be learned by the members of the less developed community itself, for they can best

mobilize the knowledge specific to their country and select the past patterns of growth experience that seem most relevant. The world community of scholars can be of assistance in its pursuit of tested knowledge of the past, but linking its results to the problems of a given country is most effectively accomplished by the members of that country's society who have direct knowledge of the distinctive features, and who can attempt to develop a consensus concerning the particular pattern of growth experience, and the particular modifications that seem best suited to their country's goals.

DISCUSSION

More Information Needed

Professor Kuznets' survey of the benefit that can be derived from studying the growth experience of the developed States evoked a number of reactions. History should be examined for the answer to certain additional queries, such as how growth started, when it faltered and why. The less developed countries cannot find a solution to all their problems in the history of the industrialized countries only. And progress in the future must come faster than it did for Western societies in the past.

In addition to studying patterns of growth, *Dr. Robert Szereszevski,* of Israel, urged the importance of finding out how growth started in the developed States—the genetics of the subject as well as its mechanics. While reviewing the growth phase, it would also be useful to scrutinize contemporary thinking about the problems that arose at the time, e.g., the literature of the Mercantilists and the economics of Friedrich List. "Another line of investigation," he said, "which might contribute to the formulation of a general theory of change is the study of arrested growth, arrested development or outright economic decline."

A general theory of social and economic transformation could be achieved, but this involves a study of experience in the LDCs as well as the developed countries. Dr. Szereszevski pointed to the wealth of economic data that have not been properly explored—"both historical, collected by colonial governments, and contemporary; unanalyzed foreign trade and budgetary statistics; unprocessed consumption surveys; and extremely interesting work-sheets of national accounts which no economist has set eyes on."

Mr. Edmond A. Lisle, of France, referred to the important role of urbanization, which "facilitates the concentration of capital and division of labor, while at the same time forming a seed-bed for nurturing entrepreneurial capacities in the population." But large urban concentrations do not always yield progress. Mr. Lisle asked, "What are the minimal urban infrastructures necessary for transforming a conglomeration of men and lodgings—or if you wish, a constellation of large villages—into a dynamic city able to develop its own means?"

Drawing attention to the need for financial institutions, *Dr. Richard Goode* of the U.S. recalled that the developed countries devote a growing proportion of their national income to uses other than the two usual alternatives, which are personal consumption and direct investment by the saver in his own enterprise.

To put it another way, an increasing proportion of income is handled either by the government through taxes, or by financial intermediaries for investment. Dr. Goode recommends comparing the relative efficiency of alternative methods in ordering the re-use of resources.

Dr. Snoh Unakul, of Thailand, admitted that useful lessons could be learned from the history of both developed and developing countries, but warned that "this would not be sufficient for concrete and detailed policy formulation in practice. What is needed is the development and establishment of local expertise."

It is easier to learn from other countries than from one's own, Dr. Unakul went on, because there is abundant material about the advanced states in publications, journals, and university courses. Thus the economist from an LDC acquires advanced economic and analytical techniques in foreign universities, only to find these techniques irrelevant to the matters needing attention at home.

"Once faced with this kind of problem, he has several possibilities. If he is very skilful and if he has been very well trained, he can sometimes go back to the country where he studied and be lost to his own society. Or else he finds refuge in international organizations, and is thus also lost to his society. If he stays on and wants to work, as he doesn't like to waste his training and background, he sometimes concentrates on low priority projects, mobilizing a lot of analytical tools which are of rather limited empirical significance."

Dr. Unakul concludes that the LDCs must develop economic faculties of their own. "We may need a few advanced and highly trained economists who are familiar with all these modern techniques.

But what is in fact required is really rather simple: an ability to handle simple statistics, to interpret even rather qualitative observations, and to present the conclusions for policy purposes."

Dr. Koichi Emi, of Japan, also advised against concentrating on over-all figures of growth. He prefers to work on narrower and more specific comparisons, e.g., by confronting agricultural development in South-East Asia with the achievements of agricultural development in Japan, whose experience is closer to the character of that region.

Dr. John Mars, of the U.N. Economic Commission for Africa, made the point that the developing countries are not conforming to all the conditions that underlay the past growth of industrialized nations. African States are too numerous and therefore too small. Twenty-five of them each have less than 5 million inhabitants, whose average income is barely $ 100 a year. Being sovereignty-conscious, these new countries are not amenable to economic projects that involve the cooperation of several States.

Population pressures have in the past promoted development. Now they are an impediment, making it necessary to spread the scarce human skills available ever more thinly over growing needs. Population accrues more rapidly than output, which is not conducive to enthusiasm for development programs especially when it is popularly supposed that a privileged few enjoy most of the advantages. Dr. Mars drew attention to the ethical component in economic development, citing as a negative occurrence the intervention of representatives from big international firms, who try to persuade Ministers in the LDCs to buy goods the country doesn't need at prices above the international level.

Several speakers gave attention to the length of time that development should take. The first to deal with this subject, Dr. Emi, referred to Professor Kuznets' assumption that three conditions of development which have prevailed in the industrialized countries—natural resource endowment, genetic capacities and historical heritage—are not necessarily unique to those countries. While natural resources can be transferred, thanks to transport and modern trade, Dr. Emi thought the other two factors, which are non-economic, will take time to grow with the aid of education.

Mr. Hanoch Smith, of Israel, said that teaching a person takes a long time, is not a well rewarded profession, and needs to be supplemented by experience on the job, which is also lacking in the LDCs. So the development of human resources involves a long pull.

Professor Raymond W. Goldsmith, of the OECD, recalled that at the minimum growth rate quoted by Professor Kuznets of 1.5 per cent a year, it will take something like 150 years before the LDCs catch up with present American living standards. To what extent can this process be compressed? It is not infinitely compressible, and Professor Kuznets has warned the LDCs that "a certain patience is necessary."

* * *

Professor Kuznets addressed himself to the same point in answering the debate. "It is quite obvious that you can get a high rate of growth by throwing everything into things you can produce rapidly, whether or not they satisfy the basic needs of the country." He predicted nevertheless that "modern economic growth is not going to take decades to come." Therefore one should not wait until a tried and tested model of growth is worked out, but should use flexible comparisons in a practical spirit, as suggested by Dr. Emi.

2

UNDERDEVELOPMENT:
AN APPROACH
TO CLASSIFICATION

By JOHN K. GALBRAITH

School of Economics
Harvard University, U.S.A.

Scholars, like the Christian theologists, have a natural instinct for a trinity—they tend to establish three classes, find three causes and propose three remedies. Werner Sombart, the German economist, sociologist and historian of half a century ago, scarcely deviated from the three causes—three consequences rule over several thousand pages of social analysis. But among students of economic development, the rule has been different. In recent years they have agreed to divide the world into two halves—the developed countries and the under-developed countries. Some, substituting blunt nomenclature for tact, speak of the rich countries and the poor.

This distinction is, of course, subject to refinement. The developed countries are more developed or less developed, in accordance with their *per capita* real income. (*Per capita* real income, by common consent, is the index of development.)[1] And there is the distinction between those that follow a broadly capitalist, free enterprise, mixed or Keynesian course—the terminology here is increasingly a matter of taste—and those committed, however distantly, to Communism.

The poor countries are also divided between the more or less poor and between the Communist and the non-Communist states. But here our determination to have one homogeneous class is especially strong. Excluding China, we speak, teach and do research on a broad category of countries that we call "underdeveloped nations." Even Professor W. W. Rostow's notable classification in his *The Stages of Economic Growth* assumes a homogeneity of social process. Underdeveloped countries may be still in their traditional mold, preparing for take-off.[2] These are important differences, but as Pro-

---

[1] Cf. Jacob Viner, "The Economics of Development," in A. N. Agarwala and S. P. Singh, *The Economics of Underdevelopment* (Bombay: Oxford University Press), p. 13. Also Bernard Okun and Richard W. Richardson, *Status in Economic Development* (New York: Holt, Rinehart and Winston), p. 236 "The size of *per capita* income is used by most writers as the criterion for differentiating between advanced and underdeveloped countries."

[2] W. W. Rostow, *The Stages of Economic Growth* (Cambridge, 1960), p. 4.

fessor Rostow presents them, they are way-stations along the same path. In his system the underdeveloped countries differ from each other only as a child differs from an adolescent and an adolescent differs from one on the verge of maturity.[3]

There are, to digress briefly, other difficulties with Professor Rostow's system. He combines imagination with—as Professor Kuznets has shown—a marked capacity for accommodating fact to framework. History does not accord with the brief take-off periods he has assigned to various countries. And as a further important consequence, he has radically minimized the obstacles to growth in the poor countries. Development and take-off into sustained growth have been endowed with an aspect of certainty and normality which is sharply at odds with reality.[4] But, as compared with much of the discussion of underdevelopment, Professor Rostow's discussion may well reflect a comparatively high level of refinement. He does distinguish between rather radically different stages of underdevelopment. A much larger part of the modern discussion deals with underdevelopment as though it were a single homogeneous category.[5]

---

[3] Simon Kuznets, "Notes on the Take-Off." Paper presented before the International Economic Association, September, 1960.

[4] Professor Rostow states that India, along with China, launched its take-off during the 1950s. *(Op cit.,* p. 9). He later cautions (p. 38) that it is still too soon to judge whether the effort will be sucessful—a suggestion of an otherwise unexplored notion that the stages of growth may be somewhat reversible. (He then concludes that as in China "the commitment... to modernization appears too deep to permit more than temporary setbacks" (p. 48) which evidently introduces a further dimension of national will.) The near certainty is that only heroic efforts, including a continuation of extensive provision of food from abroad, will prevent a deterioration of *per capita* income in India in coming years.

[5] "The purpose of this paper is to examine a modified version of growth theory... in the light of the more commonly known characteristics of *the* underdeveloped country... I suggest hypotheses about the conditions that have actually obtained in the economic growth of [the United States and the United Kingdom]. These hypotheses are then transplanted to *the* underdeveloped country... Of course, no two underdeveloped countries are exactly alike; but the descriptive literature on such countries suggests that *we may confidently describe a 'representative underdeveloped country.'*... Of course low *per capita* income and consequently low savings are the chief criteria of underdevelopment..." Henry J. Bruton, "Growth Models and Underdeveloped Economies," *Journal of Political Economy,* 1955. Reprinted in Agarwala and Singh, *op. cit.,* pp. 219–220. Emphasis added.

II

From the tendency to view the poor countries as a homogeneous group comes a companion tendency to devise common prescriptions. The economics of development is intrinsically normative.[6] To talk about the economics of underdevelopment is to consider, *pro tanto,* the steps that will overcome economic backwardness. It follows that, so long as we speak of underdeveloped countries as a class, we will tend to assume a common therapy applicable to the whole class. We will devise programs that are meant to be applicable generally to underdeveloped countries; we will continue to say, as we often do now, "This is what the underdeveloped countries should do."

Or this will be the tendency. But, in fact, there is now considerable differentiation in our prescription for the poor countries. We do not, in fact, urge the same program in India as in the new countries of Africa. And, in recent times, yet another design for development has been emerging in Latin America. There is now more differentiation in prescription than in analysis. The purpose of this paper is to urge differentiation in both.

I shall argue that the causes of a low level of income, if that be accepted as the measure of underdevelopment, are, in fact, radically different in different cases. Any system of generalization from low income which does not involve further differentiation combines unlike causes. And any common prescription is certain, therefore, to be inapplicable in some instances. If it strikes at valid causes in some places, it will fail to do so in others. And in these latter cases, it may not only fail to help but it may do harm. An infusion of capital, which is of the greatest value if capital is scarce, may divert attention from more urgent steps if a shortage of capital is not the barrier to advance. Providing investment funds may, in fact, make the necessary action more difficult. So with other measures.

Poverty has a homogenizing influence on behavior. It may well be more important in explaining how communities react—biologically, socially and politically—than any other factor, including their decision whether to be Communists, socialists, free enterprisers or some

---

[6] Once some years ago I visited Bhutan, a lovely pastoral country of high mountains, rich forests, clear streams and—it is commonly supposed—a modestly declining population. It is indubitably underdeveloped. It has no industry, airport, railroad, post offices, television, department store, diplomacy, bureaucracy or settled capital. The thought occurred to me that the world should build a fence around it and protect it from development. But I quickly recovered my sense of balance.

combination of all these. It is not easy, walking through a south Asian jungle or across the Andean altiplano, or looking into the mud hut of a villager, to determine whether the country is capitalist or Communist. These distinctions acquire enhanced emphasis only as one approaches a capital—including Washington. The people themselves are principally clear only on one point which is that they are very poor. But the causes of this poverty are not homogeneous and we must not continue to mistake homogeneity of consequence with homogeneity of cause. If we are to have an adequate understanding of underdevelopment and competent measures for overcoming it, we must have an adequate classification of countries in accordance with the principal cause of backwardness.

III

In recent years at Harvard, we have been working toward a classification of underdeveloped countries that is based on the obstacle or combination of obstacles which, in the given case, is the effective barrier to economic advance. The identification of these obstacles or barriers is not a highly scientific exercise. It involves observation and judgment, and those who assess truth in accordance with whether it depends on precise measurement will find much in the classification to which they can object. However, the classification is not based on small distinctions. For selecting the largest tree from among those of similar size, there is no substitute for measurement. But if one tree towers over the other, much can be accomplished by inspection. And all scientific method must be seen in context. The difficulties in the classification which I here offer are insignificant as a source of error as compared with the aggregation of unlike cases which we now employ. Classification still remains the first step toward science, however short the step or intractable the material.

The classification is a four-fold one. Three classes are important for present purposes; the fourth embraces the countries where there is no strongly operative obstacle to development and where, accordingly, it proceeds at a more or less rapid pace. It is pedagogically useful to give each of the classes or models an identification with the part of the world to which they are the most applicable. Their application is not, however, confined to the geographical area used in the designation. The three models of underdevelopment are:

Model I.   The Sub-Sahara African Model.
Model II.   The Latin American Model.
Model III. The South Asian Model.

As noted, the Models are set apart from each other by the barrier or combination of barriers to development which are operative in each case. In some instances, the barriers which characterize one Model are also operative in another. There are, as might be expected, intermediate or mixed cases. And the geographical designations do not include all of the countries of the area. Ceylon is not typical of the South Asian Model; Ghana is not characteristic of the Sub-Sahara African Model; Mexico and Costa Rica do not conform to the Latin American Model; and Brazil, a notably difficult case, conforms more closely to that Model in the northern than in the southern states.

IV

In the Model I countries, the principal barrier to development is the absence of what may be called a minimum cultural base. It is important, both for reasons of tact and precision, that this not be misinterpreted; the problem is not absence of aptitude but absence of opportunity. Most of the countries that are described by this Model have recently emerged from colonialism of the more regressive sort. Other countries have had decades and centuries of preparation for the tasks of economic development. These have had only a few years. "To an extent unmatched in most of the underdeveloped world, positions of skill and responsibility (in Africa) were until recently in the hands of non-Africans. ... As late as 1958 there were only about 8,000 Africans graduated from all the academic secondary schools below the Sahara, and only about 10,000 others were studying in universities—more than half of these in Ghana and Nigeria. ... in 1962 there were still few African countries where more than two hundred Africans received full secondary diplomas."[7] When the Republic of the Congo gained independence, there were fewer than 25,000 Congolese with any secondary education and only about thirty Congolese university graduates. The first university, Lovanium, had opened only in 1954 and only thirteen Africans had graduated by 1960.[8]

[7] Elliot J. Berg, "Socialism and Economic Development in Tropical Africa," *The Quarterly Journal of Economics,* November, 1964. pp. 560–561. (Mr. Berg argues with much effect that this shortage of qualified talent has not prevented—and has possibly encouraged—a number of these countries to commit scarce administrative resources to demanding experiments in socialism and planning at heavy cost to themselves.)

[8] Ernest Lefever, *Crisis in the Congo* (Washington, D.C.: The Brookings Institution, 1965), p. 9.

Professors Harbison and Myers have classified numerous countries in accordance with their resources in educated and trained manpower. Of the seventeen countries in their lowest class, all but three (Afghanistan, Saudi Arabia and Haiti) are in Africa and another twelve African countries were cited as falling in the same class. In this class, primary and secondary teachers averaged 17 per 10,000 population. On the basis of limited data, there were 0.6 scientists and engineers per 10,000 population and 0.5 physicians and dentists.[9]

The consequences of an inadequate cultural base are comprehensive —on government, the economy, internal security, communications, even foreign policy. But the most visible manifestation is on the apparatus of government. People with the requisite education, trainning and ethical standards for performing public tasks are unavailable. As a consequence, taxes are not collected except in haphazard or arbitrary fashion; public outlays tend to be the prerogative of position or the reward of power rather than compensation for service. Where this is the case, government will ordinarily be unstable; those who do not have access to public income will have a strong incentive to seek the ouster of those who do. As a further consequence, law enforcement is unreliable; so is law and order; and so, at a minimum, are essential public services. In this context, in turn, there can be no economic development that involves any sophistication in technique or organization.[10] Primitive and local trade will flourish under almost any handicap. But larger scale commerce and industry are demanding in their environment; persons and property must be reasonably secure; property must not be taxed merely because it is visible; profits cannot be appropriated simply because they are made; business cannot be transacted in the absence of such public facilities as posts, telephones and common carrier transportation. In the colonial era, firms were allowed to provide for their own security and establish service essential to their existence. With independence, such intra-territorial administration is not ordinarily permissible.

But the inadequacy or instability of government is only the most

---

9 Frederick Harbison and Charles A. Myers, *Education, Manpower and Economic Growth* (New York: McGraw-Hill, 1964), p. 38. I am indebted to Richard S. Sharpe for a useful discussion of these figures in "The Manpower Gap in Middle Africa," an unpublished seminar paper, Harvard University.

10 Cf. George H. Kimble, *Tropical Africa*, Vol. II: *Society and Policy* (New York: Doubleday, 1962), pp. 469 *et seq.*

visible manifestation of an inadequate cultural base. The shortcomings of government are paralleled in other social institutions and apparatus. And it reflects the absence of schools, colleges and cultural environment for producing or preparing people for its tasks. All discussion of economic development involves difficult problems of sequence and circularity. This is an example. How does a country get an educational system without an adequate government? How does it get a government without the qualified people that an educational system provides? But it helps to have narrowed the problem to this point. For we recognize little is accomplished by action that does not break into this particular circle. Assistance in the form of capital funds will not be useful if there is no one with the technical competence or honesty to employ it and if the environment is hostile to the resulting enterprises. Technical assistance will not be useful if there is no one to advise or assist. In the next Model progress waits on reforms which reduce the power of a vested elite. Here there is no such elite.

There is a measure of overstatement in any attempt to establish categories. No country is without some small group of honest and competent people in some area of economic activity or government. But in those countries where colonialism was exploitive and regressive—where there was no liberalizing urge that sought to prepare people for some role other than that of primitive agriculture and unskilled industrial labor—this group is very small. This Model, as a result—as in the classic case of Haiti and possibly the more recent one of the Congo (Leopoldville)—can readily become one not of advance but of disintegration with eventual reversion to tribalism or anarchy. All that is needed is for the perilously small group of competent and honest people to be overwhelmed by those who see government in predatory terms. Once the latter are in possession of the available instruments of power—the army, government payroll, police—it is not clear when (or even whether) the process of disintegration can be reversed by internal influences.

V

In the Model II countries—what I have called the Latin American case—the cultural base is, in comparison with Model I, quite wide. There is a large and illiterate mass at the bottom of the social pyramid. But at the top there is a large number of people with a diverse assortment of modern skills—lawyers, accountants, engineers, scientists, economists, managers and technicians. And back of this group there is a limited and imperfect, but still substantial, educational system. Peru, Ecuador and Guatemala are, by any calculation of *per capita* income, very poor countries. Argentina, Brazil and Chile are well below North American and European levels. But all have trained and educated personnel and facilities for its replacement that are far better than those of the new African states. As a further aspect, they have a strong intellectual tradition. As is also true of the United States, they could use more people of the highest caliber and training. Public servants of high honesty and competence are not in surplus. But in these countries—as also in the Arab states and Iran where the pattern is similar—the absence of trained and educated people is not the obvious barrier to development.

The far more evident barrier to advance is the social structure. The elite, though sizable, depends for its economic and social position on land ownership, or on a *comprador* or trading role in the port or capital cities, or on government employment or sinecure, or on position in the armed forces. Beneath this elite is a large rural mass and, in some cases, an unskilled and often semi-employed urban proletariat. The rural worker, in the characteristic situation, either earns the right to cultivate a small plot of land by giving service to the estate on which he resides or he is part of the *minifundia*— a cultivator of a small plot on which he has some form of permanent tenure. In either case he has no effective economic incentive. He naturally renders the landlord the minimum service that will earn him the right to cultivate his own plot. The latter plot was anciently arranged to be the minimum size consistent with survival. The same tends to be true of any holding to which he has title. So any possibility that he might improve his position by increasing output is excluded by what amounts to a systematic denial of incentives.[11] In a number of countries—Peru, Guatemala and Ecuador for example—the fact that most of the rural mass is Indian adds a sense of racial exclusion to this denial.

But the elimination of economic incentives is not confined to the rural masses. Beginning, at least in time sequence, with them, it tends

---

[11] "Basically, the problem [of Chilean agriculture] is lack of economic opportunities—resulting from the lack of employment alternatives, lack of knowledge and skills, and lack of collective power among workers." *An Open Letter to Chilean Landowners,* by Peter Dorner. Mimeographed, May, 1965. Professor Dorner of the University of Wisconsin has recently spent a number of years studying Chilean agricultural and tenure problems.

to become comprehensive. The landlord, since he has a labor force that is devoid of incentive, is effectively barred from opportunity for increasing production. Often he lives in the capital city and does not try. Instead of the revenues of a small area farmed efficiently, he enjoys those of a large area that is inefficiently farmed. (It is strongly characteristic of this Model that agriculture, some plantations operations apart, is labor intensive and technologically stagnant.)[12]

Income derived from government position or the armed forces is also unrelated to economic service. It depends, rather, on distribution of power, and this leads to the further likelihood of struggle over the division of power. Feudal agriculture is so constituted as to survive unstable or avaricious government. Modern industry—again unless under external protection—is much more vulnerable. So instability in government and its use as a source of personal income has a further adverse effect on industrial incentives. In this Model, substantial rewards accrue to traders. But this, also, is at least as dependent on a strong monopoly position—the franchise for the sale of a North American or European branded product or the strong position in financing and procurement of some local product—as on efficient economic service.

It is the normal working assumption of economists that income rewards economic effort. Since it induces that effort, it is functional. There has been ample dispute over whether particular functions are over- or under-rewarded, and this is the foundation of the ancient quarrel between Marxians and non-Marxians. But the problem of the adequacy of reward for service is not the issue here; the problem is that numerous claimants—landlords, members of the armed services, government functionaries, pensioners—render no economic service.[13] And the best rewarded businessman is not the one who per-

---

[12] In 1949, 20% of the population in Canada and the United States was in agriculture as compared with 60% in South America. Production per person was something over five times as great. In 1947/48 output per person was 143% of pre-war levels in North America (including Central America) and 83% of pre-war in South America. United Nations Department of Economic Affairs, "Land Reform: Defects in Agrarian Structure and Obstacles to Economic Development," New York, United Nations, 1951. Data are from the Food and Agriculture Organization of the United Nations.

[13] In certain philosophical or political contexts, this may be held to be true of the armed forces of any country. They are said to serve the wrong foreign policy, be part of the wrong defense strategy, serve only the arms race, or whatnot. But the armed forces are seriously in the service of the disapproved

forms the best service, but the one whose political position or franchise accords him the most secure monopoly. It is useful to have a term for the income which is so divorced from economic function and one is readily at hand. It may be called "non-functional income."

Not only is this income large but strong forces act to limit the amount of functional income. The rural worker gets the maximum established by custom; greater endeavor brings him no more. The landlord, as noted, is confined by a labor force that is without incentive. The efficient urban entrepreneur risks being regarded as a better milch cow by those who live on the state. He can protect himself only by developing the requisite political power; this means that his income comes to depend not alone on economic performance but also on political power. His return, or that part of it which derives from political influence, thus also becomes economically non-functional.

VI

The position of the controlling elite is commonly associated with the ownership of land. And this, certainly, has been the traditional source of power. But, in its modern manifestation, it is a mistake to identify it exclusively or even predominantly with land. The armed forces, hierarchical wealth other than land, the bureaucracy and shifting or permanent coalitions between these groups, can provide the requisite sources of power. Government will then be in the interest of the controlling groups; and since they are economically non-functional, it will not be in the interest of economic development.[14]

---

philosophical or political concepts. In Latin America no serious observer supposes that the armed services are seriously important for national defense, territorial integrity or any other such political or military objective. Their role is overwhelmingly related to domestic politics and income.

[14] This is a matter of much practical importance, especially as regards the armed forces. Generally in the United States there has been recognition of the bearing of a regressive or feudal land system on economic development. That *caudillo* government, either by itself or in association with other non-functional groups, can be equally inimical, has not been so readily seen. As a consequence, conservative, or more often naively traditionalist, officials regularly turn up defending army dictatorships in Latin America. And, in the past, military aid funds have regularly gone to support armies, which were a source of political power, at the same time that economic assistance was being given to development or even (hopefully) to land reform. It would be difficult to find a policy with a greater element of self-contradiction, despite the tendency of those who espouse support to the Latin American military to assume that pragmatism, professionalism and even an element of righteousness are on their side.

In a number of countries of this Model, most notably Argentina, Brazil and Chile, the non-functional groups are in competition with each other and more recently franchised economic groups for the available income. (In each of these countries an incomplete revolution accorded political power to urban white-collar and working classes without disestablishing the old non-functional groups. Chileans often speak of the " 'struggle' or even 'civil war' between the country's major economic interest groups.")[15] The total of these claims bears no necessary relationship to the income that is available. Since productivity is low, there is a strong likelihood that claims will exceed what is available, and this invariably is the case. The easiest way of reconciling competing claims is to meet that of each group in money terms and allow them to bid against each other in the market. As a result, in these countries inflation is endemic. In countries such as Ecuador and the Central American countries where the urban white-collar and working classes are weak, inflationary pressures are much less strong. This, however, reflects the weakness of these classes, not their better position under non-inflationary condition.

VII

With variations as to the composition of the non-functional elite and its source of power, Model II has general application in Central and South America and in Iran, Iraq and Syria. In few, if any, of these countries—and one or two Central American countries are possible exceptions—is the cultural base the decisive factor; in none would economic advance appear to be barred by the absence of trained and educated people. A shortage of capital is assumed almost intuitively by economists to be the normal barrier to advance. Iran and Iraq have rich sources of income from oil and Peru from oil and minerals. This has not rescued them from backwardness and some of the oil-rich countries are among the poorest in the world.[16]

In Latin America two countries do break decisively with this pattern. One is Mexico and the other is Costa Rica. Mexico, by revolution, destroyed its old power structure based on land ownership.

---

[15] Francis N. Schott, "Inflation and Stabilization Efforts in Chile, 1953–1958," *Inter-American Affairs* (Winter, 1959), reprinted in Gerald M. Meier, *Leading Issues in Development Economics* (New York: Oxford University Press, 1964), p. 221.

[16] Venezuela also has rich income from oil but may gradually be breaking the hold of a regressive social structure which for a long time led to the dissipation and waste of this revenue.

Costa Rica was always, in the main, a country of modest land hold-ings. Costa Rica has no army; the Mexican army is insignificant in size, cost and influence. Neither has any other strongly vested non-functional group which combines power with a claim on income. In consequence, income in both countries is—by all outward evidence —far more closely related to economic performance than in the remainder of Latin America. They are the two countries which enjoy the most favorable rate of economic development.

VIII

For purposes of identification, I have associated Model III with South Asia. The clearest prototypes are, indeed, India and Pakistan, although it has application to the United Arab Republic, in limited measure to Indonesia, and, since its characteristics transcend political organization, to China.

In this Model, the cultural base is very wide. India and Pakistan have systems of primary and secondary education that are far superior to those of Latin America. There are at least as many full-time pro-fessors in the University of Delhi alone as in all Latin America. Both countries tend to a surplus rather than a shortage of teachers,[17] administrators, scientists and entrepreneurs. In recent years, these countries have been substantial, if inadvertent, exporters of medical and scientific talent to the United States and the United Kingdom.

In both India and Pakistan there is a substantial volume of non-functional income. But it is not, as in Latin America, associated with political power. In India the political power and non-functional claims of the princes, jaguidars, zamindars and large landlords were terminated or greatly curtailed at the time of independence or in ensuing reforms. The armed forces, though costly, do not have in-dependent political power.[18] In consequence, producers can generally count on receiving the major return for their efforts. Economic in-centive is thus reasonably operative. The endemic inflation which characterizes many of the Model II countries is absent. The social structure in these countries is not at the highest level of compatibility with economic advance. But it is clearly not an operative barrier.

---

[17] Although not in all categories of teachers or with a sufficient willingness to serve in rural villages.

[18] The army is not without political power in Pakistan. However, it is not a recognized avenue to political power and economic advantage as in Latin America. And the armed *coup* which brought President Ayub Khan to power in 1959 (like his subsequent administration) bore little or no resemblance to the Latin American phenomenon.

The barrier in this Model is drastically bad proportioning of the factors of production. Demographic forces which extend deeply into the past have given these countries a large and dense population. The supply of arable land, although in India, Pakistan and Egypt it has been subject to repeated and very great increases through irrigation, is small in relation to the numbers dependent upon it. As a result, *per capita* operational production and incomes are small and, as a further consequence, savings are limited and so consequently is capital. Capital shortage, in turn, has retarded and continues to retard industrial development. The small land and capital base provides effective employment for only part of the available labor force. The advantages of gain and the costs of loss are not symmetrical in a poor society. People who live close to the margin of subsistence cannot afford any risk that they might fall below subsistence levels. This is a further inducement to backwardness.

The Model III countries are, in some respects, the most comprehensible in their backwardness. They conform most closely to the standard explanations of the economists; theirs, as I shall later describe, is the case that is most often generalized to all instances of underdevelopment or poverty.

I now turn to the normative consequences of this classification.

IX

The first result of reflection on these three Models is to destroy, one might hope without trace, the notion that, for any normative purposes, underdeveloped countries can be treated as a class. The poverty that produces common tendencies in behavior, as well as in the outward aspect of the community, proceeds in the different Models from radically different causes. For purposes of prescribing economic policy, it is at least as unwise to associate a culturally primitive country such as the Congo with a culturally advanced country such as India as it is to prescribe a common policy for India and the United States. There is equal error in associating countries with a regressive social structure such as Ecuador or Iran with those where social structure is not the operative obstacle to development. It has been the pride of economists and other social scientists in the last two decades that they have been able to refine and make more scientific the approach to underdevelopment and its remedies. No serious claim to such progress can be made so long as underdeveloped countries are treated as a class—so long, in other words, as discussion of the subject proceeds from unscientific generalization.

The practical consequences are even greater. In the Model I countries the key to progress is the widening of the cultural base. Internal effort and external assistance must center on the provision of the trained and educated people without which advance is impossible. It seems likely that this core must be substantial—large enough to dominate an adverse environment. Presumably, also, it must be pyramidal in shape—a small number with the highest administrative and technical skills, a larger number with the equivalent of secondary education, a yet larger number with basic literacy and companion preparation.

Here is the problem of the Model I countries. It requires a government of minimal competence together with a nucleus of teachers to organize an educational system. In the more fortunate former colonial countries, this organization was provided by the colonial authority and the teachers were drawn from abroad or provided as a by-product of religious proselytism. In the less fortunate countries, comparable help is still required.

This leads to the conclusion that, for Model I countries, organizations like the American Peace Corps are a strategic form of aid. And, though originally conceived in substantial measure as an outlet for youthful idealism, the Peace Corps is coming to play this role. It is having its greatest success in Africa where it is primarily a teaching organization. In 1964 approximately one-third of the 9,000 Peace Corps Volunteers were serving in Sub-Sahara Africa; of these over 80 per cent were teaching in formal educational programs.[19]

The importance of external training in the Model I countries will also be evident. So is the need to import administrators, technicians and specialists and teachers at a more advanced level than those supplied by the Peace Corps. In all instances, it should be noted, emphasis must be on what may perhaps be called active or primary participants as distinct from advisers or pecuniary assistance. Ad-

---

[19] They constitute more than one-third of all degree-holding secondary teachers in Ghana and teach over 20,000 secondary students in that country. In Malawi they provide over one-third of all secondary teachers and have helped to double the secondary school enrolment. In Sierra Leone they provide over one-half of all qualified teachers. In Liberia the Peace Corps furnished 90 per cent of all degree-holding teachers. In Nigeria 25 per cent of all graduate teachers in secondary schools are Peace Corps Volunteers who teach 40,000 students, representing 35 per cent of the total enrollment of secondary students. In Ethiopia and West Cameroun 40 per cent of all qualified secondary teachers are volunteers. Sharpe, *op. cit.*

visers are of little value when there is no going concern to advise. Money, in the absence of a competent organization to spend it, will be wasted.

Along with the requirements of the Model I countries, it is equally important to see what they do not need. The provision of capital, at least in any substantial volume, must wait upon the development of the cultural base and the companion institutions that allow of its effective use. Otherwise it will be wasted and, additionally, it may have a corrupting influence on the society.[20]

Sophisticated planning and experiments in public ownership are obviously to be discouraged in the Model I countries; if administrative resources are not sufficient for the basic tasks of government, they obviously should not be taxed with these further and more demanding responsibilities.[21] Social reform and population control are not central to the problem of development in this Model.

All discussions of Model I countries must reckon with the possibility, and indeed the likelihood, that in some instances development will be impossible. Predatory and anarchic influence will overwhelm and submerge whatever cultural legacy was left by the colonial power; thenceforth there will be disintegration without foreseeable end. Haiti, where the social fabric, political structure and living standards have deteriorated with slight interruption in the century and a half since the French were expelled, is a case in point. It will be surprising if there are not others. The world will one day have to face the relative merits of national sovereignty, allowing of predatory rule or anarchy, or some form of international administration until the requisites of self-sustaining political development are present.

X

In the Model II countries education and the expansion of the cultural base, however desirable, are not decisive for change. Neither is capital—in some cases it is abundant and misused. The power structure channels income into non-functional use. There is obvious danger that this will happen to pecuniary aid; it will further enrich

---

[20] In Laos, in the 1950s, it was U.S. policy when in doubt as to what should be done to provide more money. A conservative administration with an appropriate respect for pecuniary values naturally assumed that money must do good. In fact, in widening the economic difference between the city recipients and the countryside and proving the feasibility of winning wealth without effort, it probably did a certain measure of damage.

[21] Cf. Berg, *op. cit.*

the functionless rich and further strengthen or at least rigidify the power structure which is the obstacle to progress.[22]

This is not inevitable but it can happen. And in recent years it has unquestionably occurred to both Latin American and North American conservatives (abetted always by the politically innocent) that economic aid can be a highly welcome support to the *status quo*.

There are other temptations to the pursuit of the forms rather than the substance of development in this Model of which the most prominent, in the past, has been the preoccupation with inflation.

Inflation itself is not the operative barrier to economic advance. As noted, it is the product of much more deeply seated social and political factors—in particular, the political power of the non-functional groups, the low productivity which characterizes society which returns income to political power rather than economic performance, and the competition between groups for the income that is available. But inflation has high visibility. And regularly in Latin America it has been regarded not as the consequence of these deeper disorders but as the disorder itself. As a result, men of self-described sound views, on coming into touch with Latin American problems, have prescribed not for the disorder but for the symptom.

To a certain extent, countries have been urged to do whatever they were not doing at the moment. Thus, if prices are rising rapidly, policy is directed toward arresting the inflation. This will include budget restraint, restraint on wage and salary increases, efforts to reduce government and restriction on government and perhaps private investment. The non-functional income, as in the particularly clear case of the army, has political power. Thus, it can protect itself from any curtailment. Or, as in the case of landed income, it is beyond the reach of any effective restriction. The burden of stabilization is thus borne by the urban proletariat, white-collar workers or other vulnerable groups. It does not greatly affect *comprador* or trading enterprises or old and static industries which have no need for funds for expansion. It does force curtailment of developing industries which do need funds. So, as a broad rule, functional incomes and outlays are vulnerable to an anti-inflation policy; non-functional income is protected.

In consequence of this disparate effect, a stabilization policy

[22] A similar conclusion is argued with great skill in an important forthcoming paper by Celso Furtado, "Development and Stagnation in Latin America: A Structuralist Approach" (New Haven: Yale University Economic Growth Center), which he has been good enough to let me read.

soon becomes a source of social tension, possibly even social disorder, and a cause of economic stagnation. Those who enter to advise at this stage are certain to urge relaxation. And, in the common case, it is forced by political necessity—to continue the stabilization would be to jeopardize the position of those who hold power or would force a new coalition or, it is feared, help the Communists. The result is more inflation. This policy rhythm has now continued for many years in Brazil, Chile and Argentina.[23] It is obvious that both the stabilization and inflation phase are variants of a far more fundamental theme.

XI

There can be no effective design for economic development in the Model II countries which does not disestablish the non-functional groups—which does not separate them from political power and, *part passu,* reduce or eliminate their claim on income. This solution applies equally whether power derives from land, other hierarchical wealth, the army, the non-functional bureaucracy or some coalition of these. (The problem presented by the trader or *comprador* group is less clear for it performs an economic function.) There can be no *a priori* judgement that a particular non-functional group, for example landlords or the army, is more regressive than another. Any non-functional group which governs in its own interest will govern at the expense of economic incentives.

The problem is that the disestablishment of non-functional groups is a task not of reform but of revolution. A country does not redistribute land or eliminate an army by passing a law. Certainly it will not do so if landowners or the military are in control of the government. Nor is compensation an answer; men will sell property but they will not sell power. Such change in recent times has been under the *force majeure* of military occupation or it has involved a

---

[23] Professor A. O. Hirschman has drawn attention to other such policy rhythms, derived from a tendency to look with favor on any alternative to what is presently being done, in the field of exchange control, fiscal policy and development administration. *(Economic Development and Cultural Change, Chicago:* University of Chicago Press, 1957.) I have been impressed by the same tendency and attribute much of it to optimistic newcomers, both indigenous and foreign, in the field of economic development. Along with extremely important enthusiasm they bring a strong tendency, on seeing something wrong, to assume that change must be for the better. They cannot easily be persuaded either that present policy is the result of similar previous convictions or that the alternative policy had an earlier and equally unsatisfactory incarnation.

certain measure of violence. Such was the case with General Douglas MacArthur's land reforms in Japan and Korea—one of the more remarkable achievements of an occupying army and one that would have provoked fascinating comment in conservative circles in the United States had almost anyone but MacArthur been responsible. Such has been the case in Cuba and Bolivia. The disestablishment of the princes and other feudatories in India was peaceful (except for the police action in Hyderabad) only because those affected recognized that vast shifts in the power structure had made opposition futile.

Yet there must be such change if there is to be economic advance. And the pressures for advance, in a world where the demonstration effect of economic development is pervasive, are unlikely to abate. The choice may well be between earlier and later revolutionary change, a choice which may well coincide with that between liberal revolutionary change—which establishes conventional economic incentives—and Communism.[24]

The chance for liberal revolutionary change may not be unfavorable. It is supported in Latin America by a strong underlying pressure for constitutionalism and individual liberty. Although the surrender of non-functional power cannot be purchased, it can possibly be eased by external subsidy as envisaged under the Alliance for Progress. What is perhaps principally required in this area is the knowledge that the United States is categorically on the side of such liberal change and that reactionary or, more inimically, politically innocent officials will not think every thrust toward such change is Communist.[25] Should they be allowed to continue to do so, there is

---

[24] A case that has been argued in a different context by my colleague, Alexander Gerschenkron, in "Economic Backwardness in Historical Perspective," *The Progress of Underdeveloped Areas,* ed. B. F. Hoselitz (Chicago: University of Chicago Press, 1952).

[25] It will be the view of any close student of United States policy in Latin America, I believe, that more is to be feared from political innocence than political reaction. It has been extensively influenced in the past by a generation of professional diplomats who had no experience with the liberal leavening of domestic politics and the discovery that Negroes, the unemployed, farmers, trade union members, were not automatically enamored of the *status quo* and what best suited respectable and well-to-do white Anglo-Saxon Protestants of good family and education. Nor were they especially informed on the academic currents of liberal economic and political thought. At the same time, they drew on undoubted and lengthy experience in Latin America. This experience was all but exclusively with the elite; it led to an almost automatic identification with this point of view and a deep, self-confident and at times self-righteous con-

a very good chance that the ultimate such thrust will be Communist.

It goes without saying that not only moral but material support should be denied to non-functional ruling groups. Support to Latin American armed forces has been, as earlier noted, the most symmetrically self-defeating exercise in American foreign policy in the last half century. In the belief that power was being built up for resistance to Communism, a power was created that was strongly inimical to orderly political development and to economic progress. It helped make Communism increasingly attractive as an antidote and solution. One wonders if the Communists themselves are aware of their unwitting allies and are sufficiently grateful.

XII

In the Model III countries, prescription comes much closer to what have come to be considered the orthodox remedies for underdevelopment. The cultural base being wide, this requires no urgent attention. The political structure and the impact of non-functional power are not decisive.[26] The evident need is for more resources and for a limit on the claims of current consumption on resources. This means all feasible steps to mobilize internal capital resources—bearing also in mind that the social structure in these countries makes poverty comparatively democratic and that below a certain level consumption has a higher claim on resources than progress, for it is coordinate with life itself. It means, further, that for these countries external aid in the form of large capital transfers is of the utmost importance. It means, finally, that in this Model population control is vital. This classification is a guide to where energies on this urgent matter should be concentrated.

It has long been observed that certain countries—India, Pakistan

---

viction that the masses in Latin America did not count. These attitudes are not identified with any serious economic interest of the United States although they are, of course, applauded by American conservatives. It is for this reason that one properly associates them with innocence rather than reaction. Although sophistication is unquestionably increasing, these attitudes have not disappeared, at least from among the older generation of officers. They appear to have had an unhappy influence, at times, on recent policy toward the Dominican Republic.

[26] Technical assistance in industrial, educational and agricultural fields is, at best, of marginal importance in the Model. It has no general sanction and it is my feeling that in countries such as India it has been over-emphasized. It can be useful in specific areas where, despite the ample cultural base, specific technical or other intellectual resources are limited.

and (though less commonly) the United Arab Republic are cited—
have a high absorptive capacity for capital. They are also observed
to have an acute population problem. These, it will now be evident,
are not mere deviations from the underdeveloped norm. They are
the distinctive features of this distinct category of countries.

It is important that the capital be used with highest effect. This
means further, that there must be a plan or some other device for
establishing priorities and sequence in use and for making these
effective. The ample administrative and technical resources from
the wide cultural base make such planning feasible. It is not similarly
feasible in the other Models and is not to be recommended.

XIII

These Models are susceptible to further refinement. They are also,
unquestionably, subject to debate. It will be argued, not without
justice, that the lines between the Models are less sharp than here
suggested. The appropriate assignment of some underdeveloped countries will be less than obvious. All of this can be readily conceded.
The far more important point is that the difference. between these
countries is as great as that which divides the developed and the
underdeveloped. And the difference turns on the causes of backwardness and hence on the remedies to be applied. Accordingly, effective
remedial action—a sound developmental strategy—requires classification. It would be helped most, no doubt, by a precise and perfect
classification. But it will be helped a great deal by a classification
which reflects—as I suggest this one does—the basic elements of the
development problems.

DISCUSSION

Troika of Categories

Several speakers from the developing countries took issue with
Professor Galbraith's three broad classifications. Not all countries within each geographical zone conform to the characteristics laid down for that particular model.

Dr. Yadav Prasad Pant, of Nepal, said his country finds itself geographically in Model III, yet does not suffer from the disability that
characterizes this group—population pressure. *Mr. D. Franklin Neal,*
of Liberia, thought that classifications can be made according to

productivity, educational levels or other objective criterions. To group differences on geographical grounds may be adequate for sociological or anthropological purposes, but "as economists, and as people who must examine monetary, fiscal and trade factors of growth, we find this method lacking in many respects."

Senator A. Arca-Parro, of Peru, considered that Professor Galbraith had not taken sufficient account of 'recent developments in Latin America. The allegation that economic policy in Latin America is dominated by the landowners and the military interests may have been true up to 10 or 15 years ago. The lag in land reform legislation even explains the particular headway made, as a form of compensation, in Latin America's industrial and social legislation at that time.

Today "planning reform has taken place in most of the Latin American countries. In Peru during the last year we have passed a law for land reform, because we recognize it is necessary and because that group to which Professor Galbraith refers has lost its political power.

"Power is no longer in the hands of the landowners. It belongs to a new class that is coming up in Latin America." Senator Arca-Parro stressed that 22 per cent of his country's Budget is spent on education, and that during the last ten years a score of universities have been created in the Latin American continent. "It is a new picture that is coming out," he concluded.

Hon. Mwai Kibaki, of Kenya, said, "The classifications and the descriptions have, in the effort to try and make them distinctive, been overstated." *Dr. P. N. C. Okigbo,* of Nigeria, considered that the substitution of three model classifications instead of one adds clarity. But he took issue over the provision of a single prescription for immediate action in each case.

Professor Simon Kuznets of the U.S. likewise posed the question, what use is to be made of the three models. Are "the implications primarily for aid policy, or are they primarily for domestic policy, or for both?"

Secondly, he said, the concept that there is one immediate obstacle to be tackled, meaning thereby a factor which, if removed, would set economic growth going, is too simple, and comports dangers. "Many of the comments that have been made by people primarily from the less developed countries really bear on this implied criticism of the idea that one single group of factors may be the most immediate obstacle, and that somehow one can concentrate on its removal, forgetting the fact that its removal will bring other problems instead."

Professor Kuznets went on: "The way the obstacle is removed affects the future. In other words, granted that you have a shortage of cultural base, there are different ways of overcoming it, and these different ways will create different problems once this cultural deficiency is removed. It is necessary to have alternatives within this classification for the purpose which I assume Professor Galbraith really had in mind, namely choices of aid policy and choices of domestic policy."

Other speakers added a further elaboration to Professor Galbraith's three models. *Hon. J. M. Paturau,* of Mauritius, suggested a group he called Model IV, "which could be characterized by the smallness and isolation of the territory concerned. I am thinking of islands like Fiji, Barbados, Martinique, Malta, New Caledonia and, of course, Mauritius.

"These territories have in common a rapidly increasing population and an almost monocultural economy. They find it difficult to diversify and industrialize, because the internal market is relatively small and the export market difficult, due to the territories' geographical isolation." Mr. Paturau recommends "a close association with the larger and more advanced countries."

Professor Nicholas Kaldor, of the U.K., put forward a more traditionalist classification for Models I and II. As regards Model II, "there are countries which got stuck, for one reason or another, in the feudal stage, in which the whole of Western Europe was until it emerged from that phase, sometimes by violent revolutions."

When the Spaniards arrived in South America, they established huge latifundia and created a class of feudal landlords. These countries did not really benefit from political independence in the early 19th century. Apart from places like Mexico that underwent a revolution, "the feudal land-owning class and its paralyzing hold over society was never overcome.

"This is more or less true now even in such a highly cultured and educated society as Chile, and I realize that, in the particular case of Peru, a very important and sincere attempt is being made there to reform the situation in a peaceful manner. But I would solidly agree with Professor Galbraith that to say Latin America is in the feudal stage is a thoroughly permissible generalization, as social generalizations go."

Model I, Professor Kaldor continued, concerns countries that did not get beyond the tribal stage. "Tribalism is also a reactionary force. It is not true to say that these countries have no institutional obstacles to development to contend with. Indeed the major problem of the newly emergent African countries today is to establish a unitary State and to liquidate tribalism.

"The danger they are facing is that they will go through the same historical processes and revolutions as other countries; instead of jumping from tribalism to a modern socialist State, they may develop a feudal stage in between. It is not only that economic power leads to political power. There is also a danger that political power leads to economic power."

Mr. Hernando Arnal, of Venezuela, declared that the advanced countries should make themselves familiar with what is happening in the less developed world. An interest in this problem "is the beginning of the creation of a universal geography of development."

Indispensability of Capital

Two further points were criticized in Professor Galbraith's paper: first, the stress on training rather than capital investment as a top priority for Model I countries in sub-Saharan Africa. The second issue queried was Professor Galbraith's view that Model I countries should refrain from undertaking either sophisticated planning or experiments in public ownership.

Mr. Kibaki reproved Professor Galbraith for judging all Africa by the standards prevailing in the Congo. "We agree that in these Model I countries you do have a shortage of personnel, you do have a shortage of qualified people to run the new institutions that we want to start. But it just isn't true to say that in Model I countries you do not have enough people even to ensure law and order in the country, or even to ensure that the normal functions of government, like collection of taxes, are carried out."

Speaking of the need for teachers, Mr. Kibaki went on: "We need capital if we are to build the schools Professor Galbraith recommends, if we are to build the roads. The provision of the cultural base that Professor Galbraith wants is dependent on the provision of capital. So let us go back and say that we need capital, but it should be properly directed.

"This leads me to the next question. He overstates the point that sophisticated planning and experiments in public ownership are obviously to be discouraged. It is a fact, and those of us who are engaged in practical planning in these countries know that planning is perhaps the most essential aspect of trying to lift ourselves from this position of underdevelopment. Only by coordinated planning can you direct the efforts of the limited few who are educated, and of those who are not educated but believe, as a matter of faith, in the government that guides them. Only by that plan can you channel their efforts effectively, to transform in a short time the conditions in which they live.

"Professor Galbraith says that experiments in public ownership are obviously to be discouraged. Again, this is a theoretical statement. Anyone who has been to these countries knows, for instance, that the only agency that is in a position in so many of them either to make a useful application of technical assistance or capital, or to go into partnership with the more developed nations, is the government itself, or a semi-government corporation.

"Now if public ownership is to be discouraged, I wonder who is to play the role of initiating new development, particularly if we start from the assumption that Professor Galbraith does touch upon, that we haven't got an adequate class of people to initiate new modern development. The one agency left is the government; and therefore this dictates that the government should participate, should, in fact, go into public ownership. Not as a matter of dogma, but purely out of necessity."

Dr. P. N. C. Okigbo, of Nigeria, said, "It seems to me that the essential point is to recognize that development is a process which covers very many fronts, and that to choose a single prescription—give people training—does not provide for development just by itself. There is a shortage of trained persons, and all these to some extent require the use of resources, both local and external."

Education creates needs: "You teach people, I suppose, elementary hygiene, but you don't provide the water. You teach them to be better clothed, but you don't provide the facilities.

"As more and more education is provided, then unemployment becomes a problem that can only be handled by the public authorities."

Mr. Christopher Musoke, of Uganda, developed the same point. "You cannot educate people unless you are going to give them employment." He followed up Mr. Kibaki's defense of public enterprise, commenting: "Developing countries intervene in the private sector by undertaking industrial and other activities, not because of any ideological reason. It is because they are filling a vacuum."

Mr. David Horowitz, of Israel, agreed with Professor Galbraith that "the prescription for economic development must be adapted to the conditions of the individual country. What it boils down to is that the resources to be transferred must be differentiated.

"But it is the transfer of resources which counts," he stressed, adding: "You can buy to a certain extent skills, know-how and so on by an input of money and capital."

Teaching Comes First

An educated kernel is needed to lead the way forward. It may be created by a crash program at the secondary school level. Professor Galbraith conceded that, while recommending African countries to concentrate on education and training, he does not mean to exclude other forms of investment. But he cautioned against the "mythology of capital."

Mr. Pierre Uri, of France, felt like Mr. Kibaki that generalizations about Africa should not be based too closely on the Congo. In certain countries, "even if the cultural environment is limited, there may be a small elite which works through methods which necessarily are different from our Western parliamentary system but which nonetheless may work to the good of their countries. And this is one point on which misunderstandings, particularly in some cases, about the one-party system, may have to be avoided."

He wondered "whether national sovereignty has always really been the perfect solution and whether we didn't, a few years ago, miss a great opportunity by depriving international trusteeship of its real significance." He cautioned that a revolution in Model II countries might in some cases be less successful than in Mexico, and drag the country back into Model I. "I sometimes wonder whether Bolivia, for instance, won't be a case in point, where, after having eliminated a certain social structure, it has not been possible to find the elite or the system by which the country could be led into fruitful development."

Referring to the different stages of progress, Mr. Uri concluded by suggesting that "one of the most useful things which could be done among the developed countries is to use the expertize gained in the semi-developed countries as a relay. The people in such territories as the one which is now our host country are closer to the problems of those nations that still have to go through the whole process of development."

Mr. Abba Eban, of Israel, supported the need for giving education a proper priority in the allocation of investment. "Resources will not run away while the manpower to exploit them is being trained."

He advised that within the education field, top priority should be given to a crash program at the secondary intermediate level ("from which knowledge and skills will flow both upwards and downwards") and to adult education. This is more practical than building spectacular university campuses or enacting immediate compulsory primary education for all. "It is possible within a decade," Mr. Eban added, "for a small nation to revolutionize its capacity to mobilize technical skills. Within a decade that is possible. It is not in planning terms the kind of period which should lead to despair."

Dr. Mortimer Andron, of the U.S., warned that the lack of growth in foreign aid is due not to extreme selfishness but also to a disillusionment with results, and the recognition that there are poor people at home who need aid as well. He recommended attracting industrial companies from abroad, which would raise living standards and leave an educational impact.

Mr. Oumarou Sidikou, of Niger, also gave a warning—that the ills of the underdeveloped countries (excess population, inadequate instruction, subsistence economy) are symptoms but do not indicate the cause, "as the temperature of a patient reveals he is sick, but does not indicate either the cause of the malady or the methods of curing it."

*   *   *

Professor Galbraith opened his reply to the debate by emphasizing that, despite progress and change in Latin America as underlined by Senator Arca-Parro, the existing power structure remains the chief obstacle to advancement. "The fact that two countries where this problem doesn't exist—Mexico and Costa Rica—have shown in the last years such brilliant progress seems to me to be further emphasis on this point."

In placing the development of human resources before investment in material resources, Professor Galbraith quoted the host country of the conference as an example. Suppose Israel possessed great supplies of oil and access to capital, yet was saddled with a quasi-feudal social structure and was deprived of schools and universities— it would have remained a "comparatively poverty-stricken strip of sand, as it had been from Biblical days to the time of Israeli independence.

"The great resource, the thing that changed the map of Israel was not the capital it received, important as that was. The thing that changed the map was the combination of human resources, drawn from all corners of the world, with an egalitarian and democratic structure of society, in which the individual can see some of the worth of his own efforts. So let us not," he concluded, "be carried away by the mythology of capital."

Professor Galbraith avowed that he is not ideologically opposed to public enterprise, but he urges the importance of conserving administrative energy as a precious resource in poor countries. He reiterated the need for concentrating on the single main characteristic obstacle to growth in each of the three categories. "That doesn't imply the concentration is exclusive, and I certainly wouldn't want to imply that this concentration is without attention to complementary obstacles, or without preparation for the steps that lie beyond."

3 NARROWING THE GAP THROUGH INTERNATIONAL AID

By DAVID HOROWITZ

Governor, Bank of Israel

Narrowing the gap between the developed and the developing states is the crucial problem of our century. This is so because of its character, scope and depth.

In its character, it is the problem of a conflict between two groups of nations. In the 18th and 19th centuries, there was a vertical conflict between the "haves" and the "have nots" of each nation. Today, the problem of class conflict is less acute than that of the horizontal conflict embodied in the enormous gap between the living standards of the developed and the less developed nations.

The scope of the problem is global. About two-thirds of humanity live just on, or even below, subsistence level. The depth of the problem is reflected in the fact that the peace of the world depends to a very considerable extent on its solution. A *détente* between the two or three great ideological power blocs in the world seems impossible so long as the developing nations—suffering from malnutrition and economic backwardness—constitute an extensive no-man's-land to be conquered. Peace and economic prosperity are interdependent.

The Three Disparities

The gap between the living standards of the developed and the developing states can be measured by the difference between the *per capita* income of the richest nations—$ 2,500 to $ 2,700—and that of the poorest—$ 60 to $ 100 per annum. This tremendous gap is still widening, because the process of growth in most developing countries is too slow.

There are three main reasons for this discouraging development:

(a) Economic development lags behind demographic expansion. The specter evoked by Malthus is rising again as the less developed countries face a population explosion. Extension of health services and preventive medicine have brought about a decline in the mortality rate, whereas the birth rate continues to be high. At the present rate of increase, world population will total some six billion by the end of the century.

(b)   Prices of primary products show a secular downward trend. While the prices of manufactured goods have been rising in many industries, those of primary products have steadily declined. A report submitted to the United Nations Conference on Trade and Development which took place in Geneva (March–June, 1964) estimated the loss caused to the developing nations by a deterioration of their terms of trade at 17 per cent over a period of 11 years.

(c)   Capital investment is not taking place at the necessary rate because of inadequate capital transfers from the developed countries, slow domestic capital formation in the developing countries and the heavy burden of debt repayment. The assumption that sufficient amounts of capital will be attracted to the less developed countries at the prospect of higher returns to the invested capital has not come true. On the one hand, there is a heavy demand for capital in the developed world—new capital; intensive industries have emerged and populations have been rapidly increasing. On the other hand, there are several deterrents to investment in developing countries: insecurity of the capital invested, low productivity of the labor force and a lack of technical skills. Figures published by the OECD suggest that the flow of capital to the developing world from all sources has, at best, stagnated in the past few years. It was $ 9.2 billion in 1961 and $ 8.5 billion in each of the years 1962 and 1963. But apart from the inadequacy of the flow of fresh capital, there exists the problem of the growing burden of debt repayment. The U.S. Agency for International Development (AID) estimated that the annual debt service charges of the developing nations have risen from less than $ 1 billion in 1955 to $ 4 billion in 1964. The growing debt service burden cancels out part of the growth in aid—in 1955 only 8 per cent of the capital inflow was offset by debt service, whereas in 1964 debt service absorbed 30 per cent of external assistance.

Inadequacy of Conventional Remedies

The efforts to promote economic growth in the developing states have been far from adequate. When the United Nations proclaimed the sixties as the Development Decade, the idea was to attain a growth rate of 5 per cent per annum in real terms. Actually, the growth rate was about 4.5 per cent in the first two years, and only 4 per cent in the subsequent three. But taking into account the population expansion, a 4 per cent growth rate means only 1.5 per cent *per capita* increase in income.

Doubling the income of the less-developed countries at a rate of 1.5 per cent per annum will stretch over a period of more than 50 years. This is definitely too slow for peoples whose income is in the $ 60 to $ 120 range. In his report, U Thant, Secretary-General of the United Nations, calls attention

> to the grave danger of economic disaster in Asia, Africa and Latin America if the present trends of production continue . . . Developed countries pledged one per cent of their national output in aid, but currently less than three-quarter per cent of output is being provided. If the full one per cent of the developed countries' Gross National Product were made available, this would have exceeded the five per cent annual increase in the Gross National Product at which the developing countries aim. As it is, the gap in *per capita* income between the developed and the developing countries actually widened during the early part of the 1960s.

Capital an Indispensable Ingredient

Economic growth, to a very great extent—though not exclusively— is a function of investment, and the most important ingredient in investment is capital. Of course, there are other essential ingredients— sound and honest administration, managerial and technical skills, entrepreneurial initiative, and so forth. But still, capital is the indispensable ingredient, if progress is to be made on a very broad front. To develop agriculture and industry simultaneously, to promote health services and education, and create the infrastructure, an abundant supply of capital is essential. Development on such a scale cannot be achieved by gradual and slow infiltration of capital. A breakthrough in economic development depends on an immense transfer of capital which would create a domestic market as a catalyst for the diversification of the economy. Paradoxical as it may appear, the present experience of countries with some achievements to their credit in economic growth—such as Thailand, Puerto Rico and Israel—proves that it is easier in the modern world to achieve economic growth by a short-term, condensed process, than by a protracted effort stretching over many years.

Domestic Capital Formation Insufficient

Where should the capital necessary for a tremendous economic transformation come from? The development of Western Europe was made possible by domestic formation of capital. The conditions prevailing in the early capitalist era made it possible to squeeze out every ounce of energy and effort and surplus products for the formation of capital. The process was repeated in the early twenties in Soviet Russia by the same method—a cruel reduction in the living standards of the broad masses.

I submit that it is unrealistic to expect similar rapid formation of capital in the developing countries in the present circumstances. One reason is purely economic: $ 60 per head per annum is probably less than the average income in England, Germany and France of the early capitalism, and very little is left to be squeezed out for the formation of capital. Another reason is psychological and sociological. We live in a period of modern communication—radio, television, and so forth. The shining car passing through the poor village in India or Egypt brings with it the image of Western civilization, of a life which is not devoted just to keeping body and soul together. This image creates a revolution of expectations—it is inconceivable today to reduce the standard of living of the less-developed nations in order to promote the necessary formation of capital. A repetition of the methods of early capitalism would be possible only under a very strong totalitarian authoritarian regime—not in a democracy.

Aid from the Developed Countries

There is, however, an alternative to such methods in the world of today. One third of the world which is highly developed could, with a very limited effort, enable the less-developed two-thirds to achieve a high rate of economic growth with only modest domestic capital formation. The developed nations are required to sacrifice very little, whereas the stakes involved are very high—the connection between world peace and the economic advancement of the less-developed parts of the world has been mentioned above.

The Gross National Product of the developed world is today more than one trillion dollars. Within five years—assuming the most conservative rate of growth—it will reach the huge amount of $ 1,200 billion. One-and-a-half per cent of the Gross National Product of the developed countries exceeds $ 15 billion—nearly double the current flow of capital to the developing world. (I do not think that the less-developed countries could absorb much more at present.)

Is it realistic to expect the developed world to devote 1.5 per cent of its product to the cause of promoting economic growth in far away lands? During the Second World War, the developed countries devoted to the war effort between 25 and 30 per cent of a much smaller national product. The Marshall Aid Plan was carried into effect when the national product of the United States was incomparably lower than today, and the economy faced a post-war demand pressure—yet the aid amounted to more than 1.5 per cent of the economy's resources. Today, the developed states spend more than $ 100 billion a year on armaments. Would it not be possible and reasonable to take out an insurance policy of 15 per cent of that amount in order to prevent a war, and to liquidate that no-man's-land of misery and blight which causes restiveness and perils in Asia, Africa and South America?

The developed world is actually contending with the problem of what to do with its production. It is faced with the alternative of either to devote a modest part of its product to the less-developed nations, or to promote artificial waste and obsolescence in order to stimulate demand and prevent a recession.

How to Effect a Transfer of Capital

The flow of aid to the developing countries is far from satisfying their demand for investment capital. I have mentioned the decline in the flow of funds between 1961 and 1963. The seemingly slight decline from $ 9.2 billion in 1961 to $ 8.5 billion in 1963 marks, in fact, a substantial deceleration of the aid flow. During these three years, the population of developing countries had increased by about 7 per cent, and the prices of manufactured products purchased by them had increased by more than 10 per cent. Add to these the mounting burden of debt service and debt repayment, and it will become clear that without an immediate change in aid policy—in respect to both amounts and terms—an equilibrium point will be reached in the not too distant future, and repayments will equal the flow of capital to the developing countries.

The problem and its solution are stated in the following terms in the AID report mentioned above:

> Statistics indicate that at present loan rates AID programs risk future self-defeating spirals into impossibly huge loans and repayment costs for the recipient countries. The total foreign debt of the less-developed countries rose from $ 10 billion in 1955 to more than $ 30 billion in 1965, and will reach nearly

$ 90 billion in 1975. The mounting external debt burden of the developing countries emphasizes the need for soft loan terms. Furthermore, if development loans are made on soft terms rather than hard (that means with a lower rate of interest over long periods of time) the job of development will be finished sooner, and the United States and other donors will have to furnish less total aid. If it is concentrated in large amounts, at lower rates of interest and for long periods, the total amount needed will be much less. This follows from the fact that as loan terms harden, the net flow of resources decreases, and a decrease in the net flow of resources has two effects: it lengthens the time necessary to do a given job of development, and increase the amount of aid required to do that job.

The Horowitz Proposal

More aid is called for, and on more generous terms. It seems, however, that the trend of thinking in most donor countries is in the opposite direction. Aid is not popular even with governments, and less so with parliaments and congresses.

A way out of this dilemma, which was suggested by me at the World Bank Conference and later at the UNCTAD Conference in Geneva, is to raise the necessary capital in the financial markets of the developed countries. The governments of the developed countries will be called upon to guarantee the repayment of the amounts raised and to subsidize the interest payments, in order to cover the difference between the market rates of interest and the soft terms on which the money will be made available to developing countries. The approach to the financial markets could be facilitated if the World Bank, and its associate organization the International Development Association, were to handle the issue of the bonds and the allocation of the funds raised.

Capital Not a Universal Panacea

This chapter has stressed the importance of capital as an ingredient in the process of economic development. It has suggested that since domestic capital formation in the developing countries is extremely limited, capital transfers from the developed world should play a vital role in the economic breakthrough of the less-developed nations.

We should not like to create the impression, however, that we consider the transfer of capital a solution to all the problems of economic development. The less-developed world has some very important tasks to perform, and without the cooperation of the developing nations in putting their own economic policies in order, no amount of capital will avail. Developing countries must prevent capital flight; they must establish taxation systems that will promote the formation of capital and mitigate the extremely unequal distribution of income and wealth; they must take account of the need for land reform, and avoid spectacular investment projects which do not contribute to an improvement in the balance of payments. Developing countries should be selective in their investments and reach a balanced expansion of infrastructure and production capacity; they should allocate resources properly between economic development, education and family planning, which is an important ingredient in the whole scheme if we take into account the population explosion. Finally, they must impose on themselves monetary restraint to prevent inflation.

A two-pronged approach—a massive transfer of capital from the developed countries, on the one hand, and the application of new measures of economic policy in the developing countries, on the other—could promote the acceleration of economic growth in the less developed world, as well as better use of resources in the developed countries and a new division of labor on an international scale.

DISCUSSION

Obstacles to Trade

The lag in growth among the developing countries should not be exaggerated. But the absence of stability in the price of their primary commodities is a severe handicap to progress. A valuable remedy would be to reduce trade barriers in the advanced countries.

Dr. *Jacob L. Mosak*, of the U.N., qualified some of Mr. Horowitz' observations, stating that recent growth rates in the LDCs compare not too unfavorably with the growth rates that were characteristic of countries now developed. According to Professor Lewis, the terms of trade have improved for primary commodities, and according to Professor Galbraith, capital aid is only useful to Model III countries.

Nevertheless Dr. Mosak assented that the pace of growth must be accelerated; that the terms of trade have created "one of the greatest problems in commercial relations between the developed and developing countries in the post-war years"; and the "capital aid is certainly a strategic limiting factor in the rate of growth that might be possible in the developing countries."

He pointed to the clash between the stress on capital aid and Mr. Horowitz' list of "national policy requirements that would be necessary in order to permit such aid to be utilized effectively."

"I think it is quite clear that if all of these national policies outlined by Governor Horowitz were in fact to be regarded as an absolute prerequisite for aid, his program might require not only far more machinery at the international level than exists today, but if such machinery were employed to implement this program at the national policy level, the program might perhaps lead to an actual reduction in the amount of aid that would be possible, rather than to the massive increase which Governor Horowitz has proposed."

In pressing for a variety of solutions, Dr. Mosak thought greater emphasis could be laid on international policies. "Appropriate international trade policies could significantly reduce aid requirements. Indeed in some respects, although not all, trade could be much more effective than aid."

The U.N. has calculated that "the deficiency of foreign exchange to finance the import requirements of the developing countries, that are essential for their investment program, is significantly greater than the deficiency of savings necessary to finance that investment." It is not necessarily true, he infers, that the payments deficit is the same as the deficit between investment and savings. Estimates made by the U.N. suggest that the payments gap—concerning the target growth rates set for the Development Decade—would be $ 20 billion, whereas the savings-investment gap would be under $15 billion. This reinforces Dr. Mosak's predilection for "trade not aid." "With appropriate trade policies," he said, "one could in fact reduce rather significantly the amount of aid that might be necessary."

Mr. S. B. Nicol-Cole, of Sierra Leone, discussed the changing terms of trade. There is a limit, he said, to the possibilities of mitigating the shock of fluctuating commodity prices. Price instability creates budgetary uncertainty, and important infrastructural projects are abandoned.

The vicious circle is that lagging prices for agricultural products make it necessary to invest more capital so as to lower costs, but this is one of the most difficult areas for attracting capital—owing to the deteriorating situation of agricultural commodity prices.

"The deadlock is forcing some government bodies to enter themselves into the field of agriculture," which is "only second best." For government intervention does not commonly predicate commercial success, and "secondly the government is depleting its already scarce resources by engaging in an area which could be left to private enterprise, if only the economic conditions were sufficiently attractive.

"Above all, direct intervention by the government into commercial agriculture does nothing to solve the initial dilemma of agricultural price instability, a problem that can only be resolved by firm undertakings between the producer countries on the one hand, and the consuming countries on the other."

Mr. Nicol-Cole holds that the importance of capital has been exaggerated "vis-à-vis know-how, managerial skills and political stability . . . Many of the factors necessary to combine with capital so as to produce an economic upsurge are either non-existent or limited in scope. Grants and loans of dimensions large enough to make the necessary economic impact have to be accompanied by an idealistic plan for training the local people in the fields necessary to take advantage of such financial help, and for creating the necessary financial and commercial institutions so indispensable to economic good. Finally there should be a readiness on the side of recipient countries to accept and accommodate experts, while their own nationals are undergoing training."

Dr. Yitzchak Guelfat, of Israel, asked whether the "historic haste" of LDCs should be encouraged, opposed, or slowed down a little. Concerning the reduction of trade barriers advocated by Dr. Mosak, he notes that "we are all liberals, but each applies his liberalism to others and retains a protectionist cuirass for himself."

Dr. Max G. Mueller, of the U.S., advised that the accent be put not on the gap between developed countries and the LDCs, but on growth. The gap could in theory be narrowed by allowing the developed countries to stagnate, an eventuality that is not in any way desirable, if only because it would reduce the prospects of aid.

In any case, calculations that Dr. Mueller had made for seventy countries, accounting for 85 per cent of the world population, show that during the period 1949 to 1957 the gap in income between the developed and developing countries actually declined somewhat. Other calculations, using the parity rates published by the U.N. in the summer of 1964, show that it has widened slightly in 1961–62 as compared with 1957, but the ratio of income in LDCs to that in the advanced countries still remained more favorable than in 1949.

He concluded, "I do want to emphasize that there was economic progress during the 1950s in the underdeveloped countries taken as a whole. Many of them grew at rates which were not insignificant even compared to the rich countries. To quote a figure, India had a growth rate which was not spectacular—only one-and-a-half per cent—but it was no less than that of the United States, during the 1950s."

Is Aid Selfless?

The donor countries lack a good economic incentive that should activate their aid programs. This makes it advisable to seek the solution in a multilateral rather than a bilateral approach.

Without imputing it as an unworthy motive, *Hon. Mwai Kibaki*, of Kenya, asked whether it is not a fact that the motive of aid is political, and not a desire to raise economic standards of living. "What I am asking is whether we are at all being realistic in starting from an assumption which is so obviously not true." This proposition led Mr. Kibaki to the following pragmatic query: "Are there real economic reasons why the developed nations should promote the advancement of the less developed part of the world? In other words, if we want to start, now, a movement—internationally (because it must, I believe, become a political movement)—to convince the developed world that they must devote one-and-a-half or two per cent of their Gross National Product to the less developed countries, is there an econmic argument that we can use, a rational argument? Or must we continue merely to quote the position of the Cold War, that one side must stop the other from taking over a certain country? Or to quote the old ethical argument that we have the responsibility to look after our brother?"

Mr. Leopold Laufer, of the U.S., pleaded for a consideration not only of the capital flow but of capital utilization, which is often impeded by a lack of adequate plans, shortage of qualified personnel or hampering political conditions.

Capital exporting capabilities are concentrated among few countries in North America and Europe. But "the capacity to render technical assistance is no longer so restricted. Countries still in dire need of capital assistance are developing their own technical capacities which can be utilized for their own development and that of other nations.

"It may not be generally realized, for example, that over 20 per

cent of United Nations advisers and experts are nationals of developing nations. Similarly Israel, a country still in need of capital imports,
has developed a bilateral program of technical assistance encompas-
sing so far more than 7,000 trainees who have come to Israel and
over 1,700 experts that have been sent abroad. Turkey, Iran and
Pakistan have for years exchanged technical experts, and Turkey
may be at the point of setting up its own bilateral technical assistance
program."

* * *

Mr. Horowitz answered the debate by admitting that the transfer
of capital is not a panacea to solve all the problems of development.
"It is one of the most important ingredients. In some countries, it is
the most important ingredient; in others it takes a secondary role."
His thesis was that "instead of the formation of capital, we can now
substitute to a very great extent a transfer of capital."

Concerning the terms of trade, there has been a very accentuated
deterioration in 1964 and 1965, due among other things to the
production of synthetic materials and the decreasing role of raw
materials in production.

Supporting Dr. Mosak's views on the need to liberalize international
trade, Mr. Horowitz pointed out that the Israel delegation he headed
to the first Geneva conference of the UNCTAD had suggested the
now well known slogan, "Unilateral Free Trade." This means letting
the developed countries shift more and more to sophisticated new
industries like atomic power, electronics and chemicals, while traditional industries like textiles are taken over by the LDCs.

Aid must be used to bridge not only Dr. Mosak's investment gap
but the payments gap as well, because the industrialization of the
LDCs must take time, however much its duration is compressed. The
national policy requirements laid down in Mr. Horowitz' paper as
necessary for countries receiving aid "were never conceived as a precondition or a prerequisite . . . But the transfer of capital and the
emergence of these new policies should be a simultaneous, interdependent and interacting process." He took up Mr. Nicol-Cole's
stress on the need for ingredients other than capital, commenting that
"we must proceed on a broad front: better administration, more
skills, more know-how, more entrepreneurial initiative—but all these
prerequisites can be more easily established if we assume that there is
a broad flow of capital, and that some of it will be wasted. I am
absolutely convinced that this is unavoidable. Even in a country with

a relatively high level of skills like our own, of which I have had some experience in the last seventeen years, there is a certain percentage of waste which is absolutely unavoidable."

Mr. Horowitz concluded: "I haven't seen any country in the world which has taken off from a position of underdevelopment to development—neither in Europe in the 19th century nor in America, which was a debtor until 1914—do so without capital. 'Give us the tools, and we shall do the job.' "

Finally, Mr. Horowitz dealt with Mr. Kibaki's challenging enquiry about the motives of aid. Agreeing with his premise, Mr. Horowitz answered, "I don't very much mind the motivation, if I've got the capital. Secondly, the one way to eliminate strings and political power from aid is to move from bilateralism to multilateralism. My plan is wholly built on that. What I suggested is a direct access to capital to be obtained through the World Bank from the capital markets of the developed nations, via a subsidy on the interest rate and a guarantee—and then you don't need to go, hat in hand, every year to the parliaments and governments of the world."

As to motives, he quoted Karl Marx' Theory of Impoverishment in the 19th century, which did not come true, but did prod humanity into a fear of the dangers ahead. "We are facing the same situation now, the fear of instability, of starvation in the developing countries. That fear, together with a certain feeling of conscience—I don't eliminate the ethical motive altogether—act to some extent. We have seen that aid, though inadequate and insufficient, has nevertheless increased in six years (public capital) from $ 3 billion to $ 6 billion."

4

PLANNING AS A TOOL FOR ACCELERATING ECONOMIC PROGRESS

By Edmond A. Lisle

Deputy Director,
CREDOC, France

Fast growth rates have been achieved in some Western countries (Germany, Italy) without planning institutions. Other rapidly developing countries (France, the Netherlands) have had planning bureaus for nearly two decades. Japan and Israel set up planning agencies after consistently maintaining some of the fastest growth rates in the world. Economies with less dynamic growth rates (the U.S.A., Belgium) have no planning institutions but another of them, Britain, recently set up NEDC in order to boost its rate of growth from 2.6 per cent p.a. to 4.0 per cent p.a. (see Table 1).

This brief survey suggests that economic planning at least is not inimical to growth whereas its absence may be. Moreover we observe that both rapidly expanding and stagnating economies are going over to planning. The latter are doing so to accelerate their expansion; the former, to accelerate, to sustain or better, to harmonize theirs.

This Western—or so-called French style of planning—has three characteristics.

In the first place it is a mechanism for "reducing uncertainty"—in the very sense in which Knight used the phrase[1]—through organization and market research on a nation-wide scale.

In the second place it is a conscious attempt by society democratically to define both its long-term goals—or type of civilization it is aiming at—and the ways and means of attaining them, i.e., it is a mechanism whereby men can better visualize and control their future.[2]

---

[1] Cf. Risk, Uncertainty and Profit.

[2] "The Plan does not merely forecast what is probable, it also expresses what is desirable. It adds to a neutral anticipation an assertion of purpose... Planning thus corresponds to a deep-felt aspiration of our time according to which men want to be collectively active agents of their destiny. In so far as there exists a collective will, the plan can become an ardent obligation." Préparation du Véme Plan, Rapport sur les principales options. Loi no. 64 1265 du 22.12.64. Journal Officiel de la République Française 12.12.64, p. 44.

TABLE 1

Some International Comparisons
Annual Growth Rates of G.N.P.

Country	1950–1960	1960–1970		1965–1970 EEC
		OECD	EEC	
	%	%	%	%
Germany	7.4	4.1	4.2	4.0
Italy	5.6	5.0	5.9	5.8
United Kingdom	2.6	3.3	—	—
United States	3.3	4.4	—	—
Belgium	2.9	—	3.9	3.9
Netherlands	4.9	—	4.6	4.9
France	4.4	4.7	4.7	4.7

Source: Préparation du Vème Plan, *op. cit.*, Annexe No. 3, p. 196.

Lastly, such planning is no substitute for the market mechanism. The latter must "day by day achieve the continual adjustments entailed by the variations of supply and demand ... The Plan's function is to propose ... a common prospect of economic development in order to provide a guiding light for individuals' behavior. All long-term decisions rest upon a visualization of the future."[3] Now the traditional market mechanism does not provide such a prospect, for forward markets cover only the short-term and then only a very limited range of products. Although the plan does supplement the market on this decisive point, it does not aim at rigidly predetermining the future trend of the economy. Such a conception, which was never the French one, is less and less defensible as the economy becomes both more closely integrated with the world economy and more complex and diversified. The planned economies of Eastern Europe are themselves adopting more flexible planning techniques and are recognizing the need for short-term adjustments of supply and demand through the market mechanism.

In an advanced economy and a democratic forward-looking society, the plan thus appears a complement of—not a substitute for—the market economy. In less advanced societies, which are typically characterized by the absence of a market economy, or where the market economy functions in only a limited sphere, the plan necessarily stands proxy for the market until such time as development is sufficient for market mechanisms to be brought into play, supplementing the plan and enabling it to become more flexible.

[3] Préparation du Véme Plan, *op. cit.*, p. 40.

With a rapid growth rate and the economy consequently becoming more complex, i.e., going into greater division of labor, longer production periods, a widening range of products with a quickening rate of obsolence, planning must become more refined both as regards its real goals and as regards their monetary implications.

The highest possible growth of G.N.P. is no longer the only conceivable objective of long-term economic policy, nor the only criterion of economic efficiency. It is itself the outcome of rates of growth of output, consumption, investment, foreign trade, incomes and savings which have to be mutually consistent for a given set of prices. Planning has to define the upper and lower limits of a range of mutually compatible growth rates outside which danger lies in the form of inflation and balance of payments disequilibrium, or of recession and unemployment. This must include an "early-warning system" which will set in motion a revision of planning strategy should the economy begin skidding toward the danger zones.

In the first part of this chapter, the objective of the Fifth French Plan (1966–1970) will serve to illustrate some of the problems encountered in planning "mutually consistent" targets in real terms.[4]

The purpose of the second part of the chapter is to show how, in the light of French experience, monetary and financial planning have become an indispensable condition of stable growth, through prices, incomes and savings policies.[5]

Real Planning and Balanced Growth

The broad policy objectives of the Fifth French Plan (or indeed of any economic plan) are, in real terms: the growth rate of the economy; the distribution of the gross domestic output between investment and consumption; the desirable structure of final consumption; and the orientation of social policy and of regional development policy.

Table 2 shows how growth has been distributed in the past and how it is planned to be distributed in the coming five years.

---

[4] "Sustaining long-run expansion depends on our ability harmoniously to develop the various components of final demand. This stresses the importance of the way in which the rewards of growth shall be distributed." IVème Plan de développement économique et social—1962–1965. Annexe jointe à la loi No. 62 6900 du 4.8.1962, Journal Officiel de la République Française—7.8.1962, Cahiers annexés, p. 11.

[5] "Value programming is a development of real planning in that it applies to it price and income trends that are consistent with the political, economic and social aims of the plan." Préparation du Véme Plan, *op. cit.,* p. 51.

Throughout the fifties, public consumption and investment and residential construction grew faster than domestic output—and faster still than productive investment—thanks largely to a slower rate of growth of private consumption. But the harmony of over-all mean figures is deceptive: the apparently balanced growth of imports and exports obscures in fact the very severe internal and external financial crisis of the mid-fifties culminating in the 1958 devaluation and monetary reform. And if, in real terms, a transfer took place in favor of public expenditure and housing investment and at the expense of private consumption, this was largely redistribution through inflation, for prices rose by 90 per cent in the decade. That a growth of output should nevertheless have taken place at 4.7 per cent p.a. with a constant labor force and a declining capital coefficient partly reflects a transfer of labor from low productivity (agriculture) to high productivity sectors, partly a catching up of more advanced countries,[6] the net result being, according to OECD, a higher return on investments in France than in the U.S.A., the U.K., Germany or Italy.[7]

The dominant feature of the whole decade was, however, a tendency to overstrain resources: to maintain a high rate of increase of private consumption, simultaneously increasing the share of public expenditures and gross fixed capital formation in order further to accelerate over-all growth (Table 4). The result was a balance of payments crisis in 1952 followed by two years' slow growth and a second major crisis in 1956–1958, again followed by two years of stagnation. After the price stabilization and currency reform program had been carried through during the Third Plan (1958–1961), the Fourth Plan (1962–1965) deliberately set out to accelerate the over-all growth rate of domestic output from 4.7 per cent p.a. in the fifties to 5.5 per cent p.a., largely through a higher rate of capital accumulation. This stepping-up was to be achieved without foreign aid or balance of payments deficit and under the restraint that the new currency remain stable. The purpose of this raising of sights was to be able to devote more resources to social and urban investments, to "pay more attention to the qualitative aspects of development, reflecting thereby a less partial concept of man: The stress is laid on living conditions rather than on the standard of living. Collective investments in education, health, culture, town planning, are to progress

6 Numerous productivity missions to the U.S.A. in the fifties contributed toward this technological improvement.
7 Quoted in *Préparation du Vème Plan, op. cit.,* p. 42.

twice as fast as overall output. Regional development and town and country planning are becoming more important and ... social welfare considerations are more heavily underlined especially in the case of large families, the elderly and low income recipients." [8]

Many of the aims of the Fourth Plan will have been achieved or surpassed by the end of 1965 although in the field of urban and social investments, a privileged sector, the degree of fulfilment was

TABLE 2

Growth Rates at Constant 1960 Prices (% p. a.)

	1950–1960	1960–1965 planned	1960–1965 achieved	1965–1970 planned
Gross domestic output*	4.7	5.5	5.0	5.0
Private consumption	4.3	5.2	5.7	4.5
Public investment	7.8	5.1	5.8	6.6
Productive investment	3.9	6.4	6.0	5.7
Public investment	7.4	10.7	10.7	9.1
Housing	10.5	5.7	5.3	6.0
Imports	6.5	6.5	11.5	9.6
Exports	6.5	6.2	6.9	9.4

* A growth rate of 5.0% of G.D.O. = 4.7% growth of G.N.P.
Source: Préparation du Vème Plan, Annexe No. 2, *op. cit.*, pp. 194–195.

TABLE 3

Consumption Patterns

	1950	1960	1970
Food	41.5	36.8	28.9
Clothing	12.2	12.2	12.1
Housing	15.5	16.4	17.7
Health and hygiene	8.1	9.9	12.9
Transport	6.0	7.8	10.2
Culture and recreation	7.3	8.0	9.1
Other	9.4	8.9	9.1
All	100.0	100.0	100.0
Over-all growth	100.0	152.0	249.0
Growth p.a.		4.3	5.1
Growth p.a. p.c.		3.5	3.9

Sources: Préparation du Vème Plan, *op. cit.*, p. 198.
     Etudes et Conjoncture, I.N.S.E.E., Paris, Septembre 1964, pp. 34–35.

[8] Pierre Masse, Les principes de la planification française, Weltwirtschaftliches Archiv, Band 92, 1964 Heft 1, p. 116.

only 75 per cent. As regards monetary stability moreover, the Plan went "off the rails" quite early on, and on September 12, 1963—less than midway through its course—a price stabilization program had to be introduced. For one again in French planning experience, inflationary pressures were setting in and the hitherto favorable foreign balance was rapidly deteriorating, heavy capital imports (themselves generating inflationary pressure through an increased money supply)[9] temporarily obscuring and adversely moving balance of trade.

TABLE 4

Annual Rate of Increase of G.N.P. and Distribution of G.N.P. 1949–1963 (%)

	Increase of G.N.P. over previous year	Gross fixed capital formation	Private Consumption	Public Consumption	External surplus of deficit	G.N.P.
1949	—	21	68	11	0	100
1950	108	20	67	12	1	100
1951	106	19	68	13	0	100
1952	103	19	67	15	−1	100
1953	103	17	67	15	1	100
1954	105	18	67	13	2	100
1955	105	19	67	12	2	100
1956	106	21	67	14	−2	100
1957	105	21	67	14	−2	100
1958	103	22	66	13	−1	100
1959	103	20	65	14	1	100
1960	108	21	64	13	2	100
1961	105	21	65	13	1	100
1962	107	21	65	13	1	100
1963	105	21	65	14	0	100
1964	105	23	64	13	0	100

Source: Rapport sur les Comptes de la Nation de l'année 1964, Paris, Imprimerie Nationale 1965, pp. 338–341.

N.B. In recent years, since 1959, Gross Domestic Output in France (Cf. Table 2) has consistently been 89% to 90% of Gross National Product.

The main reason for the inflationary stress lay, however, in an increase in private consumption far more rapid than forecast. In part this was due to a once-only factor; the absorption, in 1962–63, of over one million repatriates from Algeria, whose lavish resettlement grants—though absolutely justified on ethical and psychological

[9] A similar development took place in Israel in 1963 and 1964.

grounds—nevertheless significantly added to effective demand long before the productive capacity of the immigrants increased output.[10]

Over and above this once-only factor there seems, however, to be a more fundamental reason for the French economy's tendency to skid into inflation beyond a certain growth rate, which seems to be about 5 per cent. The reason is the inconsistency of the aggregate propensity to consume of households acting in their individual capacity as consumers, with their collective propensity to invest, behaving in their capacity as citizens or producers. Correcting this schizophrenia is one of the fundamental aims of planning, if balanced growth is to be achieved.

"The experience of the Fourth Plan is instructive in this respect. When a program is drawn up solely in real terms (i.e., at constant prices), a target such as the distribution of the gross domestic output between consumption and investment is only partially operative. It is operative for public investments (carried out by government or nationalized firms) which come under the authority of the State. It is so, to a lesser degree, through induced effects, inducements and self-interest, for private sector investments. Consumption on the other hand is governed by incomes which are usually freely determined and used. The Plan's distribution target was thus a kind of hope: hope that by spontaneously not overshooting the consumption target, the investment target would be achieved without inflation . . . Western societies must solve the problem of reconciling, without inflation, public decisions drawn up first in a certain prospect, and a multitude of (subsequent) individual decisions which partly obey other criteria." [11]

The two inflationary pressures at work in a rapidly expanding economy clearly appear here: the income (or cost) push and the demand pull.

Cost Inflation

Rapid over-all growth entails distributing high prizes—wages as well as profits—to the rapidly expanding sectors, both to attract productive resources and to encourage research of new productive opportunities. But the rapid growth of new sectors or products inevitably entails the no less rapid decline of others: fast progress means high rates of obsolescence, i.e., rapid renewal of products and factors.

[10] Cf. Bank of Israel Bulletin No. 17 for an attempt to assess the "economic consequences of large-scale immigration."

[11] Préparation du Vème Plan, op. cit., pp. 52–53.

Now on account of the downward inflexibility of factor incomes—
the so-called ratchet effect—factors of production are insufficiently
mobile between sectors or too slow at reconverting within sectors.
There is a lag between the moment an obsolescent product is replaced
by a newer one and the moment its factors of production move or
reconvert. And during this lag, factor incomes are protected by
subsidies, price maintenance, import duties, detaxation and all the
well-known paraphernalia of protection of declining industries, until
the alternative (social) cost of closing down and reconverting is seen
to be significantly less than that of supporting them.[12]

Among industries that are not declining but only growing less
fast than the leaders in the expansion race—and thus offering less
glittering rewards—an income demonstration effect sets in, partly
out of sheer imitation, partly to halt the drain of the ablest or most
promising factors to the leaders, thus safeguarding one's chances of
becoming a leader tomorrow. If we assume that the annual growth
rates of factor incomes are distributed skewedly, with the mode and
median somewhat to the left of the mean, then the tendency will be,
on the part of those factors with income growth rates of mode or
median values, to exert constant pressure to achieve at least the
average national growth rate—for unless they do so they are certainly becoming relatively impoverished.[13]

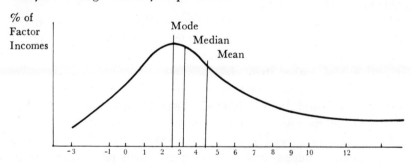

Income growth rates % p.a.

Under conditions of rapid growth the tendency to prevent or retard relative income declines will entail some transfer of productivity

[12] Cf. the agricultural policies of the U.S.A., the U.K., France, Germany, Israel, etc.
[13] The assumption of a skew distribution is a realistic one under rapid growth
conditions. The skew would obviously be less acute for slower growth rates
and we would expect a normal distribution under stationary conditions.

gains from the more dynamic to the less dynamic sectors as the accompanying figures suggest:[14]

	Activity		Real wages	
	1950	1960	1950	1960
Sectors with faster than average growth rates	100	121	100	103
Sectors with about average growth rates	100	101	100	99
Sectors with less than average growth rates	100	82	100	93

Delaying action of this sort is pursued in nominal terms and when it rigidifies the relative wage structure—and consequently hinders factor mobility—to the extent suggested by the figures, it cannot but be held largely responsible for the 90 per cent price increase that France experienced in the fifties.

Demand Inflation

On the demand side, a high marginal propensity to consume is also to be expected in a community accustomed to a rapid growth rate. In the French case three distinct factors may be isolated which contribute towards this effect.

First, 50 years' experience of currency depreciation have on the whole tended to make consumers prefer to hold tangible wealth—whether durable or less durable consumption goods, investment goods or real estate—rather than claims.

Secondly, the actual standard of living has doubled in real terms between 1949 and 1963;[15] just as households have got used to inflation so also have they become accustomed to growth.

Lastly, planning itself makes people expansion-minded and forward-looking, inducing them to extrapolate their past experience of growth and expect as a due a future improvement. If incomes are thus expected to rise, then future increments will tend to be borrowed on to finance an increase in present consumption—particularly if prices also are expected to rise.

Thus planning has introduced the time dimension and elastic ex-

---

[14] Quoted by J. Delors: Politique des revenus et stratégie du développement, Revue d'Economie Politique, Congrès des Economistes de Langue française, Mai 1965, p. 32.

[15] Rapport sur les Comptes de la Nation de 1963, *op. cit.*, pp. 334–335.

pectations into the supply and demand schedules of the market economy. Now a plan to accelerate expansion must achieve consistency in the growth objectives it assigns to the various sectors of the economy. But it is insufficient to achieve consistency between sectors. Consistency of economic behavior within sectors must also be attained. For if firms distribute higher incomes in anticipation of planned (or forecast) productivity increases; and if households spend more in anticipation of a future rise in incomes, the Plan's targets may not even be achieved in real terms—despite their initial consistency—so great is the distorting power of inflation on the allocation of resources, besides its social inequity.

It is in view of our specific experience of this in France and of the analysis of the inflationary potentialities of rapid growth, that the Fifth Plan combines real planning (or planning at constant prices) with value programming, or designing an incomes and savings policy consistent with rapid growth and price stability.

Value Programming

The report on the Fifth Plan stresses the "four basic conditions of success: competitiveness of firms; education and vocational training of the labor force; incomes policy and the financing of investment."

And it goes on to state that "carrying out the first two conditions means accentuating existing efforts. The other two conditions imply new measures and a new outlook. One of our essential tasks will be to define a set of practical measures enabling us to provide for a growth of incomes consistent with stability of production costs, and an increase of overall savings (by households, government and business) enabling the planned economic and social investments to be financed." [16]

Price Stability

A price stabilization policy implies first a decision as to the absolute annual variation of the price level deemed to be tolerable short of inflation. A rise in the index beyond such a level would be one of the signals of the "early-warning system" which would set in motion stabilization measures. The Fourth Plan had considered a "price-slide"—a nice euphemism—of 1 per cent to 2 per cent a tolerable dose of inflation. If a margin of currency depreciation is to be thus incorporated in a plan—and there is no good reason why it

[16] Préparation du Vème Plan, *op. cit.*, p. 37.

should be—it is obvious that it cannot be greater than the expected
international "price-slide." Countries whose whole economy is closely
integrated with the world economy will be far more sensitive to the
dangers of their currency slipping away from the international monetary standard through domestic inflation than economically "insular"
countries. It is noteworthy that France's spell of secular inflation occurred during a period when her economy was heavily insulated
from the rest of the world.

The second aspect of a price policy is to define a relative price
structure. Table 5 shows the relative price changes which took place
between 1960 and 1965 and which could be expected between 1965
and 1970. The latter are to some extent planned: they aim at making
agricultural incomes grow faster than other incomes, at making public
utilities more remunerative (or less dependent on government subsidies), and lastly at bringing rental accommodation—particularly of
older houses—up to the level of an economical rent.

TABLE 5
Relative Production Costs

Sector	1960–1965	1965–1970
Agriculture	100.5	105.5
Industry and Transport	96.8	95.0
Services	101.0	104.0
House rent	135.0	122.0
Average	100.0	100.0
Price increase of gross domestic output 1960/1963	116.0	—

Sources: Préparation du Vème Plan, *op. cit.,* p. 202.
Rapport sur les Comptes de la Nation de 1963,
op. cit., p. 333.

The aim in respect of agricultural prices is consistent with Common Market agricultural policy and with emigration from French
agriculture at a rate of 120,000 workers per annum.[17]

Raising rents and prices of public utilities, on the other hand, is
in keeping with French planning practice of reestablishing "truth-

[17] Between 1954 and 1962—census dates—the agricultural labor force declined
by 25 per cent at a rate of 160,000 workers per annum. To date this trend has
implied mopping up disguised unemployment and heavily increasing productivity per person employed, rather than eliminating marginal holdings. Concentration of holdings will become more important in coming years.

ful" prices, and hence both relieving the Budget of heavy subsidy payments and restoring the market mechanism.

Incomes Policy

As in the case of price policy, an incomes policy entails both a choice as to the level of aggregate income—here income growth is implied as against price stability—and a choice in respect of income distribution.

If price stability is to be maintained, households' total resources must grow no faster than aggregate private consumption—i.e., at 4.5 per cent p.a. or 3.4 per cent p.a. *per capita.*[18] The problem of restricting income growth to this relatively high level (for it implies a doubling of real income *per capita* in 20 years) can in fact only be approached by analyzing income distribution. (Distribution is understood here in the economic sense of distributive shares going to social groups, not in the sense of a statistical distribution or range of incomes). Four broad groups of income are distinguished: three groups of factor incomes, namely farm incomes, other unincorporated business profits and (non-agricultural) wages and salaries, and all transfer payments (social insurance benefits for sickness, old age, family allowance, etc.).

Table 6 shows how these shares expanded from 1960 to 1965 and how fast they can be made or allowed to rise between 1965 and 1970.

Transfer payments account for about 20 per cent of households' total resources.[19] The growth rates for factor incomes and transfer payments combined would therefore imply a rate of increase of total resources *per capita* of about 4.0 per cent p.a. between 1965 and 1970, instead of 4.5 per cent in the earlier period.

Diminishing the rate of increase of transfer payments—which would nevertheless remain the fastest growing form of income in the aggregate—is obviously within the government's direct power since these payments are financed through quasi-fiscal contributions related to wage rates. Insofar as the Common Market's agricultural price policy succeeds, farm incomes *per capita* could be made to rise faster than other incomes.

---

[18] This was the rate in real terms, through the fifties, achieved with inflation. Cf. Table 3 above.

[19] Cf. Rapport sur les Comptes de la Nation de 1963, *op. cit.,* p. 67.

TABLE 6

Income Growth by Distributive Shares
(% p.a. in Real Terms)

	1960–1965	1965–1970
Aggregate income		
Wages and salaries	6.9	4.9
Farm incomes		3.6
Other unincorporated business profits	2.8	3.5
All factor incomes	4.8	4.4
Transfer payments	8.0	6.8
Incomes per capita		
Wages and salaries	5.1	3.3
Farm incomes	3.4	7.3
Other unincorporated business profits	4.3	3.3
All factor incomes	4.0	3.8
Transfer payments	6.5	5.7

Sources: Préparation du Vème Plan, *op. cit.,* pp. 193, 203.
Rapport sur les Comptes de la Nation de 1963, *op. cit.,*
pp. 66–67.

N.B.   Factor incomes *p.c.* are aggregate factor incomes divided
by working population.
Transfer payments *p.c.* are aggregate transfer incomes
divided by total population.

The real difficulty in any incomes policy lies of course in controlling the rate of growth of non-farm wages and profits. An incomes commission, similar to the British National Incomes Commission, including representatives of government, management and
trade unions, will be entrusted with defining each year the increase
in wages and profits compatible with price stability. The planning
commissioner, Pierre Masse, himself points out that he is "fully aware
of the difficulties that will be met in setting up such new institutions
and procedures, particularly when it will come to defining rates different from the standard income trends which shall not make the
government's annual recommendations completely valueless. Yet I
am no less convinced," he adds, "that an incomes policy will tend
to become unnecessary to the very extent that everyone comes to
realize its utility."[20] The underlying hope therefore is that, as planning techniques progress and men realize the advantages but also
the implications of controlling society's future, the community as a
whole will tend to become more self-disciplined.

[20] Pierre Masse, L'évolution de la planification française, lecture delivered at
the London School of Economics, October 14, 1964.

Savings Policy

Until society achieves more maturity and responsibility in this direction, however, another aspect of value programming can help shape households' behavior in a manner more consistent with the community's planning targets, namely through an active savings policy.

The earlier French plans included the twin implicit assumptions, first that the marginal propensity to save was constant, and secondly, that savings would be forthcoming through the appropriate channels to finance exactly the amount of investment laid down in the plan. Events showed that these assumptions, naively taken over from the "General Theory," were unrealistic: the finance of investment was largely carried out by inflationary processes, which, apart from their inequity, neither ensure optimum resource allocation, nor enable the country as a whole to transfer part of its wealth abroad to stimulate progress in the developing countries.

One of the aims of financial planning must be to ensure therefore that households are induced to make their earning, their spending and their savings propensities consistent in the aggregate.

For a given increase in aggregate consumption (growing at a rate of 3.4 per cent *per capita*) it may be assumed that the pattern of consumption forecast for 1970 (Table 3) has a reasonable likelihood of being achieved, for the behavior laws it implies are consistent with past and present consumer habits in France and comparable to those observed in countries at a similar or more advanced state of development.

The maintenance of a 5 per cent output growth rate implies a more rapid increase of productive capital formation than in the previous decade (Table 2) and this, together with a much faster rate of public investment (in social equipment and urban infrastructures) requires a rise in the marginal propensity to save. Firms are to raise the self-financing of their investments from a ratio of about 60 per cent in the early sixties to about 78 per cent (the ratio had been 80 per cent in the fifties). But in a period of increasing price competition, it would be unsound to aim at a higher ratio. Moreover a higher ratio would entail a redistribution of wealth—through capital appreciation—in favor of shareholders, which contradicts both the ethics and the logic of the income policy.

The incomes policy provides for a slightly faster rise in total resources than in consumption *per capita*. In itself this will not, however, ensure an increase in personal savings. Indeed, an increase in income relative to consumption is far more likely to be spent unless an active effort is made to develop savings and this in turn requires carefully investigating the savings habits of consumers.

Present savings behavior in France is characterized by a high liquidity preference (despite inflation), a high propensity to invest in real estate and a high propensity to borrow.[21] The importance of liquid (or near liquid) asset holdings, in cash and in savings banks deposits—much more than in current banking or giro accounts—suggests a high security and speculative motive: the aim of many wage and salary earners seems to be to hold between six months' and a year's income in liquid form—a dangerously large balance from the point of view of price stability.[22] Savings policy must seek to consolidate such volatile holdings, by inducing cash holders to open current accounts, current account owners to transfer partly to deposit accounts, and both to use their savings accounts as a source from which to subscribe to investment trusts.

Households' hedge against inflation—and an important source of capital appreciation—is real estate investment, largely financed by long-term loans, and initially determined on the part of many home purchasers, by the fact that this is the only way to find accomodation. An owner occupier soon discovers, however, the advantages of holding wealth: greater security and greater freedom. Now a rapidly growing economy is also one where everybody becomes more forward-looking and expects to become more wealthy—thus discovering both more reasons for, and having more possibilities of, saving. People begin to save *for* something—their own future self-realization or pleasure, their childrens' education or career—not merely against some unforeseen (unpleasant) contingency.[23] They learn too that money saved can work for them until such time as it is needed.[24]

Having identified such habits, which emerge most explicitly under the life-cycle hypothesis of consumers' behavior, an active savings policy would aim at encouraging young and middle-aged persons to save more now for higher consumption later, the stress being laid on future consumption rather than on income or security. This would offset the urge, in a rapidly growing economy, to spend now by

---

[21] Israeli experience is similar.

[22] The interest on savings deposits—about 3 per cent—which are practically available on demand, roughly offsets currency depreciation.

[23] Against which nowadays they enjoy good *social* insurance.

[24] On this and related points, see E. Dichter, *Handbook of Consumer Motivations* (New York: McGraw Hill, 1963), p. 471.

anticipating a higher expected income. And in so far as people borrow and develop regular repayment habits preempting their incomes, the aim must be to induce them to invest—instead of spend—the sums set free once a loan has been redeemed.

But to use the forward-looking and wealth-desiring potentialities of the public in a rapidly expanding economy in this way does imply that the monetary authorities, the banking system and the stock exchange expand their markets more dynamically than hitherto: the sales promotion of claims by their natural retailers, the banking system, must become more effective than that of consumer commodities and gadgets if the marginal propensity to save is to grow. The analysts of consumer demand know that households' spending behavior changes more under the influence of producers, at any given income, than under that of any other factor, and a claim is essentially no different from any other commodity—except that, in a fully employed, rapidly growing economy its demand is not inflationary.

* * *

A rapidly growing economy tends to develop built-in inflationary forces. If planning is to accelerate growth it must also, through value-programming, offset these forces by inculcating in the community the feeling that a price stabilization and an incomes policy are both equitable and vital for rapid balanced growth. This education of minds is a long-range objective. In the short run, the inflation-offsetting weapon to be forged is a rising marginal propensity to save. It behoves the credit system to rise to the occasion.

DISCUSSION

Learn by Planning

Planners should not be sidetracked by the desire for impressive over-all production figures. They must deal with the specific problems that need attention in their country at the present time. This includes the long-term benefits of "value programing." The function of planning is illuminating, because it reveals to those in charge what can and cannot be done in terms of hard facts.

In introducing his paper Mr. Lisle took a stand against using over-all economic growth as a sole criterion for evaluating economic performance. He adapted the simile used by Mr. Sidikou in a previous debate. To judge everything according to the expansion of the Gross Domestic Product, Mr. Lisle indicated, is like saying that the lower a patient's temperature, the better his health.

Each country must list its own development objectives. Mr. Lisle showed that every one of France's successive plans had a different set of aims. The first dealt with the repair of war damage in basic sectors of the economy, like transport, steel and energy. The next two plans were devoted to raising productivity, and the fourth to infra-structure and social investments.

In evolving economies that are not yet monetized, Mr. Lisle suggests that a development plan can be an instrument for accelerating the transition to a market economy and to monetization.

Planning a steady increase in future living standards can admittedly encourage people to overspend, in anticipation of future receipts. Therefore the plan must contain a program for price stability, including an income policy and a savings policy. It is commonly said that a sound currency is needed to promote savings. Mr. Lisle put it the other way around: without adequate savings, there can be no sound currency.

Bankers must better their productivity as "salesmen" of credits to potential savers. This is difficult in an age when the industrialized countries are promoting consumption. Yet savings are feasible even in areas with an income of $60–100 a year *per capita,* because a small proportion of the inhabitants enjoy big revenues, and this is the sector that is responsible for ostentatious consumption and even for the flight of capital.

In the view of *Dr. Germanico Salgado,* of the Organization of American States, underdeveloped countries have given insufficient attention to what Mr. Lisle calls "value programming." Dr. Salgado refers to it as "financial programming," i.e., controlling incomes and savings so as to maintain price stability.

Economic planning in France presupposes the existence of a market mechanism and developed financial institutions. Dr. Salgado described the following sequence of events as characteristic in Latin America. Owing to the shortcomings of private enterprise, the public sector was saddled with a fundamental responsibility in the field of invest-ment. But the public sector failed to generate sufficient savings. This together with the speculative nature of many private business activities led to external indebtedness. In order to protect the balance of payments, private consumption was partially curtailed by restricting imports. This did generate some savings, but they were offset by the high cost of locally produced import substitutes.

Only Mexico made headway in organizing and strengthening its capital market. Private commercial banks are, in many of the countries, traditionally indifferent to development, according to Dr. Salgado. Costa Rica "ended the struggle by nationalizing the private banks; unfortunately without further attempts to adapt them to development needs."

The Latin American countries need a more complex kind of planning, which includes policies covering public sector finance, the balance of payments, financial intermediaries and monetary problems —in addition to the income and savings programs mentioned by Mr. Lisle.

Dr. Raphael Trifon, of Israel, asked Mr. Lisle "to what extent planners, in the French experience, possess the powers to see to it that their plans are executed. It seems that the act of planning is rather frustrating because politicians in the end have the option to choose those parts of the plan that seem to them politically expedient or palatable, and shelve the rest."

Dr. Trifon added that planners may be more remote from short-run problems, and therefore less realistic than the politicians.

He went on to criticize Mr. Lisle's planning formula for not making a clear distinction between goals and means. Given that the growth of output is not the sole measure of economic development, other objectives are laid down—consistent growth rates in consumption, in saving, in investment, and in foreign trade, also price stability, full employment, etc. Which of these are goals, and which means?

Then what is the scale of preferences in judging plans where some of the targets are attained and others not? Is there a social utility function by which these things can be measured?

Hon. Mwai Kibaki, of Kenya, stressed the indirect advantages of planning operations, which make political leaders understand what the problems are about. "Planning in an economy such as the French, Israeli, British or any other may be different where the ordinary man or woman, first, is already in the money economy, and thinks the pursuit of a money income a worth-while exercise; and secondly, where the problem is not so much initiating organized effort toward the attainment of targets, but rather coordinating individual efforts toward these targets."

A national plan also gives the people something to work for. "A vacuum is created soon after independence, where the one consuming goal was previously to achieve independence. If we embark on this process of planning, the vacuum, that lack of one overriding goal— a goal to which the whole population can be committed—is in fact filled in the process of having a development program. It enables the energies of the people to be quickly channelled from the old objective to this new objective, and therefore prevents the people from undergoing a time lag during which they might become disillusioned and unhappy because they are idle."

In Africa, where people are trying to plan, they are plagued by a shortage of information. "For instance, all the details which Mr. Lisle has used here in his illustrations would normally not be available, so that we have to be guided by an instinct, a kind of other sense. You feel your way as you go along, and you don't quite know how large a step you've taken." When dealing with territories where half the population do not use currency regularly, have concepts like inflation and deflation any application? What part is played by the consumption function in an economy where the bulk of the population produces its own food, and eats it without passing it through the market?

Need for Coordination

> Some LDCs are hampered in planning by an abysmal lack of statistical information. They should in that case supplement what facts there are by intelligent guesswork. At the other end of the scale, certain developed countries cannot get their plans applied by the political leaders. But the plan should not be a blueprint imposed from above. It needs to grow as a synthesis between the prevailing activities of existing political and administrative heads.

Mr. Bawa Sandani Mankoubi, of Togo, maintained that the indicative planning prescribed by Mr. Lisle cannot be applied in Africa, for lack of statistical and economic information.

Togo has used a system of extrapolation, starting with an estimate of the aid resources likely to be available over the next five years. In the circumstances, is Mr. Lisle's exposé of use to the developing States, or is it a comparison of French planning methods with socialist alternatives? Also, has planning in France been successful over the last twenty years, and can it on that score serve as a model?

Mr. Oumarou Sidikou, of Niger, dwelt on this lack of statistical information. In order to plan, the Niger authorities are first set the task of finding out the size of the population, its structure by age and sex, its geographic and ethnic distribution, its growth—all of which are not or are insufficiently known. There is similarly little material on agricultural production and the amount of livestock, on consumption in households and the proportion that live by subsistence. Statistics on foreign trade are imprecise, and no inventory exists of resources above or below ground, or of water supplies.

Now in order to have a coherent plan, it must also be continuous— yet it cannot be continuous if new facts keep coming up out of the unknown to upset the scaffoldings put up by guesswork. It is as though Israel were suddenly to discover abundant oil supplies. This would inevitably change practically all the data in the national plan.

Dr. Yaacov Arnon, of Israel, stressed that his question was posed on behalf of the developed as well as the underdeveloped countries: how do you get plans applied? "I almost do not know any group of people in the human race which is so frustrated as the people who work in planning authorities or planning organizations."

How does one organize a planning authority so that it can do more than just "know everything and publish beautiful reports, which are read by the people that have to take the decisions but which are not used further, while the economy goes on happily without planning?"

Mr. Pierre Uri, of France, offered an answer to Dr. Arnon. The secret of the French plan, he said, has been that its organization was devised to bring about a certain consistency and unity between the actions of different administrative branches within the same country. The authority is not a super Ministry, but a meeting place, with a very small staff, where experts from different sectors of the administration and the economy get together. So the plan avoids being academic because it is not made up by specialists, but is the fruit of a collective effort by all interested parties.

The developing countries should focus their interest on the first French plan immediately after the war, when the economy was destroyed and dislocated, and little statistical information was available. It was decided to concentrate on a small number of essential points, in the hope that the rest would fit in.

It is also important, Mr. Uri added, to maintain rigorously a financial equilibrium, as was done in the later French plans.

* * *

Mr. Lisle set himself to answer the question whether the French experience is useful to the LDCs. As Mr. Uri said, France was after the war a totally underdeveloped territory as regards the supply of statistics. Whether a country is developed has in fact no bearing on whether it should plan. Every nation will find others that are either more or less developed than she is. Mr. Lisle underlined Professor Kuznets' observation that one of the planning objectives needed is to increase knowledge about one's own country. But where hard facts are lacking, they must be supplemented in the meantime, as Mr. Kibaki put it, with the aid of an intuitive insight, to detect which problems are crucial and which shall have priority.

Plans always have to be revised, but it is possible to grade objectives, so that this project, say, must be attained at all costs, that one can be modified in part, and another again may be classified as less important. One of the aims of planning is to determine levels of priority. Even when you make an exhaustive plan, as France is doing nowadays, choices still have to be made and key sectors selected for privileged treatment.

A country has to set itself objectives, even if uncertain future events may make changes necessary. It is better to work out a plan that can be revised every year or two, rather than make no plan at all and sail ahead blindly. In countries that have not elaborated any national plan, there are still Ministries, each of which has its own ideas of development. So you have willy-nilly a series of different fragmentary and incoherent plans that can annul each other and lead to inflation.

"In conclusion," Mr. Lisle said, "the plan—and by that I mean the planning authority, or perhaps even the planning mystique—is an organization permitting the nation to get to know itself better through its statistical apparatus; to reflect about its own affairs better in a collective spirit; to define its future more effectively; and to adapt its collective attitude, that is, the attitude of each group of economic factors in society, to the long-term aims the community has adopted."

5

ROLE OF GOVERNMENT IN A MIXED ECONOMY

By YAACOV ARNON

Director-General
Ministry of Finance, Israel

In this chapter we will define a "mixed economy" as an economy that is capitalistic by nature—i.e., recognizes the right of private ownership of the means of production, free competition between enterprises in finding markets, and price mechanism as the main instrument for allocation of resources—but at the same time aims at Government intervention in the economic life of the country beyond fiscal and monetary measures and assistance in the development of the infrastructure. In a mixed economy Government also enters actively areas which could be dealt with by the private sector, such as development of industries, electric plants, transportation, agriculture, etc. In many cases, in countries with a mixed economy, Government is the main promoter of development through its own Ministries, through public authorities and Government companies, as well as through active participation in development banks.

The best indicator to identify a mixed economy is the ownership of production factors. In this chapter we call an economy a "free economy" if ownership of enterprises in industry, agriculture, mines, transportation and finance is mainly in private hands. We call it a "planned economy" if all means of production are in the hands of Government and public institutions. But if ownership is shared between the private sector and the public sector, we speak of a "mixed economy."

This means that in a mixed economy there are serious efforts toward peaceful coexistence between central planning and direction through price mechanism; between enterprises (including farms) owned by Government and private enterprises; and between Government or public financial institutions and private banks.

Government intervention in the economic life of a mixed economy is not aimed at keeping all production factors in Government hands as a matter of principle, but neither is there in such an economy a definite objection to Government ownership. The criterion for Government participation in certain branches is pragmatic: it is based on the need for fast development of the economy, on the one hand, and upon a lack of sufficient private capital, on the other hand.

Private ownership will get full encouragement from the Government in a mixed economy; we can even say: at least as much as it would get in a free economy. But if for some reason not enough private capital is available for the development of certain branches, the Government itself will not hesitate to act in those branches as an entrepreneur and as an owner of production factors in its own right.

Let us make it clear at the beginning that we are well aware that in countries with a planned economy or a free economy there are also elements of a mixed economy. In Communist or socialist economies, where central planning is decisive, we are today witnesses of attempts to introduce some elements of market and price mechanism. Pure capitalistic economies no longer adopt the slogan of "laissez faire," but arrange for central intervention in many fields of economic life. In this chapter, however, we will discuss only those economies where there exists a real mixture of both principles.

The Role of Government in the Development of the Economy

Before going into the special task of the Government in a mixed economy, we have to say something about the role of Government in respect of development in every type of economy.

In the past, many economies developed and grew mainly by private initiative without any direct interference by the Government in development. In many cases the Government protected young industries by means of high tariffs, ensured the supply of raw materials and export markets through an adequate foreign trade policy, and assisted in the mobilization of external and internal loans. Government removed obstacles and created the background for development, but did not interfere with it directly. Capital for development was in private hands, either local or foreign, and the Government itself did not, and did not want to as a matter of policy, own capital which could be diverted to the development of its economy.

In this framework a Government that wants to encourage development, even indirectly, has many possibilities to act. We will mention a number of measures which have been used in the past and are still effective today for the promotion of saving and investing, both of which constitute the basis for development:

   a.   Partial exemption from taxes. This can take the form of exemption from income tax for a given period (tax holiday), exemption from indirect taxes on materials and equipment for the construction of factories, exemption from property tax, invest-

ment allowances in addition to the normal depreciation allowance, etc. Such tax advances should be given only temporarily,
enabling the country to give a relative advantage to new enterprises over those which, having functioned already for a
certain period, should have consolidated their activities. The
leading principle of tax exemptions should always be a planned favorable discrimination toward economic activities which
need such special advantages, but they should be given only
to those enterprises which will be able after some time to do
without them.

b. Adoption of a suitable monetary policy and the creation of a
banking system able to give adequate credits to a growing
economy. Of main importance is that the investor, in addition
to his private capital, should be able to get loans on reasonable
terms, competitive with those in countries which have already
reached a higher level of development.

c. Development of a school system in which the whole or at least
a large part of the people can get the minimum education
required in a modern economy.

Special assistance should be given in vocational training for
development of necessary skills. Particularly in the case
of new industries, the training of suitable manpower is very
costly. Government can assist with the training of workers
in various ways, in the plants themselves or through courses
in vocational schools.

d. Protection for infant industries against competing products
from abroad by means of customs tariffs. It is desirable that
such protection should not involve too high customs tariffs
and should be kept within limits, so as to prevent the artificial
encouragement of products which in the long run could not
be produced economically under normal conditions. But in
general, protection against competing products during the
initial stages of production in new industrial enterprises is
essential.

e. Assistance in the creation of a capital market in which the
private investor can raise stock or loan capital through the
issue of bonds. Government can assist in the creation of such
a capital market through the issue of Government securities;
through suitable legislation providing protection for the individual investor and ensuring that he will get the necessary
information on securities on the market; and through the

provision of certain temporary tax exemptions on income from dividends or interest on bonds traded on the Stock Exchange.

f. Assistance to foreign investors. This can be given in accordance with the special problems of each country. It may include Government guarantees to foreign private investors with regard to general treatment, full or part tax exemption on profits made in the country and, in the case of existing currency controls, special guarantees with regard to convertibility of profits and repayment of the investment itself. Assistance can also be given in the form of information and guidance to prospective investors in their own country.

Additional Tasks of the Government in a Mixed Economy

The above-mentioned measures have proved not to be sufficient to guarantee a rapid development in new developing countries. The tremendous gap which exists in the middle of the 20th century between the developed and the developing countries, on the one hand, and the expectations of a rapid growth in the developing countries, on the other hand, have made it imperative that Governments should do more than just comply with the measures described above. Their central problem is the need for a rapid accumulation of capital, which is not, or only for a small part, available in the developing country. And even that part which is available belongs in many cases to owners who are not always willing to invest it in those branches that need to be developed for the future of the country. We have to take into account that the problem of industrialization in countries which have been dominantly agricultural is a risky and difficult enterprise. Lack of skilled labor and of an industrial tradition among both laborers and entrepreneurs add to the reluctance of the owners of wealth to invest available savings in unfamiliar branches.

In the face of such a position, intervention is required on the part of the Government, which can mobilize local capital either in a compulsory way through taxation, or by taking loans from the public that has the means but does not want to take upon itself the risk of investment. In addition, nowadays Governments can more easily than private bodies obtain capital from foreign national and international sources, and even if loans for private undertakings are available a Government guarantee is generally requested. If we add to this that private foreign capital is not always politically welcome in countries which have won their independence only recently, we have an explanation as to why direct Government influence in developing countries has become so powerful in recent years.

Responsibility for employment, which is the task of most Governments, further induces them to take the initiative in development in order to create employment. Modern economic thinking looks at unemployment as a problem of social overhead. Only macro-economic calculations and direct Government intervention are able to solve this problem on a larger scale.

This central role of the Government in the promotion of economic activity in developing countries makes it necessary to find economic tools and structures by means of which the Government can put the development projects into execution. We shall now describe the different forms at the disposal of the Government for realizing this aim.

Investment by Government Ministries

One of the principal ways of Government participation is through direct investment by Government Ministries. This applies mainly to the economic Ministries in charge of providing the infrastructure of the country, such as the Ministry of Transport, the Ministry of Posts, and the Ministries in charge of power and water.

If, for instance, the development of water resources is the responsibility of the Ministry of Agriculture, then the price of water, the kind of development undertaken, the distribution of water between different categories of consumer, etc., will be fixed not only in order to derive maximum profit, but also according to the general interests of the economy as decided upon by the Ministry of Agriculture in consonance with general Government policy. Other instances where the same principle would apply are investments in roads, railways, airports, sea ports, postal services, etc.

Those investments in which macro-economic considerations are decisive and where price returns on the investment are not derived directly from users of the service (such as in the case of roads), are best served if they are part of the activities of the Ministries themselves. It is not by chance that Public Works Departments are usually organized as a Ministry or part of a Ministry.

This does not mean that an economic analysis of every investment is unnecessary. The economic analysis has to be made, but in macro-economic terms. In other words, an investment of this type cannot be undertaken by private capital because the placement would not give the investor a positive return (which does not mean that there will be no positive economic yield for the economy as a whole).

Investment by a Government Authority

Another form of organization through which the Government can develop certain branches of the economy is the autonomous Government Authority. Such an authority is characterized by the fact that it generally receives its funds on the understanding that it will be able to return a reasonable yield on its investments.

In this kind of organization we find a direct link between tariffs for services rendered, on the one hand, and current operational costs in addition to interest and depreciation on the capital invested. Generally these authorities have a monopoly position, which makes it undesirable for the Government to give private investors a decisive role because the profit motive could easily conflict with the general interests of the economy. But the need for a commercial approach to costs and operation makes the independent authority preferable to direct administration by a Government department.

As an example, let us assume that for macro-economic considerations a decision has been taken to build a port. It will now be necessary to make a number of micro-economic calculations to decide in what way and according to what principles the different users of the port should be charged for the costs involved in the project. As we are talking about a very long-term investment in which optimum use of the facilities can be made generally only after a large number of years, the return on the investment should be calculated on a long-term basis. In our opinion, an independent authority directed by the Government will be the most suitable form to effect this purpose. Even if it is clear that the decision to build the port, its location, its size are matters for discussion at Government level, the day-to-day operations of the port require micro-economic treatment. Neither the normal Government regulations and procedures nor the psychology of Government officials are the most efficient for solving the commercial problems which arise daily in this kind of economic operation. An especially trained staff with wide executive authority should be in charge. The link with Government policy should be ensured through the election of a Board on which the different economic Ministries connected with port activities have their representatives. In certain circumstances it might be desirable to co-opt to the Board members from outside the Government who have an expert knowledge of the problems connected with the running of a port.

An additional example is the construction of an electricity plant, which is a typical monopolistic public service. The size of the investment, its timing, the location of the plant, its tariffs, etc., are matters to be decided by the Government. The decision to build an additional power station, and when to build it, should be determined by the national economy's need for electricity in the future and cannot be left to the considerations of private owners for whom the private profit motive would be decisive. But, as already explained above, the running of an electricity plant is better done by an independent authority than directly by a Government department.

Investment by Government Companies

A third form in which Government can participate directly in a development program is through a Government Company. Here the public authority appears as a shareholder and the company should act as does every company in a capitalistic economy. Its aims are to earn a return for the shareholders, and its considerations are the normal micro-economic considerations of any company based on private investment. Still, there are some differences worth mentioning:

(1) The private investor has to take into account risks which are of no relevance to the Government, such as a political risk—the danger of a change in the political stability of the country. For investments which are able to give a return in the long run only, political stability is a very important consideration for the private investor, especially if he is a foreigner. Generally he will be willing to invest only in those enterprises which give him an extraordinary high yield as a premium for running the risk. From the Government's point of view the danger does not exist at all as an economic consideration. For this reason we see that in developing countries private interests are often not willing to invest in projects that yield a reasonable return only. In those cases Government companies are imperative if development is to be unhampered.

(2) Also for non-political reasons private investors are generally unwilling to wait many years until they receive a return on their investment. Yet many of the investments in developing countries are precisely those which become profitable in the long run only.

As a result of these facts, a Government company is usually created in fields where returns are reasonable if only moderate, and are realized in the long run only. Typical examples of such enterprises are those for development of natural resources and industries based on local raw materials.

However, we want to stress that there exists a serious danger in the tendency to form Government companies automatically for projects where private capital is not available. Government should decide on the realization of such projects only after serious examination of their feasibility, both macro- and micro-economic. Utmost care should be taken that Government companies of this kind are not turned into a "socialization of losses."

Government companies are found in those areas of the country where the administration has special reasons for accelerating economic activity. They are in most cases 100 per cent Government-owned, and although their executive organization is independent, their policy will be strongly influenced by general Government policy.

As explained in the beginning, much of the accumulation of capital in developing countries can be effected by the Government only through an adequate tax policy, and foreign aid is generally made available through Government channels. If large projects have to be executed, the required capital can mostly not be found in the private sector and the Government needs to assist by supplying capital from its own resources.

As a result of this situation we find in many countries companies in which the Government is only a part-owner and in which a successful combination can be formed between a private investor with know-how but not enough capital at his disposal, and Government agencies.

In this chapter we will not go into the question of whether the Government should be a majority, a minority, or exactly an equal partner. In the history of developing countries there are examples of successful cooperation of all types. We would dare to recommend that the percentage should be decided upon according to the proportion of investment put up by each of the partners.

During later stages of growth in the developing countries, Government companies, which had been formed earlier because risks were considered too high by the private sector, become more attractive to private investors. In a mixed economy, where public ownership is not a matter of principle, the Government should be willing to transfer its shareholdings to private interests at market values, and use the proceeds to invest again in those branches of the economy where Government aid is still necessary. In our opinion this will maximize the resources of the national economy for further development.

We should like to add, as a closing remark in respect of Government companies, that generally we do not consider it the Government's task to compete with private interests in those branches of the economy in which private firms are willing to invest. Government should be a direct investor as a pioneer in development, but not as a competitor whose only aim is to achieve profits. Competition between Government companies and private ones in those sectors tends to be detrimental to a general atmosphere favorable to private investment.

Investment Through Development Banks

Another important institution for financing development projects is the Development Bank (industrial, agricultural, shipping). The role of the development bank is primarily to provide long-term loans to private enterprises which need that kind of capital and cannot mobilize it themselves. Such loans should be given to basically sound investments, even if the capital structure of the enterprise and the terms of the loans do not give enough security for commercial banks as they exist at present.

To enable development banks to function properly, they should have a much larger proportion of their total resources in the form of share capital, which should be provided for in the first stages by a Government allocation out of its budget. A certain proportion of the bank's resources can then be acquired through long-term loans from the public at large and in many cases also from foreign investors, whether international institutions or private interests.

Because of the special character of development banks in developing countries, particular attention should be paid to technical and economic knowledge, which should be concentrated in special departments. The task of the bank is not only to examine feasibility studies of the projects which the bank is asked to finance, but also to act as adviser to young enterprises in their initial stages of construction and operation. In special deserving cases where private investors have the necessary know-how but lack capital, the development bank should agree to invest as a minority shareholder, but those cases should be more an exception than a rule.

In our experience, development banks have been more efficient than Government departments in distributing loans to industry, agriculture and shipping (where long-term loans are a necessity).

Planning in a Mixed Economy

The task of planning in a mixed economy has not the same meaning as it has in a planned (socialist or Communist) economy. In the latter case the decision on a Plan, be it a five-year or other multi-year plan, is decisive for the allocation of resources within the national economy. In a mixed economy this allocation of resources is generally the result of a price mechanism, as is the case in free economies. But in view of the tremendous influence of Government activity, a multi-year Plan must be prepared to guide the Government in its economic policy, which is generally decided upon on a year-to-year basis. The task of the Plan is to recommend the desired pace of development and to fix priorities for the different branches of the economy. It has to take care that infrastructure investments are kept at an adequate level in order to prevent bottlenecks or waste in the different kinds of capital formation. The Plan should also give general guidance for the fiscal policy of the Government in all relevant areas of the economy. It should give an indication of the desired levels of consumption (private and public) and of saving. It should prepare a forecast of foreign currency needs and expected foreign currency income, in order to prevent serious difficulties and damage after certain development projects have been started. The Plan should provide valuable information for fixing priorities in the educational field, especially what kind of vocational schools should be given top priority.

In short, the Plan should provide all the information needed by the Government for its policy decisions in order to guarantee optimal results not only for a short period but also in the long run. Even if the Plan in a mixed economy cannot have the same decisive influence as in a socialist or Communist State, it is of paramount importance. It should enable the Government to decide not only about the right direction of development in the country, but also to decide intelligently about its pace. We cannot stress enough how essential it is to fix the right pace of development in a developing country. The danger is not only that too little is done. In economic life the danger of trying to do too much all at once is very real, and many developing countries have suffered heavily because they were too optimistic in estimating resources at their disposal in the future. Efficient planning should provide the new States with the instrument and the knowledge to become not only successful developing countries, but to stay independent in the full sense of the word.

DISCUSSION

Social Returns and Private Returns

Political risks in the LDCs can make private capital costly. The government should help start new enterprises, and sell them when they become profitable, using the money to launch further new development. Government companies have a particular role to play in training manpower.

If policy is based on economic considerations, Dr. Arnon laid down that "the decision about government ownership or private ownership should be taken—in every instance—on the merits of the case."

He pointed out that if a company is profitable, that is a reason not for retaining it, but for selling it to private takers. "If we want to understand a mixed economy correctly, the procedure is that the government starts certain industries, brings them to a viable and profitable level, and then sells them—not gives them away. In my opinion, to buy out private investments that exist in the country is exactly the opposite procedure of what should be done by those who believe in a mixed economy. As previously said, they should start the enterprise, bring it up to a profitable level and then sell it against the market price, using the new resources for further development."

Foreign enterprises take account of what they consider to be the political risks affecting their investments in the LDCs—risks which grow in proportion to the length of the investment period—and they expect a return for undergoing that risk. "I want to give Israel as an example. It is utterly unimportant for the State of Israel that some people think there is a risk of our being overrun, and that in ten years' time there won't be a State of Israel. We are not saying that for the outside person this doesn't appear a risk for which he expects to receive a certain return. But for us the risk doesn't exist as a factor in economic calculations. I would say that this is one of the main reasons—not the only one—why in the developing States we find a situation in which governments have to intervene in the development of branches which in developed countries are left to the entrepreneurs."

As to the type of government ownership that is most suitable, "I generally consider a 100 per cent government-owned company as perhaps the best form for those industries or for those infrastructure activities which need, I would say, almost permanent government assistance in the developing countries. If we see in certain LDCs that there will have to be a long period of development before any return can be received, then this is a case for forming a government company—but with the intention that the government will withdraw from it after a certain stage of development has been reached."

Professor Simon Kuznets listed three examples in which social returns exceed private returns, so that the latter are insufficient to mobilize entrepreneurial resources. The first case is where there is a training problem, and the enterprise cannot hold the people it trains. "A private entrepreneur investing in education gets a return from it that is much lower than the social return if there is freedom of movement of educated people away from the enterprise that trains them. In this case society may decide and should decide that, since social returns are very much larger, it would pay to supplement, or somehow intervene to optimize these returns."

Second is the case mentioned by Dr. Arnon, where there is a risk other than normal business risks. The third is the case where the returns are good, "but the sheer size of the investment—what we could call the indivisibility of the capital investment in resources— is so large that no single entrepreneur, though he may even want to, is likely to be able to undertake it." This refers particularly to the infra-structure, where "sometimes the projects are so large that nobody can undertake them except the government, and sometimes even the government cannot do it, but has to wait until it grows up to the task."

There are other cases where government ownership is necessary. One is where "the government may run enterprises largely because of the fiscal value of doing so; that is, it may monopolize tobacco factories and other plants not because it is interested in developing this particular industry, but because this is one good way of getting revenue." Here the main purpose is to siphon off the profits into government hands.

The government may develop enterprises in order to train the entrepreneurial class. Professor Kuznets mentioned that even the U.S. suffers today from a shortage of people who could have been trained in government undertakings. Governments are known to recruit people for high posts from the ranks of private business—"but it is not as good as training people in public enterprise. I still remember my own war experience, in which the people who had been trained in the WPA enterprises turned out to be the best executives in the war effort."

The requirement that governments sell out firms when they become profitable can hit up against a reluctance to make that decision. Dr. Kuznets posed the query whether an administrative device could be evolved, such as a supreme economic court or a supreme economic auditor, to decide whether a business should be shifted to private hands, and what other enterprise should be picked up.

Mr. Chanchai Leetavorn, of Thailand, while believing that the government should handle infrastructure and basic industries like power and railways, had reservations about the use of government intervention to pioneer business undertakings.

He fears the intrusion of political considerations. Private initiative would be discouraged, since no businessman seriously considers setting up in competition with a government company. Selling a successful company raises the question, who will buy it? Most LDCs do not have a stock exchange. The likely outcome is that the company will fall into the hands of certain privileged groups, who '"will reap all the benefit without having taken any of the risks in the beginning."

Mr. Ralison-Rakotovao, of Malagasy, suggested that government enterprise promote capital accumulation, facilitate the achievement of planning objectives, refrain from capital flight and train manpower. Private firms in LDCs are often reluctant to take on young university graduates because they lack practical experience.

Yet Mr. Ralison feared that the profits derived from State monopolies like tobacco and alcoholic liquors might be used not for reinvestment, but for buttressing unproductive civil service expenses.

He referred to two additional means of cooperation between State and private enterprise. First the government of an LDC can invite a foreign company to run a factory for the State and supply it with know-how, against an annual fee. Secondly there are cases where the exploitation of important natural resources like oil and minerals, or the manufacture of specialized products, involve financial commitments that are beyond the capacity of the local government, or involve technical resources and special markets that only certain big companies control. These companies may already be concessionaires from the period before independence. The government must then fall back on the conclusion of a mutually advantageous agreement with the companies, whereby the companies adapt their production programs to the country's development plans and the government shares the companies' benefits.

Mr. Christopher Musoke, of Uganda, adduced as a still further manifestation of government intervention the issue of direct subsidies and grants to private companies, which he said has done much, for example, to boost development in the southern part of Israel. He mentioned the encouraging psychological effects of offering tax holidays and fiscal concessions to foreign firms.

In deciding whether the government should be a majority or minority shareholder in a mixed economy, Mr. Musoke noted that "the more the government wants to have a major share in these companies, the less money it will have for investment elsewhere."

Making the Economy Grow

> In some cases, the government can do the job better than private enterprise, as in extending banking services into rural areas or buying petroleum in bulk. Pre-investment studies are a top priority function for the public authorities. Government intervention could take the form of international cooperation in creating a common market.

Dr. J. B. Kelegama, of Ceylon, advocated that government take over existing enterprises from the private sector in the search for more resources. This applies to insurance, banking (both of them partly nationalized in India and Ceylon), the import trade and even areas of internal trade. (Ceylon has nationalized the import and distribution of petroleum.)

Life insurance is a way of mobilizing savings, and the governments of India and Ceylon have extended it among the poorer sections of the population. Banking has been brought into the rural areas. In the case of petroleum, Ceylon economizes in foreign exchange by purchasing her fuel from certain countries at a 25 per cent discount— saving 30 million rupees a year. And the profits of petroleum trading remain inside the country, which is equivalent to another 30 million rupees a year.

These measures were taken for practical, not ideological reasons, and therefore should not frighten away private capital. Nationalization is only concerned with certain sectors, which demonstrably serve the national interest better by being in public hands.

Vice-President Antoine Meatchi, of Togo, pressed that governments should concentrate in the economic field on making pre-investment studies.

The small markets in African countries, the competition of foreign products, the risks that discourage foreign investors—these things make necessary not just government intervention, but cooperation between governments in offering larger markets over neighboring areas, and in creating common institutions. An African common market would have the additional advantage of providing security for the foreign investor.

In some sectors Africa lacks concrete projects for utilizing capital resources that are available, and in other sectors she lacks capital for well-conceived projects that need finance. This points up the urgency of establishing an African Development Bank, which should make pre-investment studies, mobilize capital, coordinate the numberless industrial projects scattered in the many so-called independent countries, and help resolve the problem of political security that affects investors.

Hon. Mwai Kibaki, of Kenya, though chairman of the session, intervened with a question before Dr. Arnon replied to the debate: Is the mixed economy a permanent way of economic life, or a stop on the road to something else? After industries have been weaned and sold off, does the economy move towards a fully capitalist or a fully socialist set-up? "I know that the short answer is to say that it is a political question. But perhaps Dr. Arnon could explain to us whether there are any guidelines as to the right division between public and private initiative."

* * *

Dr. Arnon maintained that the only authority to decide whether and when a government should sell out its holding should be the government itself. Answering Mr. Kibaki, Dr. Arnon said that as long as the government thinks there is a development job to do which no one else will tackle, it should sell whichever of its holdings will find buyers in order to free resources for the development task ahead. But "when we have reached the point where the government is satisfied that its aid is not needed any more for further development, I would not advise any government to sell its enterprises. Why should it? It would have idle funds on its hands—and that is the worst thing a government can have.

"But as I don't see that situation arising in the developing countries during my lifetime, I would propose that this subject be left for the next generation to worry about."

As regards the yardstick (for decisions as to whether and when to sell), it should be the possibility of getting a reasonable market price in return for the investment which the government has made. If such a price is offered and the government needs the money for another promising long-term venture, and if private investors are ready to buy the existing company but not to undertake the venture—then the government should sell.

Dr. Arnon emphasized that the reason for disposing of government-owned companies is to maximize the development effort. Selling them does not mean sending them out of the country. They remain within the framework of the economy. What the government has done is to increase the total resources of the economy.

Dr. Kuznets and others have said that the government can run an enterprise, such as a tobacco monopoly, to make a profit. Dr. Arnon's view is that "there are easier ways of getting at the profit of an enterprise than to earn it. I would advise every developing country not to go into business in order to earn money. If they are afraid that there is a certain branch in which people are earning too much, tax it away."

He thought a conference should be held on how to extract the maximum out of the profits of enterprises without taking the enterprise over.

There is a danger, referred to by Mr. Leetavorn, that instead of making profits, companies can become political dependencies. "I have to stress," Dr. Arnon said, "that a government company should have as its first task to run on a profit basis. If the profit motive isn't there, or if you have an enterprise in which it ought not to apply, then do not use the form of a company. Run it as a service in one of your Ministries, and if the worst comes to the worst, run it as a Government Authority, but never run it as a government company, because from a government company you expect actions which are reasonable in economic terms. Once a company gets into the habit of asking for subsidies, we have all learnt that is a habit which is very easily gotten, and very difficult to get rid of."

The anticipation that profits would be too high if a certain activity were put in private hands is not a reason for creating a government company, according to Dr. Arnon. "You can charge a high fee for licensing production, or you can impose specially high taxes. In the case of a monopoly—whose existence must be deemed regrettable in a capitalist economy—you can impose price control."

There is no rule about whether the government should be a majority or a minority shareholder—but "I personally dislike violently the 50–50 agreements." And "if the private investor is willing to invest the larger part, he should have the majority. He should have shares according to this proportion. If he is not able to do it, he should be in a minority."

Mixed companies are particularly useful in connection with know-how. It happens that a government can raise sufficient outside capital on its own, and may be tempted to do so if the cost of the capital is cheaper than the cost of the partnership; "but then it has to import the know-how." If the partnership is undertaken in order to secure know-how, it should be made clear that in due course the foreign shareholders will be bought out by local interests.

PART II   SAVINGS

There are four ways of mobilizing savings—the financial method, i.e., the money market; central planning; the fiscal method; and inflation. Each should be employed up to the point where marginal costs equal marginal social benefits.

This means that every country has to (and does) devote some resources to each system—other than the inflationary technique, which is rarely used as a deliberate policy. The financial system works best in an advanced economy, where decision-making can be decentralized. It works least well in a one-crop economy, or a country that has suffered chronic large-scale inflation.

Inflation can redistribute resources by reducing real wages, rents and other fixed charges. During the Meiji period in Japan (1868– 1875), when there was no proper banking or tax system, the government created revenue by printing a very large amount of paper money. The dispossessed feudal samurai *received these funds as loans, which they invested in industry. The resultant inflation was short-lived, because the output effect was greater than the cost effect. Subsequently as income grew, taxes replaced inflationary finance.*

Moderate inflation is found to be a concomitant of full economic activity. But it can no longer be used as a method of stimulating growth, because most sectors will not allow themselves to be victims of the "inflation tax." They demand compensation in bigger wages and higher interest rates. One country, Israel, has gone a long way towards offsetting the impact of inflation by linking wages and loans to the price index.

In countries with a limited financial sector, monetary policy cannot be effective. The money market should be expanded by upping interest rates, by aggressive banking, and by restricting credit during export booms, while expanding it when exports decline.

Savings and investment lag in Africa owing to the many uncertainties, concerning foreign trade, foreign aid, marketing prospects for new enterprises, and even the life expectancy of the person that is expected to save.

LDCs dependent on exports are hard to insulate from fluctuations in foreign trade. One remedy is to adopt a floating exchange rate. Another is to form common markets between neighboring countries to overcome economic fragmentation.

6

FINANCIAL STRUCTURES IN DEVELOPING ECONOMIES
By John G. Gurley*
Department of Economics
Stanford University, U.S.A.

As countries rise on the income ladder, their financial structures usually become increasingly rich in financial assets, institutions and markets. A financial structure, however, is only one way to mobilize savings for economic development. The extent to which a country should utilize a financial structure depends, in the broadest sense, on the opportunity costs of scarce resources devoted to it and the benefits (economic and non-economic) the economy is expected to derive from it. The costs and benefits of extending a financial system are of course different for different countries, and that is partly why some countries have elaborate systems of financial institutions and markets, while others, perhaps finding the net returns too low, have directed their efforts elsewhere. It is along these lines that I attempt to explain some of the differences one finds among countries in their use of finance for economic development. At the same time, I try to make some assessment of the role played by finance in the development process. I am aware that I have taken no more than a few tentative steps, but I hope in the right direction.

Some countries, like Sweden, Switzerland and the U.K., seem to have cornucopias of financial assets, out of which pour primary securities issued by economic units and indirect debts issued by financial institutions. Others, like Afghanistan, Haiti and Ethiopia, find the horn practically empty—even in relation to their low national incomes. And, of course, most countries are ranged between these extremes.

As the foregoing examples suggest, differences in *per capita* GNP go a long way toward explaining why some countries have a relative abundance of financial assets and others much less. The ratio of total financial assets to GNP in many of the poorest countries is probably no higher than one-half. The financial ratio rises to one and one-and-a-half for somewhat more prosperous countries—Mexico, Turkey, Brazil, Malaysia—and from 2 to 3 for other countries higher

---

* Many of the ideas in this paper belong to E. S. Shaw, who also made valuable comments on the penultimate draft. Raymond Goldsmith's empirical studies of financial interrelations ratios have also aided me greatly.

up the income scale, like France and Israel. A few economies have financial assets close to 4 or 5 times their GNPs. The United States in 1960, for example, had almost $ 2,000 billion of financial assets—two-thirds in the form of primary securities and one-third in indirect debt—which was almost 4 times her GNP for that year.

There are several reasons why the financial ratio rises as a country becomes more prosperous. The first reason is the increase, during the development process, in net issues of primary securities—i.e., corporate bonds and equities, government securities, mortgages, bank loans, trade debt, etc.[1] The net issues of these securities in the poorer countries are probably no more than 1 or 2 per cent of GNP; in the wealthier countries, these security issues are often 10 or 15 per cent of GNP.[2]

---

[1] That is, there were about $ 1,350 billion of primary securities, and approximately half of these were held by financial intermediaries. The counterpart to these holdings was an (approximately) equivalent amount of claims on the intermediaries—i.e., indirect debt. Consequently, indirect debt totaled about $ 650 billion or so.

[2] Primary security issues in the United States in each year have averaged approximately 10 per cent of GNP in the last 15 years. We can gain some understanding of the determinants of primary security issues by relating the issues to the investment and saving of the several sectors. Using annual data from 1947 to 1963, total primary issues of each of six sectors are explained by the sector's investment and saving (in the case of the consumer, corporate, and noncorporate business sectors), by government expenditures and taxes (in the case of the federal and state-local government sectors), and by exports and imports (in the case of the foreign sector). Net primary issues are positively related to the spending variable and negatively related to the income variable in each case.

The results of the six multiple regressions are:

Primary security issues of:							R^2
Consumer sector	=	-5.29	$+$	$.52\ I_h$	$-$	$.12\ S_h$	.79
Corporate business sector	=	$.48$	$+$	$.52\ I_c$	$-$	$.29\ S_c$	.78
Noncorporate and farm sector	=	-4.85	$+$	$.72\ I_n$	$-$	$.12\ S_n$	.72
Federal government sector	=	$.22$	$+$	$.98\ G_f$	$-$	$.99\ T_f$	.95
State-local government sector	=	$.56$	$+$	$.50\ G_s$	$-$	$.36\ T_s$	.92
Rest-of-world sector	=	$-.125$	$+$	$.61\ E$	$-$	$.43\ M$	.87

The results show that the first two and last two sectors tend to finance about half of their expenditures by issues of primary series (and about half by reducing their holdings of financial assets), and that these same sectors tend to retire varying amounts of outstanding primary securities from their saving (or income). The consumer sector, for example, uses only 12 per cent of its saving for paying off existing debts, the rest being used to acquire financial assets. The other sectors utilize somewhat higher percentages of their saving for debt retirement purposes.

These annual net issues of primary securities add to the accumulated stock. The equilibrium ratio of accumulated securities to GNP is equal to the ratio of net issues to GNP divided by the growth rate of GNP. Hence, if primary security issues are only 3 per cent of GNP, while GNP is growing at 4 per cent per annum, the equilibrium accumulation of primary securities is three-quarters of GNP.[3] This is perhaps a typical result for an underdeveloped country. For a wealthy country with an issues-GNP ratio of 10 per cent and an output growth rate of 4 per cent, accumulated primary securities would be two-and-a-half times the level of GNP—which is approximately the situation in the United States.

Accumulated primary securities generally rise relative to GNP during the development process because of the relative increase in investment and consumer durable-goods expenditures, the improvement in security markets, the greater desire of households and business firms to incur debt in order to hold financial assets, and the increasing amount of specialization between savers and investors.

If these factors exert their greatest impact during the earlier stages of growth, there is a tendency for the ratio of accumulated primary securities to GNP to rise sharply at first and then to taper off. This appears to have happened in the United States, where the ratio rose rapidly during the 19th century, reaching two to two-and-a-half in the 1890s; it then levelled off and has been running along a plateau ever since.

The second reason for the rise in the financial ratio is that the monetary or cash sector is often extended rapidly during development, which calls for an increasing amount of money balances for

The federal government tends to finance all of its expenditures by primary issues, and to use all of its receipts to retire debt. This sector, therefore, has only minimal changes in its holdings of financial assets. The noncorporate and farm sector tends to finance about three-quarters of its investment expenditures by primary security issues, and to use about one-tenth of its saving to retire outstanding debt. In these terms, then, primary security issues depend upon the distributions of "investment" and "saving" among the sectors and on their propensities to finance investment with primary issues and to retire outstanding debt from saving.

[3] The primary issues ratio is P/Y, where P is primary issues and Y is gross national product. The growth rate of GNP is $\triangle Y/Y$. The equilibrium ratio of accumulated primary securities to GNP is $\dfrac{P/Y}{\triangle P/Y}$ which is equal to $P/\triangle Y$. If this marginal ratio is constant, the average ratio $\dfrac{\text{(accumulated securities)}}{Y}$ will eventually be equal to it.

transactions purposes. Since this extension of cash transactions takes
place largely in the early stages of development, the big increases in
the ratio of money to GNP occur at that time, as shown in Table 1.
On the average, the money-GNP ratio rises from around 10 per
cent in the poorest countries to 20 per cent in countries with *per
capita* GNPs of about $ 300. Thereafter, the rise in the ratio is much
slower, partly because of growing competition from close substitutes
for money; however, the money-GNP ratio eventually rises to 30 per
cent and a bit beyond that.[4]

TABLE 1

Money and Time-Savings Deposits as Ratios of GNP and GNP per capita
70 Countries, 1953–1961

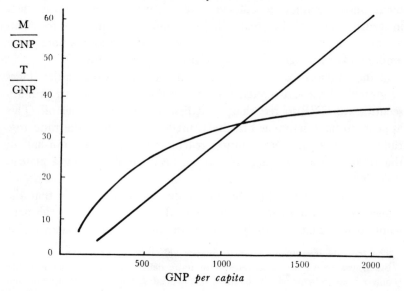

GNP *per capita*

The third reason for the rise in the financial ratio as a country
develops is the expansion of financial intermediaries—of commercial
banks, savings banks, credit unions, building societies, etc. As just
noted, commercial banks (and the central bank) are given a boost

---

[4] This curve is based on a least-squares regression, in which data for 70 countries
were used. The data are averages of annual figures over the period 1953 to
1961. The equation is: $M/GNP = -6.566 + 4.736 \ln GNP$ *per capita,* where
(.927)
M is the money supply (currency in circulation plus demand deposits), GNP
is gross national product, and the figure in parentheses is the standard error
of the regression coefficient.

by the spread of the cash sector of the economy. Commercial banks are also aided by the public's shift from currency to demand deposits during development.[5] But, finally and most important, they and non-banking financial intermediaries expand from the stimulus of a growing demand by individuals and business firms for time and savings deposits.

Table 2 shows how time and savings deposits grow relative to GNP as *per capita* GNP rises. These deposits are a negligible fraction of GNP in the very poor countries, but they rise steadily and rapidly during development, reaching 50 per cent and more of GNP in a few of the wealthiest countries.[6] The reason for this rise is principally because the growth and diversity of primary securities enable financial institutions to spread risks and to capture internal economies of scale, and because the demand for claims on financial intermediaries

TABLE 2

A Rising Financial Path as GNP per capita *Increases*

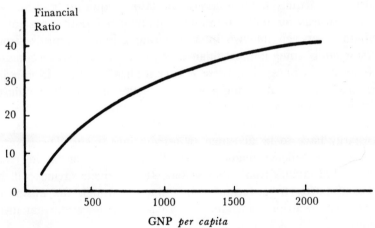

GNP *per capita*

[5] The ratio of currency to the money supply falls very sharply as GNP *per capita* rises. The ratio is 60 per cent or higher in the very poor countries, 50 per cent when GNP *per capita* is $ 300, 35 per cent at $ 1,000 GNP *per capita*. Using data for 72 countries, 1953–1961, the equation by least-squares is:
C/M=114.305—11.381 In GNP *per capita*, where C is currency in circulation,
  (7.573) (1.313)
M is the money supply, and the figures in parentheses are standard errors.

[6] Using data for 70 countries, 1953–1961, the equation is: in T/GNP= –3.528+
.980 in GNP *per capita,* where T is the amount of time and savings deposits
(.102)
in commercial banks, postal savings, savings banks, and other intermediaries.

is enhanced by the rapid growth of wealth and by a more equal distribution of incomes.

During the development process, then, countries generally follow a rising financial path, similar to that shown in Table 2, along which primary securities, money, time and savings deposits, and other financial assets grow more or less rapidly, reflecting the expansion and increasing efficiency of financial institutions and markets.

Are differences in financial ratios, then, explained by differences in *per capita* incomes? To a certain extent, yes. The United States does have a higher financial ratio than France, France than Mexico, and Mexico than Afghanistan. But the total picture does not fit together that neatly. And the reason it does not is partly because there is more than one method of accomplishing the same result. A financial system—or a debt-asset system—is only one way to mobilize savings and use them efficiently for alternative investment projects. A financial system depends upon and encourages a high degree of specialization between investors and savers, the former issuing primary securities to acquire tangible assets, the latter acquiring financial assets as rewards for not consuming, and financial institutions intermediating between the two by purchasing primary securities from investors and issuing indirect financial assets to savers. This technique of finance flourishes when there is decentralization of decision-making, specialization of saving and investment, and heavy emphasis on external rather than internal financing of investment.[7]

The saving that is mobilized by the financial technique does not necessarily have to be allocated to *private* investment. The government may, with deficit financing, issue financial assets of various types to elicit real savings from other sectors. If so, private savings will be allocated partly to government investment through the means of government securities or claims on private and governmental institutions.

However, to the extent that the savers are foreigners, or to the extent that foreign aid is substituted for domestic saving, financial

---

[7] The measure of the degree of division of labor between savers and investors is shown in the diagram above, which is basically a Lorenz-curve diagram. The lower curve shows the distribution of investment expenditures among economic units, when these units are ranked in accordance with their share in total investment expenditures. The upper curve shows the distribution of savings among the same units, when they are ranked as before. The area between the two curves as a percentage of the total area of the diagram is the measure of the extent to which saving and investment decisions are made

services are imported rather than produced at home. Consequently, a country may rely upon the financial technique for development, even though it imports part of its financial services.

As I just mentioned, there are alternative techniques for mobilizing savings. Each of these to some extent leads to greater centralization of decision-making, to less specialization of saving and investment, and so to a reduction in the extent to which investment is externally financed by the economic units involved. Each is a close substitute for the technique of finance.

The first of these centralizing techniques is central planning, under which a planning authority controls and coordinates much of economic activity, and the means of production are usually, to a considerable extent, nationalized. The significant feature of this technique, as a method for mobilizing saving and employing it efficiently, is the central direction of saving and investment and the means for bringing the two together with a minimum need of financial markets, assets and debt. A familiar device is the pooling of surplus funds and their allotment to state enterprises requiring them for investment purposes. Another is the capture by the state of a large part of national savings through appropriation of profits of state enterprises. The technique of planning may also redirect savings to investment through the control of relative prices of commodities and factors. The very process of central planning reduces the depend-

by different economic units. The two curves would be the same if each unit's investment and saving were equal, if each unit had a balanced budget.

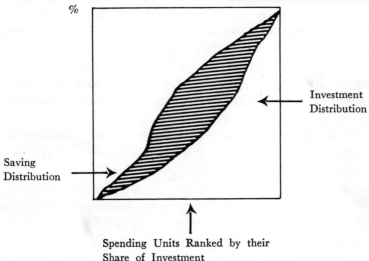

Spending Units Ranked by their
Share of Investment

ence of economic units on a financial structure; contact is made less through financial markets and financial institutions and more through planning bureaus and other central coordinating devices; the order of the day is internal finance and the use of existing money balances, not external finance and the issue of new securities.

The fiscal technique is another method for mobilizing savings, which also leads to greater centralization of decision-making and internal finance. In this system, tax payments are imposed on individuals and business firms, and a substantial part of the tax receipts is used by the government for its own investment projects or for lending (or subsidies) to private enterprises for their investment programs. The tax system is used to generate government savings which may then flow into either government or private investment.

The greater the extent to which saving and investment are brought together through the government budget, the less need is there for a financial structure to channel the smaller private savings to alternative investments. At any level of GNP, the rise in government spending and tax receipts reduces the degree of specialization between savings and investment and de-emphasizes external financing of investment expenditures.

Inflation is still another technique for mobilizing the economic surplus, although in an important sense it is part of the fiscal technique—a tax-subsidy system. It is achieved by an excess supply of money, perhaps created to finance a government deficit. As a technique for mobilizing savings, inflation is designed to alter relative prices and hence incomes with the aim of increasing savings and directing them to potential private investors. Inflation, as a mobilizer of savings, is meant to achieve a matching of saving and investment decisions, thereby increasing the extent to which investment is internally financed and reducing the dependence of the economy on a financial structure. Moreover, the rise in prices tends to reduce real demands for relatively fixed-price assets, taking still more steam away from the financial engine.

Each of these techniques for mobilizing saving and using it efficiently employs factors of production—manpower and the services of capital and land. Each technique, therefore, has a social cost in terms of the output that could have been produced if the real resources had been utilized in their next best alternative employments.

The technique of finance employs factors in the operation of financial institutions—central bank, commercial banks, savings banks, insurance companies, small loan companies, moneylenders, and so on—

and in activities of financial markets, like the stock exchanges, bond and mortgage markets, etc. Factors are also utilized, less directly, in the management of portfolios throughout the country, an activity that may involve a large fraction of the population for much of the time.

Central planning uses factors of production in planning bureaus and in the many coordinating and regulating agencies. The fiscal technique employs them in activities associated with the government budget—tax administration and compliance, agencies directing government investment programs, trust funds, and in debt management. Inflation has few direct costs in real resources, since it is generated simply by an excess supply of money. However, there may be indirect costs associated with it in the form of misallocations of resources. Additional factors may be employed in more frequent wage payments, in constant re-calculations of prices, in more frequent shopping forays, and in numerous other ways. Misallocations, of course, may accompany the use of any other technique too; if so, these costs should be added to the total costs to society of mobilizing savings in that way.

Each of the techniques also has social benefits, measured by how well it achieves the goals established for it. These goals may be economic ones—such as a more efficient allocation of resources, a more equal income distribution, a higher growth rate, more short-run stability—or they may be non-economic, like the extent to which the technique serves as a cohesive force for society, how many "freedoms" are derivable from it, or whether it is generally compatible with the ideology of the country.

Taking the non-economic goals and ideologies as given, though they may of course rule the day, factors of production should be employed in any technique up to the point where their marginal social cost is equal to their marginal social benefit. Consequently, in principle, economies should devote at least some real resources to each of the techniques, and this is in fact what they do.

However, as I have already noted, each of the centralizing techniques is a close substitute for the financial one. This means that, as more real resources are employed in any of the centralizing techniques, the payoff to the inputs in finance declines. Thus, as more resources go, say, into central planning, the resources in finance become less useful and at the margin do not pay their way. For this reason, an economy may rationally concentrate resources in one or more centralizing techniques, as in France, instead of spreading them out rather evenly between the two opposing forces.

Such choices, however, are subject to change as the balance of benefits and costs is altered over time. Thus, some countries may find it profitable to use tight central planning through many stages of development, until it finally becomes more profitable to decentralize decision-making to some extent. In this case, some real resources would be moved from planning bureaus to financial institutions and markets. Still other countries may find the balance of benefits and costs shifting in other directions, perhaps because of a changed emphasis on the goals of society (less emphasis on income equality, say, and more on efficient allocation) or because technological advances have altered the relative costs of the techniques—high-speed computers may make central planning relatively more efficient, for example.

Thus, benefit and cost considerations lead countries to move along one financial path or another; and such considerations may dictate changes later on, causing a country to swing from one path to a higher or lower one.[8] Economic considerations, of course, may not be decisive in the choice of technique. But they always play a role, and often account at least for small changes within the context of any effort toward development.[9]

At any moment in the development process, a country will have some optimal size of its financial structure which depends on all the forces affecting the marginal social benefit and cost curves of finance. Among these forces are those, already mentioned, which lie behind the long-term growth of primary securities, money, and other indirect financial assets. Such forces will generally trace out over time a rising financial path for any country, similar to any of the paths in Table 3.

Thus, over time, the United States has moved along a path close to the one denoted by Table 3.

But the optimal size of the financial structure also depends on the

---

[8] In terms of the set of equations in Footnote 2, a rise in G and T means a reduction in the other spending and income variables, at any given level of GNP, which would tend to reduce primary security issues. At the extreme, if G and T were each equal to GNP, primary issues would be insignificant, assuming the regression coefficients remained unchanged.

[9] Thus "Libermanism" in the Soviet Union may be dictated by the increased payoff in recent years to some decentralization of decision-making. Another example: if a country does not have a good capital market, it is because it chooses not to have one out of considerations of costs and benefits. At some cost, any country can have an efficient capital market. The same is true for a well-administered income tax, etc.

amount of real resources devoted to the alternative techniques for
mobilizing saving. If, as I have mentioned, an economy has heavy
concentration of resources in central planning, it will generally have
few resources in finance, and so financial assets will be small relative
to GNP. Such countries will tend to follow a lower financial path,
similar to the one labeled 1 in Table 3. This lower path, or perhaps

TABLE 3

Alternative Financial Paths

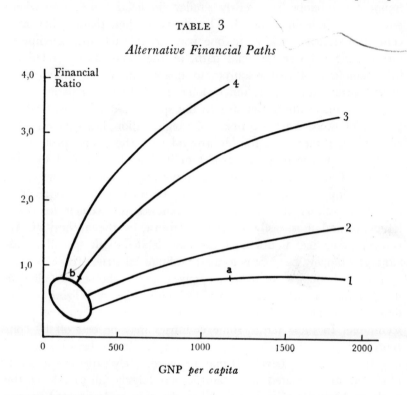

GNP *per capita*

path 2, will also be occupied by countries with strong commitments
to the fiscal and inflation techniques for development, for these
techniques reduce the value of inputs in finance and so reduce
the optimal size of the financial structure.

Some countries may have exceptionally large amounts of inputs in
Finance and thus unusually high financial ratios. If so, these countries will move along a path similar to the top one in Table 3.

In summary, I am suggesting that the size of a country's financial
structure, as measured by its financial ratio, depends on the factors,
already mentioned, which accompany the growth of income *per
capita,* and on the commitment the country has made to one combination of techniques or another for mobilizing its economic surplus.

A centrally planned economy, for example, may be well along path 1, at *a*, but its financial ratio may be lower than that of a much poorer country that is just starting out on path 3, at *b*. In each case, the country will experience a rising financial path as it develops, but the paths the two countries follow may differ widely.[10]

Very poor countries, before they have really embarked on development, probably have fairly similar financial ratios, somewhere within the circle in Table 3. The choice is then theirs: they may centralize decision-making in one way or another and attempt to move along a lower financial path, or they may devote relatively large amounts of real resources to finance in an environment of decentralization and try to move along one of the higher paths.

Does it make any difference to the speed of development which path is followed? This of course is the big question, but I have no big answer. So rather than fumble around with this grand problem, I propose to pursue only one aspect of it—the dark side of finance. The gist of my remarks is that one cannot always count on the financial technique to come through; it may be inferior in many respects to its competitors; it has inherent weaknesses as a vehicle for development; and it is easily subject to misuse by the authorities. Of course, other techniques may also be debited with special disadvantages, but my purpose is to analyze financial structures.

The particular way in which any country chooses to allocate its resources among the various techniques for mobilizing saving depends, in the broadest sense, on the benefits and costs of each technique. In these terms, some countries may be best off by concentrating on techniques other than finance, simply because finance may have too low a payoff. It may be inordinately expensive in terms of skilled and educated labor, and it may largely fail to achieve the goals established for it—compared to the costs and expected performances of other techniques.

Finance is at a relative disadvantage if a country has had a history of inflation so persistent as to reduce, for some time, real de-

10 Although the data are far from complete, what I have seen (mainly from Raymond Goldsmith's work) suggests that the U.S.S.R. (Central Planning) and Chile (Inflation) are on path 1; Yugoslavia is on path 2; the U.S., France, West Germany, Italy, Mexico and Guatemala on 3; and Switzerland, Japan and the U.K.—all with the most elaborate and sophisticated financial structures—are on the top one. Switzerland and to a lesser extent the U.K. have financial assets out of proportion to their incomes because they serve as financial intermediaries for other countries.

mands for financial assets. This lack of confidence in the financial system could be overcome, but the cost in real resources might be too great to justify the action. It might be better to by-pass finance by seeking development through another combination of techniques.

Finance is often handicapped by the narrow range of primary securities which emanate from equally narrow economic structures —one-crop economies, etc. In these cases, a financial system is at a relative disadvantage because of the strong linkage of risks among primary securities, precluding opportunities for intermediaries to spread risks among highly diversified portfolios. The result is higher risks of operation and reduced abilities of finance to attract saving. In addition, at low levels of operation, finance may be relatively inefficient, with high average costs of operation and little opportunity to realize the internal economies of scale often associated with financial activities.

Given these and other drawbacks, other techniques may look more promising. Some economies, for instance, may have such a simple structure of production as to make central planning most profitable relative to finance and other techniques. Other countries, perhaps because of the importance of foreign trade in their economies, may be able to collect taxes easily and cheaply on commodity flows and thus make substantial resources in the fiscal technique pay their way. Still other economies may find themselves so short of skilled and educated labor as to make the costs of planning, fiscal policy, and finance prohibitively high. If so, the technique of inflation may be chosen as the least expensive way to achieve higher saving rates and economic development.

If a country cannot organize an efficient financial system, if it opposes centralism and if it does not have the skills for fiscal methods, it may still get along after a fashion with branches of foreign financial intermediaries. A country that cannot afford to produce all of its financial services may buy part of them from abroad. But foreign intermediaries might have the drawbacks that they leak local saving to abroad, do not pursue competitive methods and so on.

Finally, even if finance meets the requirements of development, it may still fail to achieve other goals established by society. In particular, it may not achieve a more equal distribution of income, a more efficient allocation of resources between, say, private and public goods, or greater short-run stability of economic activity, not to mention its possible deficiencies in meeting the non-economic aims of society. Other techniques, such as fiscal policy, may be cheaper and more efficient in that they are able to gain successfully a multi-goal objective.

The financial technique works most efficiently when there is a substantial amount of decentralization in decision-making. However, decentralization may lead to lower levels of investment and saving and to poorer allocation of saving to investment than would exist if more concerted action were taken or if more relevant information were available to the parties involved. But it is not easy for a decentralized economy to make the corrections. This argument has three parts.

First, as Scitovsky has shown, in a decentralized economy, rates of return on individual investments will tend to be underestimated owing to the subsequent profitable feedbacks to the investor which are generally not taken into account at the time the investment is made—because current prices do not reflect these later feedbacks. Consequently, each investor tends to invest less than is warranted by the "true" rates of return. The lower rates of return that investors "see" will also be seen by savers and so will tend to reduce saving to the depressed level of investment. However, even if investment and saving are not reduced by this factor—because, say, investors proceed anyway on the basis of high hopes regarding feedbacks—there is still likely to be misallocation of saving to investment, for current prices, which do not include subsequent feedback effects, cannot be accurate guides to efficient allocation.

Second, if a government attempts development, within the framework of decentralization, by exhorting the population to save more in order to "double income in ten years," the result may be less saving than would otherwise take place. For any person, if he believes that the government propaganda will influence others to save more, has an incentive to save less now in view of such bright income prospects ten years from now. He would then have the best of all possible worlds—continued high consumption with the sacrifices of others ensuring grand prospects for the future. Since each person has such incentives, all will tend to act in this way, reducing the current rate of saving in the economy and slowing down development. Development by exhortation to a decentralized economy may easily backfire.

Third, not only may saving and investment be depressed in a decentralized economy for the reasons just noted, but, from the standpoint of growth, saving may be allocated inefficiently to alternative uses through financial intermediaries. Financial institutions, which intermediate between savers and investors in a decentralized economy, will tend to make "too many" loans that do not assist materially in economic development.

Given the amount of resources devoted to alternative techniques and the structure of the economy, resources should be employed in finance to the point at which their marginal productivity, in accelerating growth of the capital stock (if development is the aim), compensates for their marginal cost. A private financial system, however, may pay its way without "accelerating growth in the capital stock." Additional resources in finance (e.g., additional branches of banks, establishment of new intermediaries, enlargement of existing institutions, increase in the quality of services offered, expansion of middlemen activities in security markets, etc.) will pay their way if they induce additional financial flows from which a net profit can be made by the financial system (and by the economy as a whole). The extra financial flows, however, may result in more loans that are not highly conducive to economic development, like consumption, trading and speculative loans, and in less investment loans. For example, more real resources in finance may stimulate some people to acquire more financial assets and to reduce their own real investment, and other people to borrow more for consumption purposes. This would represent a more efficient allocation of resources, perhaps, but it would also signify a slowdown in the growth of the capital stock—a slow-growth situation achieved in the most efficient way. Thus the financial system may expand in profitable ways (even to society as a whole) which are inimical to economic development.

This outcome is quite likely in the earlier stages of development in many countries because consumption demands are so intense; a "better" financial system may simply service these demands more efficiently. This, of course, is not an optimal situation from the standpoint of economic development, and it may require some sort of controls over the lending activity of financial institutions. Controls can be justified not only in the interest of development but they will often be to the advantage of the financial system itself. It is in the interest of each financial institution and lender to continue making high-yielding consumption, trading and speculative loans in the hope that the other lenders will make long-term investment loans to build up the capital stock and stimulate development; for, if they do, the higher income levels in the future will induce large financial flows which will redound to the profit of the financial system. But since each lender has an incentive to behave in this way, all will do so, with the result that there will tend to be more "no-go" loans than would really be desired by the lenders themselves. Each might be willing to curtail such activity if he knew the others would be compelled to do the same.

A financial system may be inadequate because it does not meet the demands of a development program. It may also be inadequate because, given the resources in alternative techniques and the structure of the economy, too few resources have gone into it, or the resources in it are inefficiently employed. This may come about because the spirit of entrepreneurship in finance is weak; entrepreneurs may be slow to recognize credit gaps in the economy. Further, the financial industry may have overtones of monopoly or oligopoly, so that private benefits of concentration in power are put ahead of social benefits from competition and dispersion of power.

Whatever the reason, if finance is suboptimal, the authorities could respond by trying to improve the performance of finance (which would generally require the use of real resources), or by putting more resources in one of the centralizing techniques for mobilizing savings so that finance is partly by-passed. If neither of these actions is taken, the economy will respond by centralizing itself—but in inefficient ways. Enterprises lacking adequate finance will merge with other, larger firms. Many businesses will reduce dividend pay-out ratios, which will tend to centralize saving and investment decisions. There may be consolidations of government units, so that deficits and surpluses within larger decision-making groups can be cancelled against one another, to avoid having to finance them through inadequate capital markets and financial institutions. Individuals who cannot find external financing will tend to regroup with their families for the purpose of securing "internal" funds. Funds will tend to be reinvested in existing businesses rather than in new ones, since the latter require more external financing. Economic units will tend to put their savings in their own investment projects, rather than seeking more productive ones through financial markets, or they will simply consume more.

An economy, in brief, will tend to centralize itself when it faces an inadequate financial system. These centralizing responses, however, may be much less efficient than if real resources had been purposely devoted to one or more of the centralizing techniques for mobilizing the economic surplus. But once these inefficient centralizing responses have been made, the financial structure will seem optimal in terms of the lowered efficiency of the economy.

A private financial system, guided in its development by market forces, may be inadequate for development goals and for other purposes. If the State intends to rely on finance, there is some justification for State intervention in this area. However, a financial system may easily be misused by the State, resulting in its continued poor performance or even in its deterioration. I propose to discuss just one example of this.

If a country has experienced price inflation, nominal interest rates will ordinarily rise. However, if interest rates in the organized financial sector are controlled by the State, the rise in rates will occur only in the unorganized financial sector, where small loan companies, moneylenders, etc. operate. Consequently, real deposit and lending rates will decline in the organized sector, leading to a decline in funds supplied to the sector. Its assets and liabilities, in real terms, will decline, and so will rates of return on capital invested in the sector. Potential savers, who have withdrawn funds from the organized sector, may redirect them to unorganized finance, inducing more real resources in this area, step up their consumption, or employ the funds in their own real investment projects. Since leaders in the unorganized sector are prone to make consumption and similar-type loans, the deterioration of organized finance is accompanied by a rise in consumption, a fall in investment and saving, some misallocation of saving to investment, and inefficient use of real resources in the financial area. The retrogression of organized finance is accelerated if foreign exchange is undervalued, for then funds tend to move out of domestic institutions for purchases of goods and assets abroad.

The decline in domestic saving widens the gap between the development goals of the economy and its ability to achieve them. If this leads to attempts to bridge the gap with further increases in nominal money, organized finance, and along with it saving and investment, will continue their descent toward oblivion.

Summary

I have made three main points. The first is that it will generally pay a country to put more real resources in its financial structure as it climbs up the development ladder.

The second point is that, while each country will follow a rising financial path, the paths may be quite different for different countries, depending on the resources allocated to the alternative techniques for mobilizing the economic surplus. And this choice largely turns on the relative costs and benefits of the alternative techniques.

The third point is that the financial technique has many drawbacks and failings, and it is easily misused. It is not likely to be the best technique in all circumstances; it is apt, under many conditions, to lead to relatively low levels of saving and investment and to misallocation of saving; and it is subject to deterioration if misused by the State.

DISCUSSION

External Finance Goes With Private Enterprise

The choice is between self-finance through central planning òr inflation, and external finance through a capital market. Also possible is a combination of both. It depends on the needs of the economy, and the quality of the financial institutions the country has.

Mr. Roman A. Cruz Jr., of the Philippines, listed a number of further considerations when choosing which financial system to use. First, the availability of personnel specialized in finance, and their division as between the Government and private sectors. The less qualified manpower exists, the more advisable it is to centralize these services, whereas "the more formidable the financial skill at the command of the private sector, the weaker is the case for centralizing the finance function."

Next, the relative importance of the Government and private sectors in the economy will determine the scope for private as against centralized financial control. "Investment banking or securities underwriting make little sense where most of the enterprises are government-owned."

The financial needs of the country also have bearing on the subject. "As asset structures change, financial requirements also change. The pertinent question is, as development proceeds and financial requirements become more complex, can the centralized techniques enumerated by Professor Gurley keep up with these complex requirements, or would they eventually become a bottleneck?"

Mr. Cruz gave as an example the emergence in the last year or two of an investment banking system in the Philippines, together with a stepped-up growth of the local securities market—because, owing to a rather unyielding central bank policy, business firms could no longer look to the commercial banks for finance.

Conrado Pascual Jr., likewise of the Philippines, said, "The economists' approach of deciding between alternative financial systems by equating marginal social costs and marginal social benefits involves complicated problems of quantification. In practice the choice is complicated by other considerations. Prevailing ideologies might simply rule out central economic planning as an alternative. And then, of course, considerations of stability for incomes might preclude inflationary finance."

The cost of the financial technique is high in the LDCs because the markets and the financial instruments are not there. But in the long run, the cost would decline. So a time dimension ought to be introduced. "We cannot usually appraise these problems by simply taking a short-term point of view. The long run is just as important."

Professor H. G. Johnson, of the U.S., took issue with Professor Gurley on several points of emphasis. The fact that current prices fail to reflect subsequent profitable feed-backs does not discourage investors overmuch, because financial services take all information into account including predictions of future earning. As concerns the argument that people are stopped from saving by government forecasts that incomes will double in ten years, this benefit "will only affect the individual if either he improves his own skills so that he participates in the more productive processes forecast for the ten years ahead, or if he saves and acquires an ownership participation."

Professor Johnson disagrees with the strictures against consumption loans. First, a loan has to be repaid, and if you borrow for consumption purposes, you have to pay out of future income. Secondly, expenditure on labor-saving devices in the household can permit labor to move out of domestic activities.

Financial intermediaries help poorer people get access to the higher yielding investments that are generally the province of the rich.

Dr. Haim Ben-Shachar, of Israel, indicated that his country has passed through several phases of capital formation—first via inflation, then through central planning, whereas today there is a growing organized capital market.

The growth of the capital market system as a method of mobilizing savings is contingent on its success as a technique for *investing* resources.

Dr. Snoh Unakul, of Thailand, regretted that Professor Gurley had not discussed ways and means of strengthening the financial system. After the private sector has developed beyond a certain initial stage, the financial system becomes dynamic to the point of causing inflation, as in India. It also outlives the preoccupation with consumption loans, and diversifies its portfolio as the capital market becomes more experienced. Dr. Unakul maintains that private finance is not any more subject to misuse by the authorities than central planning or financing by inflation.

Dr. Barend de Vries, of the World Bank, said, "We should focus this analysis on the countries with a *per capita* income of $300 to $600 a year, because these countries are having to make key decisions for the direction of their economic future. It would be useful to study relations between the behavior of financial assets and other variables, such as the structure of the economy, the role of exports and the behavior of prices—and to do this, as Mr. Pascual suggested, over a period of time. A country may rely heavily on financial assets because of the dominant role played by the export trade."

This distribution between the fiscal and financial sectors is sometimes blurred. A government can sell bonds in the private market and allocate the funds to the public sector. Or the banks may be required to use deposits for the purchase of government bonds or for investment in specific items of the State budget.

Dr. de Vries pointed out that inflationary problems can in the long run be detrimental in that they discourage the formation of capital market institutions. The capital market has an important role for the LDCs, because it can be a channel for overseas capital, including medium- and short-term credits.

Mr. Hak Men Say, of Cambodia, said, "Governments in the LDCs are burdened with heavy expenses on social services, the infrastructure and defense. The State thus appears at the center of the most important decisions. Lack of savings is not occasioned by institutional inadequacies, but by poverty and by the propensity of the rich to luxury and speculation.

Inflation releases resources, because there is a delay before wages catch up with prices. Mr. Say estimates this lag at a fall of 25 per cent in purchasing power. It is then necessary to channel resources released by these inflationary methods to investment. In order to avoid destroying confidence in the currency, the authorities have to engineer alternate phases of inflation and stability. The whole thing is a dangerous method of financing.

Dr. Mortimer Andron, of the U.S., added what he considers another important advantage of the financial system, that along with its growth, "there grows a complex of individual freedoms for the citizens of the nation, so that a developing country with an undeveloped financial system has a smaller area of freedom."

Financial Assets and Total Wealth

Which mechanism allocates funds to investment more efficiently? Central planning, even when occasioned by the lack of a capital market, can hold up the development of a financial system.

Dr. Raymond W. Goldsmith, of the OECD, classified Professor Gurley's paper as perhaps the most important in the conference, because it offers the interesting new approach of regarding finance as one of several alternative means for handling the increase in a country's stock of capital.

The costs of different systems are not an important factor of comparison, in Dr. Goldsmith's opinion, because the whole financial system, even in a developed country, absorbs only 1 or 2 per cent of the labor force and even less of the capital. The essential point is a comparison of allocative efficiency.

Professor Goldsmith suggests using as a ratio financial assets divided by real assets. "This ratio is simply the finance ratio of Professor Gurley (the ratio of financial assets to GNP) divided by the capital/output ratio."

The monetization rate measures the financial superstructure in relation to the real infrastructure of the country. For the developed States, it is in the neighborhood of unity, but in the LDCs it is usually one-third to one-half. Another real factor is the capital formation ratio. "The higher the capital formation ratio, other things being equal, the higher the finance ratio." Finally there is the ratio of new issues to capital formation.

"Layering" (where one financial institution has claims against another financial institution) is higher in the LDCs, where the banking system is more important, dominating all financial bodies—and where the central bank is large compared with the commercial banks. In developed countries, a bigger role is played by savings institutions and insurance companies.

Professor Don Patinkin, of Israel, suggested that financial assets should be related to total real wealth rather than to the GNP or even current savings. Foreign debt is one form of financial asset. Another is the discounted value of future tax collections.

The economics of "layering" need to be studied. Is roundabout financial investment more productive than direct financial investment? What percentage of the labor force in different types of economy is occupied with financial intermediation in the broad sense of the term, including all the connected services? Planned economies are not free of the necessity to make financial adjustments. Thus the banking system in Russia is one of the main vehicles used by the planning bureaus for applying their policies.

In Israel, 60 per cent of current investment has been financed through the Development Budget. "Now which comes first? It isn't at all clear that because there was government activity, therefore the private security market didn't develop. To a certain extent in Israel it was the other way around: the private security market didn't develop, and therefore the government stepped in. Both of these things occurred—it hasn't been a one-way interaction."

Professor Patinkin queried Dr. Gurley's assertion that the more resources go into central planning, the less profitable is the financial system. Where a lot of activity is absorbed in central planning, those resources that remain are particularly suitable to capital market operations and should therefore show a relatively high marginal productivity.

Professor Simon Kuznets, of the U.S., pointed to technical difficulties in comparing the financial systems of different countries when each country uses separate systems.

The choice between financial mechanisms should start with the question, what are the savings and investments necessary at different stages of development—domestic savings, foreign capital, etc.—and how can the largest amount be mobilized in the most profitable way? Then comes the question, what kind of mechanisms and institutions are available at these different stages?

* * *

In summarizing the debate, Professor Gurley divided the system into external finance—which is done by the financial system—and self-finance, which is done under central planning techniques. In China profits made by nationalized industries are ploughed back through the manipulation of relative prices. That is self-finance. Inflation is also a form of self-finance, a system of the last resort; but it is perfectly possible for the outcome of inflation to be an increase in external financing among the various economic units.

7

IS INFLATION
A RETARDING FACTOR
IN ECONOMIC GROWTH?

By HARRY G. JOHNSON

Department of Economics
University of Chicago, U.S.A.

The question set as the subject for this chapter is an apparently simple one, demanding a choice between two widely held views of inflation. This apparent simplicity, however, is deceptive, and the necessity of choice invalid; for the question exploits the fact that both the word "inflation" and the word "development" (or "growth") have multiple meanings in current discussion. In particular, both may be used to refer either to economic facts or to economic policies; and indeed the first half of the question uses the word "inflation" to refer to a fact and the second half uses it to refer to a policy (or the outcome of other policies). Furthermore, "inflation" defined broadly in the factual sense of an upward trend of prices, includes the possibilities of both mild and rapid, and steady and erratic, upward price movements; and each of these distinctions is connected with important differences in the economic consequences of inflation. It is therefore neither necessary nor correct to regard the two propositions of the question as exclusive alternatives; on the contrary, the two can be discussed virtually independently. In this chapter, it will be maintained that a moderate degree of inflation—specifically, inflation at an annual percentage rate that can be counted on the fingers of one or at most two hands—is likely to be an inevitable concomitant of a development policy that seeks efficiently to mobilize an economy's resources for economic growth; but that a policy of deliberately promoting development by inflationary means, though it has theoretical and practical attractions, is likely in fact to retard rather than foster economic growth.

Before entering on these arguments, however, it seems desirable to discuss briefly the naive interpretation of the question, according to which the problem is whether inflation is associated with rapid or with slow economic growth. The available historical and comparative evidence on this point is fairly conclusive; there is no convincing evidence of any clear association, positive or negative, between the rate of inflation and the rate of economic growth. This is particularly true of the longer-run historical evidence; an impressive contribution in this respect is provided by the recently published *Monetary History of the United States,* by Friedman and Schwartz,[1] which finds that the United States has grown at relatively high or low rates in periods of both deflation and inflation. Comparative studies based on shorter periods of experience, such as that of the *Commission on Money and Credit,*[2] have tended to find at most a slight inverse association between the rate of economic growth and the rate of inflation *or* deflation among countries, for rates of inflation or deflation lying outside a modal range of zero to low rates of inflation.

The absence of any marked historical association between observed rates of growth and of inflation is only to be expected. In the longer run, one would expect an economy to adjust to whatever rate of monetary growth it experiences largely through price movements, or conversely to adjust its monetary growth to its growth and price trends, depending on whether its exchange rate is variable or fixed. Moreover, it has become increasingly clear that the main determinants of economic growth are to be found in the growth and application of knowledge, through technical and managerial change and the improvement of human capacities, rather than through the saving and investment of capital in the narrow sense. These are aspects of economic life over which monetary developments exercise little direct and obvious influence, except when monetary disturbance—either deflationary or inflationary—disrupts the system of economic organization. For the same reasons one would expect differences between countries to be dominated by social and cultural differences, and cross-country comparisons to provide little clear-cut evidence on the relation between inflation and economic growth, except again for experiences dominated by monetary disturbances.

Historical experience is, however, not a very useful or relevant guide to the issues under discussion, since that experience predominantly reflects the influence of chance or natural developments, whereas contemporary concern with these issues is promoted by the deliberate adoption of policies of manipulating the economic environment so as to mobilize resources for and foster the achievement of economic growth. To be relevant, therefore, historical and comparative analysis would have to go beyond the simple correlation of growth

[1] M. Friedman and A. J. Schwartz, *A Monetary History of the United States, 1867–1960,* a study by the National Bureau of Economic Research (Princeton, N.J.: Princeton University Press, 1963).

[2] Commission on Money and Credit, *Money and Credit: Their Influence on Jobs, Prices and Growth* (Englewood Cliffs, N. J.: Prentice-Hall, 1961).

rates and rates of price change, into an analysis that would seek to isolate the influence of inflation on growth from other contemporary growth-promoting or growth-inhibiting influences. In the absence of detailed empirical analysis of this kind, it is necessary to resort to theoretical analysis combined with empirical observation. This is the approach employed in the remainder of this chapter.

The first question to be discussed is whether the mobilization of an economy's resources by development policy inevitably involves inflation. It is contended here that some degree of inflation—but a moderate degree only—is the logical concomitant of efficient economic mobilization. The argument rests on two propositions. One is that, so long as inflation proceeds at a rate low enough not to disturb seriously the general confidence in the stability of the value of money, its effects are primarily to redistribute incomes, and to do so to an extent that does not involve serious social consequences, rather than to produce significant misallocations of resources, such as occur when people come to expect inflation and seek to protect themselves from it by holding goods instead of money and by using political means to safeguard their real incomes. The other proposition is that, owing to the various rigidities and immobilities characteristic of any economy, but particularly of underdeveloped economies, upward movements of wages and prices can help to reallocate labor and resources and to draw labor out of tradition or subsistence sectors into the developing sectors of the economy. It is important to notice that this proposition, like the first, presumes a general expectation of stability in the value of money, as a precondition for the offer of higher wages and prices to serve as an inducement to mobility.

The second proposition implies that some inflationary pressure in the economy will assist the task of mobilizing resources for development; the first implies that such inflationary pressure will not introduce offsetting distortions causing significant real losses to the economy as a whole, but will instead mainly involve transfers of income within the economy, the social consequences of which will be small enough to be acceptable. Efficient policy-making will therefore involve arriving at a "trade-off" between the mobilizing and redistributive effects of inflation that will involve some positive rate of inflation. The indicated optimum rate of inflation is likely to be significantly higher for an underdeveloped than for an advanced economy, for two reasons: first, the sophisticated financial system of an advanced economy provides many more facilities for economizing on the use of money in face of expected inflation; and second, the superior mobility of resources of an advanced economy implies that the increase in total output achievable by inflationary means is relatively much smaller. Thus one might expect that whereas "tolerable" price stability in an advanced economy is frequently defined as a rate of inflation of no more than 1 to 2 per cent a year, the tolerable degree of stability for an underdeveloped economy might be in the range of a 4 to 6 per cent annual rate of price increase. (My colleague Arnold Harberger has suggested that a 10 per cent annual rate of inflation represents the outside limit of inflation justifiable by this line of argument.)[3] This analysis, of course, relates to purely domestic considerations and ignores the balance-of-payments or exchange-rate implications of internal price trends.

The foregoing remarks relate to the question of inflation as a consequence or aspect of economic development policy, and to the argument that some degree of inflation is the necessary price of rapid development. It has been argued that a modest rate of inflation is a logical part of an efficient development policy, in the sense that the "price" may purchase gains in efficiency of resource allocation and utilization that outweigh the costs. The argument now turns to the second problem raised by the question, the effectiveness or otherwise of inflationary financing of development programs.

The deliberate use of inflationary policies to promote economic development has been recommended on theoretical grounds by certain economists; and the fact that many underdeveloped countries have for one reason or another resorted to such policies has led a number of other economists to condone or find merit in inflation as a means to economic development. This chapter will not attempt to survey all the theoretical arguments—in particular, it will not go into the structuralist *vs.* monetarist debate over inflation in Latin America —but will instead outline the major theoretical and practical arguments for inflation as a means to development, and discuss the major defects of inflationary development policy in practice.

The main theoretical arguments for inflationary development policies derive from two systems of economic thought, the Keynesian theory of income determination and the quantity theory of money. The Keynesian approach to the question (which derives from the Keynes of the *Tract* and the *Treatise* as much as from the Keynes of the *General Theory*) argues that inflation will promote growth in

[3] Arnold C. Harberger, "Some Notes on Inflation," Werner Baer and Isaac Kerstenetzky, eds., *Inflation and Growth in Latin America* (Homewood, Ill.: Irwin & Co., 1964).

two ways: by redistributing income from workers and peasants, who are assumed to have a low marginal propensity to save, to capitalist entrepreneurs, who are assumed to have a high marginal propensity to save and invest; and by raising the nominal rate of return on investment relative to the rate of interest, plus promoting investment. Neither of these arguments, however, is either theoretically plausible or consistent with the facts, at least so far as sustained inflationary processes are concerned. Both rest on the arbitrary and empirically unsupported assumption that entrepreneurs realize that inflation is occurring, whereas the other members of the economy do not, or not fully. As to the first, the theoretical prediction is that all sectors of the economy the prices of whose services are upwards-flexible will come to anticipate inflation, so that no significant redistributions of income will take place; and this prediction accords with the mass of the available evidence. As to the second, the theoretical expectation is that free-market interest rates will rise sufficiently to compensate holders of interest-yielding assets for the expected rate of inflation; this expectation also accords with the mass of the available evidence. This argument for inflation, therefore, is valid only in two possible sets of circumstances: first, in the early stages of an inflationary development program, while the mass of the population (especially the workers and the savers) still has confidence in the stability of the value of money; and second, when inflationary financing is accompanied by governmental policies of holding down the wage and interest costs of business enterprises. Such policies would generate distortions in the allocation of resources, which might offset any benefits to growth from the inflationary policy; in particular, the contrary view has been argued that inflation will discourage the supply of saving for investment.

The quantity theory approach, on the other hand, adopts the more realistic assumption that in a sustained inflationary process the behavior of all sectors of the economy will become adjusted to the expectation of inflation, and that consequently the effect of inflation will be, not to redistribute income from workers or savers to capitalist entrepreneurs, but from the holders of money balances—who are the only losers from an inflation that is anticipated—to the monetary authorities who issue money the real value of which steadily depreciated. Inflation imposes an "inflationary tax" on holdings of money, which consists in the real resources that the holders of money have to forgo each period in order to restore the real value of their money holdings. The presence of this tax, in turn, encourages the public to attempt to evade the tax by reducing their real holdings of money, by shortening payments periods, holding inventories of goods instead of cash, and so forth; these efforts involve a waste of real resources and a reduction of real income, the "collection cost" of the inflationary tax. On the other hand, the real resources collected by the inflationary tax are available for use in the development program; and if they are used for investment, the inflationary policy may accelerate economic growth. It should be noticed, however, that in the transitional stages of an inflationary development policy, or in the process of acceleration of such a policy, whatever contribution to growth there is may be outweighed by the increased waste of resources produced by the increase in the inflationary tax.

In practical experience, resort to the inflationary tax as a method of financing economic development is generally prompted by the inability of the developing country to raise enough revenue by taxation and by borrowing from the public to finance its development plans —either as a result of the low income and taxable capacity of the economy, or more commonly as a result of inability to command the necessary political consensus in support of the necessary sacrifices of current income. Unfortunately, the same characteristics of underdevelopment that limit the capacity to finance development by orthodox fiscal methods also place rather narrow limits on the possibility of financing development by inflation. Especially, underdevelopment implies a relatively smaller use of money than is common in advanced countries, and therefore a relatively smaller base on which the inflationary tax can be levied.

Before discussing this point in detail, it is appropriate to refer to a related question that figured large in the development literature of about a decade ago, the question of the extent to which development can be financed by monetary expansion without producing inflationary consequences. The answer, clearly, is that such financing can be safely pursued up to the limit set by the growth of demand for money consequent on the expected growth of the economy at stable prices, plus the growth of demand for money associated with the monetization of the subsistence sector (where relevant), minus the portion of the growth in the money supply that must be created against private debt. The magnitude of the resources that can be made available for financing development by this means, however, depends on the magnitude of the absolute increase in the money supply permitted by these factors, or to put it another way on the rate of growth of the demand for money, the ratio of money to income, and the portion of the additional money that can be used to finance public spending. Thus, for example, with a rate of growth of demand for money of 6 per cent, half of which can be used to finance public spending, the budget deficit financed by monetary expansion would be 3 per cent of the initial money supply. If the ratio of money supply to national income were in the neighborhood of two-fifths, as is common in advanced countries, this would make 1–2 per cent of national income available for development investment; if, on the other hand, the ratio of money supply to national income were in the lower neighborhood of one-fifth, as is common in under-developed countries, only 0.5 per cent of national income would be available for development investment.[4] The difference in the order of magnitude of the money-to-income ratio explains both why budget deficits in underdeveloped countries are more frequently associated with inflation, and why in such countries inflationary financing of development is more frequently resorted to than in advanced countries.

In the same way as it limits the scope for non-inflationary deficit financing of development, the restricted use of money in underde-veloped countries limits the extent to which inflation can make re-sources available for economic development through the inflationary tax. Ignoring the possibilities of non-inflationary financing by mone-tary expansion due to the growth and monetization of the economy, the yield of the inflationary tax as a proportion of national income will be the product of the money-to-income ratio, the rate of inflation, and the proportion of the increase in the money supply captured for financing development. Thus, with the assumed money-to-income ratio of one-fifth and capture rate of one-half, a 10 per cent rate of inflation would secure 1 per cent of national income for the develop-ment program, and so on. The money-to-income ratio, however, is not insensitive to the rate of inflation, but is on the contrary likely to decrease appreciably as the rate of inflation rises, thereby setting limits to the possibilities of development financed by these means. (Note also that insofar as development financing depends on a growth of de-mand for money resulting from monetization of the economy, in-flation is likely to reduce that growth by inhibiting monetization, so further reducing the net amount of resources gathered for deve-lopment finance through inflation).

[4] The illustrative numbers used are derived from J. J. Polak, "Monetary Ana-lysis of Income Formation and Payments Problems," *International Monetary Fund Staff Papers*, VI, No. 1 (November 1957), pp. 1–50. Table on p. 25.

In a recent article, Professor R.A. Mundell has used a simple model of inflation, economic growth, and the demand for money to estimate the contribution that inflationary financing might make to economic growth.[5] His results, which are based on rather generous assumptions about the magnitudes of the determinants, designed to produce a maximum estimate, give a maximum inflationary tax yield of 3 per cent of national income and maximum increase in the growth rate of 1.5 per cent on one formulation of the influence of the rate of inflation on the demand for money, and a yield of 3.2 per cent of national income and increase in the growth rate of 0.8 per cent on another.

Contrary to Mundell's own judgment, these are not negligible figures, when compared with the savings ratios and growth rates characteristic of underdeveloped countries. But they are extreme estimates, and likely to exceed substantially the contribution that inflation could make under even the most favorable circumstances.

The circumstances in which inflation is resorted to in underdeveloped countries, however, are far from the most favorable conceivable; and their inflations are extremely likely to proceed in such a way, and to be accompanied by such other economic policies, as to exercise a serious retarding influence on economic growth. Specifically, inflationary financing may impede growth in three major ways, each contrary to the assumptions of the "inflationary tax" model.

In the first place, contrary to the assumption that prices throughout the economy adjust freely to inflation, the government of a developing country employing inflationary development policies is likely to be under strong political pressure to protect important sectors of the community from the effects of inflation, through control of food prices, rents, urban transport fares and so on. Such controls inevitably distort the allocation of resources within the economy, and particularly their allocation to private investment in growth. Fixing of low prices for food inhibits the development of agricultural production and the improvement of agricultural technique; control of rents, on the other hand, may unduly foster the construction of new housing to accommodate those who cannot find rent-controlled housing or to enable landlords to evade rent controls. All three policies tend to promote urbanization, which involves expenditure on social overhead and may increase the numbers of the urban unem-

---

[5] R. A. Mundell, "Growth, Mobility and Inflationary Finance," *Journal of Political Economy* (April 1965).

ployed. Moreover, control of prices of food, and particularly of fares on state-owned transport facilities, may involve the state in explicit subsidies, on the one hand, and budget deficits, on the other, so that the proceeds of the inflationary tax are wasted in supporting the consumption of certain sections of the population rather than being invested in development. Such phenomena are widely observable in the underdeveloped countries of the world. (They are also observable in advanced countries, but the latter can more easily afford the waste of resources involved.)

In the second place, contrary to the assumptions of the "inflation tax" model, inflation typically does not proceed at a steady and well-anticipated rate, but proceeds erratically with large politically determined variations in the rate of price increase. These variations in the rate of inflation divert a great deal of the effort of private business into forecasting and speculating on the rate of inflation, or hedging against the uncertainties involved. They also destroy the possibility of rational calculation of small margins of profit and undermine the incentives to strive constantly to reduce costs and improve performance, which striving is the key to the steady increase of productivity in the industrially advanced nations.

Finally, the inflation tax model assumes either a closed economy or a country on a floating exchange rate system. In reality, countries —especially underdeveloped countries—are exposed to competition in and from the world economy, yet they display a strong propensity to maintain fixed exchange rates and to defend them to the limit of their exchange reserves, borrowing powers and ability to use exchange controls. In this kind of setting inflation introduces a progressive tendency toward exchange rate overvaluation, balance-of-payments difficulties, and resort to increasing protectionism, which in turn results in the diversion of resources away from export industries and toward high-cost import-substituting industries, and a consequent loss of economic efficiency. While the appearance of growth may be generated by the establishment of import-substitute industries, the reality may be lost in misallocation of resources produced by protectionism and the inefficiency of exchange control procedures. Moreover, eventually the increasing overvaluation of the currency is likely to force a devaluation, coupled with a monetary reform involving drastic domestic deflation. This experience, in addition to the disturbing effects of deflation in interrupting the growth of the economy, has the long-run effect of damaging the stability and confidence of expectations on which the process of investing depends.

ummarize, this chapter has argued the following propositions. efficient development policy should plan on some modest degree of inflation as a means of more fully mobilizing the economy's resources; in this limited sense, inflation is an inevitable price of rapid development. Second, while a policy of financing development by deliberate inflation has strong attractions theoretically and politically, the possibilities of stimulating economic development by these means are quite limited. Third, inflationary development policies in practice are unlikely to achieve this stimulating effect, but on the contrary likely to retard economic growth, by distorting the allocation of resources and wasting the inflation-gathered development resources on consumption, by increasing uncertainty and reducing incentives for innovation and improvement, and through their balance-of-payments effects by fostering the inefficiencies of protectionism and exchange control.

DISCUSSION

Pros and Cons of Inflation

Inflation is bad because it causes a misallocation of resources. On the other hand, it does not necessarily put a stop to economic development.

Professor Johnson drew attention to the fact that events in the political, administrative and social as well as the economic field affect inflation. There tends, for example, to be a division of functions between Treasuries and central banks. Treasuries like to keep interest rates low, which can be inflationary. Central banks —and the International Monetary Fund—dislike inflation, because it reduces the value of money. They insist on keeping exchange rates fixed for as long as possible, making it necessary to apply exchange controls and import restrictions.

How to halt inflation? Under IMF rules, it has to be stopped drastically. This can create depression and unemployment—which is likely to shock the country back into inflation again.

Dr. Barend A. de Vries, of the World Bank, regretted that little empirical material exists on the effects of inflation. Wages today start moving up as soon as prices do, so that the role of the "inflationary tax" in transferring resources to development breaks down. "I think that any government which plans on a modest degree of inflation ends up with very serious inflationary problems, and I know of no government—and I have dealt with many—that has actually planned a modest inflation, and has been able to manage modest inflation."

Therefore financial policies should be concentrated toward absolute stability from the start, especially in smaller countries dependent on foreign trade. "This does not mean that you will end up with absolute stability, but I think that policy as such ought to be directed toward it."

Does inflation help development, at least? The question is irrelevant. What governments ought to be concerned with is using resources in the best manner and channelling savings efficiently. If there are inflationary consequences, "I would regard these as secondary."

It does not follow that inflation prevents economic development. "We know that the most vigorous developing part of the world is Latin America. Despite the disadvantages of feudalism, as Professor Galbraith emphasized in Model II, we find in Latin America a spectacular industrial development, a spectacular development of urban centers and of an urban culture, and a spectacular development of commercial agriculture." Peru for example has increased its fisheries export from zero to $200 million in the seven years. It is possible to avoid the dislocations commonly ascribed to the inflationary process. Rents are frozen in Brazil, and this has checked luxury building.

"Yet there is an enormous problem of inflation in this part of the world. Heavy industrialization programs would add to the inflationary pressure because the production and supply of goods lag behind the expenditures involved while industrializing. A remedy is to maintain flexible exchange-rate policies, as Professor Johnson suggests, because it is the freezing of exchange rates in Latin America that has made their foreign trade stagnate.

"Once countries follow a policy of concentrating their resources on efficient, high-yielding investments and maintain a flexible exchange-rate policy, I think you can have development, even though there may be a heavy dose of inflation; and this does not imply by any means that inflation is good. I think inflation is bad."

A particular problem of stabilization concerns countries that have passed through ten or 15 years of industrialization and inflation, emerging with a good infrastructure. As returns on investments are lower in infrastructure than in the private sector, the tendency is

to squeeze private business. "I think this runs contrary to the interest
of development in the country concerned. More resources should be
put into the private sector because returns are higher; and the over-all
development of the country, given a certain stage of development in
the infrastructure, can move faster ahead."

Dr. Joseph Attyeh, of Israel, stated that full employment is inflationary because, to entice a person from one job to another, one
has to pay him more than the value of his product. The entrepreneur
finds compensation for this cost in the government's inflationary
policy, which is a form of extra credit to the business sector. Hence
to mobilize fully the resources of the economy, some price increase
is unavoidable.

In developing countries, labor is less mobile. More inducements
are needed to bring manpower from subsistence villages to the towns.
The authorities ought not to depend exclusively on monetary incentives, but should encourage this mobility by providing better facilities, such as, to take a basic example, building roads to the subsistence areas.

Inflation can be made a tool of development if consumption is cut
and resources diverted to investment. This can be accomplished by
deficit financing and the allocation of credits to the entrepreneur. It
is also possible to tax inflation, i.e., tax money holdings, though little
revenue will accrue.

But the deliberate use of inflation in this way can only work for a
limited period of time. In 1949–1965, Israel used deficit financing as
a means of pushing investment, and achieved a remarkably large increase in the national product. Subsequently there came balance of
payment difficulties, followed by devaluation and some unemployment, with a fall in the rate of growth to more normal proportions.

Dr. Francisco Aquino, of El Salvador, opposed inflation as a
planned policy. "With an inflationary rate of more than 5 per cent,
I would be plain worried, because I believe that then the forces inherent in the process could easily get out of hand."

The problem of controlling inflation is made more complex by
the impact of the external sector. "The monetary and credit policies
of the highly developed countries affect us in a very direct way, and
we have to deal with these inflationary or deflationary influences as
best we can."

High rates of economic growth in the LDCs usually lead to a
payments deficit rather than to inflation. This subject is vital to any
discussion of monetary expansion in developing countries.

Keeping It Moderate

Inflation can be, if anything, a stimulus—on condition that all the countries in a trading group undergo a parallel price rise. Boom policies help expand the market in a developing economy. But how do you keep inflationary pressures in check?

Two views exist in Latin America on the subject of inflation, according to *Dr. Josue Saenz*, of Mexico. There is the Kubitschek view, named after the former President of Brazil, which says, "Let's get the thing built and to hell with prices or exchange rates." Then there is the IMF view, which bans inflation outright, treating the subject "as a sort of sacred cow."

"There is, I think, a general agreement that, if there are feasible alternatives to inflationary finance, inflationary finance should not be used. But I stress 'if there are feasible alternatives.' "

Mexico has achieved sustained growth. However, if it had followed financial orthodoxy in certain periods of its history, the country would never have emerged from stagnation. Thus "at certain crucial times in a nation's history, if a choice has to be made between sacrificing growth and sacrificing the exchange rate, unquestionably the exchange rate should be sacrificed."

Dr. Saenz stresses that inflation is not only a national question; it is fundamentally an international problem. You can have parallel inflations in a coordinated group of countries without the need for devaluation. Inflation can then be a stimulating influence toward growth.

"Autonomous inflation" can occur in economically powerful countries that are able to inflate with impunity over long periods without suffering balance of payment difficulties, because their money is a key currency. This situation would call for a series of adjustments among their satellites, i.e., the other nations which form part of these constellations; but such adjustments are purely compensatory and cause no damage. So "a developing country should allow inflation, or perhaps even plan inflation, at least to a degree similar to other countries in the same constellation." This helps maintain effective demand, offsets high interest rates, stimulates the marginal efficiency of capital, maintains the profitability of investment, and attracts foreign capital.

Rates of inflation should be made compatible with the aid of import controls, export incentives and exchange rates. There is the problem of competitive exports, so perhaps the best solution is "a moderate world-wide inflation parallel in all countries, which will have the advantage of giving a general stimulus to all."

Dr. *Bernard Ryelandt,* of Congo (Leopoldville), said that administrative collapse (provoked by the sudden departure of the colonial power), combined with a maldistribution of the national income in favor of certain sectors of the public service, have led to galloping inflation in the Congo. During the first 16 months after independence, prices rose by 30 per cent, and in the following 16 months by 150 per cent.

There are positive aspects to these events: first, the growth of an internal market, previously limited almost entirely to the Europeans. This has permitted industrial development, thanks to the existence of a healthy industrial base inherited from the past. Also in areas favorably situated, agricultural trade has grown rapidly—as much as threefold in the Lower Congo betwen 1960 and 1964. The monetization of the traditional society constitutes a structural change of the first importance.

Dr. Ryelandt concluded by stressing that all the negative aspects outlined by Dr. Johnson exist as well, causing grave distortions in the economy.

Mr. *Conrado Pascual, Jr.,* of the Philippines, said that economic development is an urgent objective of economic policy. The most vexing hindrance to growth is the inability of the developing world to form the requisite volume of capital. How do we fill the gulf between the investments needed in an age of rising expectations and the savings available?

Mr. Horowitz suggests a capital transfer, i.e., the import of foreign savings from developed to developing countries. Professor Johnson suggests a measure of coercive savings, by fermenting a modest degree of inflation. Both approaches are helpful, in Dr. Pascual's opinion. He drew attention to the possibility of also increasing voluntary savings in the LDCs. The magnitude of assets hoarded greatly exceeds estimates, and there is room to discuss monetary and fiscal measures for mobilizing resources of this kind by voluntary means.

Hon. *Unia Gostel Mwila,* of Zambia, said, "Taking into account that Zambia has had what Dr. Johnson would call a mild inflation of 5.4 per cent this year, how can one be sure that the trend will continue to be moderate? Any program of slow inflation is unlikely to remain slow for long. As people come to expect a steady price increase of, say, 3 per cent annually, they will soon take steps to circumvent it—which must speed up the price rise further.

"Secondly, must rapid development always go with the rise in price levels, or can these two factors be dealt with separately? Everything depends on controlling the growth of incomes, and securing a proportion of the additional earnings for savings and investment instead of consumption. Mr. Mwila was emphatic that inflation can cause hardship in countries where a great majority of the people are simple farmers. He observed that the achievement of non-inflationary development is easier in an economy which possesses spare productive capacity."

Mr. D. Franklin Neal, of Liberia, took up Mr. Mwila's point, adding that, in a dual economy where you have a reserve of labor in the subsistence sector, development does not necessarily involve inflationary wage increases. Mobility of labor can be achieved at existing wage rates. In any case it is difficult to up wages in countries that are competing in international export markets. Rising wages and rising prices likewise bridle budgetary expenditures, impeding investment in the infrastructure.

Mr. Christopher Musoke, of Uganda, does not support inflation as a deliberate policy for economic development. It is a form of expediency. If it gets out of hand—"and there are very few countries which have tools efficient enough to keep inflation under control"— it leads to a misallocation of resources. People buy more consumer goods and invest more in real estate.

Developing countries which use inflation as a method of economic growth put themselves deliberately into a balance of payments crisis. The multiple exchange rate system encourages a measure of uncertainty. This and other factors discourage foreign investors. Inflation penalizes the small saver, the people who buy bonds, the people who buy insurance policies. In summary, "Cannot the governments of developing countries employ better and more realistic methods and tools for achieving their social economic objectives?"

* * *

Professor Johnson concluded the debate by contradicting the imputation that he favors inflationary policies. When attempts are made, he said, to use inflation as a means of mobilizing resources, distortions are introduced which render the net effect negative rather than positive.

"I don't recommend the deliberate use of modest inflation. I'd say instead that development planning, which tends to maximize what you can get, would, on a rational calculation of the advantages and disadvantages of growth versus inflation, involve some modest inflation," he said.

Concerning the balance of payments, a subject that ran through the debate, there are two kinds of LDCs. The first is countries like the Philippines and Zambia, which are tightly linked to a major economic power that takes most of their exports and provides most of their capital. Such countries may well have an advantage in maintaining an absolutely fixed exchange rate with the currency of that dominant country—and they must therefore avoid inflation.

The second type of LDC does not have that need. Their problem comes from "trying to maintain a fixed exchange rate and yet enjoy an autonomy that you cannot achieve unless you have a floating exchange rate to save them from the balance of payments problem."

Dr. Johnson then set himself to answer the questions posed by Mr. Mwila. First, how do you stop inflation from getting out of hand? "I believe inflation cannot get out of hand unless you make it get out of hand. In other words, inflations that get out of hand do so because the government of the country prefers to inflate more and more and more, rather than to stop it.

"You can steal a lot of resources if you start inflating after perhaps having got used to stable prices. This is typically the mechanism of wartime finance in advanced countries, where you deliberately rob the people and you can do it for a short period in a big way, but you can't keep doing it, because people get wise to it."

Mr. Mwila's second question was: Must rapid development always go with a rise in the price level? It depends which causes which. If we ask: Does inflation always generate rapid development?, the answer is no. It might possibly accelerate development a little if the situation were handled right, but no more than that.

If we ask: Does rapid development always generate inflation?, the answer depends on the circumstances. You may have underemployed resources to utilize, or you may have a pool of unemployed during a big depression, in which case you can move forward without inflation.

Using labor from the subsistence sector does generally involve some inflation, because the labor "is not simply lying there, fully trained, adequate human capital and so forth, just waiting." Finally, if rapid development can proceed without inflation, isn't deliberate inflation morally wrong? It depends who benefits from the morality. "In my own country, Canada, there was a period of something like five years with 7½ per cent unemployment, as the result of an effort by the central bank to stop inflation. It seems to me that, taking 3 per cent as a normal figure for idle labor, to throw 4½ per cent of the population out of work in order to prevent a 1 per cent a year deterioration in the real value of the monetary assets of the civil servants and others who were implementing this policy, was clearly immoral.

"The issues of morality here are not morality versus immorality, but one kind of morality versus another. I happen to favor the morality of developing people, and raising their incomes, over the morality of protecting my own savings from inflation."

8

SAVING AND INVESTMENT THROUGH THE GOVERNMENT BUDGET

By KOICHI EMI

*Institute of Economic Research
Hitotsubashi University, Japan*

For the purposes of economic growth, the central problem of public finance lies in what kind of revenue should be selected for financing the expansion of government activity. Theoretically the source of funds ought to correspond to the expenditure purpose. Taxes as current revenue are used to finance ordinary administration, and borrowings or public debt are very often used for extraordinary purposes, either military or productive. Saving and investment through the government budget have two alternative channels, that is, taxes to finance ordinary public investment, and borrowings to finance urgent loan or investment projects. Under the normal conditions of economic development, the former channel is the major one and the latter is supplementary. However, during rapidly changing phases of a country's economic and social structures, current sources of funds cannot meet the urgent need for government activity to lead the private economy to new circumstances. This function has to be enforced by the extraordinary part of the government budget which substitutes for the private banking system. In other words, the function of public finance should be extended to set up a new saving-investment scheme for the national economy beyond its original framework.

Here we can point to two typical cases of such government fiscal activity in modern Japan. The first is the role of government financing in the economic shift from a feudal to a capitalistic society in the opening decade after the Meiji Restoration (1868). The second case is the rehabilitation process from the war economy to a peacetime pattern of production after World War II and subsequently.

Government Budget in the Opening Decade of Modern Japan 1868–1875 (Case I)

To clarify the process of transforming the economic system through the government budget, Table 1 is presented. Revenue and expenditure correspond with each other under their two separate heads— ordinary and extraordinary. Giving attention to the revenue side

138

for the first four fiscal years of the new Restoration government, it is known that the ordinary part accounts for only 30 per cent of total revenue, and that the government depended on extraordinary sources, namely paper money issue and borrowings. Especially we should notice that such heavy dependence on paper money issues was concentrated in the first two years and then decreased sharply. So it is a notable fact that the initial motive power was produced by the enormous spending of paper money which is shown as 70 per cent of total revenue. The important point is the correspondence between extraordinary sources and extraordinary uses of funds. Much of these funds were directed to loans to the former *samurai* (feudal warrior class) for occupational change or for promoting the establishment of new industries. This had a similar role to that of the present Treasury Loans and Investment Program, but the funds were lent directly to the borrowers, rather than through intermediary financial institutions. Therefore the economic effects could be expected to appear swiftly.

The problem is what kind of impact such a credit expansion would have in transforming the economic system. Under a full employment economy, it would immediately bring about rises in prices. However, in the situation of the Japanese economy when the feudal society was in the process of liquidation, there did not exist full employment in terms of capitalistic production. In other words, both natural and human resources were relatively ample in the first decade, so they could react positively to credit expansion and could stabilize the initial impact of rises in prices by increasing supplies. In the circumstances, the accepted role of monetary policy in an "industrially underdeveloped and rapidly expanding" country could be applied.[1] Furthermore, the case of "unlimited supply of labor at subsistence wages" pointed out by Professor W. A. Lewis,[2] is also suggestive for the starting period of Meiji Japan. Of course, we should also appreciate the deflationary effects of gold and silver accumulated during the preceding feudal age. Almost every year in the opening decade, they flowed to foreign countries to pay for excess imports.

Next to paper money issues, the ratios of borrowings are significant in 1870. They were raised from two sources, namely domestic

---

[1] Alvin H. Hansen, *Monetary Theory and Fiscal Policy* (New York: McGraw-Hill Book Co., Inc., 1949), Ch. 12, p. 167.

[2] W. Arthur Lewis, "Economic Development with Unlimited Supplies of Labor," *The Economics of Underdevelopment,* ed. A. N. Agarwala and S. P. Singh (New York: Oxford University Press, 1958).

TABLE 1

Sources of Revenue and Purpose of Expenditure of Central Government, 1868–1885

(A) Revenue

Fiscal Year	Total Revenue (million yen)	Percentage Distribution								
		Ordinary				Total	Extraordinary			
		Total	Land Tax	Customs	Others		Paper Money	Borrowings	Return of Funds	Others
1868	33,089 (100)	11.1	6.1	2.2	2.8	88.9	72.6	14.3	0.0	2.0
1869	34,438 (100)	13.5	9.7	1.5	2.3	86.5	69.6	2.6	13.1	1.2
1870	20,959 (100)	47.9	39.2	3.1	5.6	52.1	25.5	22.8	0.8	3.0
1871	22,145 (100)	64.8	51.2	4.8	8.8	30.7	9.7	—	19.5	1.5
1868–1871	110,631 (100)	30.5	22.5	2.7	5.3	69.5	50.2	9.4	8.1	1.8
1872–1875 [a]	295,719 (100)	84.3	70.3	1.9	12.1	15.7	6.0	3.7	2.5	3.5
1875 [b]–1881	440,755 (100)	91.4	68.3	3.7	19.4	8.6	*	*	1.7	6.9
1882–1885	295,442 (100)	93.0	58.7	3.4	30.9	7.0	—	1.7	0.2	5.1

Source : Ouchi, Hyoe and Tsuchiya, Takeo (eds). *Meiji zenki zaisei keizai shiryo shusei* (Collection of Historical Data of Finance in the First Half of the Meiji Era). Vol. 4, Tokyo, 1932.

Notes: (1) In the years immediately after the Restoration, the accounting period was irregular, so the absolute amount of each year should be compared after adjusting the number of months. For two accounts of 1875 in the table, they are respectively the first half (a) and the second half (b) of 1875.

(2) Asterisks* indicate that figures do not appear in the Closed Accounts of the central government. But the issue by the government of 27 million yen and borrowings of 15 million yen from the Fifteenth National Bank were financed for the military expenses to suppress the Satsuma Rebellion in 1877. Such financing should in fact be taken into account here.

140

(B) Expenditure

Fiscal Year	Total Expenditure (million yen)	Percentage Distribution										
		Ordinary					Extraordinary					
		Total (a)	Public Works	Compensation (b)	National Debt	Military (e)	Total (a)	New Industries (c)	Loans (d)	Return of Old Debts	Temporary Allowances (b)	Military (e)
1868	30,505 (100)	18.0	2.6	1.1	—	3.5	82.0	2.3	59.5	3.6	1.6	14.8
1869	30,786 (100)	45.0	7.0	8.2	—	7.4	55.0	4.9	21.5	9.0	3.4	11.1
1870	20,108 (100)	48.5	4.4	11.6	—	7.5	51.5	16.4	3.3	13.1	5.3	6.1
1871	19,235 (100)	63.6	4.7	16.4	2.3	16.9	36.4	13.1	5.7	9.0	0.5	0.5
1868–1871	90,634 (100)	40.6	3.9	9.1	0.5	8.1	59.4	6.6	26.9	8.1	2.6	8.1
1872–1875	268,813 (100)	76.6	3.6	32.8	3.1	15.1	23.4	7.3	3.0	3.5	4.4	1.8
1875–1881	432,801 (100)	90.3	5.3	8.8	28.9	15.5	9.7	1.5	1.1	—	1.8	0.3
1882–1885	293,405 (100)	80.1	2.1	0.7	29.3	22.0	19.9	1.1	—	—	—	3.7

Source : Ibid.

Notes : (1) Same with Notes (1) of (A) Revenue.
(2) (a) Includes "others."
(b) Both are transfers to the former samurai.
(c) They are expenses for establishments of new industries and for agricultural development.
(d) They are expenses for loans financed to the former samurai to encourage them to enter new occupations. However, a fair part of the loans was diverted to military expenses.
(e) Military expenses in the ordinary part were directed for organization of new industrial forces and those in the extraordinary part were costs for civil wars in the first decade except those for the Satsuma Rebellion and other extraordinary military events.

141

and foreign loans. The first borrowings in 1868 were mostly supplied by domestic wealthy merchants, but they were generally directed to expenses for military action to subdue *samurai* of the feudal regime. However, loans in 1870 which amounted to one million pounds (4.88 million yen) were provided by foreign indebtedness floated in London, and they were positively used for railroad construction. In the year after the Restoration when the domestic financial market was not established yet, it is noticeable that the first issue of public debt was floated in the foreign market and all the funds served for the creation of social overhead capital.

The ratio of land tax to total revenue shot up in 1870, after the Restoration, and subsequently current revenue in the second period (1872–75) increased greatly. The former came from the political stabilization after the chief remaining feudal elements had been wiped out, and the latter was systematically developed by the Land Tax Reform in 1873. With these events, the weight of extraordinary financing contracted sharply. This means the major sources of revenue made it possible to shift from paper money issues or borrowings to regular taxes, so that borrowings could be repaid and the burden of public indebtedness could be readily borne. In 1873, the second series of foreign loans amounting to 2.4 million pounds (11.71 million yen) were floated in the United Kingdom, again for the purpose of having funds to compensate the former *samurai* for giving up their feudal stipends. However, it can be seen in the table that the greater part of compensations to ex-*samurai* in the second period and the redemption of national debt in the third period were financed within ordinary government funds.

Turning back to the problem of saving and investment through the government budget, its initial function of promoting industrial production decreased in the third and the fourth periods and was gradually switched to the private banking system. At this stage, the purpose of government loans and investments shifted from the establishment of private enterprises to the proper function of creating public works and other social overhead capital. In the second decade after the Meiji Restoration, this role of the banking system was greatly advanced, as can be seen in the establishment of the Yokohama Specie Bank in 1880 and the Bank of Japan in 1882, the issue of convertible bank notes in 1884, and the enforcement of the silver standard in 1886. With this preparation of the fiscal and monetary system, it can be said that capital accumulation in the 1890s "was greatly promoted."

Government Fiscal Activity in the Recovery Process After
World War II (Case II)

In the confusion of a political turning-point, enormous expenses
were incurred in transferring from the old system to the new order,
as occurred at the beginning of the Meiji period. In that case,
most current revenue was absorbed for very urgent administrative
purposes, and positive government investment and loans had to
depend for their source of funds on the extraordinary financing in
addition to current revenue. A similar situation is observed in
the general account of the central government for several years after
the end of World War II.

As seen in Table 2, the biggest item of expenditure in 1947–1950
was expenses for the termination of war. This included such military
expenses as the quartering of U.S troops so that such expenditures
were greatest in the immediate post-war years. Next to this, three
items of expenditure, namely subsidies for price adjustment, public
works, and investment, are more or less related to saving-investment
activity through the general budget. Needless to say, public works
are a proper field for government investment and were urgently
necessary to reconstruct war-devastated areas quickly. However, the
items which played a positive role in encouraging the reopening of
production were two other outlays. The first was to compensate key
industries for the difference between the prices fixed for sale and
producer's actual cost. Under the intensifying inflation, such price
support served greatly to make the production of basic materials
and commodities profitable for entrepreneurs. Second, investment and
subscriptions have as a purpose to mobilize private funds for supplementing the government investment itself and stimulating business
further in a broader sense. All this helped in the task of rapidly reconstructing key industries. Here, as also in Case I, a huge amount of
money was thrown into the immediate post-war economy to reopen
peacetime production. It was the special function of the Reconversion Finance Bank together with the central bank which carried out
this policy. In other words, the Reconversion Finance Bank issued
its debentures to have loanable funds for industries, but these were
held for the most part by the Bank of Japan and the economic
effects were the same as the issue of inconvertible bank notes.
However, the initial monetary policy based on free market economic
principles was not altogether successful under the condition of bottlenecks in physical resources, even though this situation was caused
by the post-war inflation which spread during the half-year after the

termination of the war owing to the extraordinary military funds left over.

TABLE 2

Ratios of Major Expenditure Items of General Account, 1947–1955

Unit: hundred million yen

		Percentage Distribution				
Fiscal Year	Total Expenditure	Expenses for Termination of War %	Subsidies for Price Adjustment %	Public Works %	Investment and Subscriptions %	Refund of National Debt %
1947	2,143 (100)	30.0	11.1	6.9	3.3	3.5
1948	4,731 (100)	22.6	13.2	10.5	3.9	2.1
1949	7,410 (100)	16.9	24.2	8.4	12.1	1.8
1950	6,646 (100)	16.4	9.6	15.5	3.8	12.5
1947–1955	20,930 (100)	14.3	2.0	13.9	6.4	3.8

Source: Ministry of Finance, Statistical Yearbook on Public Finance, 1962 and 1964.

Theoretically speaking, the conversion from a war economy to peacetime production does not mean a quick switch from a controlled economy to a situation of free competition. Therefore the economy was actually in a condition of full capacity during the rehabilitation period. This point does differ from the situation in Case I, and an enormous money increase worked to intensify the rise in prices. However, the Reconversion Finance Bank itself was established to provide concentrated funds for the key industries such as coal, iron, electricity, shipbuilding and marine transport and chemical fertilizer. The greatest priority was given to coal production. It was expected that greater production of coal would induce more production of iron and the area of activity could be gradually enlarged. This policy finally led the ruined economy into production increases, for the initial monetary policy was soon revised to accompany the decontrol of commodities and encourage savings.

TABLE 3

The Rate of Increase of Taxes, Currency, Price, Production and Income to Previous Years, 1947–1955

Year	Taxes %	Currency Issues %	Wholesale Price %	Manufacturing Production %	Real National Income %
1947	416.9	132.8	195.7	24.3	6.1
1948	131.8	61.5	165.5	33.7	17.2
1949	62.6	0.3	64.0	32.5	15.7
1950	–13.9	18.8	18.1	25.2	18.6
1951	26.6	19.9	38.7	41.2	10.0
1952	21.6	13.8	1.9	8.0	9.7
1953	10.2	10.7	0.6	23.8	5.9
1954	2.1	–0.9	–0.6	9.6	2.8
1955	1.8	9.0	–1.7	8.3	11.4

Source: (1) The Bank of Japan, Statistics Dept., *Economic Statistics of Japan,* 1957.

(2) The Economic Planning Agency, *White Paper of National Income,* 1964.

(3) Ministry of Finance, *ibid.*

Note: Real national income was computed on the fiscal year basis.

To see in brief how the initial monetary policy created a process leading to final success, such indices as taxes, money, prices, production and national income are compared in Table 3 in terms of rate of increase. As clearly seen, the rapid increase of currency issues in the first two years resulted in a sharp rise in prices, as the quantity theory of money suggests. However, the rise in prices soon reduced speed, inflation ceased, and then output effects grew to be larger than price effects since 1950. Real national income also showed a steady growth. To realize the above tendencies, the increase of taxes which was enforced through the balanced budget by Mr. Dodge's Stabilization Program (1949) and the subsequent tax reform by the Shoup Mission (1950) contributed a great deal. The Korean War broke out during the period of this fiscal and monetary stringency. Therefore it was important to decide how to support the rapid increase of production in private enterprises so as to offset inflationary tendencies under the new circumstances. Of course, tax revenue increased automatically in the war boom, making possible bigger expenditure on government investments. However, the reconstruction of key industries was not accomplished yet and, furthermore, new demands sprang up to develop further industries. Therefore, at the second stage, government loans to and investments in industries were still continued in a special form beyond the framework of the general account, namely via the Special Account of the U.S. Aid Counterpart Fund. These funds were also directed mostly to the four big key industries (coal, iron, electricity and shipbuilding) as well as government enterprises—telegraph, telephone and national railways. The characteristics of the funds differed from the inflationary money of the Reconversion Finance Bank since the increase in the supply of money was offset in a deflationary manner by the counterpart sale of commodities imported under the U.S. Aid Program.

The third phase of reconstruction begins with political independence from the occupying authorities in 1952. At this stage, the Japan Development Bank as a quasi-government organization took over the leading role to supply funds to industries. In the first two fiscal years, financial resources were kept up mostly by contributions from Government sources, but afterwards the bank could not expect to receive such supplies of funds from the public account, with the expansion of expenditures, especially military-related expenses. Henceforth the greater part of funds for investment derived from the public debt or other kinds of borrowings. The main new source was the accumulation of funds which the government commanded—that is, postal savings, postal insurance and postal pensions. This was meant to mobilize spontaneous private saving for public investment in relation to government agencies. Here saving and investment in relation to government activity are not only limited to channelling a reallocation of financial resources. It could be said that the borrowings from such savings are a kind of public debt, even though they are not officially named as government bonds.

The characteristics of government funds loaned for key industries can be summarized over the three stages as (1) inflationary money, (2) increase of taxes and the U.S. Aid Fund and (3) borrowings from the public. Of course, tax revenue provided the source of industrial funds for every stage in the form of loans or subscriptions, but it can be said that it was relatively important in the second stage. Broadly speaking, this sequence is similar to that of the Meiji case which can be summarized as (1) paper money and borrowings from wealthy merchants, (2) foreign loans and land tax and (3) issues of public debt. However, there are some differences between these two cases. First, the supply of funds in the post-war situation was mostly directed to key industries closely related to the increase of production, whereas the Meiji period placed importance on the construction of social overhead capital and land cultivation. Second, government loans and investments in the post-war period were provided through the government financial organizations, but those in the Meiji epoch were supplied directly to borrowers as already stated. Third, the government authorities in the post-war case intentionally adopted a fiscal policy for reconstructing the ruined economy, while the authorities in the Meiji Restoration government were not fully aware of the economic effects of their policy.

Every fiscal year since 1953, the Japanese government announces the Treasury Loans and Investments Program, in which loans through the Japan Development Bank are included. These government fiscal activities are considered as a form of public finance combined with banking business beyond the normal area of government activities. This means that it is not enough to carry out normal fiscal functions within the framework of the general account under the present mixed economy. Thus public finance serves as a balancing factor through economic fluctuation and then supports a steady growth of the economy in the long run by supplementing the banking system.

Conclusion

Many problems remain when comparing government fiscal activities in two periods far apart in time and in their degree of capitalist development. However, public finance did show common characteristics during periods of rapid change in the political and economic system, according to the Japanese experience. In other words, the role of public finance is not only to perform its own saving and investment, but also to establish the initial saving and investment channels for private industries, taking the place of the banking system. These activities are necessarily enlarged beyond the area of the general account of public finance, but they then contract to normal proportions with the growth of the private economy.

9 VALUE-LINKING OF LOANS IN ISRAEL[1]

By Amotz Morag

Eliezer Kaplan School of Economics
and Social Sciences
The Hebrew University of Jerusalem, Israel

As an introduction to evaluating the practice of the linkage of loans in Israel, I wish to state briefly my general approach toward escalation of incomes and assets. I have argued elsewhere[2] in favor of the extension of the form of escalated payments to all possible spheres of a monetary economy; that is, all nominal incomes except profits, and all nominal assets (and liabilities) including money balances. The logic of that extreme proposal is that in a completely price-linked economy, a rise in the level of prices would be almost economically harmless, unless the economy is ready to pay a high price for the very stability of its foreign exchange rate. But I cannot see any good sense in that attitude for most countries of the world; certainly not for countries with "soft" currencies.

The proposal involves administrative nuisances, but has many economic merits. Since in a fully escalated economy no one will benefit from inflation, it is also clear that no one will suffer from it. The relevance of the rate of inflation loses thus most of its poignance, yet it is not at all obvious that it will increase. Since a rise in the price level will be compensated for, expectations of such a rise should not increase the velocity of circulation of money which is a major factor in the dynamics of inflation, nor should it decrease liquid savings or encourage capital flights abroad or distort the structure of investments toward the "hedges-against-inflation" types.

The main intention of this proposal, which is admittedly extreme, is to reduce the fear from inflation not in inflationary periods, but in economies that are still partly unemployed, while the fiscal and monetary policies take too many precautions not to overshoot the mark and create inflationary excess-demand.

In the above-mentioned publication, and in an article written much earlier, I objected to escalation to any specific price, and espe-

---

[1] Parts of this survey are based on Haim Ben-Shahar's *Rates of Interest and the Cost of Capital in Israel* 1950–1962, a mimeographed manuscript.

[2] See Amotz Morag, *On Taxs and Inflation* (New York: Random House, 1965), pp. 154–173.

cially to the prices of gold and foreign exchange. This is not only because there is indeed an implication of an "abdication of the local currency" in such linkage, but for purely economic causes.

To begin with there is no economic logic in linking local payments to the price of a foreign currency. All it will achieve is a complete frustration of any devaluation of the local currency even when clearly needed. Secondly, even if one accepts the "purchasing-power parity" theorem (in its average or marginal versions), devaluations are made only periodically. It is clear therefore that borrowers who had received loans after a devaluation and repaid it before the next one do not pay any escalation charges (and the lenders do not receive any), while borrowers whose loans were granted just before a devaluation would be charged with tremendous additional payments. Also, from a psychological point of view, holders of bonds linked to the rate of foreign exchange may wrongly expect that the value of their assets will rise on the very date of a devaluation at the rate of the devaluation itself. This will not be true, owing to the rate of discount, in all cases where the redemption of the bonds is due only several years later.

Linkage to a general local price index—and there may be several alternative suitable indices—does not create any of these difficulties, and is completely justified on moral or patriotic grounds. It is clear that if all private loans were linked to such an index, inflation would not any more change the distribution of wealth between private lenders and private borrowers. With all incomes also linked to the same index, the base of the inflation tax would be limited to the amount of money and the public debt. This would still be an arbitrary tax, but much superior to the inflation tax in any escalationless economy.

Index-Escalation Savings and Investments

The propensity to save in all economies is determined, at least for personal and business savings, by the size and by the distribution of disposable incomes, and by the expected rates of return. A very mild inflation may, under favorable conditions, increase total savings by transferring incomes from other groups (rentiers, debtors, employees) to profit receivers. But when a rather high rate of inflation is built into general economic expectations, liquid savings in the economy will obviously be drastically reduced (thus accelerating excess-demand), while consumption or investments are increased. As far as households are concerned, they do not have many channels for their savings. A highly negative rate of interest on hoarding tends to increase dissaving and purchases of real estates or durable goods even if they hardly bear any real rate of return. In many countries stocks have flunked the test as a hedge against inflation. There cannot be any doubt that under the circumstances, the introduction of index-linked bonds would increase savings and decrease wasteful expenditures.

It should be also noted that in some countries there is a maximum legal rate of interest, so that when the rate of inflation exceeds that rate, ordinary bonds cannot offer legally any positive real rate of interest. Depending on the laws concerned, escalation charges may be formally excluded from the calculation of effective interest rates, thus enabling the economy to elude some of the undesirable effects of such Interest Laws.[3]

Since index linkage narrows the base of the inflation tax, and since there are recurring arguments that inflation might promote growth by increasing investments, it follows that were those arguments true (or where they are true), linkage would have reduced total investment (and, necessarily, total saving). Even if such arguments were valid, which is far from being clear, it is clear that the productivity of investments does not depend only on their quantity but on their composition as well.

The Israeli Experience

Israel has been one of the few countries in the world (including Finland, France, Chile, China, Brazil, Greece, Iceland and Austria) to have attempted linking of loans. Its experience could be instructive for other countries, though it has not been always a happy one.

Most loans in Israel are linked either to the U.S. dollar (the major part), or to the cost-of-living index, or to both bases together.

The first public loan linked to the dollar rate of exchange was issued by the Jewish Agency in May 1948,[4] the very month of the establishment of the State of Israel. Both interest payments and the principal were linked to the official dollar rate, and the money market

---

[3] Indeed, the Israeli Supreme Court has decided that linkage charges are capital expenses, not to be included in interest payments that are annually deducted for income tax purposes. While linkage charges on foreign-exchange-linked bonds may be considered capital expenses (or gains) even from an economic standpoint, it is clear that linking charges on index-linked loans are ordinary incomes and expenses from that point of view.

[4] "The National Loan."

easily absorbed the IL45 million issue. Naturally the series of devaluations of the local currency in the years 1952–1955 have increased the price of those bonds considerably. The official rate of exchange of the U.S. dollar became IL1.8 in July 1955; and did not change until February 1962, when it was increased to IL3 per dollar.

While the public sector has been borrowing funds internally since the establishment of the State, it has also been lending funds, mainly through the channels of the Development Budget in order to encourage investments in housing, irrigation, industry and transportation, especially in the so-called Development Areas.

Loans granted within the framework of the government Development Budget after 1954 were linked to either the dollar exchange rate or the consumers' price index, the so-called "cost-of-living index," unless explicity exempted from the escalation charge.[5] The rate of linkage increased with the duration of the loans: no linking in loans up to two years, 50 per cent for loans granted for over two years but less than five years, 60 per cent for loans granted for over five years but less than eight year, and 70 per cent for loans for longer periods. Borrowers could choose either one of the two bases for linkage.[6]

In 1953 when the country used a multiple exchange-rates system, the problem arose which rate should be applied for the linkage purposes. The lenders claimed for the highest rate of the dollar, 1 IL = $ 1, while the government was ready to pay according to the lowest rate of the dollar, 1 IL = $ 2.8. The Supreme Court decided in favor of the lenders, and the bonds price-index reached 300 in 1953. The demand has also increased for a second issue of dollar-linked bonds (Tavei Dollar) which had been offered by the government in mid-1951 only against gold, foreign exchange, and foreign securities held by the public (which was required to hand over to the government all such assets).

Another series of dollar-linked bonds was issued by the government approximately at the same time. "The Dollar-Linked Saving Certificates" were sold at a discount (83½ per cent of their nominal value) when paid for in foreign exchange. The redemption terms were inferior to those of "Tavei Dollar," and for lack of demand the issue was closed at the end of June 1952.

---

[5] Such concessions were given on loans to new settlements, or for land development, public works and public building. Until April 1958 they were given also to industries established in the Negev area of Israel.

[6] It is not clear why the more favorable linkage terms for short loans were granted to the index-linked loans.

In 1958 the rate of escalation on mortgages was raised to 100 per cent, and from August 1960, the rules of linkage on government loans were changed as follows: if the base for linking was the dollar's rate of exchange, the rate of linking was also raised to 100 per cent, while the linking rate for index-based loans was unified to 80 per cent. In spite of the choice that was left to borrowers almost until the smell of the forthcoming devaluation was already felt in the air, most of them chose the dollar base, as Table 1 illustrates:[7]

TABLE 1

Linking Base Chosen for Loans from Government Budget, 1962

Linking Base	Balance of loans from government budget	
	3/31/1962 (millions IL)	% of total
Exchange rate of Israel pound to dollar	328	16.9
Consumer Price Index	17	0.9
Not linked	187	9.7
Linking base undecided	1,410	72.5
Total	1,942	100
Dollar-linked bond as a % of all linked bonds		96.8%

That choice seemed stupid from an economic point of view, at least from 1957 onward. The effective rates of the dollar were already much higher and increasing in those years, so that a choice of the base of its official rate as a base for linking instead of choosing an index base with no retroactive element should have been considered very strange indeed. When asked to explain their choice of the dollar base, many have answered that "whatever will happen to the rest of Israel will happen to them," and that "the Government cannot afford to ruin the economy." The course of events has proved them right.

The public sector continued to borrow extensively in linked terms. For several years no ordinary bonds were issued, and the prices of all stocks were extremely low, implying not only real but also nominal capital losses for their holders. On the other hand, from 1956 on both the public sector and some private companies offered many issues of linked bonds.

---

[7] According to *Loan Report 1962*, The Ministry of Finance, The Accountant-General.

TABLE 2[8]

Various Securities as a % of Total Israel Currency
Securities Listed on Tel Aviv Stock Exchange, at par value

	1960	1961	1962	1963
Dollar-linked loans	35.4	44.3	46.7	34.6
Index-linked loans	34.4	10.6	15.7	19.5
"Mixed" link loans	0.9	11.4	10.2	7.4
Total value linked loans	70.7	66.3	72.6	61.5
Non-linked loans	15.3	11.6	7.2	5.0
Ordinary and preference shares	13.9	22.0	20.3	33.5

It is clear from Table 2 that the ordinary lender preferred dollar-linked issues. Still it ought to be clarified that the major customers for index-linked loans bonds are not represented here, i.e., the provident funds, the insurance companies and the National Insurance. For these institutions index-linked loans solved one major problem: how to protect their funds against inflation.

TABLE 3[9]

Effective Rate of Interest on Dollar-linked Loans Given
at 8% Direct Interest (%)

Date of Granting loan	Duration of loan (years)						
	3	5	7	8	10	12	20
1/1/1955	8.0	8.0	8.0	8.8	10.1	10.4	10.5
1/1/1956	8.0	8.0	9.3	9.9	10.8	11.0	10.8
1/1/1957	8.0	8.0	10.5	10.9	11.6	11.6	11.2
1/1/1958	8.0	10.0	11.8	11.9	12.5	12.3	11.6
1/1/1959	8.0	12.1	13.2	13.1	13.7	13.1	11.9
1/1/1960	13.3	14.3	14.8	14.4	14.2	13.9	12.5
1/1/1961	28.2	24.4	21.5	20.6	18.8	17.6	15.0
1/1/1962	41.8	30.7	25.3	23.6	21.1	19.4	16.0

[8] According to Bank to Israel *Annual Reports*.
[9] From Haim Ben-Shahar, *Rates of Interest and the Cost of Capital in Israel*, *op. cit.*

TABLE 4[10]

Effective Rate of Interest on Index-linked Loans
Given at 8% Direct Interest (%)

Date of Granting loan	Duration of loan (years)						
	3	5	7	8	10	12	20
1/1/1955	10.6	10.5	10.9	10.9	11.4	11.4	11.4
1/1/1956	10.6	10.3	11.0	10.9	11.4	11.4	11.3
1/1/1957	10.4	10.3	10.8	10.8	11.4	11.3	11.3
1/1/1958	9.8	10.2	10.6	11.2	11.2	11.2	11.2
1/1/1959	10.0	10.2	10.6	10.5	11.2	11.2	11.2
1/1/1960	10.9	10.7	10.9	10.9	10.6	11.5	11.4
1/1/1961	13.5	12.7	12.3	12.2	12.0	11.9	11.7
1/1/1962	11.0	11.0	11.0	11.0	11.0	11.0	11.0

Tables 3 and 4 illustrate that the effective interest rates on dollar-linked loans granted shortly before the 1962 devaluation were as high as about 42 per cent per year for three-year loans, while the effective interest rates on 3-year dollar-linked loans granted up to 8/2/1959, on loans for seven years granted up to 8/2/1956, and on loans for five years granted up to 8/2/1957, did not differ from the nominal rates.

After the devaluation panic struck that part of the population with liabilities linked to the rate of the dollar, but very briefly afterwards, the government made serious retroactive adjustments to lighten their burden. The adjustments were not uniform. The lowest concessions were granted to industry and to citrus growers: the duration of their loans was increased by one-third of the period remaining until repayment times the rate of linking, but the loans remained linked to the dollar. Even assuming no further devaluation before the redemption date, this concession left the effective rates of interest very high (though reduced). The biggest concessions were given on loans to agriculture granted as compensations for natural disasters; in this case all linking was cancelled. On other loans to agriculture linking to the dollar was retroactively replaced by linking to the c.o.l. index. Moreover, linking charges to the index up to the devaluation and later on were to be debited as an unlinked obligation bearing 3 per cent interest, to be paid after completion of the original repayment and in similar instalments.

In the case of dollar-linked loans by the government for housing

---

[10] From Haim Ben-Shahar, *Rates of Interest and the Cost of Capital in Israel,*
op. cit.

purposes, several alternatives were offered to the borrowers. They could either repay the loans within a few months after the devaluation without any linking charges, or exchange the linking base from the dollar to the index one, or postpone repayments according to the terms offered to industry. Loans for housing of new immigrants were not debited at all with linking charges for the period preceding the devaluation.

Index-linked loans did not raise any problem either economically or politically. Thus those borrowers who had behaved more rationally and chose that base did not benefit in comparison to those who chose the dollar base for linking. In some cases, they were even discriminated against.

All this concerns the public sector as a lender of linked loans. As a borrower of linked bonds, it kept the terms agreed upon, and holders of dollar-linked bonds fared better than holders of index-linked loans, and the more so the closer the period they bought the bonds to the devaluation date.

It is well known that one of the factors determining the rate of the devaluation in 1962 was the rather big amount of government debt linked to the exchange rate of the dollar, and the even larger amounts of assets of foreign exchange deposits (of several kinds) held by the public. The fear of an uncontrollable monetary expansion, encouraged by the very act of the devaluation, was a major reason in deciding upon the new rate of exchange, which was indeed much higher than the previous official rate of exchange, but not much higher than the effective exchange rates granted to exports before the devaluation.

In any case, the government has learned from its own experience, and no further linking to the rate of a foreign currency was allowed after the devaluation. The index base is the only base for linking in all internal loans, and the escalation is complete—100 per cent. But in loans from public funds to agricultural purposes the borrowers enjoy a privilege of paying a 3 per cent annual premium instead of an index-linking; borrowers from the industrial, transport and tourist sector may choose to pay a premium rate of 4 per cent (increasing the nominal rate of interest to 11 per cent in the first case, and to 12 per cent in the others). This "premium" changes, of course, the whole meaning of an index-linked loan; it turns it into just a loan with a higher interest rate. Linking charges were not recognized as current expenses for income tax purposes (although they are clearly interest payments from an economic point of view).

Index-linked Bonds and the Cost-of-Living Allowances

Since almost all wages and salaries are linked to the "cost of living" measured by the same consumers price index which serves as a base for linking assets and liabilities, attempts by the government to prevent a rise in that index or to moderate it (in order to moderate wage increases) have also decreased the attraction of bonds linked to that index.

But it should be stated at once that if and as long as the index expenditures weights are representative of the true weights of expenditures in the index population, changes in relative prices which imply also changes in the index-absolute price level cannot be condemned even if they are achieved by increased subsidies or decreased indirect taxes.

Probably suspicions that the weights of the c.o.l. index in Israel differ from the weights of the expenditures of that part of the population to which index-linked bonds have been offered was one reason for the relative failure of those bonds in the markets. More important, I believe, were two other factors: the extremely high rates of returns (mainly in the form of capital gains) received on almost all stocks during the years 1958–1963, and the high gains on dollar-linked loans after the devaluation took place.

Taxwise, linkage charges on either dollar-linked loans or index-linked loans were not recognized as ordinary payments (or receipts), for income tax purposes, although, at least in the case of index-linked bonds, they clearly are such from an economic point of view. On the other hand, a special amendment to the Income Tax Law allowed special deductions of not linking charges on loans granted to industry, agricultural, building and the tourist industries. Specifically, it was allowed to deduct such charges from incomes in four equal parts, to the extent that they were paid after the 1962 evaluation. Naturally, a distinction was made between the different bases for linking. In all cases the deductions were allowed from 1962 onwards, but for index-linked loans deductions are allowed on linking charges due to the rise of the index from January 1, 1959 to December 31, 1964, while on linked dollar loans there had been obviously no linking charges until the 1962 devaluation took place. Since another amendment has offered revaluation of the amounts of depreciation for income tax purposes, borrowers whose loans were linked and used for the purchase of depreciable assets had to choose between the revalution of these assets and the deduction of the linking charges.

DISCUSSION

Neutralizing Inflation

Linking bonds to the price index would encourage long-term saving. It may inure bondholders too much against the gradual depreciation of their assets, the latter being a socially desirable trend. In any event, the system is generally too sophisticated for the LDCs.

In the absence of Dr. Morag, *Dr. Yosef Attyeh* read out the opening statement on his behalf. He said that "if everybody's income and assets were protected against inflation, then inflation itself would be non-functional, that is, deficit finance might still raise prices, but no one, not even the public sector, would be the better or worse for it."

It has been argued that "if a government issues bonds linked to an index, that implies it expects the price level to rise. Inflation does throw a doubt on the value of a national currency, but the attempts to sterilize it (and linkage terms of loans are included among them) do not. Linkage is a measure needed when the national currency is not any more highly respected as a unit of value."

Dr. Morag thought the only reasonable objection to a linkage is that "it might perhaps accelerate the rise in prices. But it need not. The very activity of linkage lowers the turnover in the means of payment. And suppose it does accelerate the rise in the level of prices, who will be harmed?

"The main area that conceivably might be affected is the balance of payments. At the worst, if other countries' prices rose much less, devaluation might be necessary. I do not think that devaluation is a tragedy, especially not for most of the countries represented at this conference. In order for a devaluation to be successful, it must be accompanied by deflationary monetary and fiscal policies. The chances of such policies to succeed are no less in a linked than an unlinked economy."

Leaving aside the comprehensive linking of all obligations, which is unlikely to be generally adopted, *Dr. Richard Goode,* of the U.S., spoke about the linking of government bonds and long-term government loans. This has the advantage of attracting savings to the government, and of preventing capital flight. The system could be extended beneficially to private mortgage finance.

It could be objected that these loans will compete with non-linked bonds. Also they secure too firmly the wealth of those owning money claims, preventing its re-distribution through the inflationary process. Keynes remarked that inflation is the method by which a generation can disinherit its predecessor's heirs. Dr. Goode prefers to do that by taxation.

It would seem that linkage is good for an advanced community where the population is accustomed to entrusting its savings to financial intermediaries or buying government bonds. But the link to a c.o.l. index is a very elaborate kind of instrument, unlikely to find a response in the LDCs.

Dr. Goode felt less critical than Dr. Morag of a link with the exchange rate, which reminded him of the Gold Clause (a link with gold), applied to U.S. government bonds in the latter part of the last century. A link to the exchange rate would be an effective check against capital flight.

While favoring the selective use of linkage, *Dr. Ernst Lehmann* of Israel does not hold that a universal linkage of all obligations is a suitable substitute for a stable currency. Linking short-term obligations would end in a repudiation of the currency by the inhabitants. So value linking should be confined to long-term debts, savings and securities. Furthermore it should only be applied if there is continuous uncertainty about the future stability of the currency.

In LDCs, the governments take foreign loans for development which have to be repaid in foreign currency. But the government lends the money in local currency, and it may like to pass on the risk of devaluation to the ultimate debtors. Also a linkage tempers the appetite of would-be borrowers, whose unlinked debts are cheapened by inflation. "It is a paying proposition, for instance, to purchase some heavy machinery against long-term unlinked credit, not only for the purpose of putting the machinery into operation, but in the anticipation of realizing a capital gain when there is a future devaluation." If the loan is linked, then the deal is not worth making.

Provident and pension funds cannot, under inflationary conditions, be compelled to invest all their reserves in long-term debentures if these are not linked. Life insurance in Israel came to a complete standstill, and revived a few years ago only when it became possible to link both the life insurance policies and the investments of the companies' reserves.

Professor Abba Lerner said that one cannot object to linkage, any more than one can object to insurance. "It is nothing more than a guarantee that the creditors and debtors shall not be hurt by changes in price." The practical difficulties occur if the scheme is applied piecemeal. Then you get innumerable problems of people shifting between things which are guaranteed more, and things which are guaranteed less. If it is desired just to slow inflation down and make it more gradual, a linkage system could be introduced allowing for a decrease of 1 or 3 or 5 per cent per annum in the value of the scrip.

Professor H. G. Johnson was chary of a system that intends to protect those who participate in the market against the redistribution of wealth normally done via inflation. Israel's experience with linking has not been sufficiently examined. He drew attention to the failure of the link with foreign exchange at the time of devaluation, and defined the whole system as an *"ad hoc* attempt to preserve the public against the worst evils of monetary mismanagement. It is unlikely that the public is going to be satisfied with the result—and I think that the Israeli experience certainly demonstrates that this is the case."

Dr. U Tun Wai, of the IMF, opened by saying that "instinctively I do not like this linking idea." He pointed out that the Latin American countries "don't have linking as in the Israeli experience, but they do have exchange-rate adjustments along with domestic inflation, and this is a *de facto* linking which Latin American countries have given to foreign investors. It is, in my opinion, one of the main reasons why, despite inflation in Latin America, foreign investments still continue to flow in there. So that if domestic prices and exchange rates move more or less parallel—I mean if the domestic price index is computed in such a way that it would move exactly the same as the exchange depreciation if there is a free market—then there is not much to be said between the choice of one index versus the other."

For the African countries and a large majority of Asian countries, the practical disadvantages of linking—the administrative problems, the question of computing the index, etc.—would outweigh whatever benefits there might be.

Mr. Haim Duvshani, of Israel, said that linking can have a positive effect on savings in the LDCs if there is stagnation on the financial market. Small investors "know there is an inflation, they don't know what they can do about it, they don't know how to judge it, so if you give them a simple thing by which you promise that they will not be hurt by any price increases, they usually do accept it; and we feel it does increase savings."

Mr. Edmond A. Lisle described the various linkages that have obtained in France—with gold, with the Napoleon, with the index of shares in the Paris bourse, with foreign exchange. In the private sector links were made with the activity of the borrowing organization, e.g., the volume or value of kilowatts sold by the electricity company. Such securities had a fixed interest, plus the variable rate as a "kicker," giving a kind of participation in the growth of the industrial branch. Since the financial reforms of 1958, linkage is forbidden. "The question remains whether it was wise to eliminate any possibility of linking, since, after all, prices have continued to rise for about five years, and long-term lenders may be discouraged."

Mr. Lisle thought therefore that the linkage should be used for "overcoming what seems to be the main difficulty in our world—even in developed countries, but more so in the developing States—and that is that we may have a lot of short-term savings, but it is terribly difficult in all the countries which have gone through inflation (and even more so in countries which, because they are too young, have not yet built up their credit system) to obtain long-term savings. It seems to me that the particular utility of linking would be to try to arrive at a situation gradually whereby savings would be invested on a long-term basis."

Dr. Joseph Attyeh said that insurance companies in Israel stagnated until linkage was introduced, so there was here an increase in savings. A save-for-housing scheme linked savings to the index of building costs, and this has been very successful. On the other hand, the comprehensive linkage system recommended by Dr. Morag does away with the price mechanism as a regulator, and leaves the price level to move up or down in the wake of any chance price changes.

Senator A. Arca-Parro, of Peru stated that for countries which have undergone devaluation, some sort of linking is necessary. Cases have arisen in Latin America where social security funds became decapitalized because their reserves were not protected against the depreciation of the currency. So contracts in the private sector and even long leases refer to the exchange value of the dollar or some other currency, somethimes to the benefit of those people that have the money. "So I think the State has to take a position (in the control of linkage arrangements) to regulate the situation for the benefit of the public."

10

ROLE OF THE MONEY MARKET IN SUPPLEMENTING MONETARY POLICY

By U Tun Wai[1]

African Department
International Monetary Fund

A money market, whether organized or unorganized, enables individuals and institutions with surplus funds to lend money to others to finance their expenditures. To the extent that the borrowers use the money for investment one can assume that there will be economic growth. If, however, they use the money to finance consumer expenditures, especially for non-durable items such as clothing and food, then there is unlikely to be additional economic growth. Even where the loans are for investment, the effect on economic growth will depend on various other factors such as the terms and conditions of the loans (e.g., interest rates), the use made of the funds between productive and unproductive investment, the level of final demand and the internal and external financial stability of the country.

In the unorganized money markets of developing countries, most of the borrowings are for financing consumer expenditures. About 80 to 90 per cent of the supply of funds comes from non-institutional sources such as professional moneylenders, traders, shopkeepers, landlords, relatives and friends who charge exorbitant rates of interest. Furthermore, the link between the unorganized and the organized money markets is poor and central banks are unable to influence the terms and conditions of loans in the former. Therefore, for the purpose of this chapter, attention will be focused only on the role of the organized money markets.

A money market can be defined broadly to include not only the lendings of commercial banks but also those of specialized development financial institutions and the transactions of stock exchanges. Unfortunately, in most of the developing countries, there is no stock exchange and even the market for treasury bills and bonds is hardly established. The savings habit is also not developed with the result that the amount of financial savings is small in relation to investment needs and also in comparison to those in developed countries. Thus

[1] U Tun Wai is a member of the staff of the International Monetary Fund. The opinions expressed are those of the author and do not necessarily reflect the views of the International Monetary Fund.

even where savings banks and development banks have been established the amount of funds available to finance investment is very limited.

This chapter will survey the nature and size of the money market in developing countries and examine the role it has played in financing investment, directly or indirectly. It will also study existing institutional arrangements and analyze how the evolution of a money market enhances the efficacy of monetary policy in developing countries.

Nature and Size of the Money Markets

As mentioned above, one can define "money market" to include all kinds of financial institutions. If narrowly defined, it would consist only of the commercial banks and the central bank. This narrow definition may be used as a starting point for making international comparisons as all countries of the world have both types of institutions and developing countries do not have too many kinds of financial institutions. The size of an organized money market, narrowly defined, in any country may be indicated by either or both of the following ratios, although neither measurement is perfect: the ratio of deposit money to money supply and the ratio of the banking system's credit (mostly loans, advances and bills discounted) to the domestic sector to national income. The first ratio views matters from the liability side of the balance sheet of the banks and the second from the asset side.

The ratio of deposit money to money supply actually measures banking development rather than the development of the money market. However, to the extent that the development of commercial banking is synonymous with the development of the money market, this ratio may be used as an indicator of the growth of a money market. The ratio of the banking system's credit to the domestic sector to national income is a more reliable indicator because in most developing countries there are hardly any other lending agencies of importance besides the commercial banks. There are no discount houses or acceptance houses, and savings institutions (including life insurance companies) are in the early stages of development. In most developing countries, commercial banks supply about three-quarters of the short-term loanable funds in the organized money markets, inclusive of loans made by governments.

As is to be expected, both ratios are lower in a developing country than in a developed one. While it is common for deposit money to be two-thirds or three-fourths of the money supply in a developed country, it is quite often about half or even less than half the money supply in a developing country. As regards the ratio of domestic bank credit to national income, it varies between developing countries themselves with a median of 28 per cent. In 1963, it ranged about 40–45 per cent for such countries as Argentina, Brazil, Ceylon, Greece, Philippines, Tunisia and United Arab Republic, while it was less than 20 per cent for others such as Ghana, Jamaica, Jordan, Korea, Malaysia, Mexico, Nicaragua and Sudan. The percentages differed between countries partly because of variations in institutional structures and partly because of differences in the stage of development of the money market and in the level of income. In developed countries such as the United States, United Kingdom, Switzerland, France, Germany and Japan the ratio of domestic bank credit to national income ranged between 47 and 148 per cent.

In the overwhelming majority of the developing countries, the major proportion of domestic bank credit represents loans and discounts given to the private sector and only a small amount represents credit to the government. There are important exceptions for Afghanistan, Burma, Ceylon, Haiti, India, Indonesia, Pakistan and the United Arab Republic, where bank credit to the government was much larger than that to the private sector at the end of 1963. For some of these countries, such as Burma and Ceylon, it was due to the socialistic nature of the economy, while for others such as Indonesia, it reflected central bank financing of large budget deficits and general inflationary pressure.

Most of the domestic bank credit to the private sector is for short-term loans for commerce and industry, and to a lesser extent for financing agriculture. Occasionally there are medium-term loans for financing housing construction or for the purchase of equipment for factories processing agricultural products, e.g., rice mills, coconut and groundnut-oil mills, sugar mills and jute mills. Short-term loans do not finance investment directly in developing countries. However, as the firms making investments in the modern sector, whether in plantations or in factories, are invariably also the ones which are engaged in export-import trade, the availability of short-term bank credit influences investment decisions. During the Korean War boom, the expansion in private investment was facilitated by the availability of short-term bank credit, for example, in Malaysia and in Thailand. With the collapse of the boom, investment fell off; in some countries such as the Philippines, investment fell despite the fact that bank credit was not reduced between the end of 1951 and the end of 1952. An example of a cut in domestic bank credit causing a fall in gross investment is to be found in the Dominican Republic between 1959 and 1960. Bank credit to the private sector fell by 10 per cent and gross investment fell from 103 million pesos in 1959 to 73 millions pesos in 1960.

Bank credit extended to the government sector varies in duration. Commercial banks in developing countries are reluctant to purchase government securities unless they are short-term or unless there is a guarantee by the central bank to repurchase them. However, these banks have been persuaded or legally made to hold larger portfolios of government securities. Many governments have required commercial banks to hold a certain percentage of their deposit liabilities in government securities, as for example in Ceylon, Colombia and the Philippines. Furthermore, the bank credit to the government, even through short-term treasury bills, has very often been renewed so that in effect governments have obtained long-term credit from the banking system. Most governments of developing countries have established a capital budget in addition to a current budget, which is usually in balance or in surplus (except for countries such as Indonesia with serious inflationary pressures). Therefore, one can conclude that domestic bank credit to the government has financed a part of government investment. Sometimes this financing of budget deficits by bank credit has been self-defeating, when savings have been insufficient to prevent inflation.

Since the money market, narrowly defined, in developing countries can indirectly finance investment, it is of interest to know whether money markets have grown in the past decade and a half in developing countries. Judging by the ratio of domestic bank credit to national income, it appears that in the majority of developing countries there has been a significant growth in money markets. In the early post-war years, the percentage was less than 15 per cent in most developing countries. By 1963, the ratio had exceeded 20 per cent in a large number of countries (20 out of 27 countries). The countries with a significant growth in money markets include Colombia, Costa Rica, Ecuador, El Salvador, Guatemala and Honduras in Latin America; Burma, Ceylon, India and the Philippines in Asia; and Tunisia in Africa.

This trend is to be expected because as an economy develops, the size of the typical business and industrial unit is likely to expand;

the amount of self-financing tends to decline, and greater use is made of the money market to finance business operations. The net result is that domestic bank credit tends to increase more rapidly than national income. When an economy reaches a very advanced stage, the size of the typical business enterprise may grow to such an extent that more and more of the required funds will be financed internally rather than from the market, as occurred in the United States in the past few decades. But even in such a situation, any decline in bank loans to industry for investment may be partly offset by loans to consumers for financing private consumption.

In developed countries, there are many non-bank financial inter-mediaries. In developing countries, they consist mainly of savings banks, development banks and occasionally of life insurance com-panies. The development banks usually have only small deposit lia-bilities and do not create credit. They, however, provide long-term loans to finance investment. They receive funds from Government lending funds, from the central bank and make loans to the private sector. They sometimes, especially in Latin American countries, ob-tain funds from the sale of bonds to banks or to the private sector. These institutions are generally not very important, especially in low-income countries. Thus, of 35 developing countries with a *per capita* income of less than $ 200 per annum, only 8 countries (Ecuador, Guatemala, Haiti, India, Korea, Peru, the Philippines and the United Arab Republic) had non-bank financial intermediaries of some importance. Domestic credit granted by these institutions was around 10–15 per cent of domestic bank credit in 1963 in India and the United Arab Republic, and between 30 and 40 per cent in Guatemala and Korea. Out of 19 developing countries with a *per capita* income of between $ 200–500, there were only 10 coun-tries (Argentina, Brazil, Chile, Colombia, Costa Rica, Dominican Republic, Greece, Mexico, South Africa and Spain) with such insti-tutions in 1963. Furthermore, in Brazil and Chile they were of negligible importance; domestic credit of such institutions in 1963 was less than 1 per cent of domestic bank credit. In Mexico and South Africa these institutions were more important than banks and in Colombia, the Dominican Republic and Greece they supplied between a quarter to a half of domestic bank credit. In the developed countries, these non-bank institutions are very important, and in such countries as the United Kingdom and the United States they are equally important as commercial banks.

Stock exchanges exist in only 10 developing countries, namely

Ceylon, Chile, India, Israel, Mexico, Peru, Philippines, Portugal, United Arab Republic and Venezuela. On the other hand, there are stock exchanges in most of the developed countries. These exchanges play a vital role in the mobilization of capital and the channelling of investment. While it is true that they have sometimes facilitated speculation in stocks, especially during a period of inflation, on the whole they have performed a useful function in promoting economic development. As the amount of capital required for a business enterprise increases, one finds that individual private fortunes are not sufficient to finance investment in industries requiring modern equipment. The joint stock company with shares open to the public for subscription is therefore needed. The subscription to the capital of joint stock companies will be more easily available if there are stock exchanges where an investor can follow the activities of his company and if need be sell his shares for cash without undue loss of capital. In addition to providing a market place for the purchase and sale of existing shares, a stock exchange also facilitates the flotation of shares of new companies and new shares of existing companies. While only limited information is available on the working of stock exchanges in developing countries, it is evident that they are not as important as their counterparts in the developed countries.

Financial Savings Through the Money Market and Investment

In order that an economy can develop without inflation or balance of payments difficulties, domestic investment should be financed by domestic savings or by an inflow of foreign aid and capital from abroad. Since the available amount of foreign aid and capital is limited, a country should rely on domestic savings to finance increasing amounts of investment. Apart from foreign financing and allocations for the wear and tear of fixed capital, domestic investment has to be financed by domestic savings. Domestic savings consist of savings made by the Government, by public corporations, by private corporations and by household and private non-profit institutions. Savings of the first three sectors are usually used internally to finance investment and only a small fraction, if any, is channelled through the money market to finance investment by others. It is, therefore, the savings of the last named sector, the households and private non-profit institutions, which are used to finance investments made by other sectors.

Savings of the households and private non-profit institutions take many forms in the developed countries, including savings and deposits with banks and other financial institutions, purchase of bonds (government and private), and premiums for life insurance policies. In developing countries these various items are not as important as in developed countries. Furthermore, there are savings in the form of hoarding of currency or of gold in developing countries which do not exist in developed countries. Comparable data are available only for savings deposits kept by the private sector with commercial banks and with savings institutions. It can be assumed that these savings deposits are kept mainly by households and non-profit institutions.

There are two factors which would tend to influence the ratio of savings deposits or financial savings of households and non-profit institutions to economic savings, as recorded in national income accounts. On the one hand, one would expect the volume of financial savings in developing countries to be small, as the banking habit is not widespread, while in developed countries such financial savings would be large. On the other hand, other forms of financial savings would also be very small in developing countries, while in developed countries with bond markets, life insurance companies, etc., other forms of financial savings would also be large. Thus the actual percentage of savings deposits to economic savings would depend on the actual circumstances of each country. In fact, for the period 1953–58 and the period 1959–62, one finds a rather wide range in both developing and developed countries. In the first period, the median value in twelve developing countries was 19.5 per cent while in fourteen developed countries it was 23.2 per cent. In the second period, the median values were 34.5 per cent for developing countries and 32.7 per cent for developed countries. However, there were relatively more developed countries with percentages above 40 than for the developing countries.

The interesting point to note is that in both groups of countries, there has been a greater growth of savings deposits relative to economic savings between the two periods 1953–58 and 1959–62. This trend is of great significance to the developing countries where total domestic savings are not large relative to domestic investment. There have, of course, been notable exceptions where savings deposits have not grown relatively, for example in Canada, Japan and Sweden among the developed countries, and in China (Taiwan), Costa Rica and Greece among the developing countries. Considerable progress has been made in Jamaica, Korea and Colombia where savings deposits have expanded rapidly.

The growth of both financial and economic savings of households and non-profit organizations depends upon many factors, not the least among which are the rate of interest, financial stability and the growth of *per capita* income. For the period 1953–58, there were three developing countries (Chile, Peru and the Philippines), where despite some increase in savings deposits of the household sector, economic savings as compiled in national income accounts were negative. In Chile the phenomenon continued in 1959–62, and it was undoubtedly linked to the rapid inflation in that country and perhaps also to a flight of capital. The Philippines had negative domestic savings of the household sector every year during the period 1953–58, and this trend continued into 1960. Beginning around 1961–62, however, such savings became positive partly due to the program of financial stabilization and exchange reform introduced at that time.

The growth of financial savings enables the banking system to finance investment without inflation. Therefore, governments should encourage the establishment of savings banks, commercial banks with savings deposit facilities, and also expand the number of post offices with savings accounts in the rural areas. Raising interest rates on postal certificates, government bonds and savings deposits might increase the flow of domestic savings, though it would raise expenditures of the government. However, offering too high a rate could discourage investment. Given the fact that domestic savings are small in developing countries, and that the rates of interest in the organized money market of developing countries are often lower than those in the developed countries, it seems that interest rates should be raised in developing countries to increase the flow of domestic savings.

Monetary Policy and the Evolution of Money Markets

Central banks, through appropriate use of monetary policy, are able to influence the level of investment and economic growth by determining the cost (interest rates) and the availability of credit. Traditionally, central banks in developed countries have influenced the availability of credit through purchases and sales of government securities. When a central bank desired to expand money and credit, it would buy government securities in the money market so as to increase the liquidity of banks and to encourage them to lend more money to their customers. At the same time, such purchases had the effect of raising bond prices and lowering rates of interest. When a central bank desired to restrict or even to contract the supply of money and credit, it would sell government securities. In this case, the cash reserves of the commercial banks would tend to be reduced, prices of bonds would fall and interest rates would rise. These developments tend to force the commercial banks to restrict their lending.

In addition to open market operations, i.e., purchases and sales of government securities, central banks have changed the bank rate as a means of influencing the cost and availability of credit. These two instruments of monetary policy have been widely used in the developed countries whereas in developing countries the former instrument has hardly been used but the latter instrument has been used with some success.

Open market operations have not been used in developing countries to any great extent because the amount of government securities held by banks, private corporations and individuals is not large and there is no real money market in government securities. Attempts have been made by many central banks in developing countries to establish a market for these securities but with hardly any success. Occasionally, as in the case of the Philippines, the banks have been encouraged to buy some securities, but only at the expense of the central bank agreeing to repurchase the securities at the option of the banks.

Many central banks in developing countries have begun to use the central bank rate as a means of influencing the rates of interest in the money market. Between 1953 and 1962, about 19 developing countries made about 50 changes in the bank rate, sometimes adjusting the rate upwards and sometimes lowering the rate. In the Philippines, the central bank made 11 changes during this period. Despite the fact that the central banks did not supplement the use of the bank rate with open market operations, they have generally succeeded in influencing the market rates of interest and also the supply of credit. The central banks have used moral suasion to make the changes in the bank rate effective. The commercial banks are aware that central banks have other ways of controlling credit, such as raising reserve requirements and placing credit ceilings. During the past decade, the rate of credit expansion was checked when the bank rate was raised in Brazil, Costa Rica, El Salvador, India, the Philippines and Peru. In the reverse case, that is, when the bank rate was lowered, the rate of credit expansion increased in El Salvador, Ceylon, the Philippines, Thailand and Turkey. In Chile and Nicaragua reactions were the opposite, while in Guatemala the change in the bank rate had little effect either way.

Many developing countries have adopted the device of making commercial banks hold reserves against their deposit liabilities either in the form of a blocked deposit with the central bank or in the form of government securities. The former is more effective in controlling the total supply of credit while the latter may only limit credit to the private sector and not credit to the government. The latter has been favored by some central banks as a means of establishing a government securities market, but the disadvantage of this method is that unless these securities are attractive for investment, the banks will unload them on the central bank once the regulation is removed. Furthermore, the commercial banks are likely to economize their cash reserves in order to comply with the requirement of holding government securities and therefore there may be an over-all expansion of credit.

Reserve requirements are placed either in the form of an average or in the form of a marginal requirement, i.e., based on the increases in deposit liabilities after a given date. They may be either in the form of a fixed percentage or may be variable, i.e., subject to change by the central bank. Obviously, the variable reserve requirement gives a central bank very wide powers, because it can eliminate any excess reserves immediately, especially if the requirement is in the form of a blocked deposit at the central bank. During the past decade and a half, more than 40 developing countries have used this instrument at one time or another, and some have made a large number of changes in the reserve requirements according to the needs of monetary policy, as, for example, in Colombia, Ecuador and Korea.

Besides reserve requirements, there are selective credit controls which limit credit for a special purpose. One instrument used quite widely in post-war years is the import deposit. According to this, importers have to deposit a certain fixed percentage of their intended imports with the commercial banks which in turn have to redeposit the money with the central bank. This instrument has been used to restrict imports and to solve balance of payments difficulties through credit control. Apart from the usual drawbacks which apply to all selective credit controls, such as that one cannot distinguish between funds used by integrated businesses for different purposes, there is the disadvantage that the import deposit system tends to release these deposits once the level of imports is reduced; this will then tend to increase the demand for imports.

Besides selective credit controls there are other instruments ranging from moral suasion to actual credit ceilings. The latter is used in

France and in many African countries which have inherited the French system where the central bank supervises the demand and supply of credit, and where commercial banks rely on central bank credit to finance about half their loans. This is the case in the countries of the West African Monetary Union comprising Dahomey, Ivory Coast, Mauritania, Niger, Senegal, Togo and Upper Volta.

From the above, it appears that there has to be a money market before a monetary policy can be effective. A money market in a developing economy does not necessarily have to be as developed or take the same form as that existing in the developed countries such as the U.K. and the U.S.A. It was noted that in developed countries, the central bank influences the lending policies of the commercial banks by open market operations. In developing countries, the methods used are mainly moral suasion and selective credit controls and only partly the central bank rate. The central bank can influence commercial bank credit even in developing countries. However, if the amount of commercial bank credit is small in relation to investment and to national income, then even a large percentage cut in commercial bank credit is unlikely to have more than a small influence on investment and growth. It was noted earlier that the ratio of commercial bank credit to national income was much smaller in developing countries (median ratio is 28 per cent), whereas in the United States, United Kingdom, Switzerland, France, Germany and Japan it ranged between 47 and 148 per cent. Therefore, one of the tasks of the monetary authorities is to increase the size of the money market and commercial bank credit without endangering internal financial stability and without creating balance of payments difficulties. This can be achieved by restricting credit during export booms while expanding credit during recessions provided the central bank has accumulated foreign exchange reserves during the booms. This accumulation of foreign exchange reserves is necessary because credit expansion during recessions will increase the demand for imports which is likely to cause balance of payments deficits; the deficits would have to be financed by accumulated foreign exchange reserves.

DISCUSSION

Organizing the Money Market

Aggressive banking can promote initiative among potential entrepreneurs. The challenge is to start putting up the infrastructure of financial institutions, and get credit flowing.

Dr. U Tun Wai recalled that, with the establishment of central banks in the newly independent Asian States, they began to use their foreign exchange reserves (hitherto invested overseas) to finance their own development programs. Gradually they ran through these reserves and found it hard to reverse their credit policy, "partly for political reasons and partly because the financial investments were on projects only half completed."

So it is advisable for the African countries to allow an aggressive credit expansion policy so long as they have reserves, but to trim the investment program to the availability of resources, so that when the reserves are used up it is possible to level off, and "that is difficult. You can only level off provided the government sector does not take too much of the permissible credit expansion." If you pre-empt too much credit to the government by cutting the private sector, the latter reacts by increasing the speed of money circulation, which offsets part of the intended contraction of demand. You end up with inflation and balance of payment difficulties.

Dr. John Mars, of the ECA said that the unorganized money market mentioned by Dr. U Tun Wai, of "moneylenders and traders, landlords, relatives and friends," charge in African countries as much as 300 per cent interest. They should be replaced by a proper monetary system as far as possible.

When bank credit is limited and there is no capital market, monetary policy can still influence the price level by controlling the supply of money. Deposit banks in the LDCs "should help to induce any kind of saving made anywhere to pass through the money market, so as to decrease the total amount of self-finance. Self-finance is inefficient practically everywhere. Very seldom does a company, or another group of people having savings, think of all the possible investment opportunities."

Deposit banks should help reduce lenders' and borrowers' risks. They should seek out potential borrowers and brief them on investment opportunities. They should show them how to increase their credit-worthiness. They should help the government create collateral securities—e.g., by registering land titles, as was done in Kenya. They should promote feasibility studies and pre-investment studies. Some banks in developing countries have in fact established cadres of competent managers and technologists, to whom they refer inquiring investors.

"This is aggressive banking," according to Dr. Mars. "But most of the bankers, having been imported from the developed countries, just sit in their offices and wait until the people come to them."

Dr. Mars described an investigation he made in 17 African countries, separating domestic savings from foreign savings (i.e., foreign aid). He found an almost perfect correlation between savings per head per annum and income per head per annum. Savings start appearing in the very low income range, "which is a very encouraging fact. Anybody who has proved by his continuous savings that he is credit-worthy should then be in a position to obtain loans for a good investment project."

It is important that the banks should prove themselves worthy of the public's confidence, which has been achieved in several African countries. And government policy in financial and fiscal matters should be reasonably predictable. In many loans to local entrepreneurs, interest rates are lower than their "shadow price" (i.e., than the true cost of capital), wages are higher than the value of labor output, and land is more costly than is justified by its profitability— because land is a traditional investment object.

If the interest rate were fixed at, say, 10 per cent, more profitable investment projects would be selected, and there would be some increase in savings.

Mr. R. A. Cruz, of the Philippines, criticized academic discussions and drew attention to the fact that what needs doing is to "take several steps beyond the neat models we are constantly obsessed with and really go into the organizational planning of financial institutions with as much obsession as we devote to planning out and organizing investments in physical productive assets. The point has already been made that the physical development of the LDCs must go hand-in-hand with financial development, because eventually it is the finance function that becomes a bottleneck.

"This preoccupation with models can perhaps be seen in the way central banks in most developing countries today devise their monetary policy. Many of them are preoccupied really with aggregates, with money supply totals, with domestic credit totals and consumer price levels. What is needed is for these economists to start 'disaggregating' their aggregates—to go from money stocks (to get out of this lazy pre-occupation with the quantity theory of money) into specific financial flows. The financial requirements must be traced, both of existing businesses and new projects, and they must then be translated into the types of financial institution and instrument that must be designed."

Referring to the difficulty of selling government bonds in cases where the government's revenue position does not make it too credit-worthy, Mr. Cruz suggested as an alternative that "the central bank issue its own debt instruments and then turn around and lend the money to the government. In such a case the central bank, which commands much more financial respect than, perhaps, a good many governments, can put its own prestige behind these debt instruments and then channel the funds to the government."

In conclusion, Mr. Cruz recommended that "in future conferences of this nature, it might be more useful to make it an assembly of countries that are more or less at the same stage of development, and then we can get right down to the concrete and specific problems which are common to all." At the present conference "the papers usually take one prototype of an underdeveloped country and then concentrate the analysis on that particular prototype. So you have a lot of disagreements on papers, though the differences are not really based on the papers themselves but on the fact that the commentators come from different types of developing country, and therefore find no application or no relevance in the papers to their own problems."

Dr. Marshall Sarnat, of Israel, said, "The central banks in the developing countries, in their striving to create research departments, in their training of personnel and in the dissemination of technical banking services, are probably making in the long run their most important contribution to the economic growth of these countries."

Even a rudimentary capital market, according to Dr. Sarnat, makes for a good allocation of resources, as is shown in Israel's experience. Despite wide spreads between prices, low turnover and, it is said, overt price manipulation—all characteristics of a rudimentary market —the Tel Aviv stock exchange shows a very strong correlation between the long-run rate of return to investors in common stocks and the underlying profitability of the business firms themselves.

Mr. Asher Shlein, of Israel, argued against the executive use of credit restrictions. Governments should disinflate via fiscal policy, influencing the demand for credit. To cut its supply means that the government must subsidize the interest rate for certain chosen projects, and new pressures are created on the short-term credit market, with the result that "the managers of enterprises devote much of their time and energy to the procurement of credit."

Mr. Haim Duvshani, of Israel, said that money markets should be started by governments which can later withdraw again. "History tells us that most government debts have been created out of wars, so there is no objection to creating a large national debt for development purposes instead of wars.

"As a big national debt is created by the government for development purposes, this market can be developed. The government can, as it did in Israel, take funds from the money market, invest them in private companies, and not be ashamed to sell its investment later to private hands, even as an anti-inflationary measure. One can make an offer of a company which was created ten years earlier by the government and financed through bonds."

Government Bonds Hard to Sell

> Development needs cheap capital, but good interest rates are required to attract savings. Expatriate banks lack inducements to open up in the small villages.

According to *Mr. Conrado Pascual,* of the Philippines, demand for government securities in that country is low. The solution is to "package" the offers properly. Commercial banks require a flexible and liquid portfolio. Non-banking financial institutions invest in real estate mortgages bearing high interest rates. All these factors must be taken into account. "And the very absence of an organized market in such obligations makes it thoroughly difficult to package the issues intelligently, since there is hardly any feedback of market information which can be utilized in the packaging process."

The difficulty is enhanced by the fact that governments borrow money usually in times of financial strain and do not offer competitive terms. Secondly, liquidity is achieved by giving the purchaser an option to sell the bonds to the central bank. This results in most of the bonds finding their way back to the central bank. Yet without the option there is no liquidity, owing to the absence of an active market.

Another approach is to make speculative investments in such assets as real estate less attractive. This can be done by taxation, e.g., by making the carrying expenses of land ownership expensive. Or credit can be channelled away from the property business.

Mrs. Suparb Yossundura, of Thailand, described the development of the Thai money market. Her country now has 29 banks with 460 branches. Capital is an important source of bank funds, and the central bank has laid down a capital assets ratio.

There is an active call market. "Sometimes the foreign banks want to expand credit but they cannot attract enough deposits, so they make use of some of the idle deposits made available to them by domestic banks." Bank credits have on occasion exceeded their deposits. This is because "both the local banks and the local branches of local banks made quite considerable use of short-term facilities in New York, particularly during the busy export season. This has been possible because official reserves are strong. Twenty years ago exactly, we had no official reserves at all." Now they run at over $600 m.

"In order to foster the sale of government securities," Mrs. Yossundura said, "we allow the banks to use them as part (at present 50 per cent) of their legal cash reserve. We use moral persuasion. For example, we meet regularly with the Thai Bankers' Association, and we say, 'Look here, according to the clearing bank figures, your bank has too many bounced checks. If you come into line, we'll give you a dinner party'."

For a time government bonds were paying 8 per cent tax free—on condition that the security was held for 10 years. The government has no need to borrow at the present moment, but nevertheless issued some more bonds in the last few weeks "to keep the market going: we cannot have the market with nothing to buy or sell."

Mr. E. Yameogo, of Upper Volta, observed that several countries south of the Sahara belong to a monetary zone, so that interest, credit, etc. are fixed outside the country. If inflation takes place in the metropolitan territory, it spreads inevitably to the LDC. Under the circumstances, is it not desirable for each country to create and control its own currency?

Mr. Jean Nsele, of Congo (Leopoldville) said that bank deposits in his country constitute 54 per cent of the total money supply. They mostly belong to foreigners, and are kept in the country by exchange control. The credit ceiling is evaded by foreign companies, which carry out loan transactions among themselves, outside the banks. How can the indigenous sector of the economy be developed under these conditions?

Mr. Ralison-Rakotovao, of the Malagasy Republic, said that the central bank in Malagasy does re-discounting for the commercial banks, which lack sufficient deposits to finance agricultural and other trading activities. The main promoter of industry is the National Investment Corporation.

The economy still depends on long-term, low-cost credit from international institutions for work on the infrastructure, "but this is not always easy to get." There is concern with the question whether it is feasible to create an organized money market, if only to prevent a decline in the value of existing stocks and shares.

Mr. Christopher Musoke, of Uganda, asked whether there is any good central banking reason against borrowing working capital from abroad or using the foreign currency reserves to supplement the lack of local savings. He spoke of the difficulty in persuading expatriate banks to open up new branches inland. "However many inducements we have offered to these banks, they say they are just not interested, because there is not enough business to justify their opening up branches. Have other countries found that the government had to create institutions of its own, as Uganda had to do, because the existing expatriate banks do not show a pioneering initiative?"

Mr. Musoke described the difficulty of selling a bond issue recently, that was aimed at the low-income groups but did not possess the liquidity which is essential for this kind of market. In addition, "if the person, after buying these bonds, finds after five years that an inflation of 10 or 15 per cent annually has halved the value of the bonds, then I'm wondering whether such a person would not regard government bonds as another form of taxation." Would value linking be a help here?

Concerning interest rates, Mr. Musoke pointed out the dilemma that "we want cheap money—but we want development resources." Therefore "should government bond yields be determined by the market rates, or should this be determined deliberately by the government?"

Can consumer credit, which people receive by giving post-dated checks, etc., be converted into credit for development? Referring to Dr. U Tun Wai's recommendation that governments aid the creation of collateral, Mr. Musoke raised the problem that part of the land in his country is owned collectively. Can anything be done about that? And what follow-up is used to check that money which has been advanced for one specific purpose is not being used for another?

* * *

Dr. U Tun Wai said, "If I may be permitted to underline the consensus of opinion, it seems to me that there is need to develop the financial infrastructure. It is true that the developing countries have made some progress in having the commercial banks as a nucleus, but there seems to be the need to develop institutions such as life insurance companies, development banks, agricultural banks, specialized banks. And rather than going in for model building and trying to see what theoretical models one can build, the time may now be ripe for action to get back to more pedestrian methods of institution building."

Referring to the National Investment Corporation in the Malagasy Republic, Dr. U Tun Wai indicated that "many countries have established investment institutions and I am sure that, if a conference on such things were convened, with delegates coming to give of their experience about these attempts that have been made at infrastructure building and the problems they had to face, it would be rather useful."

It is important not only to build a "financial infrastructure," but also to make the best use possible of existing facilities. Thailand's experience suggests that the interest rate can be used to mobilize savings. "The point is the choice of the correct interest rate. You see, underdeveloped countries have this dilemma. On the one hand, you want low interest rates to encourage investment; on the other hand, you want sufficiently high interest rates to encourage savings. Thailand has more or less succeeded. The rate seems high by other developing countries' standards, and now this most recent move of lowering it from 8 per cent to 7 per cent, I think, is welcome. With a few years at 7 per cent, they still can generate as much as before, and in another couple of decades I can picture Thailand getting down to 5 and 4 per cent, when they have generated a sufficient flow of savings. By that time they would be far, far ahead."

He praised the BCAO* area in West Africa, where seven countries share one central bank. It participates in the capital of specialized development banks. This is possible because there is no inflationary financing in this area (e.g., borrowings from the central bank are limited to not more than 10 per cent of the previous year's State revenue). It is the mixture of measures that does the job, with a healthy balance kept. Dr. U Tun Wai is not sure that the creation of a stock exchange is a top priority task for the LDCs. As to the use of foreign banking loans, "my position on whether it is good or

* Banque Centrale de l'Afrique Occidentale.

bad depends on whether the economy still has a certain amount of sluggishness and you really wish to have bank credit expansion."

In summary, "there is no particular institutional arrangement that is good or bad, in my opinion. It's rather that you have to put down the figures as to how much they are doing and compute the flow of funds, so to speak, and what is the extent of total credit expansion in one form or another that the economy can stand. If, for example you have more put in by the central bank or the development banks for credit expansion, you must then allow less to go in from the commercial banks."

11

POTENTIALITIES AND LIMITATIONS OF MONETARY POLICY

By JOHN MARS

Special Adviser to the Executive Secretary on Economic Policy and Integration United Nations Economic Commission for Africa, Addis Ababa

Monetary policy is a course of action taken by public authorities (central banks, ministries of finance, exchange authorities, etc.) and by financial intermediaries (deposit banks, discount companies and other specialist banks, insurance companies, etc.) in pursuit of certain objectives concerning monetary phenomena which relate to the amounts and prices of various financial assets and liabilities, and to the impact of changes in them on economic activity in general.

The scope of this chapter is intentionally limited to avoid overlapping with the other chapters that make up the present volume. Here are discussed only those monetary policies to which the authors of other contributions have presumably not given primary consideration.

Objectives of Monetary Policies of Developing States

Most objectives of monetary policies of industrialized market economics are acceptable to developing countries but these have also specific objectives. Below is a list of the major objectives, several of which are conflicting. This problem is well known in industrialized states. It is solved in developing as in industrialized countries by trade-offs among the conflicting objectives.

Internal Monetary Objectives

  1. Creating confidence in the currency, especially confidence in paper notes. (It is to a large extent a political problem, i.e., confidence in present and future governments.)
  2. Stabilization of the internal price level and a growth policy for factor incomes compatible with the stable price level for goods.
  3. Control of the supply of money (legal tender and bank money) to stabilize the domestic price level.
  4. Developing short-, medium- and long-tem capital markets for fixed interest and equity securities. Reducing the imper-

180

fections of these markets to a minimum and thereby making interest rates as effective as possible in determining the supply and demand.

5. Reducing lenders' and borrowers' risks and uncertainties which are incomparably higher in developing countries than in developed countries.

6. Raising the propensity to save even among the lowest income groups. Eliminating chronic indebtedness.

7. Promoting creative risk-bearing, i.e., promoting additional productive real investment versus ostentatious treasure hoarding or purely monetary investment.

8. Integrating the segregated economic behavior systems in developing countries. The basic systems are: (a) the modern production system and its financial superstructure, (b) the government economy and its financial superstructure and the marginally monetized traditional sector. As long as the pluralist economic behavior system is not unified, monetary policy will be restricted to (a) and (b) and will be to a large extent ineffective.

9. Indigenizing the banking and insurance assets and repatriating funds unnecessarily invested abroad as far as this is compatible with the need to assure the convertibility of currencies.

10. Creating new monetary institutions to promote development, such as deposit insurance, credit insurance, hire purchase credit for businessmen, post office checking accounts ("giro" system), mobile banks, etc.

11. Improving the climate of expectation-forming from the monetary side, i.e., establishing confidence in monetary aspects of development plans and lengthening the foresight period.

12. Contributing to a reduction of visible and disguised unemployment through creation of jobs via investment.

External Monetary Objectives

13. Aiding the balancing of external payments and thereby aiding the stabilization of the foreign exchange rate.

14. Manipulating the money capital movements in and out of the country in the interests of balancing the external accounts and accelerating development. Flight of capital can effectively be prevented only by high profitability of invest-

ment, predictability of economic progress, confidence in the currency and capital security comparable to that existing in industrialized countries. One of the more difficult tasks for monetary authorities is the prevention of international over-borrowing.

15.   Insulating as far as possible the domestic monetary and price and income system from erratic and cyclical disturbances imported from the world market and introduced to developing countries via the international banking system.

Major Limitations of Monetary Policy in Africa

The major limitations of monetary policy are dictated by the specific monetary conditions prevailing in developing countries. This section will be confined to the specific monetary conditions existing in Africa which are better known to the author than those in other parts of the developing world. The specific monetary conditions in Latin America and Asia will differ from those in Africa partly due to the fact that the latter continent is in an earlier phase of development.

We enumerate below 14 basic facts of the African economic background which affect monetary policy. They will be arranged in a descending order of the magnitude of their divergence from conditions prevailing in industrialized countries.

Pluralist Economic Behavior System

(a)   The modern production system and its financial super-structure are closely akin to the economic system in industrialized countries. This sector consists of expatriate producers, large scale indigenous enterprises, including government enterprises, and modern banking and insurance companies, both foreign and domestically owned. The economic motivations for economic decisions are as much rational and as little irrational as in any industrialized society. The foresight period for production, purchase, sales, finance and investment planning is somewhat shorter than in industrialized societies because of the higher uncertainties. The standards of business ethics are largely comparable to those in industrialized societies. Generally, a period of less than five years for recoupment of capital is expected. Owing to the smallness of the markets, both markets for goods and for loans, the imperfections in all markets are incomparably greater. The money and capital markets in particular are much more imperfect than they are in industrialized countries.

(b) Although it is generally professed that the government sector among other objectives also supports the private effort in promoting development, yet this sector is by and large inspired by political motivations, which often override purely

     economic considerations. For instance, investment projects are sometimes undertaken for prestige reasons and to earn political support. With respect to some investment projects the social time preference in the government sector is low, especially for prestige projects. For other projects the foresight period is extremely short, as quick returns are preferred to higher deferred returns. Governments do not confine themselves to real investment projects but are often engaged in monetary investment projects such as the purchase of land, existing businesses and existing houses.

(c) The marginally monetized traditional sector. This comprises the indigenous small scale and handicrafts businesses and the indigenous farming communities. Pure 100 per cent barter has died out completely, except perhaps in nomadic tribes. All of these economic units contrive to receive some money revenue from the sale of products or services, varying from 5–50 per cent or more. However, the motivation is largely non-economic. There is a non-monetary propensity to save which is determined by social customs such as financing traditional festivities on the occasion of births, circumcisions, marriage and death. In some areas this investment and saving in kind is very substantial and amounts to 25 per cent of total investment. The social time preference in the traditional sector is high and the time preference rates increase steeply with futurity. This is largely the effect of the short life expectancy (see Table 1) which has lengthened since 1945 but is still so short as to preclude a return on investment in human skills over a sufficiently large number of years. In 15 out of the 26 countries the life expectancy at birth is still below 40 years, a fact which is not generally recognized.

This low life expectancy at birth also explains the short foresight period. Three years seem to be almost an eternity. Paradoxically, the rural population behaves as if time is not money, i.e., as if it has

TABLE 1

Life Expectancy

Life Expectancy at Birth	Number of Countries
Under 30	1
30 — 35	2
35 — 40	12
40 — 45	2
45 — 50	5
50 — 55	3
55 — 60	0
60 — 65	1
	26

Source: Table 26, U.N. Demographic Yearbook for 1963.

no opportunity cost. This attitude of mind can be explained only by the fact that disguised unemployment in the countryside comprises often up to one third of the total population. Many decisions which in industrialized societies would be subject to a cost-benefit analysis are judged by uneconomic criteria.

In periods of high export prices, simple hoarding is practiced. Lack of technical knowledge and economic opportunities in general explains a preference for monetary investment in land, existing houses, existing businesses and gold. African entrepreneurship must be prodded to develop its full potentiality which is as great as anywhere else.

Smallness of the National Economies

The following table shows the populations of 35 of the 37 independent countries of Africa. It will be seen that 23 of the 35 states have a population of less than 5 million in 1965. In addition it must be recognized that the gross domestic product of the 35 independent states was estimated recently at only US$ 27.5 billion. This corresponds to four-fifths of the gross domestic product of Italy in 1962. The average income per head is only in the neighborhood of $ 100 per head per annum. It is obvious that the markets for goods, services and capital in the 23 countries with a population of less than 5 million and an income per head of $ 100 are tiny markets which for that reason alone are imperfect.

TABLE 2

Population of Independent African States
(excluding S. Africa and Gambia), 1965

Population Size (in millions)	No. of African States	
Under 1	3	
1 — 2	4	23
2 — 3	6	
3 — 4	5	
4 — 5	5	
5 — 10	4	
10 — 20	5	12
20 — 30	2	
over 30	1	
	35 countries	

Practical Impossibility of Isolating African Economies from World Economy

The small economic size and the fact that on an average exports are equal to 19½ per cent of gross domestic product and imports are equal to 21½ per cent of gross domestic product make it quite impossible to pursue economic and especially monetary policies to isolate African economies from the fluctuations of world economy. Apart from the extreme cases of Liberia which has no currency of its own, and Somalia, where a 100 per cent statutory foreign exchange cover applies, many countries have automatic narrow statutory limitations on currency issue, which prevent them from implementing a truly independent monetary policy. Owing to imbalances of payments the free convertibility of African countries is either achieved by large foreign aid or by means of an exchange guarantee granted by an industrialized country (e.g., France).

Expectation-Forming Frustrated by Uncertainties

Inter-temporal decisions are made extremely difficult and are often impossible because of the prevailing degree of uncertainty. For the sake of convenience of exposition four types of uncertainty will be enumerated.

(a) *Political Uncertainty*

In some African countries it is impossible to predict the complexion of future governments and their programs of action. The unpredictable and possible vast scope of political changes is responsible for disincentives to investment, preference for monetary investment in land, houses and gold and flight of capital and currency.

(b) *Monetary Uncertainties*

The purchasing power of money, the savings propensities of households, businesses and public authorities, the future trend of lenders' and borrowers' risks, the solvency and liquidity of financial institutions, all these present great monetary uncertainties. Opportunities for risk spreading are limited.

(c) *General Economic Uncertainties.* They can be enumerated as follows:

Balance of payments developments are not predictable. Foreign exchange budgets either do not exist or are impossible to prepare. The international indebtedness and the commitments arising therefrom are very often not accurately known. The present and future convertibility and transferability of currencies is uncertain. The continuance of foreign aid is uncertain and subject to erratic changes chiefly caused by changes of political attitudes. The belief in the implementation of existing development plans is usually very weak. At least the urban African population is very conscious of the effect of the population explosion on the growth of visible and disguised urban unemployment. The steady inexorable increase of unemployment and the absence of any effective policy for halting it or reducing it is one of the greatest economic uncertainties besetting African countries.

(d) *Producers' Uncertainties*

The uncertainties which entrepreneurs have to face in Africa do not differ in kind from similar uncertainties in industrialized countries but there exists a great difference in degree. The prices of factors and of products and the probable profits are much more uncertain in African countries, especially, of course, in pioneer industries where there are no past experiences available to guide decisions concerning investment in fixed and circulating capital. Import duties and taxes change in unpredictable fashion. All of these factors make entrepreneurial decisions extremely difficult.

Peculiarities of the Supply of Money and its Control in African Countries

The expansion of bank deposits depends both upon the supply of domestic cash and of foreign exchange. Treasury bills and commercial bills have little influence on the expansion of bank deposits. Open market operations are impossible in most African countries.

Money is here defined as media of exchange which are generally acceptable and are not subject to capital loss. The following assets qualify as money in Africa:

(a) Domestic coins and notes.
(b) Convertible foreign notes *de facto* permitted to circulate.
(c) Domestic current deposit liabilities in those African countries only in which the banking system is stable in the sense of having stable cash ratios, liquidity ratios and proved solvency.
(d) Foreign deposit liabilities.

No other financial assets qualify as media of exchange.

The velocity of circulation in Africa is at least physically limited by the time required for transferring money from the receipt point to the expenditure point. Velocity is furthermore limited by the small number of financial intermediaries.

The cash ratio of African banks is far in excess of the cash ratios in industrialized countries. In some areas where the account holders are an insignificant proportion of total population, cash ratios may be as high as 25 per cent. This naturally increases the rate of interest which is charged on bank advances.

The seasonal trade credits are chiefly supplied by the banks of export-buying countries and are withdrawn when imports into African countries are financed out of export proceeds.

Peculiarities of the African Banking System Affecting Monetary Policy

The asset structure of African banks differs from those of Euro-American banks.

The high cash ratio is necessary because bank money is but a moderate percentage of total money, i.e., 35 to 60 per cent, and bank clearings are to be found only in a few capital cities.

African banks discount a variety of bills with a maturity of nine months or less, such as bills for financing exports and imports secured on receipt of goods, treasury bills and promissory notes. They also grant advances against securities.

At least in francophone areas credit rationing is global. Limits (ceilings) are fixed for credits (discounts, advances, short- and medium-term credits) to be created by each bank, to be granted to each business enterprise and for each category of credit. Francophone banks limit in particular the purchase of treasury bills. The law establishing the Bank for West Africa (BCEAO) lays down that bank credit granted to any member government cannot exceed either of the following two limits:

1. The central bank's advances plus the central bank's and commercial banks' holdings of Treasury securities shall not exceed 10 per cent of the actual fiscal receipts of the member government during the preceding year.

2. The commercial banks' holdings of Treasury securities at any time shall not exceed 10 per cent of the average deposit liabilities to private businesses and individuals during the preceding twelve months.

The expatriate firms, especially import and export businesses, grant often substantial trade credits which are usually obtained from overseas banks. These trade credits are large by comparison with bank credits.

Most economically active areas in most African countries are "under-banked." Some central banks (e.g., of Somalia and Ethiopia) undertake to open small commercial bank offices in areas to be developed.

The Effectiveness of the Interest Rate in Africa

Owing to the extreme imperfection of the loan and capital markets and the prevailing high rate of uncertainty in Africa, the interest rate is even less a regulator of supply and demand of loanable funds than in Euro-America.

As far as the long term is concerned, the gap between the rate of interest and the acceptable minimum net profit rate is much larger in Africa than in Euro-America. This is due to several causes: the uncertainty of the total surplus of a business and the consequent even greater uncertainty of the equity owner as residual claimant. Unlike most Euro-American businesses, an African business cannot grow continuously. There is no inducement to consent to a lowering of the acceptable minimum net profit rate as there is no market share to defend or to conquer and no novel products to be sold for which consumers' tastes need to be developed.

The short-term interest is without any effect whatever on attracting or repelling foreign short-term loans in the form of currencies or gold, or in increasing or decreasing liquidity preference. This effectiveness presupposes active money and capital markets which are lacking in Africa.

The short-term rate has, however, a limited usefulness as a regulator of short-term loans to finance exports, imports, domestic trade, working and liquid capital of modern industry and public works.

Supply of and Demand for Loanable Funds in Africa

Loanable funds in Africa comprise domestic gross savings, net foreign loans and donations and net direct investments by foreign businesses.

Domestic savings arise in eight sectors of the African economy each with different savings habits. These sectors are:

(a) The government. Government savings are defined strictly as tax revenue plus currency issue profit minus current exhaustive and transfer expenditure. (Foreign aid must not be counted as government revenue in ascertaining government savings).

(b) The modern large scale and non-agricultural production enterprises. These may be owned and managed by: the African government, expatriates (European) and private African persons.

The retained domestic gross savings of such enterprises are equal to gross profit after tax minus dividends minus retained profit transferred abroad.

(c) Large scale agricultural enterprises and medium scale non-African farms. These are owned and managed by African governments and non-Africans.

(d) Expatriate households (exclusive of savings transmitted abroad).

(e) African small or medium scale, non-corporate enterprises in urban areas. These enterprises sell part of their output for cash, and the remainder is either consumed by the owners and their families or takes the form of capital formation for own use.

(f) African middle and high income earners. This group comprises the political and administrative, as well as the managerial and professional classes.

(g) African urban wage-earning households. Some of them may be engaged in subsistence farming and construction of their homes as a side line.

(h)   The African rural population. This population comprises both farmers and artisans. Both groups consume part of their produce whereas the remainder is either sold for cash, or takes the form of capital formation for own use.

In addition to the above mentioned sources of saving, the following sources of investible funds should be referred to (items (b) to (e) are not savings proper):

(a)   If insurance premiums, social insurance contributions, trade union dues, and similar payments are not regarded as savings by the payers, the corresponding "institutional savings" must be regarded as a separate category of savings.

(b)   Increments of the fiduciary part of the currency. These need not be inflationary.

(c)   Dishoarding of money hoarded in the past.

(d)   Selling foreign assets owned by residents to foreigners and selling home assets owned by residents to foreigners.

(e)   Using part of the foreign exchange reserve (in the widest sense of the term) as investible funds.

The savings of the first seven groups of savers are already being tapped but are capable of yielding larger contributions to gross domestic savings. The most important source of savings should have been the government. However, very few African governments nowadays realize any savings and those that do provide only a small fraction of total domestic savings. If foreign aid to African countries is included in government revenue, governments contribute substantially to capital formation, as much as or more than 50 per cent in many cases; but these savings are supplied by the foreign sector.

Business savings are managerial decisions predominantly without reference to consumers' time preferences.

Only the savings of private households imply an intertemporal equilibrium between more future utility against the sacrifice of less present utility. The most numerous African households are the indigenous rural households. As a group their net savings are mostly zero because the net savings of the one group are dissaved by the other group for sumptuous traditional feasts at the time of birth, circumcision, marriage and death. Also dowries and payments to the bride's family devour savings.

It is difficult to believe that these penurious farmers can and will save. Their life expectancy as shown above is so short that extreme impatience to consume must result. They seldom earn a surplus above mere biological maintenance consumption.

Yet economic development requires that this most populous group should save in spite of its poverty. Contrary to widespread opinion it can be done, as the Comilla Academy of Village Development in East Pakistan has shown. The Comilla Academy performed the miracle of inducing unbelievably indigent farmers to save one rupee a week by adding to the one rupee saved three rupees as a repayable loan (obtained from the Ford Foundation). This made the realization of the goal of savings possible in a quarter of the time. The savings not needed to repay pre-existing debts were most productively used and the savings habit grew even stronger.

Changing the traditional bouts of overconsumption into some productive investment activity seems highly desirable The payments on the occasion of marriage could, for instance, take the form of buying shares in the local farmers' cooperative.

Domestic savings could be increased by any of the measures described above. But that is only half of the problem. The other half consists in preventing the dissipation of investible funds on nonproductive uses.

Unfortunately the investible funds are susceptible to at least 13 different uses inside the African economy which will be called "leakage from real investment," i.e., these uses do not result in gross domestic capital formation. These 13 leakage uses are as follows:

(1) Remittances of expatriates out of their savings.

(2) Donations in money or in kind by home country to foreign countries.

(3) Loans by home country to foreign countries.

(4) Repayment of foreign loans.

(5) Excess private consumption. (Hire purchase credit).

(6) Purchase of non-productive ostentatious assets, such as gold ornaments and jewelry.

(7) Simple hoarding of money (burying money) or sophisticated hoarding of money (i.e., keeping unnecessarily large cash balances), not counter-balanced by credit expansion in the banking system.

(8) Destroying a portion of state money or bank money in existence. The government may use tax money to buy back the fiduciary backing of currency.

(9) Excess government consumption, i.e., the current government expenditure is in excess of current tax revenue.

(10) Augmenting the foreign exchange reserve by acquiring gold and foreign exchange or foreign bank balances.

(11)   Paying capital subscription to international political, econo-
       mic or cultural organizations.
(12)   Purchase of financial assets by residents from foreigners.
(13)   Repayments to private sector of loans previously granted
       to governments. (If the private sector invests these repay-
       ments productively, this would not constitute a leakage of
       investible funds to non-productive uses).

The leakage of investible funds from productive uses must be
stopped or minimized as a vital part of monetary policy.

Population Explosion, Savings, Investment and Unemployment

The population explosion all over Africa affects savings and investment decisions to a large extent. This fact is not usually realized.
In terms of factors of production economic development can be defined as a process in which modern factors of production such as
machines, irrigation installations, industrial managers, technicians and
skilled workers increase much faster than the unskilled working
force. But the factors of production just enumerated cannot grow
much faster than they are growing at the present time. Hence, unless
the growth of population is held back, the modern factors of production per occupied person will only slightly, if at all, increase.

It is time that a concept of "warranted population growth" is
developed. Let r be the increment of capital endowment per em-
ployee during the current year. Let k be the capital endowment per
worker during last year. Let y stand for the growth rate of net
domestic product and c for the average propensity to consume. Let p
be the growth rate of the population and s the marginal propensity
to save. The following equation holds:

$$(y - cp)s = \frac{\triangle I^t}{Y^{t-1}} \tag{i}$$

Where the expression on the right hand side shows the ratio of the
increment of investment during t compared with investment during
t-1, Y^{t-1} stands for the net domestic production during the last year.
Let the employment during last year be written E^{t-1} and the desired
increment of employment as specified in the development plan be
written E^t, we would then have the equation

$$I^{t-1} + \triangle I^t = rE^{t-1} + (k+r) \triangle E^t \tag{ii}$$

If the rate of growth of net domestic production, average propensity
consumed and marginal propensity to save are given, the increment

of investment in equation (i) in the current year depends upon the rate of population growth (p). This determines the warranted population growth rate.

Income Policy

The incomes policy is an essential part of price stabilization policy. Many African incomes are politically determined incomes and are not related to productivity. One of the most unfortunate inheritances from the pre-independence period was the expatriate salaries. In most countries, the African executives who took over jobs from expatriates were at once paid expatriate salaries. Thereafter, their salaries were increased for political reasons. There can be no doubt that if the expatriate salary was the rate for the job, a great many of the executive African officials fully earn this rate. However, the number of these executive jobs was much increased and the salary scales for most new posts were above the relative productivity. The same sort of situation arose in private industries where executive positions were Africanized. The direct consequence of this situation is, of course, that of vastly increasing current budgetary expenditure. In the early fifties the highest percentage of expenditure was generally absorbed by the economic services. In recent years general and social services have become predominant, while recurrent budgets are more often than not in deficit and require equilibrating grants from abroad.

Trade union policy also tends to create political rates of pay. Unionized government workers everywhere have been able to raise wage rates of anything up to eight times the national average.

These political salaries which are unrelated to productivity constitute a major type of cost-push inflation. It is, of course, politically impossible to reduce these rates. It should, however, not be beyond the ingenuity of African leaders to find a solution. A radical proposal might consist in establishing an upper limit of cash payments per annum, say $ 1,500 per annum, and paying the remainder of the salaries in the form of interest-bearing bonds of a government investment trust. This trust should be concerned only with investments in revenue yielding projects. The bonds should be irredeemable and non-negotiable for a period of perhaps ten years.

Unreliability of Fiscal Support for Monetary Policy

Monetary and fiscal policy must reinforce and support each other to have any chance of success. Unfortunately, in many African countries monetary and fiscal policies are formulated separately without much effort at integration and the implementation differs from the planned policy. It is not an overstatement to say that the monetary authorities do not receive reliable fiscal support for their policies.

Aggregate Supply Deficiency and Lack of Scientific and Technological Knowledge

Africa is the continent of classical supply deficiency. What demand deficiency there is is completely negligible. Monetary policy in Africa should contribute to overcoming this supply deficiency by increasing the supply of investible funds and directing it into productive uses.

These include:

(a) The creation of more modern factors of production.

(b) Assuring that the investment projects are input-output interrelated and arranged in a proper time sequence.

(c) Influencing the expectations of the entrepreneurs and making them aware of the increased profitable investment opportunities.

(d) Contributing to the spread of scientific and technological knowledge through helping to finance technical assistance for feasibility and pre-investment studies on a large scale.

Inflationary Pressures

The African types of inflationary pressures do not differ from those experienced elsewhere but there is a difference of degree. In particular, what might be called physical scarcity inflation resulting from a constant or rising factor incomes stream compared with a decreasing physical goods stream from one period to the next is a peculiar feature of African economic life.

Four aspects of demand inflation stand out:

(a) The increment of investment expenditure multiplied by the propensity to consume is usually greater than the extra supply of domestically produced and imported consumption goods.

(b) The retained domestic savings plus foreign savings minus imported investment goods are usually smaller than the actual investment expenditure.

(c) Government consumption and government investment expenditure is usually larger than government revenue minus transfer payments.

(d) In years of rising export prices the export revenue exceeds the cost of production by an inflationary windfall profit.

The three typical aspects of cost inflation are as follows:

(a) The increments of factor incomes are in excess of increments of productivity.

(b) The rise in import prices usually exceeds the rise of prices of domestic goods and of export goods.

(c) The indirect tax rates including import duties and excise duties rise much faster than the prices of domestic goods.

In some African countries in which the actual rate of price inflation was substantial an expectational inflation raised its head.

Lack of Legal Institutions

Monetary and banking legislation is inadequate in practically all African countries. Such legal institutions as checks and other bills of exchange are not properly defined, nor are the rights and duties of banks. Insolvency laws which penalize the irresponsible debtor and lighten the consequences for the *bona fide* debtor meeting with misfortune are practically non-existent in most African countries. Ghana is one of the few countries which possesses an excellent insolvency act.

Monetary Policies for African Countries in External Monetary and Payments Equilibrium

(a) Accelerated monetization of the subsistence economy, which requires specialization of production, transport facilities and organization of markets as well as special monetary institutions, e.g., a postal checking system.

(b) Curbing inflationary forces, especially political rates of wages and salaries, removing physical scarcity of consumption goods during a period of heavy investment expenditure, checking reckless government expenditure, etc.

(c) Unifying the pluralist financial structure, involving reducing borrowers' and lenders' risks and lowering social time preference, integrating interest structure, developing habits of thrift, replacing traditional by economic motivation, etc.

(d) Increasing the propensities to save of households, business and public authorities, creating institutional savers such as insurance companies and social insurance funds to cover domestic risks in domestic currency and domestic portfolio investment.

(e)   Increasing the international net inflow of capital. This im-
      plies an efficient preparation of feasibility and pre-investment
      studies, accurate cost-benefit analysis and efficient imple-
      mentation of projects as well as adequate, but not excessive,
      economic concessions to foreign pioneer industries.

(f)   Preventing overborrowing from abroad, i.e., receipts of loans
      which do not add to productive investment.

(g)   Promoting productive investment through feasibility and
      pre-investment studies, improving the bankability of projects
      and the credit-worthiness of prospective borrowers, applica-
      tion of a rational system of investment criteria.

(h)   Promoting the adoption of mixed technology as a device
      for reducing capital output ratio and at the same time
      increasing the creation of jobs while yet bestowing upon
      the country the benefit of advancing technology. The opera-
      tions for which advanced types of equipment must be used
      are those upon which the international competitive quality
      of the products depend. The initially non-mechanized opera-
      tions would, of course, be successfully mechanized as wage
      rates rise in future years. The character of mixed techno-
      logy is also partly determined by the requirement that prices
      of products must be internationally competitive. Generally
      speaking, it is not applicable to the chemical industries which
      operate with continuous flow processes in closed pipes, stills
      and towers. Mixed technology will result in the maximum
      practical creation of jobs.

(i)   Reducing the social time preference and enlarging the time
      horizon of equipment planning. When Africans in distress
      are forced to borrow money from money lenders they may
      pay an implied annual rate of interest from 60–300 per cent.
      African businessmen may borrow from banks at rates up to
      15 per cent per annum. Expatriate businessmen can borrow
      from overseas banks at rates varying from 6–8 per cent.
      There is no single rate of time preference in existence.

Modern large scale and medium scale businesses in Africa can
largely finance themselves out of their own retained profits and in
addition can call upon foreign private loans and funds from overseas head offices for investment purposes.

The investment decisions of modern large and medium scale
businesses in Africa differ from those of African governments in three
respects:

1. The business firms take account only of the private productivity of investment and not of the social benefits which the remainder of the national economy can directly or indirectly derive from it.
2. They take account of the highest risk rate payable to private lenders plus premiums for uninsurable uncertainty.
3. They fix the amount of investment so as to equate the marginal private productivity of investment with the minimum expected return stated in the preceding item.

Only the African governments are in a position to apply a social time preference rate which ensures maximum economically justifiable investment. The governments consider the social productivity of investment which includes an allowance for increased factor incomes, for the induced growth of auxiliary industries, for stimulation of technical progress (which in turn will lead to further technical progress and further creation of additional skills).

It is one of the tasks of the African governments to pursue policies which will induce the private savings schedules to approximate the socially determined savings supply schedule.

Monetary Policies of African Countries When There is Disequilibrium in the External Monetary and Payments Situation

The imbalance of external payments of the majority of African countries is characterized in three ways. It is chronic, unless export prices rise substantially; it is everywhere represented—and hence perpetually latent—by such measures as foreign exchange and import control; it is primarily a chronic imbalance in extra-African trade though some African countries have also a chronic imbalance in the payments relations with fellow-African countries, especially land-locked countries in West Africa.

The monetary symptoms of such chronic imbalances are: flight of capital, drying up of foreign loans; dwindling of foreign exchange reserves; foreign speculation against the currency; domestic inflation and consequent overimportation at pegged exchange rates; default on servicing of international debts; continuous difficulties of the treasury to meet its expenditure commitments, etc.

Most developing countries in external disequilibrium do not of their own free will attempt a fundamental cure but merely suppress the outward signs of a chronic imbalance. Some succeed in this.

Only few developing countries adopt growth-neutral and employment-neutral adjustment policies of the kind mentioned below when the first signs of possible chronic imbalances appear.

(a)   Borrowing international liquidity to enable adjustment of exchange rates to be in moderate steps over many months.

(b)   Lowering or a least preventing the rise of incomes and prices so as to become once more internationally competitive without causing a restriction of output.

(c)   Inducing a capital influx and discouraging capital repatriation through creation of good prospects of high rates of return net of tax.

The above growth-neutral and employment-neutral adjustment policies are under the control of the developing countries themselves.

Fundamental cures of external imbalances are, however, possible only with the active cooperation of the industrialized countries. Let it not be forgotten that 35 independent African states (exclusive of South Africa and Gambia) have only an aggregate gross domestic product equal to four-fifths of that of Italy. It is intuitively obvious that much of the action for rescuing African and other developing countries from their chronic external imbalances must come from the industrialized countries. What policies have to be pursued were clearly outlined by the U.N. Conference on Trade and Development.

Among the many policies adopted, a purely monetary one may be specifically mentioned here. It is consolidation of the individual indebtedness to many countries into one consolidated indebtedness with lengthened repayment periods and lowered rates of interest payable partly in soft currencies. Such a consolidation agreement might be preceded by a standstill debt-service during the period of negotiation.

Monetary Integration Policies

The economic fragmentation of Africa is a great handicap to accelerated development. Developing countries in Central America, the Caribbean, Middle East and Oceania are in a similar position. Even if outright political fusion is impossible, economic integration taking the form of an economic union or at least limited economic cooperation should be attempted to achieve larger markets which could absorb the outputs of optimum size plants and provide other economies of scale, e.g., of public administration.

Monetary integration policies can pursue many objectives among which are:

(a)   Mutual consultation and cooperation among central banks.

(b)   Formation of a supra-national bank and a number of other common monetary institutions such as common regulation of exchange control, common exchange stabilization fund and common regulations for money markets.

(c) Creating a monetary union between a region of developing states, e.g., Africa, and a single or a group of industrialized states to overcome inconvertibility problems.

(d) Creating a multi-national, a sub-regional, or a regional payments union at first for intra-regional trade and later on also for certain areas of extra-regional trade.

(e) Establishing a regional (e.g., African) branch of the International Monetary Fund with the express duty of helping the developing countries concerned to achieve free and secure convertibility of their currencies.

(f) Coordinating financial aid from industrialized countries and ensuring maximum efficiency of its use.

DISCUSSION

Accent on Restraint

A good development plan attracts business. Smaller wages, a lower birth-rate, "mixed technology," and a ban on "over-borrowing" would help economic growth.

Dr. Mars said that out of the 37 countries in Africa, four have no development plan at all, and 12 had a plan which collapsed "because it turned out to be wishful thinking." The remaining countries have development plans which are either fully or largely implemented. The very best one is probably Tunisia's. It has been found that the existence of a good plan "does affect very strongly the expectations of the investors, and this is very important. Unless investors can form firm expectations, you cannot expect them to be willing to assume risks and uncertainties."

Also "I must confess that whenever the bigger private companies in Africa do believe there is an intelligently drawn up development plan, their willingness to invest in new manufacturing enterprises in the country is much greater than if the development plan is just a form of wishful thinking."

The amount of legal tender in circulation is related to the size of the foreign exchange reserve, which depends on the balance of payments. As "these foreign exchange reserves move up and down very rapidly, the whole money system is uncertain and subject to fluctuations." The foreign sector operates mainly with foreign deposit money, i.e., checks drawn on foreign banks. The active creation of money by banks is thus done abroad.

More than 60 per cent of expatriate salaries are transferred to foreign countries. "The willingness of expatriates to have their money, let us say, in the local savings accounts or to buy local securities or equities depends very much upon the political atmosphere, and also upon whether there is a feeling that a real sort of inter-racial harmony exists. Now some African countries have succeeded excellently in that. The snobbish foreigners have left, and in some of the countries the Europeans that have stayed behind are very happy to be there, and are very pleased to work for an African government—and they are the people who leave their savings in the country. That group will, I hope, increase in the future."

Wage disparities could be eased by limiting salaries to a maximum in cash of £1,500, with the rest paid in bonds. Such a measure would promote savings. In addition "the large mass of the population has experience of a very slight increase, if any, in consumption standards. They see that the high income earners are able to gain anything up to £2,800 or £3,000 per annum, and then they say: 'Well, development is for the benefit of that group, not for our benefit.' "

Concerning the population explosion, Dr. Mars said, "I have made a radical proposal—which, of course, my African friends object to— that for about five or six five-year plans, they should try to hold the population constant by having only as many babies as people die. Now every year in Africa 6 million people die, so they could still have 6 million babies—and this, to my mind, is a little ocean of babies. It would mean that an African wife would only have an average of three children. Savings would then rise, and the governments would be spared a lot of expenditure." As things are, "I calculated that on an average one can create jobs at the most for one-half of the annual addition to the work force. The remaining addition to the work force is just an addition to unemployment." About one-third of the people in agriculture in Africa today are victims of disguised unemployment. A job costs at least £1,000 to create. "Even if aid were doubled, it would be impossible to create as many jobs as people are added to the work force."

Dr. Mars advocates "mixed technology" using modern machinery where this is essential to achieve quality, but otherwise labor-intensive methods (e.g., in haulage).

The African trade unions should devote themselves to raising productivity, so as to be able to increase wages without putting up prices or ruining the business. They should even interest themselves in birth control, to keep in check the flood of work-seekers. The unions today demand the same rate for the job from small indigenous African-run enterprises as they do from big expatriate firms.

High protective tariffs allow poor quality local goods to be sold at prices that belong to top-quality products—which is another cause of inflation. "You keep the price but you reduce the quality. You have therefore reduced the cost, and you get a profit appearing that way."

A check ought to be placed on "over-borrowing," i.e., loans that do not result in a net addition to productive investment.

Dr. E. Sheffer, of Israel, said that a first task for the LDCs is to create monetary institutions. The job of a central bank is to sponsor the establishment of banking facilities and other financial intermediaries, not just for creating objects of control, but to encourage savings and provide organized credit services for the producer.

But monetary policy such as a contraction in the quantity of money or credit cannot solve structural problems or chronic balance of payment deficits, nor can it cure the evils of excessive budget deficits. The impact of monetary policy is particularly limited where the monetary structure of the economy is narrow. This emphasizes the need for coordination between Treasury policy and central bank policy. Commonly "the government creates the inflation and leaves the task of putting out the fire to the central bank. This, of course, cannot work."

Selective credit control can help the quantitative control of credit, i.e., it is possible to limit credit for house construction or consumption, while extending credit to export. But this policy needs careful handling, particularly to ensure that the authorized credit goes to its designated purpose.

Dr. Placido Mapa Jr., of the Philippines, recalled that historically, monetary policy has been used effectively to achieve stabilization, but always at the expense of economic growth. So it has to be supplemented by fiscal measures. The Philippines could be productivized further with more investment in her infrastructure. This requires new taxes, but the decision depends on politics, which is responsive to human considerations.

If credit controls were relaxed, the banks would increase activity in the industrial sector. Industry is more congenial to the banks than agriculture, because manufacturers can more easily give collateral, and they are immune to the hazards of weather and epidemics. But industry requires more imported materials than agriculture, so a credit relaxation leads to foreign exchange difficulties. An alternative to reforms in fiscal policies is to allocate central bank credit to the government for increased capital expenditure, although that raises questions of deficit financing.

Dr. Ernst Lehmann, of Israel, suggested using high liquidity ratios for the banks. This would allow the central bank to remit the liquidity rules for a proportion of the frozen deposits, provided they are allocated to purposes having a high priority.

There are pitfalls. The system may become too rigid, and may handicap the central bank in its function of ironing out seasonal fluctuations in the supply and demand of money. Secondly, if inflationary pressures are strong, the economy may try to circumvent the system by bill brokerage, for instance, which results in a growing volume of credit transactions executed outside the banking system and hence outside the monetary and credit control of the central bank.

Dr. Max G. Mueller, of the U.S., referred to Dr. Mars' point that high export prices result in hoarding. If he means hoarding in domestic currency, this gives scope for additional development expenditure, because hoarding is deflationary. The use of financial intermediaries is of course a better form of savings, because there is always the danger of dishoarding, which could become inflationary.

Hoarding of gold or foreign exchange is not helpful, except that it creates an accumulation of resources within the country that could be mobilized in time of need. In all, hoarding is still better than dissipating resources in consumption.

Serious Investors Needed

Forming a monetary union has advantages, but many problems remain. One of them is how to attract serious investors. Tax holidays and other concessions should be standardized throughout Africa.

Mr. Ralison-Rakotovao, of the Malagasy Republic, referred to the difficulty of getting supra-national coordination, e.g., for creating the African Development Bank or the Asian Development Bank. He took issue with Dr. Mars' plea for salary restraint. "Wages are not just toys in the hands of economists and politicians. Wages, even 'political wages' are linked to living standards, and are defended by strong social pressures. Therefore I wonder if we would not do better to be realistic, and see existing salaries as irreducible minima."

Mr. Ralison quoted Professor Kaldor in support of his view that 'wages of misery' hold back progress and that an incomes boom acts as a catalyst to economic advancement.

Hon. Sheriff S. Sisay, of Gambia, said his country has no central bank as yet, and one commercial bank. It is expatriate and confines itself to financing the export and import trade, which is to a large extent handled by expatriate firms. The bank does not extend the same facilities to indigenous business men, is unwilling to finance agricultural development, and does not invest in industrialization "even to the modest degree which Dr. Mars would be prepared to support in African countries."

So the government had to form public corporations, like the Gambia Marketing Board, and to organize producers into cooperatives. These bodies build up reserves to finance business activity, reducing their dependence on bank loans which, to the extent that they were available, carried a high rate of interest.

If African economies combined, "it would be possible with a larger unit to carry out monetary operations and all the other things more rationally. And of course even if all of Africa were to become one political unit, one monetary unit—it is still going to be part of the world. For this reason it is bound to be affected by the day-to-day fluctuations or even the seasonal fluctuations in prices."

Discussing the fall of prices for primary products, Mr. Sisay observed that, if neighboring countries got together, they would be able to borrow capital from outside or generate capital locally for setting up industries to process the materials at present sent abroad (and often re-imported at a considerably higher price after processing). He stressed that the formation of an economic union would not mean either that the price of African products would suddenly shoot up, or that Africans would cease exporting such products. The problems must remain, except that the Africans' bargaining position would be strengthened.

Mr. Sisay took issue with Dr. Mars' observation that investors face uncertainties owing to unpredictable changes in import duties and taxes. Pioneer industries enjoy tax holidays, and if there are import duties, they are intended to protect the local product, which means they are an additional aid to the investor.

"The difficulty has been in inducing the right kind of people to take an interest in industrial development." Applicants negotiate terms for exploiting local resources, secure concessions, receive documents to that effect, and only then do they go round with these documents to persuade other people to produce the necessary capital. In the case of a fishing project, it emerged that "these people had nothing of their own for development'" but wanted to use the concessions as an instrument for seeking funds. "And if for example one later encounters such a person, he would not agree that that was the reason for the failure of the undertaking. He might say he was not satisfied with the results of his negotiations with the Ministry of Finance or with some other authority in the country. And to some extent, the picture of our country and of our readiness to cooperate with foreign investors is being blackened."

Concerning the lack of insolvency legislation, Mr. Sisay remarked that "legislation of every sort was the responsibility some time ago of a metropolitan power which did not regard these countries as places of intensive financial or monetary activity. And on achieving independence it is difficult to choose between the catalogue of so many things one has to do, and to say that monetary legislation is the first and most important thing which ought to be done." But in spite of all that, there do exist courses open to any person who gives credit, under the existing legal system, to take the necessary legal action.

Mr. Sisay suggested that discussions be devoted to what is lacking in the concessions worked out for attracting the investor, because "with all the concessions we are prepared to give, we don't know what is stopping people from coming and taking an interest. We know that in some cases the potentialities are there and ought to be exploited. It is in our interest that they should be exploited." In conclusion, Mr. Sisay supported Dr. Mars' plea for regional monetary integration: "I think this is vital," he said.

Mr. John Sackah Addo, of Ghana, expressed disappointment that Dr. Mars found it necessary to paint the African picture so black, though "we all agree that Africa is the darkest continent." Attempts are being made to adapt some of the traditional monetary instruments to African economic conditions. After all, "whether Dr. Mars likes it or not, the politician makes the decisions, not in Africa alone—in every country." So the Bank of Ghana cannot control government expenditure, but it does try to control the private sector.

Before Ghana's independence, the banks brought in their reserves from overseas to finance the purchase of cocoa from the farmers, and during the off-season they transferred their reserves and profits back to the U.K., as did the commercial firms, to invest in the more active British market. The central bank has stopped this traffic by passing the Exchange Control Regulations in 1961. Then it floated Treasury bills and other government securities to mop up the seasonal surplus of cash.

Mr. Addo took vehement exception to Dr. Mars' "population-stop" theory. While more education is admittedly needed for the increased population, its growth cannot be halted by just saying so.

* * *

In replying to the debate, Dr. Mars conceded that generalization about the policies of thirty-seven African countries cannot do justice to all the exceptions. In addition to South Africa and the U.A.R., there are other African countries with highly developed monetary institutions, such as Morocco, Algeria and Rhodesia.

He reassured Mr. Sisay that he had recommended not isolating Africans, but insulating African countries from the fluctuations of the world economy. Dr. Mars urges the negotiation of an African Convention, about the sort of concessions that should be granted to foreign companies. This would stop governments outbidding each other in the terms they offer, and would also prevent giving more concessions than are necessary to attract the amount of capital they want.

In criticizing uncertainties about what import duties and taxes will be, Dr. Mars emphasized the need that, for example, a company erecting a textile mill should know what tariff they are going to pay on imported dyestuffs.

He pointed out that the ECA has drawn up an African Payments Union plan, suggestions for establishing an African Monetary Fund, and suggestions for an African Bank of International Settlements— a sort of mutual aid club of central bank governors.

The population-stop policy is only proposed for a limited period during which unemployment would disappear, until it became possible to finance new jobs for a rising population.

PART III TAXES

The object of taxation policy is to shift resources or encourage their shift from low-priority to high-priority uses. Fiscal measures should be designed to maintain stability and foster growth. They should stimulate savings, investment, hard work and efficiency.

Revenue is low in the LDCs partly because incomes are low, but also because tax systems are antiquated. Poor societies often have a higher potential tax yield than would appear, since they harbor pronounced economic inequalities. The richer inhabitants can be brought to contribute more to the exchequer at the expense of sumptuary consumption.

The taxation of land rents can stimulate a more dynamic use of agricultural resources. A full economic price needs to be charged for the services of public utilities like railways, ports, posts, water and electricity. Recommended are income-elastic taxes, which are progressive and therefore bring in automatically more revenue as incomes rise. But they are complex to apply.

Competition between LDCs in offering tax rebates to foreign investors can be self-defeating if the object is to step up the production of a valuable export mineral, since its output depends on world demand. But "tax holidays" are useful for inducing foreign companies to put up an undertaking that will serve the internal market.

Taxes imposed on the profits of big foreign companies can be evaded by profit-shifting and the use of tax havens. There is here a need for international cooperation—which could be valuable also in coordinating the allocation of tax concessions.

Governments can contribute to the accumulation of savings by budgeting for a specified surplus, instead of leaving it as a residual item after all other outlays have been met. The difficulty is that so much revenue is needed for the governments' mounting administrative expenses, due to rapid population increase.

12

TAXATION IN DEVELOPING STATES

By NICHOLAS KALDOR
King's College, Cambridge
Great Britain

Although the countries generally referred to as "developing" differ widely in many respects they have many common problems in the field of fiscal policy. They all, for example, urgently need to increase the proceeds of public revenue so as to finance programs designed to accelerate the rate of economic growth and to increase the standard of living of the inhabitants. While foreign aid is important—and often essential in the early states—it is likely to be effective only if it is complementary to finance which a country can raise from domestic sources.

The economic and cultural development of a country requires the steady expansion of a large number of non-revenue yielding services —schools, hospitals, communications systems—which are most important for long-run development but which are, unfortunately, expendable in the short run when lack of revenue may force economies in public spending. Effective taxation (or other compulsory levies) is a means of providing the revenue required for these services, and, at the same time, it can be the means of diverting expenditure from consumption to expenditure on investment. In other words, taxation may provide the means of generating the domestic savings needed to supplement foreign aid for the large capital formation projects, needed both to attain higher productivity in industry and agriculture as well as educational and cultural facilities for the majority of the population. Taxation is, indeed, the only alternative to inflation which is, by comparison, a clumsy and ineffective means of mobilizing resources.

The Taxation Potential of Developing Countries

It is generally believed, however, that the proportion of national income which a poor country can divert to public purposes through taxation without setting up intolerable political and social pressures, is much smaller than in a rich country. It is undeniable that at present the proportion of tax revenue to gross national product in the so-called underdeveloped countries is much lower than that of the advanced countries—the former may be typically around 8–15 per cent, the latter 25–30 per cent. But the reasons for this are not to be sought mainly in lack of "taxation potential" due to this poverty; it is also due to a failure to exploit this potential effectively.

Taxes can, of course, be paid only from the economic surplus—the excess of production over the minimum subsistence needs of the population—and if this surplus is already being used for productive investment, taxation will reduce the rate of capital accumulation of the community with adverse effects on development. The taxation potential of a country therefore depends on the excess of its actual consumption over the minimum essential consumption of the population. In practice, "minimum essential consumption" cannot be measured as it will depend on social conventions and habits and the prevailing standard of living in the community, and governments have to work within these limits. If this were not so, taxation potential would vary enormously with the actual level of real income per head. For this reason, therefore, the taxation potential of a country depends to a large extent on the existing inequality in the distribution of the national income and this is closely connected with income derived from, and the degree of concentration in, the ownership of property. As between two countries, with the same real income per head, the accustomed standard of living of the bulk of the population will evidently be the lower in the country in which a larger share of total income accrues to a minority of wealthy individuals.

With the major exception of Africa, the statistics that are available for the developing countries show that, despite their very considerable diversity in the economic and social spheres, the degree of concentration of property and the inequality in the distribution of income in the poor or semi-developed countries of the Middle East, Asia or Latin America are comparable to that of the countries of advanced capitalism in Western Europe and North America. In fact, the share of the national income which accrues to property owners of all kinds is probably considerably larger in countries like Mexico, Chile, India, Turkey or Persia than in the United States or in Britain. While average income per head in the underdeveloped countries is low therefore, there is a small minority of individuals whose share of the national income is out of all proportion to their number and in addition a high percentage of that income tends to be spent on personal consumption rather than be saved. The extent to which this is so in a country depends partly on the efficacy of the taxation system but also on the extent to which wealth is derived from the land or from industrial or commercial enterprises. The owners of land are high spenders and as a consequence a high ratio of resources of these countries is often devoted to unnecessary consumption. Similarly, in countries which are in the earlier stages of industrialization, where fortunes made in the course of industrial development virtually escape taxation, a much higher proportion of profits is devoted to personal consumption. This is borne out by the national income statistics of Chile (one of the developing countries for which adequate national income statistics exist) which in the 1950s showed that the personal consumption of the property-owning sector accounted for over 20 per cent of gross national product.

The level of national income per head in the underdeveloped countries therefore is not a good indication of taxable capacity. If a large part of a country's resources is taken up in inessential or luxury consumption, then there is plenty of scope for increasing the tax revenue. For example the taxation potential of the semi-developed countries of Latin America (with income per head of $ 200–$ 300 a year) must be as great as that of the highly developed countries, although their actual tax revenue is approximately one half as large—e.g., 9 per cent of gross national product in Mexico, 14 per cent in Chile, 10 per cent in Brazil and 16 per cent in Venezuela.

The efficient utilization of the tax potential of an underdeveloped country raises problems which vary with the circumstances of each country but there are certain fundamental changes in the taxation systems of all these countries which, if adopted, would make it possible to increase public revenue and reduce some of the inequalities which now exist.

The Importance of Agricultural Taxation

Developing economies typically have a high proportion of their total population in the subsistence agricultural sector—varying between 80–90 per cent in the poorest and most backward countries to 40–60 per cent in the more developed areas, compared to 10 per cent or less in the agricultural sector in the highly developed economies. The proportion of the population engaged in the provision of food supplies for domestic use is therefore a rough guide to the stage of development of a country. As development proceeds this proportion is steadily reduced and the proportion engaged in secondary and tertiary industries steadily increased. This means that the proportion of food sold outside the agricultural sector must also be increased to make expansion of the non-agricultural sector possible; but as post-war experience has shown, an increase in agricultural output does not occur automatically with the process of development. The agricultural sector does not respond to economic incentives in the same way as industry or commerce; the reaction in the agricultural sector may be the opposite of what is required; that is, a price rise may reduce, not increase output. In such circumstances, additional taxes levied on the agricultural sector act as an incentive to economic growth. The economic history of countries with such widely differing social institutions and economic circumstances as the Soviet Union or Japan show similar dependence on heavy agricultural taxation to enlarge the supply of "savings" required for economic development.

At present, however, with the exception of plantation agriculture, the agricultural or subsistence sector in underdeveloped countries virtually escapes taxation. An annual tax on land expressed as a percentage of the value of the produce per acre is one of the most ancient forms of taxation in both Europe and Asia and up to the early part of this century it provided the principal source of revenue in countries in the Middle East, Asia and many other areas. It is still collected in most underdeveloped countries, but owing to political pressures combined with monetary changes, its yield has been reduced from the traditional one-tenth of the value of the produce of the land to negligible proportions; its current yield in India is only about 1.5 per cent and in Turkey 0.2 per cent. Yet heavier agricultural taxation would, without doubt, accelerate the rate of development in the underdeveloped areas; an annual tax on land would yield not just revenue but the right kind of revenue; it would enlarge the supply of foodstuffs to urban areas and thus enable more employment to be offered outside the agricultural sector without creating inflation.   •

The main objection to the tax is that it is socially unjust in its incidence. This objection could be overcome, however, by making it progressive, and since in most of the relatively over-populated countries where land is scarce the distribution of the ownership of land is very uneven, it would be possible to exempt the very small farmer from the tax altogether and yet still collect adequate revenue from the owners of larger holdings. The problem of frequent valuations which is the basis of another objection to the tax, could be overcome by basing the tax on a combination of (a) the potential fertility of the land (assessed on more or less permanent criteria) and (b) the average value of output per acre. Such a tax would be a tax on the "potential output" of the land and would give the maximum incentive for efficient farmers to improve their land and expand their output. In addition a tax of this kind would encourage the transfer of land ownership from the inefficient to the efficient and in so doing raise the average productivity of land.

Taxation of Non-Agricultural Sectors

Failure of the developing countries to tax the agricultural sector efficiently has meant that in general a disproportionate share of the burden of taxation has fallen on the monetized or market sector. In addition the incidence of taxation in most developing countries is regressive; indirect taxes—the majority of which fall on articles of mass consumption—make up a large proportion of total revenue while far more of the direct tax revenue is obtained through tax deducted at source from wages and salaries. For although progressive income taxes and inheritance taxes exist on paper in most of the underdeveloped or semi-developed countries, there are few cases in which such taxes are effective in practice. There are a number of reasons for this, among which the following should be mentioned:

(a) Defective tax legislation. In the majority of cases, there is no single comprehensive tax on all income but the so-called "cedular" system of income taxation is in use. This system has administrative advantages but while it imposes separate taxes on different sources of income, it leaves many important sources entirely untaxed.

(b) Anonymity in the ownership of wealth—mainly "bearer" shares in the case of companies, or the system of "benami" in India. This legal loophole prevents any effective taxation of incomes derived from capital or of wealth (either in the form of inheritance taxes or of annual taxes on capital).

(c) Inefficient (and perhaps corrupt) administration which prevents the enforcement of the existing tax provisions.

As a consequence of these it is probable that the typical underdeveloped country collects in direct taxation (excluding wages and salaries) no more than a small fraction of what is legally due. (Such a broad generalization would naturally have to be qualified when applied to individual countries or regions). Successful attempts have been made by some countries in recent years to improve both legislation and tax administration, but unfortunately in others the situation is going from bad to worse brought about by the steady erosion of ancient taxes or the paralyzing effect of corruption.

The effective administration of a tax on the income and wealth of individuals or corporations requires a carefully thought out legal code and a corps of capable and honest administrators. Although it may seem, and it is often argued, that simpler forms of taxation are more suitable for the less developed countries, these taxes, e.g., commodity taxes, can never succeed in mitigating growing economic inequalities or in reducing the resources devoted to socially unnecessary luxury consumption in the same way as progressive taxes on income and wealth. The same commodities are bought by people of very different means and to get maximum revenue, articles of mass consumption have to be taxed while many items bought by the wealthy cannot be effectively brought into the taxation system—for example domestic service, foreign travel, etc.

This is not to deny, however, that commodity taxes may be superior to direct taxes at some stages of economic development; for example, whenever the economy is comprised mainly of small enterprises with few employees in each. The most appropriate forms of taxation will differ as between an economy where commercial and manufacturing activities are carried on by small traders and one where they are concentrated in the hands of large scale enterprises. Insofar as commodity taxes are levied on imported and exported goods, they are often a more effective method of taxing the profits of the importer or exporter. This is particularly useful in the case where the local exporting company is a subsidiary of a foreign company, and where, therefore, export levies provide an easy means of taxing the benefits derived. On the other hand, once export duties are imposed, they may be fixed at such high levels that the development of the export industries will be impeded.

Advantages of a Value-Added Tax

At the same time a variant of the general tax on sales or on turnover which avoids their distorting effects, can provide a firm base for administration of the whole tax system. Such a tax is the value-added tax, i.e., a tax on sales less the purchases (of fuel and materials and possibly also of capital expenditure) of each enterprise. This has already proved highly successful in France and Brazil and is now being introduced in a number of other countries (such as Denmark and Sweden).

A tax of this kind may be looked upon in two ways. On the one hand, it could be regarded as a proportionate direct tax on the gross income generated by each enterprise or as a universal and uniform tax on that part of the national expenditure which represents consumption. As a tax on consumption expenditure generally it would have the advantage that it would not (or need not) enter into the costs of either investment or exports.

From the macro-economic point of view the over-all incidence of the value-added tax may differ little from that of the corporation tax. Both tend equally to be "shifted" but the incidence between firms is different in the two cases. The former would have the effect of encouraging the growth of the efficient firms while penalizing the inefficient, because with a value-added tax of equivalent wield the firms which pay most of the profits tax would improve their position and those that pay little profits tax would carry more of the burden. A system of a high rate of profits tax combined with numerous exemptions is really a tax on marginal profits and has the effect of shielding inefficient units from competition. The introduction of a value-added tax would therefore improve the allocative efficiency of the economy.

Such a tax also has the added advantage of being self-reinforcing, and is a potent weapon against tax evasion. A universal comprehensive value-added tax would make it possible to obtain continuing comprehensive information on the sales and purchases of each enterprise, thus providing a framework which would be the basis for the administration of all direct taxes. Apart from this, the system would also provide an invaluable aid to economic planning and forecasting. It could provide an up-to-date transactions matrix of the whole economy in a degree of detail, the importance of which to economic planning and policy generally needs no emphasis. Its use for the latter purpose may not be too difficult with the aid of modern electronic computers.

Taxes on Income and Wealth

The importance of progressive taxes on income and wealth are more clearly seen in semi-developed countries where large scale industrial and commercial enterprises operate and a wealthy domestic capitalist class exists. The detailed requirements of tax reform vary considerably with the circumstances of each particular country but as a result of studying the problem in a number of countries, I am convinced that, in all countries which have attained the stage of development at which the need for an effective system of direct personal taxation arises, there are no insuperable technical or administrative obstacles to its introduction.

Nor is it tenable to argue, as is sometimes done, that progressive taxation of industrial and commercial wealth slows down the rate of development by reducing both the means and the incentive to accumulation. While it is true that in the United States and Britain progressive taxation was imposed only after the process of industrialization was largely completed, it does not follow that if progressive taxation had been imposed earlier, the course of development in these countries would have been very different. Profits, it is true, have always been the main source of industrial and commercial capital accumulation but experience has shown that taxes on profits affect consumption out of profits far more than business savings. Progressive taxation, far from slowing down the rate of economic development, may do the opposite; the kind of growth that occurs when a large part of a country's investment is in industries which mainly cater for the rich, merely serves to make the rich richer and does not improve the standard of living of the mass of the population. Progressive taxation is important, therefore, as a deliberate corrective to spontaneous economic forces which produce steadily growing inequality.

An effective income tax system should, in my opinion, comprise a comprehensive income tax which would cover capital gains as well as all ordinary forms of income, including imputed rent. Exemptions (e.g., on income from government bonds) should not be allowed. In addition, the rate schedule should be simple and moderate with a small number of income brackets; the rates should move up by steps of 5 per cent (from a minimum of 10 per cent) to a maximum of 40–45 per cent. High tax rates are inefficient and relatively unproductive—they are the main reason for the process known as "tax erosion," the whittling away of the tax base by concession and exemptions of numerous kinds.

Apart from a tax levied on the income of individuals and of companies, to make direct taxation effective, taxes on wealth must be administered conjointly with income tax. Different individuals possess disposable wealth and money income in widely differing proportions and a tax assessed on net wealth which is additional to income tax is a more equitable method of allowing for such differences. Taxes on wealth may take two forms:

    (1)   An annual tax on net wealth (at present in use in India and Ceylon as well as in the Scandinavian countries) which is appropriate for tapping additional taxable capacity inherent in the possession of wealth as such, in a manner that is fairer and more effective than the differentiation between earned

and unearned income. (A combined system of an annual tax on wealth and on income also has the advantage of making tax evasion and concealment more difficult).

(2) Inheritance tax—ideally a single tax on all gratuitous transfers payable by the individual recipient of the gift, bequest, or inheritance levied on a progressive scale dependent on the total wealth of the donee. Taxation based on the wealth of the recipient rather than the donor is obviously fairer but this method does raise considerable administrative difficulties, as also does the effective taxation of income derived from property. These difficulties are by no means insuperable, however, in this age of technology.

Taxation of Foreign Enterprises

An important problem in many of the developing countries is the tax treatment of foreign enterprises. There are two separate problems which must be faced in this connection:

(1) the extent to which underdeveloped countries should offer tax concessions (immunity from taxation, etc.) so that foreign capital is attracted to their country and

(2) the most appropriate method of taxing foreign enterprises when they are not exempt.

First then, the question of tax concessions to foreign investors. As a means of paying for greatly enlarged imports of equipment and materials in the early stages of industrialization, foreign investment is often indispensable as these imports are needed before there can be any increase in export capacity. In addition, foreign enterprise is often essential for importing the know-how necessary for the efficient development of local industries. For many countries, too, it is the production and export of valuable minerals found in their area which is their best hope of generating the economic surplus needed for their internal development. That the production and, possibly the processing, of such minerals must be encouraged is appreciated by the governments of the developing countries and so is the fact that the finance and expertise must come from foreign concerns. However, in the case of many important minerals the total amount of investment undertaken by large international concerns will depend on their overall view of world market requirements; competition between the developing countries in the concessions offered is not likely to increase this total. While one country may with advantage offer special concessions to attract a larger share of foreign capital, competition from other countries, each hoping for a larger slice of such investments, will cause special concessions to be copied, and they will largely cancel out without any compensating benefit to the countries concerned.

This reasoning does not apply, of course, to concessions offered to foreign enterprises for the purpose of developing domestic industries serving, mainly, the internal market. Tax concessions granted in such cases may well increase the total flow of international investment, i.e., a particular project such as the development of a local textile mill may well be undertaken when tax concessions are offered whereas it would not be considered without them.

The second problem, that of the best method of taxing foreign enterprises, is a more complex one. An export duty is, of course, an effective form of taxation but one that may inhibit development if carried beyond certain limits. A far less discouraging method from the point of view of the international investor is a tax on profits since in the latter case, the liability to tax depends on the success of the operations. The difficulty for the taxing country, however, is to know what the true profit of a company is, for it is well known that an international concern operating through a chain of subsidiaries in different territories can easily "shift" its profit from one place to another merely by changing the price which the subsidiaries charge to one another. There will be little incentive for "profit shifting" so long as profits everywhere are subject to tax and the rates of tax in each of the countries concerned are not very different. Since the war, however, there has been an increasing use of "tax havens" —international companies have established associated companies or subsidiaries in territories where profits are not subject to tax (or only at nominal rates) or where profits earned in overseas operations are not charged against resident companies. "Tax havens" combined with "profit shifting" allow international concerns to escape a good deal of the taxation of profits both in the country of their domicile and in the countries in which they operate.

The best manner in which problems of taxation of profits of foreign companies, and also the question of tax concessions, could be dealt with would be through international cooperation between the developing countries, and also between the developing and the advanced countries. It would be greatly to the advantage of the developing countries as a group if they could agree on a uniform treatment of tax concessions and at the same time reach some agreement on how to deal with the problems of profits taxation so that companies operating within their territories make an appropriate contribution toward the public revenue.

Problems of Administration

It is not only reform of the tax laws themselves, however, that is required to improve the revenue position of the developing countries. Tax laws, to be effective, must be capable of being enforced and this can only be done if there is an able administration consisting of persons of competence and high integrity. Many underdeveloped countries suffer both from an insufficient number of personnel, and the relatively low ability of personnel, in the tax administration departments. Persons of ability and integrity can only be found for these jobs if the pay, status and prospects of promotion are high enough to attract the best talent and also at a level sufficient to establish the professional standards and etiquette associated with a public service that enjoys a privileged social status. Any additional outlay incurred in improving the status and pay of the officials of the revenue department is likely to yield a very high return in terms of increased revenue.

DISCUSSION

Taxation Should be a Stimulus

A land tax can be used to precipitate land reform. The fiscal system has to be simple. Important also is what the money is used for after the tax has been collected.

Professor Kaldor said that the use of taxation to reduce economic inequality not only mobilizes more resources but, diminishing the income and power of the big landowners, stimulates agricultural productivity. Israel has achieved a record pace of economic development. "I submit to you that this process would have been quite impossible had society in Israel not been set up from the beginning so as to provide social cohesion. This was done by shunning rather than encouraging large accumulations of individual wealth, whether on the land or in other sectors, and by maintaining a considerable economic equality, despite the fact that this society was, in terms of income, at a moderate level of development or underdevelopment to begin with."

In feudal societies such as exist in Latin America, "when you see progress, it is progress of the wrong kind. You have a privileged elite which gets richer, whose living standards are growing, whose wealth is growing, whose capital is growing, and all this is reflected in the national income statistics. But as far as the great masses of the people are concerned, no noticeable progress is taking place. Their housing standards do not improve, their consumption standards do not improve—in fact, they are not participating in economic progress."

The question is, can this situation be changed, and if so, how? There are technical problems, but they are small, and soluble. Needed is the political will for change. "In my experience as a tax adviser to the Government of Turkey, I put forward a scheme which was in my view eminently sensible, to finance a progressive tax on the potential value of the land, varying with the size of the landholdings. The ruling parties—not one, not two, but three such parties—would not hear of it, and in no case countenance it."

Land reform and land taxation are complementary. Progressive agricultural taxation reduces land values. It makes the big landowners sell at least a part of their holdings. It makes for freer markets in land. The lack of economic progress in many LDCs "has nothing to do with their commercial or industrial sectors. It is a superficial view to say that lack of industrialization is the trouble. It is agricultural stagnation which is the trouble. If you can get rid of agricultural stagnation, then marketing centers will bring an accelerated rate of industrialization, and an accelerated rate of capital accumulation also, from internal sources. Competitive conditions cannot be achieved in agriculture as they are in industry, if the soil is already owned by certain people and nobody else can try his hand at farming."

One way of assessing the land tax is to let the owner do his own valuation. People should be given an option to buy the land if it is assessed too low—and then the owner should be allowed to re-value the land to beat that option. Such a scheme incidentally allows the emergence of a professional class of valuers, who can perform the useful service of making up-dated land valuations.

A country's success in development does not depend on whether it possesses natural resources—witness the progress of Japan. "What matters is what sort of government you have. If you have a good government, every other obstacle to economic development can sooner or later be overcome." Western Europe and North America succeeded where South America, Asia and Africa failed, and "I am absolutely convinced that the long-run explanation is not climate, geology, geography, the habits and thoughts of the population, or their inlaid abilities. The answer is to be sought in the nature of the governments they have."

Mr. Pierre Uri, of France, said that the taxable capacity of a country is a function of inequality in income distribution. The need is "to encourage the right kind of savings and investment, not as against consumption, but as against sumptuary consumption and wasteful investment." We should do away with the unitary tax idea, using instead a combination of value added taxes, income taxes, capital gains taxes and inheritance taxes, "which provide a kind of mutual control on their assessment and collection."

Mr. I Gal-Edd, of Israel, cautioned that when advising that the LDCs copy the tax structure of the developed countries, it should be borne in mind that the developed countries are not themselves agreed on what is the best system. Professor Kaldor's own country has not adopted the value-added tax.

As concerns the LDCs, small farmers and traders have not the bookkeeping arrangements for this tax. Mr. Gal-Edd recommends instead a kind of standardized income tax, based, not on the actual earnings achieved by the particular small undertaking, but on a formula for calculating what would be the normal income of such a business.

The standardized tax is a way of getting revenue when the record keeping that would be desirable just does not exist. The LDCs could consult on methods of drawing up this special kind of assessment, "and perhaps could also consult together as to whether it would be possible to introduce some simple form of record keeping, which would be of value to all of us."

Mr. Gal-Edd favors levying taxes where the revenue can be got. Reacting to the emphasis placed by Professor Kaldor and Mr. Uri on direct taxation, he commented: "There is too little regard to the fact that the customs and purchase tax systems do represent a large proportion of the taxes which are collectable in the LDCs. It does not really solve their problems to suggest that other forms of taxation can be used to replace these very large sources."

He concluded by quoting the reaction of a person from an oil country after a lecture recommending the introduction of income tax: "Ten years ago the only income in my country was from royalties. The royalties went to the ruling classes who bought Cadillac cars. Today we have an income tax system. The income tax goes to the ruling classes who buy Cadillac cars." Mr. Gal-Edd underlined that a mere change in the system of taxation does nothing unless you have done something to change the allocation of the income.

Using Revenue Wisely

> Taxation should not be such as to discourage investment. It should not bear heavily on small farmers. Agricultural reform makes necessary credit for the new farm proprietors.

Dr. Stephen Enke, of the U.S., said, "Where there is a fair degree of inequality in income size, which is the normal case, usually more taxes can be collected than people often seem to believe.

"In fact if a country cannot finance its own government, it hardly warrants political independence, and in practice it will soon be a protectorate or colony again."

He took issue with Professor Kaldor's assumption that governments are bound to use fiscal revenues wisely. In a study of several countries over a period of ten years Dr. Enke found that for every extra $ 10 of revenue collected during that period, only an extra $1 or $2 went to productive investment, the rest being devoted to transfer payments (social welfare, army, police, etc.). Thus bigger taxes do not necessarily mean bigger public investment.

If a government takes more taxes from investment-prone, well-to-do people who have a 30 per cent propensity to invest while the government has a 10 or 15 per cent propensity to invest, then the country's investment has been quantitatively reduced.

Whether governments spend these funds wisely has to be studied, but one area is neglected in Dr. Enke's estimation: planned parenthood. Investigations he made lead to the conclusion that the investment of 10 cents a year per head of the population on birth control can reduce the birth-rate by one-third over a decade. "Various calculations suggest that each dollar invested in reducing the number of births may have an impact on *per capita* income over a period of years anywhere up to a hundred or so times more than a dollar of resources invested in factories, steel plants, irrigation systems and the like."

Dr. Enke presses the need for simple taxes. Complicated systems that require highly qualified tax office personnel will use up educated manpower needed elsewhere. Exports should be taxed on value and not on the profits of the exporter, because price fluctuations in minerals, for example, make profits vary enormously at different times.

Mr. Cosme Hounkponou, of Dahomey, maintained that large-scale agriculture can be taxed but to impose levies on farmers at their beginnings "could break the eggs before they are hatched." There should be a tax on the proprietors of uncultivated land.

He accentuated the need for civic education in fiscal matters, to get across the connection between tax payments and the proper functioning of the State. Chronic deficits are caused in some countries by the accumulation of unrequited tax dues that in due course become irrecoverable.

Mr. Bawa Sandani Mankoubi, of Togo, suggested that instead of choosing between direct and indirect taxation, the accent be placed on the relative utility of alternative taxes in tapping new revenue.

He reinforced the claim that fiscal techniques should be simple by recalling that in many LDCs the expatriate personnel that used to run the tax departments in colonial times have gone home. Complicated taxes could well cost more to administer than the revenue they collect.

Dr. P. N. C. Okigbo, of Nigeria, thought there was some danger in Professor Kaldor's verdict that a price rise in agriculture may cause a fall in output and vice versa. A decline in prices can accelerate harvesting perhaps, because the people need more money. But this does not necessarily apply to new planting, and in West Africa a price decline has almost invariably retarded new plantings. So before adopting novel prescriptions for agricultural taxation, one has to be very careful about the effect they might have on new investment.

Agricultural communities in West Africa are relatively highly taxed, owing to the use of the marketing boards as a fiscal instrument. They have often withheld as much as half the export returns from the producers as a reserve against fluctuations. Of course, most of the reserves have disappeared by now, owing to the continuous decline in export prices.

Mr. Oumarou Sidikou, of Niger, expressed his opposition to increasing the tax burden on agriculture, which is too poor in arid lands to carry new imposts. A progressive agricultural tax is hard to apply owing to difficulties in evaluating cultivated areas and determining what were the selling prices. As a transitional measure, the Niger administration fixed the tax at cantonal level by making a rough inventory of agricultural wealth within each canton. The distribution of the tax as between individuals is left to the cantons, which are handling it as a kind of poll tax, until they become equipped in the future to assess family incomes.

Mr. Emmanuel Oudraogo, of Upper Volta: While it is said that the industrial revolution in England, Japan and even Russia was accomplished on the backs of the peasants, this cannot be done to the same extent in the LDCs of today.

Fiscal revenue is no longer intended merely for assuring the operation of administrative departments, but is now also utilized for modifying the country's economic structure. Hence the new investment codes, and the advantages offered to enterprises from abroad. Foreign companies are reluctant to come forward and undertake industrial and commercial activity unless they are guaranteed political security and a financial return.

Hon. Mwai Kibaki, of Kenya, said that the LDCs have inherited a tax structure and a tax administration. If it seems to work, "that in itself becomes the political argument why it should not be changed."

In making land reforms, it happens that "only the class of people who own land at that time may have the capital to buy more land. You do not really want your land tax to force land to be sold just among those who are rich, as would tend to happen. Therefore, if you are really going to have the social revolution that Dr. Kaldor suggests, it is essential that the government or any other credit organization provides the capital to those who want to develop land and put it to productive use."

Also needed are agricultural extension services, if the land is going to be passed on to people who were formerly agricultural laborers, or just unemployed.

Disagreeing with another speaker, Mr. Kibaki was emphatic that rich people must undergo forced savings through taxation, because what Dr. Enke fails to realize is that in these parts persons with means are not interested in creative investment, and the "money does not fructify in their pockets." Mr. Kibaki concurred with Dr. Enke that governments do not necessarily invest the money as usefully as might be. In order to direct capital to investment, governments must go into joint ventures—again, despite Professor Galbraith's opinion that governments should not get involved in public ownership.

Mr. S. Souvanlasy, of Laos, addressed several questions to Professor Kaldor. LDCs need funds not only for administration and investment in production, but also for non-lucrative placements in the development of basic amenities, like schools, hospitals and roads. In such a case, do fiscal burdens act as an obstacle to private investment?

Some countries do not have exact information on incomes, and the taxes are often based on appearances, which leads to an incoherent and inequitable fiscal system. What is the most appropriate fiscal mechanism for such a territory?

A problem particular to Laos is that a part of the population is subject to Communist propaganda, which aims to prevent people from paying taxes. What is the best administrative approach in the face of that problem? Mr. Souvanlasy feels that the answer is to opt for showing a quick return to the affected inhabitants for their taxes, by concentrating on the construction of roads, schools and other visible infrastructure amenities. The Laos government avoids personalizing taxes, and therefore focuses its program on indirect imposts, which make up 80 per cent of budget revenue.

Mr. Phan Thul, of Cambodia, added his support to the view that agriculture supports the biggest part of the population and affords the lowest incomes, so that raising taxes in this sector would have adverse results including unfavorable political repercussions.

Rural indebtedness is widespread. Extending Professor Kaldor's argument, usurious exactions should stimulate farmers to raise their productivity; but it hasn't happened so far. Farm workers are already migrating to the towns, where the meanest employment offers them a better living. To raise their fiscal dues would discourage agriculture further.

Mr. Thul advocated a policy of expansion, sponsoring a better allocation of land use with generous agriculture credit and government-planned development. During this phase an indirect tax on the sale of agricultural produce would be better than a levy that hits the farmer directly.

There are many factors to distract owners of capital from productive investment—the lack of a capital market, the possibility of making usurious loans, of speculating in trade and property, of exporting the capital abroad or of indulging in sumptuary consumption. Therefore the tax system should be supple. It should avoid being too progressive when applied to productive enterprises—which need to be fostered tactfully. On the other hand, it ought to be heavy on property deals when it comes to penalizing speculation. As concerns the need for social justice, indirect taxes should be kept progressive by applying them heavily to luxury consumption.

Mr. Afxentios Afxentiou, of Cyprus, underlined that taxation is important for mobilizing funds in many LDCs precisely because an organized capital market does not exist. Not uncommonly, local capital is placed overseas to assist in effect the development of the advanced countries. "In such a case, the question might arise: why offer incentives to attract foreign capital, when we know that our own capital is being exported?"

High prices have increased farm output in Cyprus—and farmers should be taxed on their swollen earnings. But excessive tax rates sometimes achieve nothing, because "the higher the tax rates, the higher the tax evasions." Lowering taxes can in certain circumstances increase revenue.

Dr. Y. P. Pant, of Nepal, agreed with Dr. Kaldor's predilection for simple, comprehensive taxes. As for the capital gains tax, it is too complex, requiring a check on all property transactions, valuations of all taxable property, and so on.

Tax paying has to become a matter of habit. At the beginning it is a hardship. The masses should be introduced to it gradually, as part of a pattern of social, political and economic reform.

"Fiscal Dumping"

Tax the means of production—land, building and tools—to get the best use out of them. An Investment Code is needed to fix the concessions necessary for encouraging foreign investment.

Mr. Pierre Mendès-France was in accord with Professor Kaldor that taxation must be simple, even though this necessity may lead to formulations which are not altogether satisfactory—though Mr. Mendès-France stressed they must always be such as are in line with the over-all objectives.

What is the main objective? The fiscal system must stimulate, it must encourage and aid production. So it is a good idea to tax the means of production in order to make their owners use them more actively.

He recalled that in eighteenth century France there was a tax on land, especially fertile land. This levy turned out to be useful at the time for promoting agricultural development. The system penalized landholders who left their property barren, or who did not make an optimum use of it.

This applies even to water, according to Mr. Mendès-France. In a certain previously colonial territory, water made available at the public expense through dams and channels was offered to big foreign plantation-owners almost free of charge. Today the country is independent and these properties have returned to the nation—yet the water is still distributed free of charge which means it is wrongly used and even wasted. Water is an asset, and should be paid for at least according to its cost.

The payment of taxes *in specie* is desirable, because it helps monetize the economy. However in rural areas where dues are necessarily minimal, it is possible to supplement them by contributions made in kind. Between agricultural seasons, work could be mobilized without pay for local tasks such as road construction, drainage, digging a well, measures against erosion, and even putting up a school building.

Mr. Mendès-France went on to speak about "fiscal dumping," whereby countries compete with each other in making concessions to attract outside investors, so that a perfectly beneficial project can be watered down to the point where it makes almost no positive contribution to the local economy. As a result, a country like France makes an effort to aid a particular underdeveloped country, only to find in the end that the only beneficiary is a foreign business company which is anything but underdeveloped. An international institution like the U.N. or the World Bank ought to work out an Investment Code, to lay down rules for the import of capital in the LDCs.

* * *

Professor Kaldor, in closing the debate, reaffirmed his belief in simplicity, asserting that he favors a personal expenditure tax—but considers it inconveniently complicated for the LDCs.

Concerning the tax on land, he went on, "I did not mean to imply that my recommendations on agricultural taxation are in any way dependent on some perverse relationship between agricultural prices and agricultural output. A tax on land has by no means the same effect as a fall in price in the same circumstances. When there is a fall in price, the elasticity of supply is a combined result of income and substitution effects, to speak the technical language of economists. The land tax, however, is concerned with the income effect and not the substitution effect."

The land tax falls on the owner, not the cultivator. It applies first of all to countries with big landowners, that do not use this asset properly, as in Latin America and some Middle East countries. Also imposing taxes at the source, where the profits are earned (as in the case of the land tax) gets the revenue before the capital can be exported. Professor Kaldor pressed for the land tax as an ideal solution for dealing with small farmers as well—and perhaps a wealth tax could be used for small traders. "It is easier to tax the small trader on his wealth, which is a tangible thing, than on his income."

Concerning Dr. Enke's preference for leaving money to be used in private investment, instead of siphoning it off into the hands of the government, Professor Kaldor commented: "Private savings may be high, but if they are invested in millionaire flats and luxury yachts and other things, they have not got the quality which public investment may have in schools and hospitals, even though the sums may be, as a proportion of total expenditure, smaller in the one case than in the other."

Dr. Enke recommended taxing exports rather than the profits of exporting companies. The trouble is that "a country which imposes heavier duties than another country on exports, prices itself out of the world market." The departure of experienced fiscal administrators at the end of colonial rule can be repaired with the aid of technical assistance. The marketing boards in West Africa mentioned by Dr. Okigbo are an excellent example of the use of taxation to apply incentives. The fact that the grower could take his cocoa to the nearest depot and get a steady 60 shillings a bag for it—whether the price was above or below that figure—constituted an outstanding stimulus to production.

The value-added tax has been labelled as too difficult, yet it is not really more complex than the turnover tax, which has been found acceptable in a number of LDCs. Each business has to deduct the tax from its sales, and subtract from that the tax which had already been paid on its purchases. The beauty of the value-added tax is that each business must collect a slip of paper from its suppliers attesting to the tax already paid—"and that makes it more difficult for each business to evade the tax it is supposed to deduct from its sales."

13 OBJECTIVES OF TAX POLICY

By RALPH K. DAVIDSON

Associate Director, Humanities and Social Sciences, Rockefeller Foundation, U.S.A.

Taxation policy, like other forms of social and economic policy, reflects and expresses the general economic views, social aspirations and goals of the citizens of the country; it reflects also the country's social and cultural institutions. Each country does have a unique set of social, political and economic institutions, therefore it is not possible to design a general tax structure that is ideal for all developing states. There are, however, some general observations that are relevant for most developing countries.

The aspirations of the people of developing states are clearly focused on economic betterment. The achievement of a maximum rate of economic growth to provide the basis for a better social, cultural and political life has now become a central objective everywhere in the world. The central issue of economic development is the problem of mobilizing all allocating resources for growth in such a manner that growth becomes self-sustaining. The rise in the aspirations of the people has been accompanied by a belief in the desirability and possibility of economic improvement as a result of increased governmental activity. There has been a very rapid expansion in the belief that many things cannot be left to the workings of the underdeveloped market system but rather that it is the duty of the government to provide the desired goods and services, either by purchase or by production and to carry through substantial programs of redistribution of real income between different sectors of the society. Accompanying the increasing reliance on governmental activity has been a very rapid increase of population[1] and an emergence of national governments which are responsive to public pressures for more social goods resulting in a rapid rise in government expenditures.[2]

---

[1] "Relatively rapid population growth has been a salient feature of all developing regions," *World Economic Survey, 1963* (New York: United Nations, 1964), p. 20. The rate of population growth during the decade 1950–1960 varied from as high as 2.8 per cent in Latin America to as low as 0.5 in the European Free Trade Association area. See also the *United Nations Statistical Yearbook 1963* (New York: United Nations, 1964), pp. 23–41 for individual country data and p. 43 for area summary data.

[2] *United Nations Statistical Yearbook, 1963, op. cit.,* pp. 565–625.

The goal of a rising real level of income could be achieved by a fuller and more efficient use of existing resources including manpower, a greater rate of investment and an injection of more capital, a shift in investment from largely non-productive to productive investment or the introduction of more efficient kinds of investment goods. The additional resources required to stimulate growth, maintain a high level of income or more productive investment can be acquired by an economy either through bringing into production resources that are currently not being fully utilized or by reducing consumption expenditure, including both private and public, and transferring the resources into investment, or by receiving additional resources from abroad either by way of gifts or borrowing so that there is a net addition to the resources available to the developing states, thereby enabling them to carry out the programs of investment while still maintaining the current level of consumption. However, the amount of outside resources available to the developing states by way of aid or loan is relatively small, and the bulk of the growth needs must be satisfied from internal sources.[3]

Tax Structure a Tool for Growth

Within the context of stimulating a higher rate of growth, the tax system is an exceedingly important tool which can be utilized by the developing states in such a fashion as to stimulate economic development by channelling more resources into more productive use and thus leading to a higher rate of growth of the economy as a whole. In the developing states, taxation has been assigned a far more positive role than in already developed countries in stimulating the process of technological change, investment and capital formation. Particularly important has been social investment which many would argue is an absolutely essential ingredient of economic development, especially the provision of education for the society at large.

In the past there has been a variety of so-called goals for tax policy, including allocative efficiency, economic growth, stability, full employment and a redistribution of income in accord with some social policy. Not all of these may be consistent at any one time. It has

[3] An interesting exercise in the *United Nations World Economic Survey, 1963,* suggests that if present trends continue, the gap on current account of the developing countries will rise to $20 billion by 1970 (pp. 29–41). From 1951–55 to 1960–62 the net annual flow of long-term official and private funds from the developed market economies and multilateral agencies increased from $2.6 billion to $6.0 billion. *Ibid.,* p. 225.

been argued that in the circumstances today, the goal of economic growth and development is tending to receive a much greater weight than previously. The objectives of growth, however, need to be weighed against other social objectives, such as fairness or equity, acceptability, simplicity, efficiency and full employment.

The tax structure is of key importance in the drive for development. Each of the developing states must provide its own answer to the question: can its tax structure be designed to stimulate the growth of its economy in a manner which is economically and politically feasible, subject to the limitation of administrative feasibility and a general lack of relevant data. As we have pointed out, these additional resources needed for development may come from increased internal savings, that is, reduced internal consumption, from external sources, from foreign borrowing or aid, from reallocation internally from less to more productive investment and from bringing previously idle resources into productive uses. Within the market structure, taxation affects the mobilization and allocation of resources by transferring funds to the government to cover government expenditures and by influencing decisions concerning savings and consumption, exports and imports, investment and industrialization and a host of other individual and group decisions which determine the use of resources. Financial transfers are only a means to an end—the shifting of real resources to meet the needs of growth in the economy. The tax system can be utilized to provide incentives to shift economic behavior in such a way as to stimulate economic growth, such as providing incentives for desired actions—to induce more resources to enter the market, to increase savings, to increase investment for growth, to work longer periods and/or more efficiently.

Because of the rising demand for government provision of goods and services and social overhead, it is clear that to meet the long-run growth of government expenditure, it is desirable that the tax system as a whole should be income-elastic in character, that is, that as income grows the government receipts should grow at a higher rate. In order to achieve this, the tax structure could be so arranged that each individual tax would have its yield increase faster than the increase in national income, that is, on the pattern of a progressive income tax rather than a poll tax. Or the tax structure could be so arranged that individual taxes whose yield responds proportionally faster than the rise in income could predominate in the over-all structure of taxes.

Basis for a Successful Tax Policy

Very broadly conceived, the task that faces the developing states consists in first measuring the existing resources available and actually disposable for the program of increasing *per capita* real income. Secondly, the states must find ways of measuring or assessing the wide-ranging claims on the available resources. Thirdly, the states must outline the alternative ways in which the demands can be reconciled with the resources available in such a manner as to give the optimum integrated development program consistent with the social goals of income distribution and maintenance of consumption. It has often been argued that sacrifices will only be made if it can be seen that the gain will accrue to those who are making the sacrifices.

A successful tax policy must of necessity be based on factual knowledge concerning not only the growing real income, the government expenditure policies, but also a good factual knowledge of the inter-sectoral relations of the economy, the key flows of goods and services between agricultural, industrial, commercial exports and imports. In the absence of such information, tax policy must be based upon guesswork which may or may not be appropriate to the existing situation.

The enforcement of the tax system needs to be carefully examined to eliminate inefficiency and dishonest practices. In many cases additional revenue can be raised without increasing tax rates by administering the existing system more efficiently and honestly. But administrative skills are scarce and expensive, indicating that the system should be designed with the scarcity of administrative skill in mind as well as the low level of literacy and record keeping in many of the developing states. As a general principle, one can say the tax system needs to be administered efficiently and honestly with the goal of raising the necessary revenue with a minimum of real cost, at the same time providing the maximum incentive for growth possible. In many instances the social and political structure is of such a nature and the shortage of administrative skills is so great that a complex and comprehensive tax structure simply cannot operate within the existing social conditions of many of the developing states.

If the tax structure is income-elastic, that is, arranged in such a manner that receipts increase at a rate faster than national income, we immediately face the problem that the yield is likely to be elastic downward as well as upward; that is, if income falls, yields may very well fall faster. Fluctuations of this kind are to be expected in many of the developing states with their substantial dependence on exports of primary products.[4]

Another difficulty encountered in framing the tax structure is that the type of tax or structure of tax which most successfully diverts to the government an increasing portion of national income or, as we could state it, a portion of the rising gains of real income, is a type that will most likely interfere with incentives needed for growth. The difficulty with incentives is encountered most strongly with direct taxation rather than indirect but, as has been pointed out from time to time, it also occurs in the use of indirect taxation where the ability of producers to buy desired consumption goods might very well be a strong incentive to enter the market on an increasing scale.[5] In addition, the tax structure itself in a developing state normally must be such that it cannot have a high degree of perfection, and it must be relatively simple, in order to operate with greatest efficiency in an economy that normally has a relatively low level of literary and record keeping, inadequate numbers of trained tax personnel, limited use of the credit system, a substantial subsistence sector in the over-all economy, perhaps in many of the countries an unsatisfactory land titles situation and a general difficulty in assessing the exact amount of income, the exact amount of wealth, or the exact increase for a particular year.

Direct and Indirect Taxes

At present the developing states seem to rely most heavily upon indirect taxes.[6] However, with the growing demand for social investment and rising government expenditures,[7] it has seemed to be inevitable that the tax authorities must look to the day when they

---

[4] *Ibid.*, p. 14, 9/10 of the exports of the developing countries consist of primary commodities. See also discussion on stabilization, pp. 140–174.

[5] P. T. Bauer, "The Economic Development of Nigeria," *Journal of Political Economy* (Chicago: The University of Chicago Press) LXIII (October, 1955), 399–408.

[6] For example, in 1963 Bolivia received 72% of its government receipts from indirect taxes; Ceylon, 66%; Ghana, 65%; Uganda, 50%; Sudan, 51%; and Kenya, 47%. Other developing states relied equally heavily on indirect taxes. See *U.N. Statistical Yearbook, 1963.*

[7] For the same six countries, but slightly differing time periods, the increase in government expenditure has been:
Bolivia, 1956–1963, 731%; Ceylon, 1954–1963, 114%; Ghana, 1956–1963, 79%; Uganda, 1957–1963, 42%; Sudan, 1954–1963, 270% and Kenya, 1957–1963, 27%. *U.N. Statistical Yearbook, 1963.*

can develop an efficient system of direct taxation—some form of either an income or an expenditure tax in combination with taxes on capital gains, wealth and gifts. This, however, must remain in the future for many countries. Thus far an expenditure tax, although the logical grounds for it are strong, has been ruled out on the grounds of administrative complexity.

Income tax

In the developing states there is great difficulty in defining and measuring income for the country as a whole as well as for many of the individuals who make it up. Nevertheless, for the top income and wage-earner groups that do have a standard of literacy and record keeping, particularly the employees of the government and of the large companies, an income tax is certainly feasible and continues to be utilized extensively. The danger here is that with the relatively high standard of record keeping among this group, the actual tax incidence may be proportionately higher than among other groups where tax collection is less because of the lower level of record keeping. It is certainly exceedingly difficult to apply an income tax to the subsistence sector. However, in East Africa the personal tax is successfully utilized at a relatively low level with the assessment being made either by a committee of county and village officials or non-officials who are familiar with local conditions. Where the taxpayers are the typical, semi-subsistence farming group, the assessment is normally based upon external criteria such as acreage or number of cows, which are relatively easy to determine.[8]

With respect to the growing numbers of corporations in developing areas, an income tax is obviously a first choice, but again it does have some difficulty in that companies that are internationally mobile do have the choice of withdrawing their investment from one country over time and moving it to another country. They are concerned with the net return in the alternative locations, and if one country has a rate of tax very much higher than another, it will act as a deterrent to the international flow of capital to that country and thus may very well slow down development internally. In many countries not only has this been kept in mind, but investment incentives have been created such as giving tax holidays for particular kinds of investments that are declared to be in the national interest. This again creates problems as it is difficult to say what is in the national interest

---

[8] See U.K. Hicks, *Development from Below* (Oxford: Oxford University Press, 1961), for an excellent discussion of African local government and finances; also, John F. Due, *Taxation and Economic Development in Tropical Africa* (Cambridge: The M.I.T. Press, 1963).

and it does take a good bit of time to make the decision. And, equally well, there are tax losses as a result of giving the tax holidays which may not offset the additional investment gains. An additional wide variety of tax concessions has been made concerning loss-carry-forward, accelerated depreciation, tax holiday type, all of which are designed to utilize the tax system to stimulate investment and thus economic growth and development.

With the difficulty in designing and administering a system of income taxation, it is widely argued that indirect taxation should play a major role in tax structure of developing economies, and in most of the developing states indirect taxation does account for the bulk of tax revenues, largely because it is administratively much simpler to collect. The major tax sources are, in fact, import and export duties.

Over the years export taxes have served a variety of purposes, including the provision of fiscal revenue through moderate or low level export taxes, the protection of domestic industries that utilize domestic raw materials, the protection of local resources by export taxes designed to conserve the rate of utilization of natural resources, and the improvement in the quality of exports by imposing relatively substantial taxes on lower qualities of the domestic product, and use of the export tax as a means of shiponing off part of monopoly revenue profits to the local government. After the Korean war, various governments saw export taxes as a way of siphoning off part of the windfall profits due to the rise of commodity prices on the world market. This has been criticized from time to time because of the impact on the net income received by the producer and the relative influence it has on the production of cash crop for the market or subsistence crop for the producer's own use.

In some areas of production, it must be pointed out that the use of the export tax does increase the cost of production to the local producer and thus reduces the net rate of return and over time may well result in restriction or closing down of operations. This is one of the implications of export tax which must be considered in analyzing the over-all tax structure. When the burden of taxation reduces the profitability of operations in one country, the operations may very well shift to another if the particular company is internationally mobile. International mobility seems to be a characteristic of capital entrepreneurship and certainly of some kinds of labor skills that are in great demand in developing countries.

Equally important, and in many countries more important, are the indirect taxes levied on imports. The use of selective import taxes is a way of making the tax structure more progressive in that items that are consumed by higher income groups may be taxed at a higher rate. There is a difficulty, however, that taxes on incoming raw material and intermediate products that will enter into manufacturing or commerce may very well inhibit the development of local industry. Therefore in some countries it has been the practice to either eliminate the import duties on items destined to go into production domestically or to import them at a lower rate. On the other hand, there also exists a danger that high-cost, inefficient domestic producers may be sheltered by the wall of the import duty. If this is not desired, it can be eliminated through the use of excise taxes on the domestic industry which tax domestic production at the same rate as the imports and thus eliminate the inefficient domestic production. Custom duties have constituted the primary form in many countries and the whole administration of such a tax is relatively simple. In the same way, a domestic excise tax is, by and large, relatively simple in that it can be charged at the point of production.

In many of the developing states, the scope for the income tax is fairly limited. While export and import duties are very substantial, the governments must rely also substantially on excise taxes that are really taxes on consumption. As was pointed out very briefly in connection with import duty, the pattern of excise taxes can be adjusted in a way that will make them relatively progressive in that generally there are differences in consumption patterns in various income levels; the luxury goods or semi-luxuries that are consumed by wealthier individuals can be taxed at a higher rate than staple goods.

In many countries taxation based upon real property and land has been neglected as revenue sources largely, it appears, because of the political influence of landowners and owners of urban property. But equally important has been the erosion of the tax base, particularly in many Latin American countries, through inflation plus the lack of updating of the valuation base. Year after year the valuation remains the same while, for a variety of reasons, the price level rises and the real return of the tax on property and land continues to fall. There is a real problem involved in updating the valuation, but this does appear to be a source of revenue such as the Japanese economy once tapped for its development.

Total Analysis Required

Each of the direct and indirect taxes utilized to make up the total system, usually with some combination of an income tax, import and export duties, internal excise taxes and property taxes, etc., needs to be carefully analyzed with a primary goal of a stimulation of economic growth. However, the tax structure cannot be looked upon in isolation from the expenditure structure of the government. We have been directing our remarks primarily to taxation. In operation it cannot be isolated from the use to which the tax revenues are put. In many developed countries, a budget is decided first and then sufficient taxes are found to cover the needs. In many of the developing states it is the reverse. The needs for expenditures on social overhead and development and maintenance of the operation of the government are so great that expenditures are limited by the amount of taxes that are economically and politically feasible to raise. Thus, unless the expenditure is used in such a fashion as to stimulate additional growth, which in turn will produce additional income and thus further taxes, the self-stimulating development will be frustrated.

It is generally accepted that in the long run the system should be income-elastic in character; that is, that the increase in tax revenue would be proportionately greater than the increase in income. This generally also means that the developing states are faced with embarrassing short-term fluctuations in revenue that create grave problems for rational development planning, since additional income in many underdeveloped areas exhibits fairly wide short-term fluctuation. Ideally the developing states should have a tax system that is income-elastic for upward but income-inelastic for downward fluctuations. At this point this does not seem to be possible. Another problem is that the tax that is income-elastic may also be the tax that is likely to interfere with incentives. The whole structure needs to be carefully examined in order to reconcile the alternative goals of tax policy while achieving a desired rate of growth of real income with a minimum of real cost. The rise in aspirations of the inhabitants of the underdeveloped countries appears to be creating pressures which can only be met, in the long run, by direct taxation which really means an income tax. Thus one of the problems of development is the transition from a tax structure which is primarily based upon export and import duties and other indirect taxes to a tax structure which is largely based upon direct taxation.

14

IMPACT OF FISCAL MEASURES

By RICHARD GOODE

Director, Fiscal Affairs Department
International Monetary Fund

Fiscal policy, in the broad sense, comprises the deliberate use of taxes, government spending, and public debt operations to influence economic activity in desired ways. It is concerned with the effect of fiscal operations on variables such as employment, saving and investment, national income, the price level and the balance of international payments. The paramount goals of fiscal policy are stability and growth. Fiscal policy is an important part of public finance but not the whole of it. Fiscal policy does not take in tax incidence and equity, budgetary procedures, treasury management, and many other topics that fall within the sphere of government finance.

Short-Run Stabilization

Fiscal policy, as a term and a body of doctrine, came into prominence in the industrialized countries during the great depression of the 1930s. The pioneers in fiscal policy argued that unemployment could be reduced and production stimulated by raising aggregate demand through deficit spending. The contention that budget deficits were helpful in the circumstances, rather than a sign of weakness and profligacy, was an enlightening and liberating idea.

Later, particularly during World War II, the application of fiscal policy to inflationary conditions was developed. The theory thus emerged in symmetrical form as the principles governing "a policy that uses public finance as a balancing factor in the development of the economy."[1] Often called "compensatory fiscal policy," it focused on fiscal actions as offsets to fluctuations in private spending. Over the past three decades, the basic principles of compensatory fiscal policy have come to be widely accepted and have been applied to a considerable extent.

The developing countries also face short-run instability, but the possibilities of compensatory fiscal policy are more limited in these countries than in the industrialized countries. This is true because

---

[1] Gerhard Colm, "Fiscal Policy," in *The New Economics*, ed. Seymour E. Harris (New York: Alfred A. Knopf, 1947), p. 454.

of differences in the origin of fluctuations and in other economic characteristics.

The principal sources of economic fluctuations in the less developed countries are variations in harvests due to weather and other natural conditions; changes in the relative prices of exports and imports which alter the terms of international trade; and political uncertainty. In industrialized private-enterprise economies, on the other hand, the leading cause of the business cycle is fluctuations in investment.

Variations in agricultural yields and the terms of trade represent changes in the amount of real income that can be produced by using a country's labor, capital, and natural resources with a given degree of intensity. A primary-producing country cannot prevent a bad harvest or a deterioration in its terms of trade by stabilizing aggregate demand, and of course it would not wish to prevent an increase in real income due to a large crop or rising export prices. In contrast, booms and recessions in industrialized countries reflect to a great extent changes in the employment of labor and other productive factors due to fluctuations in effective home demand. These fluctuations can be reduced by fiscal measures that help stabilize aggregate expenditures.

It does not follow that a less developed country should pursue a passive or neutral fiscal policy, taking no account of short-run fluctuations. Fiscal policy, in conjunction with monetary policy, can facilitate adjustment to variations in havest and the terms of international trade. This can be done by actions that influence in appropriate ways the level and composition of government and private expenditures.

Technically, the situation that is easiest to deal with is a sudden and temporary increase in export receipts due to an unusually large crop or especially high prices. If the government takes no action, export producers will realize additional income, imports will rise, and the prices of home goods will also tend to rise as the expansionary influence is transmitted through the economy. The authorities may consider it in the general interest to capture a large part of the temporary increase in real income in order to make sure that it is devoted to socially important uses and to prevent an increase in domestic prices and incomes that will be painful to correct later when export receipts return to a more normal level. They may also wish to guard against an investment boom in the export sector that will bring into existence productive capacity that cannot be profitably maintained under normal conditions.

In this situation, a temporary export tax or production tax can appropriate part of the additional income and allow the gain to be spread through the community and over time. These objectives can be realized only if the government makes wise use of the revenue. Usually, some increase in government expenditures will be warranted, and some accumulation of foreign exchange reserves or repayment of external debt will also be indicated. It is important that the temporary taxes be ended when export conditions become less favorable. Otherwise, permanent injury may be done to the country's export capacity. While the technical problems are fairly simple, a government needs political strength and prudence to carry out a policy of the kind described.

A decrease in export receipts presents harder problems. The community is now faced with a cut in real income, which cannot be made up in the short run by expanding the output of home goods owing to the lack of certain productive factors and other obstacles to rapid changes in output. If neither foreign exchange reserves nor external credit is available, total real consumption and investment will have to fall as much as export receipts. Government expenditures or tax reductions intended to compensate for the decline in domestic money income accompanying the fall of exports would only create inflation and accentuate the balance of payments problem or the fall in the external value of the currency (the exchange rate). Indeed, the government may be well advised to follow the austere course of raising tax rates or cutting public expenditures in order to make up for a revenue loss due to the decrease in exports and imports.

If the country has foreign exchange reserves that can safely be drawn down or if external resources in the form of official or private credit or other assistance are available, a less restrictive fiscal policy will be appropriate. A fiscal deficit may be the means of partly compensating for the fall in domestic income accompanying the decline of exports and facilitating the use of reserves or external resources. At a later time, however, a fiscal policy tighter than would otherwise be required is likely to be needed to hold back demand for imports and thereby allow the rebuilding of reserves or the repayment of external loans.

Capital inflows or outflows pose problems similar to those associated with changes in export receipts but impinge less directly on domestic income. Appropriate fiscal adjustments are similar but may be smaller in magnitude.

Long-Run Growth

In recent discussions of fiscal policy, attention has shifted to some extent from short-run stabilization to long-run economic growth. This brings closer together the orientation of policymakers in the industrialized countries and the developing states. But significant differences of emphasis remain.

A fiscal policy for growth in a high-income industrialized country might be directed almost entirely toward the maintenance of the appropriate level of aggregate demand. The objective would be to keep demand high enough to minimize any shortfall of actual production below potential production but not so high that inflation or balance of payments difficulties would result. Reliance would be placed on the private sector to obtain an efficient use of resources and to provide for growing productive capacity. While this might not be the ideal policy for growth, it would be an intelligible one.

A more aggressive fiscal policy is required to satisfy the aspiration of an underdeveloped country. Here emphasis has to be placed on the enlargement of productive capacity, and without government intervention the pace at which potential output grows is likely to be slow. Inadequate demand is rarely a problem. Even when there is much unemployed or under-employed common labor and unused land, an increase in spending will call forth little if any increase in total production. This is true because the necessary skills, capital equipment and organization are lacking.

The usual prescription for a developing country is to direct fiscal policy toward the increase of saving and investment in the public and private sector combined. A better formulation prescribes an increase in the proportion of resources used for high-priority developmental purposes, a classification which is in some respects broader than physical capital formation but which excludes certain investments in physical capital. A well-balanced development program must include substantial expenditures for education, research, health and other services that improve people's productive capacity and add to knowledge. Although these expenditures are usually not considered investment, it is increasingly recognized that they are as essential to growth as is ordinary investment and even less likely to be spontaneously provided. On the other hand, investments in splendid public buildings, luxury housing and inefficient industries may contribute little to economic progress.

The government of a developing state must undertake large expenditures for developmental purposes, and many of these outlays must be made long before a substantial return in the form of additional national income is realized. Even a generous social yield, moreover, does not automatically provide the government with the resources needed to carry forward its development program. Non-developmental expenditures of governments can also be expected to increase, especially in the newly independent states, in response to public demand and the standards set by the example of rich countries.

The main task of fiscal policy in a developing state is to finance large and growing government expenditures in an orderly, efficient and fair manner. Of course, the financing of expenditures is only the monetary counterpart of the mobilization of real resources in the form of labor, land and materials. Financial limitations, properly understood, are indications of economic, administrative and political obstacles.

The orderly financing of government outlays requires cooperation among ministries and other organizations and the coordination of financial planning with general development planning. Efficiency comprehends effective low-cost administration and, more fundamentally, the avoidance of unnecessary interference with production. Fairness implies consistency with the community's standards of social justice. Since efficiency and fairness are relative terms and since they may conflict, compromises and sacrifices of one for the other are unavoidable.

Opportunities for financing government expenditures by non-inflationary borrowing at home are narrowly limited in the less developed countries. Private savings usually are small relative to income, and a large part of the total is invested by the savers in their own farms and business enterprises. Much of the remainder may go into residential and commercial construction or foreign assets. In a progressive, mixed economy, there will be urgent claims from private business enterprises for any savings that the public is willing to invest in securities or to entrust to financial intermediaries.

Most government domestic loans, in these conditions, will be placed directly with the central bank or with the commercial banks on the basis of an accommodating expansion of central bank credit. The government borrowing therefore will result in an increase in the stock of money and a net addition to claims on output. Although this does not necessarily condemn the borrowing, it raises serious questions.

Ordinarily it may be assumed that, in reasonably stable conditions, people will wish to maintain a fairly steady ratio of money holdings to money income, with perhaps a slow upward trend as income grows and wealth accumulates. If so, the money stock in a developing country can be expected to grow only a little faster than national income, the excess growth reflecting mainly the transfer of production from the non-monetized sector to the market economy. Purely as an illustration, a 5 per cent rate of growth in gross national product (GNP) might call for a 6 per cent annual increase in the money stock. Since the money stock equals less than one-fourth of GNP in most underdeveloped countries for which information is available,[2] a 6 per cent growth of the stock would ordinarily amount to no more than 1.5 per cent of GNP. Increases in commercial bank credit to finance foreign and domestic trade may absorb a good part of this sum. If foreign exchange reserves are being accumulated, they will serve as the counterpart of some of the domestic credit.

Without trying to be more precise, it may be concluded that the amount of non-inflationary finance that the government can obtain by claiming a share of the annual increase in outstanding credit that corresponds to the normal growth of the money stock is likely to equal only a small fraction of developmental expenditures.

When the expansion of domestic bank credit to the government and private sectors combined creates more money than the public wishes to hold under existing conditions, total spending increases faster than the available supply of goods and services valued at stable prices, and inflation occurs. Prices rise, and a balance of payments deficit appears unless prevented by rigorous controls or depreciation of the exchange rate.

Credit creation to finance developmental expenditures of government or capital formation strictly defined is no less inflationary than credit creation to cover non-developmental expenditures of a current nature. In the short run, both kinds of outlay add to money income without increasing the supply of goods and services on which the income can be spent. A deficit in the capital budget or development budget poses the same problems as a deficit in the government's current account.

---

[2] For 32 less developed countries for which information is readily available (mostly for 1963 but in some cases for 1960, 1961 or 1962), the ratios of the money stock to GNP were distributed as follows: below 0.10, 5; 0.10–0.14, 13; 0.15–0.19, 5; 0.20–0.24, 5; 0.25 and above, 4.
Source: International Monetary Fund, *International Financial Statistics,* June 1965. Money includes currency and demand deposits; the values used are averages of those for the beginning and end of the year.

Inflation, of course, is a means of transferring command over resources. While experience shows that inflation and development are not necessarily incompatible, inflation is inefficient and unfair, and it loses effectiveness when prolonged or accelerated. Inflation gives rise to many social and economic problems. At best, it is the consequence of developmental expenditures that outrun a country's ability to redirect resources by preferable methods; often, it results from miscalculation or indecisiveness.

An underdeveloped country that is determined to avoid both stagnation and inflation will have to find ways of raising large and growing amounts of tax revenue. For this purpose, many tax systems are antiquated and too weak. Modernization of the tax system is an essential part of modernization of the economy. In tax reform consideration must be given to revenue productivity, administrative feasibility, effects on economic incentives, and compatibility with popular sentiment. Political resolution, common sense and technical expertise are all required.

There are no general rules for determining how much revenue a country may reasonably attempt to obtain. Deductive considerations and observation suggest that the ratio of taxation to national income should tend to rise with income per head though not uniformly among countries or over time.

A large subsistence sector holds down the ratio whereas a large volume of foreign trade tends to raise it. Since attitudes toward taxation depend on what people are accustomed to, a country with a history of low taxation may have to move slowly toward a higher level.

The most convenient way of raising the ratio of taxation to income over time would be to rely on taxes whose yield grows faster than national income without changes in rates. Such taxes are said to have a high income elasticity of yield. Elastic taxes help avoid the political controversies associated with frequent increases in tax rates. These taxes include excises and import duties on certain consumption items, progressive income taxes and profits taxes. Taxes on essential consumption goods, land taxes, stamp taxes, licenses and fees tend to have inelastic yields. Excises and customs duties that are assessed at specific rates usually are less elastic than *ad valorem* taxes, and the real yield of the specific taxes may fall when the price level rises, unless rates are frequently adjusted.

Unfortunately, the taxes with elastic yields generally are more complicated than other taxes. The elastic taxes usually account for only a minor part of the revenue in less developed countries. An increase in yield elasticity is a proper objective of tax reform. Care should be exercised, however, to avoid excessive complexities and tax formulas that take too large a share of the rewards for growth-producing activities. These dangers are greatest in connection with income and profits taxes but exist also with respect to consumption taxes.

An objective of fiscal policy in a developing state is to limit private spending in order to allow resources to be diverted to high-priority uses in the public sector. Generally, a tax system that holds back consumption and favors saving and investment will be advantageous, but a greater degree of selectivity is desirable. Consumption expenditures required to maintain health and working efficiency merit higher priority than investment catering to luxurious consumption. Perhaps the traditional principle of taxing luxuries and other non-essentials more heavily than essentials offers as reliable guidance as any simple rule.

Remunerative prices for railways, ports, postal and telegraph systems, power projects, irrigation works and other public enterprises are a source of revenue that is often neglected. Frequently these enterprises not only fail to cover depreciation and interest on their capital but suffer operating deficits. Users of the services are subsidized at the expense of taxpayers. Although this is not always wrong, the subsidies raise questions of equity and often displace other government expenditures that would contribute more to development. There is a strong presumption in favor of prices that will cover full costs, including capital costs, and in many cases return a surplus to finance expansion of the enterprise.

Conclusion

Owing to differences in the kinds of economic fluctuations experienced, the developing states have less scope for compensatory fiscal policy than do the industrialized countries. Primary-producing countries, nevertheless, can use fiscal measures to facilitate adjustment to variations in harvests and changes in the terms of international trade.

The main task of fiscal policy in the developing states is to finance large and growing government expenditures in an orderly, efficient and fair manner and to limit non-essential private spending. This requires the modernization of tax systems and remunerative prices for government enterprises.

DISCUSSION

A Question of Priorities

> "Elastic taxes," that grow as incomes grow without the need for upping tax rates, are complicated to apply. Consideration should be given to letting the LDCs receive the full price for their exports as paid by the consumer, including the duties charged on those goods when they enter the country of destination.

Dr. Goode said, "The objective of fiscal policy is not, as it is sometimes suggested, to raise the level of savings and investment in the economy. I think a better statement is the one that Dr. Kaldor gave this morning, and that is that fiscal policy should be devoted toward the rechannelling of resources from low-priority uses to high-priority uses."

Thus "I include in the category of low social priority not only the luxurious flats of the wealthy people, but the palatial presidential residence, which is part of capital formation (and is included as such in the statistics). I include in low-priority items the capital that is devoted to inefficient industries that have little hope of ever being self-supporting. And I include in high-priority uses of resources not only education and health services, but the amount of private consumption which is essential for the development of a vigorous labor force, and which offers reasonable incentives to people to better their lot in society.

"High social-priority use of resources by the government does not necessarily result in an immediate increase in the national product. Sometimes there is a long gestation period. Education is a good example. It takes many years before the yield is shown in higher national income. Even when the national income is increased, that does not necesarily increase the revenues of the government. There is no automatic assurance that the revenues of the government will grow equally with the growth in the nation's income."

In talking of "elastic taxation," Dr. Goode said that customs are not elastic, particularly if they are specific in nature instead of *ad valorem*. "Typically, as you go through the process of development, there is a change in the composition of your imports, and you import more capital goods and maybe raw materials for the industries that have been founded. Most countries do not wish to impose high customs duties on capital goods and basic raw materials for their industries, so the yield of customs duties tends to stagnate as economic development proceeds." But he added that customs "will probably continue to be the largest part of the tax system in most of the countries in an early stage of development."

Elastic taxes are difficult to apply, and "I am very much afraid that Ministers of Finance are going for a good many years to have the disagreeable duty of appearing periodically in parliament and calling for new taxes and for higher tax rates, if the developing countries are going to obtain the volume of revenue which is necessary."

In pleading that an economic price be charged for services (like posts, electricity and water, that are often sold below cost), Dr. Goode noted that "if this is not done, the task that I described for the Minister of Finance, which is difficult at the best of times for obtaining more revenue, will be complicated all the more. Surely if the persons who use the services of the public enterprises do not pay the costs, the taxpayer will have to. The people who are buying the services of the enterprises are more likely to be willing to accept a tariff which covers costs than the taxpayer to pay more levies, because the user of the services can see the direct connection between his benefit and the tariff he is paying."

Dr. U Tun Wai, of the IMF, said that countries that tend to inflation and seek stabilization ought to adopt the relatively modest objective of "holding the line"—just keeping expenditure from going up. As all economies grow and national incomes keep increasing, a policy of freezing expenditure—rather than the much harder task of cutting it—would leave the budgetary outlay a declining proportion of the national income.

As concerns expansion, since governments do not know when export prices may boom and yield new resources for investment, they should plan projects for keeping in cold storage, "to be taken out as and when their resources, both internal and external, permit them to do so."

Finance Ministers have tended toward expansion. Dr. U Tun Wai took figures from the U.N. book on national accounts for the years 1956 to 1962. "There are only data for about twelve countries. Running through the statistics I found that, of course, there are some countries where you have both a government budget deficit as well as a private sector deficit, and thus a balance of payments deficit year after year. We have deficits in both sectors for Thailand, Vietnam and Korea, and also for Ecuador. Then we have other groups of countries, like Burma and Costa Rica, where the government sector was in deficit and the private sector in surplus. Others, such as Honduras and Jamaica, had the government sector in surplus and the private sector in deficit. And lastly there were the Philippiness, Panama and Morocco, where in some years you had deficits and some years surpluses—there is no fixed pattern."

Dr. U Tun Wai drew a line between countries whose revenues are 5 per cent or even 3 per cent of income, where the accent has to be on increasing taxes, and countries like Morocco and Burma, where revenue is 20 or 25 per cent of the GNP.

Mrs. Gerda Blau, of the FAO, saw the tax problem in agriculture as follows. The agricultural export sector, harassed as it is by low prices, has to supply the means for subsidizing the subsistence sector, in order to make a start at raising its productivity. In these circumstances the land tax does not seem to fit the needs of the case.

A potential source of revenue and foreign exchange is the duties charged on these export crops by the developed countries that import them. If such tariffs were abolished, the loss to the developed countries would be greater than the gain to the LDCs, because as demand is inelastic, sales receipts would not increase greatly. On the other hand "the gain to the exporting countries would be a real gain in terms of foreign exchange, while the loss to the exchequer of the importing countries would be partly a book loss in terms of redistribution of income."

The possibility should be studied of leaving these tariffs unchanged and handing over the revenue to the exporting countries. This would do away with the situation that exporting countries dare not tax their own exports because competitors that do not apply such taxes may catch a larger share of the market (as once happened in the tea trade).

Combating Fluctuations

Compensatory fiscal policies are needed to counter not only variations in demand, but fluctuations occasioned by export prices and poor crops or other natural causes. Foreign loans are not inflationary provided the foreign currency content of these credits is used fully, to add more resources to the economy.

Professor Abba Lerner, of the U.S., followed the point made by Galbraith and Kaldor that investment in the manufacture of luxuries for consumption by the rich is not better than consumption by the rich. It ensues in reverse that "consumption by the rich is no worse than investment in the building of luxuries for the rich. A proper understanding of that means that we are not talking about consumption versus investment at all, but between consumption by the rich and consumption by the poor. So we have high and low priorities in investment. And this way of looking at it solves a puzzle which I have not seen as clearly before, and that is why there is so much stress on shifting to investment, apparently without paying any attention to the preferences of the consumers."

Concerning the prices to be charged for public utilities, Dr. Lerner said: "I agree with Dr. Goode that many of the authorities charge prices which are lower than they should be, but also there are many which charge prices that are higher than they should be. Both cases are due to the existence of strong prejudices, neither of which seems to be much more defensible than the other. One is the prejudice that public goods ought to be free, like water, for which I think there is no basis. The other is that they ought to cover their cost, for which, again, I think there is no basis. The proper basis from the point of view of the full utilization of resources is that the price should be equal to the marginal cost. The charge which just covers the marginal cost performs the traditional function of prices in bringing about the most efficient use of resources. Departures from that price I like to call subsidies or taxes. Now it is possible, and it might be desirable, to charge more than the marginal cost, as a way of taking money away from people, if this is in the interest of the economy as a whole. But then I think the burden of proof is to show that this is the best tax available. It may well be. But I think that one should beware of assuming that it is a good tax just because of the prejudice that a price ought to cover the average cost."

Professor Nicholas Kaldor, of Britain, said, "The strongest pressure of vested interests is always exerted to keep the price of public services so low that the government has to pay a considerable part of its tax revenue in order to cover the subsidies on their cost, let alone provide any return on the capital invested. The real reason is that the greater part of the services are not bought by final consumers, but they are bought by the business sector. And of course by making the profits of public enterprises negative, the profits accruing to private enterprises are that much larger."

Dr. Kaldor found two things wrong with Dr. Lerner's assertion that price should equal marginal cost. The first is, nobody knows what marginal costs are. Secondly, the *private* sector does not charge marginal costs. If there were perfect competition, average cost and marginal cost would be the same. But there isn't; and if marginal cost were below average cost, no private firm charging marginal cost could stay in business. So if the private sector does not charge marginal cost, then the public sector cannot either.

Professor Kaldor explained that, were the private sector subject to the law of diminishing returns under ideally competitive conditions, and supposing that increasing returns were confined to the public sector, then it would be correct to say that the formula "price equals marginal costs" in the public sector gives the ideal allocation of resources between the private and public sectors.

But in the real world, all industries are subject to long-run increasing returns, so that marginal costs, being below average costs, can never be a proper rule for pricing. And if they were used for the public sector only, it would lead to a misallocation of resources.

Hon. Mwai Kibaki, of Kenya, asked how fiscal policy can help ensure that people who save money re-invest it in their own country. Between Dr. Enke's recommendation not to tax wealth and the alternative that the State take the money and do the investing, there must be a third alternative.

Mr. Asher Shlein of Israel, analyzed what is involved in taking a foreign loan. If it is intended to finance the government's investment plans but not to finance imports for those plans, then it is no different from printing money.

Following the case through, the creation of new money will create inflationary pressures. As the foreign currency counterpart of the loan taken from abroad is kept in the central bank, it can be used to increase the supply of imports which will mop up the new purchasing power created by the loan. "To conclude this point, we have not really one question as to whether to take a loan from abroad to finance government expenditure, but two questions: first, whether to create inflationary pressures by printing money; and second, whether to overcome inflationary pressures by taking a foreign currency loan and financing additional imports."

It can be necessary to prevent capital inflows from generating inflation. "A fiscal policy is important to ensure that the capital inflow into the country is not consumed and is not used only to increase the standard of living." He urged the importance of fiscal as against monetary policy. "Suppressed inflation is a combination of a loose fiscal policy and a very strong and deflationary monetary policy. The result is misallocation of resources."

* * *

Dr. Goode agreed with the suggestion that, "however weak compensatory fiscal policy may be in the primary producing countries, it is probably more powerful than monetary policy, because the size of the banking sector and the money stock is relatively small, so there is less room to manoeuvre here. I also agree with the comment made that there is some advantage in fiscal policy in that you attack not only liquidity but the flow of income, whereas monetary policy addresses itself to changes in liquidity.

"It is a good thing that fiscal and monetary policies be broadly consistent. It is a bad thing if, at a time when the Minister of Finance was trying to have a tight budget, the central bank was allowing a liberal credit expansion. I find that in most countries there are channels of communication between the central bank and the Finance Ministry. There are differences of emphasis between the two that I do not regard as inconsistent with common-sense policies, since each has special responsibilities. It seems to me that these problems are not in practice so very serious in most countries, and that they work themselves out one way or another."

Dr. Goode explained the policy of short-term stabilization for primary producing countries. It involves "appropriating in times of export boom, when export receipts are large, a portion of the increase in income, and using that for saving and investment. It can be saving and investment at home, or it can be saving and investment in foreign assets. By and large, I think you would want to divide it between the two. You spread out the thing. Instead of letting it all flow into the hands of the export sector, you spread it throughout the community. Instead of consuming it all in one year, you would try to spread it over several years. In bad times, if you have accumulated some foreign assets or if you have open to you a new line of credit, you can afford to maintain government expenditures in excess of current revenues, which has the effect of making a higher level of money income than would be possible if the government's budget were annually balanced. And you can do that without creating inflation because you draw on your foreign assets or you use your credits to allow an increase of imports, which counteracts the inflationary effects of the government's deficit.

"So you maintain a more stable level of income if you use your resources over the years instead of allowing a big spurt whenever you have a good year and then tightening your belt and raising taxes and reducing government expenditures when you have a bad year."

The same results cannot be achieved by "stabilizing" on the domestic investment front, as one speaker suggested, because you cannot get investment projects started and stopped quickly enough, and you have not got the reserves of skills and management. If you did, the country would cease being a primary producer.

It may be important to prevent capital flights by exchange controls. "I must, however, in all candor go on to say that I am not particularly sanguine about the success of these, because experience shows that the ingenuity of people in evading exchange controls on capital movements is very substantial. If you limit overt capital movements, they very often take place in the guise of current transactions; and it is generally a very difficult subject to control effectively. I would much rather create conditions in which people do not want to take their capital out of the country than to rely on exchange controls to prevent them from doing so."

In agriculture, Dr. Goode favors taxing the consumer goods that the farmer buys rather than taxing his output, which might hamper incentive to producing for export, or taxing his land, which is not always feasible when land titles are not clear.

Comparing a foreign loan with a central bank loan, Dr. Goode reasoned that "a foreign loan allows you to import more than you would otherwise have imported. It puts into your hands additional real resources, and they can be used either for particular investment projects, or for anything else in the economy." Borrowing from the central bank channels existing resources but does not add to them. "It is permissible, when a foreign loan is available, for the government to spend more than its local tax receipts, because the inflationary excess of that government expenditure is cancelled out by the additional flow of imports made possible by the foreign credit."

15

CONTRIBUTIONS OF FISCAL POLICY TO DEVELOPMENT

By STEPHEN ENKE

Deputy Assistant Secretary of Defense
U.S.A.

Three important ways in which fiscal policy can contribute to the growth and development of comparatively poor and backward countries are described below. In such less developed countries it is crucial that there be (1) increasing useful investment, (2) a suitable money and banking system, and (3) adequate financing of government through taxes. These are all related to what might more generally be termed fiscal policy.

Increasing Useful Investment

Useful investment in a country occurs because "someone" provides funds and "someone" decides where to invest. Domestic sources of finance include the government (through taxes or inflation), the private banks (extending commercial loans), firms (reinvesting their surpluses), and private savers (investing directly or indirectly through firms, banks or the government). The domestic "someone" who decides where to invest may be a private firm or government agency. There are obviously many combinations of who provides funds and who decides investment. Three aspects of certain of these combinations deserve discussion.

Government Financing of Public Investment

Governments of many recently independent LDCs often act as though the only useful accumulations of capital resulted from government financing of public investments. The sources of funds have sometimes been taxation, but more often inflation of the currency, in which case government borrowing from private savers is minimal. Favored investments have been transportation infrastructure, power utilities and irrigation projects, plus a few spectacular industrial facilities.

Official pronouncements often make it seem that extra tax yields will be saved and invested. The truth though is that four-fifths or more of extra tax receipts usually go to extra operating expenses of government and not to what might be termed investment. This is partly the result of rapidly increasing populations in these countries.

Nevertheless, the marginal propensities of LDC governments to save and invest extra tax receipts is low, and very possibly lower than that of better-off families called upon to pay extra taxes. Thus government schemes of investment-from-taxes may have a negative productivity on balance.

Usually, despite unused tax capacity, most government investment is financed through inflationary forced saving. The morality of this policy, in countries where the aged, infirm and other dependents have sought protection against poverty through savings accounts, bonds and insurance, need not be assessed here. It is more important to determine whether the customary price inflation seriously lessens development.

It must be remarked that several Latin American countries, despite theories of conservative economists, grow and develop in spite of continual and rapid inflation. Whether they would do as well or better without inflation is anyone's opinion. However, conceptually at least, one would expect that various costs are incurred.

Advanced economies have found that a wide variety of financial instruments are needed—stocks, bonds, savings accounts, endowment insurance policies, etc.—if maximum savings are to be called into use. Nearly all these ways of indirectly translating savings into investment are most vulnerable to inflation. The effective yield of the creditor-lender may with inflation be negative in retrospect. It is therefore no wonder that many saving-into-investing channels atrophy in countries suffering inflation.

Another frequent cost of inflation are the rigidities that almost inevitably result from ensuing government controls. Inflation brings rising prices, especially of food and other necessaries, and this leads to political discontent. The government seeks to remedy the situation with compulsory prices ceilings. Market shortages are thereby increased. Rationing of food grains and allocations of housing are next invoked. Exchange controls follow. The price system is partially thwarted in performing its functions of allocation. And, over a period of years, a serious misdirection of national resources develops.

Government Rankings of Public Investments

Judging from economic development literature, private investors rank alternative possibilities according to their expected rates of return on investment, while government officials supposedly favor projects with low capital-to-output ratios. What private investors try to do is sufficiently well understood. But what is this capital-output ratio?

Some modern economists would have government officials estimate, for each potential investment project, its expected investment cost (K) and its anticipated value added after deducting cost of purchased materials (V). Projects with low K/V ratios are allegedly preferable. And labor intensive projects, which have high payroll costs but low capital costs per unit of gross value added, usually appear profitable of course. This approach gets the government maximum extra gross value added per year in the near future for a given aggregate investment this year by the State. But it does not take into account that labor may not be a free good in the economy at large. And, unless *net* value added is considered, short service life projects may be uneconomically favored.

These same notions are often applied macro-economically in development planning. Officials, in estimating how much extra output is yielded by a given nation-wide public investment, commonly use so-called "incremental capital-output ratios" (ICORs). Thus, if over the past decade extra value of output in constant prices was $\triangle V$, while additions to the country's stock of capital were $\triangle K$ during this same period, $\triangle K/\triangle V$ is the ICOR. Typically, this may be 2 or 3, and sometimes this is mistakenly thought to mean that the rate of return on investment in this country is typically 50 or 33 per cent respectively. This would only be true, however, if labor were a free good to employers, willing to work for nothing despite job disutility, and irrespective of whether the marginal product of their work is zero.

An economy's extra output ($\triangle V$) must ordinarily come from extra employed labor ($\triangle L$), extra useful and used capital stock ($\triangle K$), and extra productivity ($\triangle \Phi$) in the sense that given factor inputs now produce more output. There is no more justification in attributing all the $\triangle V$ of some past period to $\triangle K$ alone than there would be in attributing it all to $\triangle L$ alone. The macro-economic use of ICORs by development planners often understates the capital needed to attain a stipulated $\triangle V$ by a factor of about 3.

It is time government projects that sell output be ranked in the same way as private firms assess their investment possibilities. Labor is normally a valid financial and economic cost. Only when the State is investing to produce outputs not for sale, e.g., toll-free highways, is there any reason for ranking public investments differently from private ones. However, when such external economies are significant, capital to output-ratios cannot be applied because output cannot be valued.

Government Financing of Private Investments

Although bitterly opposed by all socialists, and indeed by most government officials who enjoy the power that control over large investments brings, much can be said for having the State finance development banks and other institutions that are privately managed. Mexico, and other countries, have established variants of this idea.

Several advantages can theoretically be listed for such institutions.

First, the management that determines what investments to make is presumably less influenced by uneconomic political considerations than would be a government investing agency.

Second, a development bank ordinarily will invest in the private sector, which, apart from certain direct private investments, may find it hard to tap the savings of families.

Third, government can subsidize the participation of private deposits in the development bank, as follows. The development bank may pay a higher interest rate to certain classes of depositors than it charges certain classes of borrowers. This differential interest rate can be met by the government. Through such subsidization the government's contribution may increase extra saving and investment by more than its own contribution. It depends partly on the combined interest elasticity of the demand and supply of loanable funds. Another consideration is the extent which savers can invest directly. Because such circumvention of the market is common in primitive economies, this proposal has merit for truly "emerging" nations.

Such development banks, with the government providing or subsidizing funds for others to manage, runs counter to the prevalent culture of today. It is analogous to having the State provide funds in support of privately conducted schools, for instance. But some observers remain convinced that private direction of such matters is likely to be more efficient. Hence, if government initially can obtain funds for investment more readily than private firms, such development banks may be worth a more extensive trial.

Suitable Money and Banking Systems

The desirable characteristics of a national money and banking system are familiar.

First, a government must ensure that a means of payment exists in circulation that will facilitate trade and more or less maintain the real purchasing power of fixed debts. Provision of a means of payment is necessary to encourage division of labor, productive specialization and general efficiency. Maintaining the value of money-defined assets and liabilities is a matter of social justice.

Second, in every economy, profitable opportunities to invest are constantly coming into existence. Seizing these opportunities could not only benefit those that invest but also those who will become employed as well as those who will obtain extra output at lower prices. But such opportunities are often recognized first by those without capital to invest. And those with capital are not always the first to recognize such opportunities. Hence much of development has historically consisted of entrepreneurs with vision obtaining financial support from lenders who must in turn be convinced that there is a profitable risk. A good banking system is one that facilitates this backing by commercial banks of what to them appear good investment bets in the private sector. Growth through private entrepreneurship otherwise tends to be limited to what a few wealthy families wish and can finance and manage.

Third, economic happenings abroad can drastically affect prices and incomes of residents, so that domestic economic activity is often closely linked to foreign events. This can be especially important in the case of one-crop countries with only a few exports. However, through exchange operations, commodity stockpiling and credit regulation, a central bank can somewhat insulate the home economy from untoward happenings overseas.

The central and commercial banks of advanced nations have long performed some of these functions. Over the decades, certain techniques of regulation have been evolved, through altered rediscount rates, varied reserve requirements, open market operations and so on. And the commercial banks have, together with other financial intermediaries, financed a rapid rate of economic development. But many of these practices depend upon circumstances to be found only in advanced countries and not in the less developed ones. Unfortunately, despite these differences, the money and banking systems of many LDCs are imitations of those to be found in the United States, Great Britain and France. It is therefore important to understand the kinds of regulation that are appropriate to the circumstances of still underdeveloped countries.

Commercial Bank Loans and High Cash Drains

In the least developed countries, goods and services are purchased with legal tender notes and coinage and not with checks on bank demand deposits. One per cent or less of the families own such deposits anyway. This means that the cash drain on the banking system is very high indeed. Thus, if the commercial banks create credits, they will lose perhaps 90 per cent soon in cash payments to the public. (In the U.S. this would be 10 per cent or less.)

A serious consequence is that the commercial banks as a whole are almost incapable of creating demand credits to finance worthwhile projects in the private sector. This important function of modern banking, an ability that was perhaps an essential condition of growth in Western Europe and North America, remains unnecessarily stultified in most LDCs. Only the government has recourse to credit, as a means to command resources for investment or operating purposes, and this essentially through printing legal tender currency.

One possible solution—now alien to Western nations—would be to permit licensed commercial banks to issue bank notes of their own that would be legal tender for all private transactions but not for inter-bank settlement at clearing houses. Thus the cash drain would not limit banks in extending credit. But the clearing house drain would still inhibit one bank loaning more rapidly than the others.

These legal tender private bank notes could superficially all be similar, as are Federal Reserve bank notes of the same denomination in the United States, except for a small symbol identifying the issuing commercial bank.

Most of the liabilities of the private banks would comprise their note issue, plus demand deposits, against which certain reserves would have to be maintained with the central bank. Their main assets would be their loans and these same credits with the central bank. Clearing house settlements among banks would be through transfers of these central bank credits.

The main point of such an arrangement, until such time as most firms and families come to use demand deposits as their principal means of payment, would be that commercial bank managers could lend more to private borrowers. These, despite absence of the banking habit, could be substantial in the aggregate. Otherwise, the banks can only loan approximately what is deposited with them, instead of many times more.

Government Credit Regulation

In socialistically inclined countries, the government often operates the banking system. But in most of the underdeveloped world there have long been private banks that continue to be part of the banking system. Their regulation is often necessary and important.

This can be readily done, in a system where private bank notes are legal tender for most purposes, by requiring each commercial bank to maintain some fraction of its total note and deposit liabilities with the central bank as a credit. This fractional reserve is, of course, subject to change by the government monetary authorities. And the central bank can extend overdrafts to the private banks with interest.

How do commercial banks otherwise gain central bank account credits? One method for a single bank is to have a positive balance at a clearing house. The private banks as a group can gain such credit accounts, assuming there is a foreign exchange control system, by selling exchange that they acquire through their customers to the central bank. Thus, unless government increases legal reserve requirements, a favorable balance of payments on international current and long-term accounts taken together is likely to result in expanded means of payment within the country.

One means of regulation that central banks in LDCs cannot effectively use, but which is often employed in the U.S. and Great Britain, are open market operations. In these latter two countries, the central banks can absorb purchasing power by selling securities from their portfolios on the open market, thereby directly or indirectly forcing the commercial banks to make payments to the central bank. This serves to reduce or eliminate excess reserves of the commercial banks (in the U.S.) or to require private banks to rediscount with the central bank (in Great Britain).

Open market operations are impractical and ineffective in LDCs because they lack a substantial local capital market in which securities that are denominated in local currency are bought and sold. If the Bank of Ceylon wishes to sell securities, most will be denominated in pounds, and a few perhaps in dollars. If it sells them locally in Colombo for rupees it absorbs some local currency, but it is also engaging in foreign exchange transactions. Thus it cannot divorce exchange stabilization transactions from domestic credit control. Alternatively, if it sells securities denominated in local currency to residents, the market is likely to be so thin that these securities' prices may fall drastically. This serves to raise yields in the case of bonds sold. Thus, with locally denominated currencies, it is hard to separate the effects of open market operations on credit and upon interest rates.

Clearly, there will be times when the central bank wishes to tighten credit, support the domestic currency on foreign exchange and raise interest rates altogether. Then it can combine open market operations, higher posted rediscount rates, exchange stabilization transaction and higher legal reserves in some combination. But the open market operations, without an international capital market to hand, will be relatively unimportant.

Adequately Financing Government Through Taxes

A nation that cannot or will not finance its essential government services—e.g., maintenance of law and order—hardly warrants political independence. Many recent colonies have not increased their taxes sufficiently to both replace grants from the former imperial power and support the various social services that have been expanded. There have been instances of riots against new levies although taxable capacity existed. This bodes ill for development.

A rational tax system should have conscious objectives. If an LDC's economy really has a growth potential, its major taxes should be designed to foster growth as described below. The primary goal should certainly not be redistribution of existing wealth and income if this inhibits increasing total employment and output. Goods and services must be produced before they can be distributed. Metaphorically, a large total pie usually results in most people getting more to eat, even though some may get a smaller fractional slice.

A tax system to promote growth probably has the following characteristics. It should (1) discourage production as little as possible, (2) reduce less essential consumption, and (3) be economical as regards collection expense. Other things equal, taxes should not bear so heavily on certain goods or activities that they are practically terminated, and the economy distorted. An income elastic tax system that collects proportionately more as national income rises is more desirable than one that does not.

Taxes on Rents

A tax on pure economic rent—i.e., a tax on income attributable to natural resources that are not being depleted—cannot be shifted. If all the landowners died tomorrow, the land would still be there, adding to output. Hence there is theoretically no loss of production unless the rent that is taxed really includes a return on labor and capital as well as upon land itself.

Where a few landowners control nearly all valuable natural resources, rents received per owning family are large. Then a tax on these rents will also tend to reduce non-essential consumption by these families. This is not the case where land ownership is fragmented, of course.

A progressive tax on the rent income of families might encourage large owners of land to sell some of their holdings. Where large landowners supply few or no important services—such as credit, equipment or marketing to their tenants—such a tax may be beneficial. Historically, landowners have sometimes become useful capitalists through selling their land, receipts from sales being invested in new domestic industries.

The equity of abruptly increasing taxes on land depends upon how present landowners or their ancestors acquired these assets. If acquisition was centuries ago, and by conquest, there is no moral problem. The difficulty then is more political.

Taxes on land are economical to collect and they cannot distort the economy.

In countries where agriculture supplies half or more of the gross annual product, land rent taxes must supply a considerable fraction of government receipts, even with exemptions for smallholders. In overpopulated countries, land rent cost will be a large fraction of the value of agricultural output, and accordingly offer a broad tax base. Where prices have risen rapidly, past assessments on land for tax purposes will understate the capitalized value of its income, so newer assessments or higher rates are needed.

Import Duties on Luxury Goods

Countries that are undeveloped and small in population ordinarily import most of the durable consumer goods that are used by residents. Entry of these goods is usually through a few ports or over one or two railways or main roads. There is always a wide range of durable consumer goods, from watches to automobiles, that can be taxed to advantage.

Hence, duties on luxury imports are economical to collect, and superficially they lessen non-essential consumption. If the government's object is maximum duty revenues, and assuming the country has no monopsony power, the duty should be such that the government's marginal revenue from duties plus marginal costs equals the import supply price. However, if the government is especially anxious to save foreign exchange, duties should certainly be heavier.

The home market demand for a good now imported may be adequate to support one or more domestic producers if completely protected from foreign competition. Thus, government might set a prohibitively high import duty, excluding all imports, yet safeguard home consumers by setting a maximum price on the sale of domestic output not much above the cost of unrestricted imports. Minimum qualities might have to be established also. Such a policy is a more reasonable variant of the old infant industry argument. But the result in this case is not so much to discourage non-essential consumption at home as to save foreign exchange and increase local employment through import substitution.

Care must always be taken so not to discourage non-essential consumption through import duties that more enterprising residents, who raise their incomes through special productive efforts, find there is little in the way of imported "luxuries" available to enjoy. Well-stocked stores, with exciting consumer goods from abroad, can stimulate desire and earnings. Otherwise, families would cease exerting themselves once they were fed, clothed and sheltered.

Taxes on Turnover

An effective tax in LDCs where firms keep few reliable accounts is a tax on turnover. At the retail level this is the familiar sales tax. It would probably not apply to intermediate and final goods that are basic necessities (e.g., food).

Turnover taxes are compounded where there is little vertical integration, with different business concerns at almost every stage. But, if accounts are complete enough, a more sophisticated tax can be on value added at each stage. Then the turnover tax in effect becomes a tax on incomes of factors of production, and especially upon labor incomes where production techniques are primitive.

A tax on turnover is regressive, in the sense that it will bear relatively more heavily on lower income families, but in the over-all tax system this feature may be offset by progressive taxes on land, income, etc.

Taxes on Income

Taxes on income become important in the over-all tax system only when a country is already emerging. Enforcement is difficult except where family incomes are received as payments for services or output and the family keeps some records. Thus few families in the subsistence economy can practically be taxed. It is corporations, self-employed professionals, salaried employees and industrial skilled workers that can most economically be taxed and have the capacity to pay. These become relatively numerous only as a nation's economy develops. But even so, a generous exemption is necessary to avoid an impossible administrative burden.

Conceptually, although discrimination is often difficult, the various kinds of incomes a person receives can be taxed at different rates. Thus so-called unearned income from land and capital can be taxed at a higher rate than earned income from labor. The rationale is that a tax on unearned income will not inhibit output. In the case of income from land this is so. But the willingness of capitalists to invest in other means of production than land, and assume more speculative but promising risks, will be lessened to some extent by taxes on income from invested real capital.

A progressive income tax on earned income may not discourage individual efforts at the low end of the income scale. The reduction in disposable income may even cause people to work harder. But this is not so of persons with incomes in the high tax rate brackets, who often have abilities especially scarce in most underdeveloped countries, and who are inclined to choose more leisure because of the tax.

Some LDCs have considered levies on wealth. One version is a general property tax, excluding land but including houses, furniture, cars, jewelry, etc., and such a tax does discourage consumption to some extent. Another variant is a tax on the market values of productive capital investments such as plant and machinery. This latter version is hardly an inducement to invest and produce. And, incidentally, it is always translatable into a tax on income from capital, assuming some normal rate of return on investments.

Adult Poll Taxes

There is much to be said for a yearly adult poll tax. Especially is this so if the tax, instead of having to be paid in cash, can be worked off on nearby government projects or be bought off by supplying certain quantities of staple food grains. Each family will then meet the annual levy according to its comparative advantage.

In really primitive economies an adult poll tax (but in the form of statute labor on roads) is one of the simplest to enforce. For this reason, it was used a century and more ago in much of Europe. In this form it was also used in Canada and Australia, during this century, commutable by payment.

Another, and rather peculiar, advantage of poll taxes, is that on balance they probably encourage productive output and work. The marginal utility of disposable income or output is increased. But the marginal disutility of labor is unaffected.

Poll taxes are politically unpopular in many underdeveloped countries because they are regressive in incidence and often smack of recent colonialism. But people have the right to vote because they are alive and adult. Why should they not have a duty to pay yearly a small uniform tax for the same reason?

DISCUSSION

Soaking the Rich

Taxes can inhibit production. On the other hand, leaving private enterprise untaxed will not help create the infrastructure. Countries whose tax capacity is limited are not able to base all their development on fiscal policy.

Dr. Enke offered three comments. First, taxes are destructive. "Almost without exception, all taxes inhibit production. Among the main exceptions are, of course, a tax on pure economic rent. Unfortunately in countries where land ownership is very fragmented, it is hard to tax pure economic rent without causing hardship. A poll tax can encourage output to a limited extent, I believe. A tax on wealth need not discourage production, if wealthy people intend to consume all the output they earn, which is usually not the case. Therefore when we argue for higher taxation, the burden of proof, I think, is on the person making the proposal.

"My second point is that soaking the rich is really a negative policy. Anyway there aren't so many rich people—and there is always the question, what do you do after you have soaked them?"

He referred to one speaker's observation that investments are not good if they are used to satisfy the consumption of the wealthy. Dr. Enke commented: "I think the real test is not whether the consumption is of people who are wealthy, but whether it is of people who are making a useful productive contribution to the economy. In other words, I would distinguish between a wealthy landowner who inherited his land and, say, a successful innovator, who perhaps was responsible for establishing an entirely new industry."

Thirdly, instead of soaking the rich, Dr. Enke suggested helping the poor, and the best way to do that is by providing them with the knowledge and techniques for limiting the size of their families.

He concluded: "I do think that when we discuss economic development, we tend too often to think just in terms of *per capita* GNP. Whom is economic development for? Is it the average person, or are we really trying to alleviate poverty—which means that perhaps we should be focusing more attention on contributions we can make to those suffering poverty."

Mr. Pierre Uri took exception to Dr. Enke's ideological support of private enterprise. Dr. Enke questions the morality of taxing assets which are not inherited, but forgets about the moral problems of extreme inequality. Mr. Uri criticized the view that "the rich, unless they have inherited their wealth, are deserving—and it is too bad for the poor.

"There is the assumption that in a great many cases public financing means inflation. Well of coure, it is going to mean inflation if we have so many arguments against any kind of taxation. But we all know that development cannot take place unless some infrastructure is established, and this basic infrastructure cannot bring in a monetary profit or be financed directly by private capital.

"We must not forget that the real problem of our century is that we cannot accept the extreme degree of inequality which alone made development in our Western countries possible in the nineteenth century, because there were such differences in income that some people, either after they had consumed a lot or because they were rather puritanical, would invest—and development took place that way."

Mr. Uri queried Dr. Enke's suggestion that commercial banks be allowed to issue money. "Is it really implied that the issue of paper money by a central bank or a government-controlled bank is inflation, whereas if it is paper money issued by private banks, then it just accomodates the normal requirements of trade?"

Mr. H. R. Monday Jr., of Gambia, quoted Dr. Enke's statement that four-fifths of extra tax receipts go to extra operating expenses of the government. According to Mr. Monday, money is used to cover, first, the obligations that have to be undertaken by independent governments in such fields as defense, and secondly, the recurrent costs that follow from capital investment in the social services. High birth-rates are not always a contributory cause, because in many African countries the population is not augmenting rapidly.

The subject of inflationary finance has not been fully dealt with. Before starting on this method of development, the authorities have to take many factors into consideration, such as the propensity to import; whether import-substituting industries can be established so as to minimize the leakage of foreign exchange; and the feasibility of increasing agricultural output for domestic consumption, where the marginal demand for foodstuffs is high.

Development banks should have clear instructions from the government, to ensure that their lending operations chime in with the State's development policy. "I agree with Dr. Enke in recommending heavy import duties on luxury goods. I would only add that non-luxury imported consumer goods should be taxed as well, though not at high rates, so that the mass of the population who cannot be dunned for income tax can make some financial contribution to government revenue."

Mr. Monday stated that in countries whose tax capacity is limited, there is no point in basing all expectations on fiscal resources. "Fiscal policy in this context should be used to supplement internal and external borrowings, grants from abroad, and monetary policies.

"Borrowings from currency boards, central banks and marketing boards can supplement external borrowings to finance loanworthy capital projects. Fiscal measures can be taken to encourage investment in the country of profits made by foreign enterprises. For example, that part of the profits or income of the foreign concern which is invested in the country might be exempted from income and profits tax."

Professor J. G. Gurley, of the U.S., said that Dr. Enke believes that fiscal policy should not interfere with private enterprise, hence he "more or less gives up on fiscal policy for growth purposes, and relies on monetary policy."

Discussing the suggestion that interest rates be subsidized, Dr. Gurley made the supposition that deposits pay 10 per cent, and loans are charged 5 per cent. Some people may reduce their investments in order to hold deposits instead. Others may borrow money from a bank at 5 per cent in order to deposit it in another bank for 10 per cent. Some people may borrow just to hold financial assets cheaply, or to consume (which could easily be disguised).

Dr. Germanico Salgado, Organization of American States, said that it is superficial to lump together all forms of current expenditure as having a lower priority than investment. Agricultural extension work is current expenditure. So are the subsidies Dr. Enke recommends to cheapen credit for the private sector.

If these subsidies are sound, why is another form of subsidy, given to the same private sector through low prices charged by basic enterprises, unsound? Concerning the private issue of currencies, "I do not see anything that a central bank cannot do better than commercial banks in the creation of credit."

Dr. Mortimer Andron, of the U.S., said the conference has brought out the importance of non-economic factors in development, mainly birth control and education. In public utilities we must measure the non-market effects. A road leading from the city to a resort area might benefit only the consumption of the rich, which is not the best use of investment in infrastructure.

The Will to Develop

Family planning will not come until machines replace labor in agriculture. Taxes are equitable if they help give a fair livelihood to everyone. The most vital task is to make people see their land and possessions not as aspects of status, but as assets which have to be developed.

Hon. Mwai Kibaki, of Kenya, said that Dr. Enke's reflection that development will take generations makes this conference superfluous as well as the planning offices and all the efforts of a responsible society to speed up development—since "it would come about by itself in any case in about the five generations that Dr. Enke has in mind.

"We start off from the basic conviction that it is possible to speed up the rate of development, the rate of capital accumulation, the rate of training qualified manpower. All these factors, their evolvement, can be speeded. We start from that assumption."

The rich do not have to be "soaked" just for the sake of it, or even primarily for social justice; but because the savings they accumulate are not being spent to promote development. "By definition, taxes can only be paid by those who are able to pay them. All this has nothing to do with the slogans of soaking the rich, all of which originated in Western Europe, and we hope we don't have to take them over in our countries."

As to population control, Mr. Kibaki agrees that it is a legitimate objective. But unlike in China or India, population growth is not the only obstacle of growth. "Those of us who are involved with these practical problems in the underdeveloped nations know all too well that really you cannot talk in terms of *the* solution. You have to agree that there are three or four or five or six lines of attack always to the development problem."

As to the tax on land, "the criterion we have used all along is again not equity. It is not a question of how anyone acquired his land. Our argument is that people who have more land than they can usefully develop need to have it taxed on the basis of the potential productivity of the land, so as to cause one of two things to happen.

"Either they will part with it, and the land will go to people who will develop it, or alternatively they themselves will be forced by this taxation to develop the land. If it was a question of equity, Mr. Chairman, I do not see that really we need go back to asking how somebody acquired his piece of land. The equity aspect of it is whether we are dispossessing the landowner to the point of making him a pauper, or whether we leave him with enough means for him also to have a fair livelihood as well as everything else in the society."

When adopting mathematical criteria for measuring the effectiveness of investments, Mr. Kibaki pleaded for the following recurrent expenditure, whose return cannot be calculated mathematically: "I refer here to the first thing you have to instill in the minds of these people, which is the will to develop, the will in fact to think in terms of a standard of living, the will or attitude of mind which leads the ordinary peasant farmer to think of land not as merely an aspect of status, not just as something that he will leave to his children, but to begin to look at it as an investment, as a business. The attitude of mind which leads a farmer to keep records of what yield he is getting from his cow. The attitude of mind which leads a businessman to calculate what profit he is making. The attitude of mind which leads an official employed by the government to think not merely that he is employed to collect taxes, but to think of the development that results from what he is doing.

"I would like to urge that this is the fundamental investment that has to be made, if the other developments we are talking about are really to come true, because until we change the attitude of the 90 per cent of the people who live today as they have always lived, development will remain confined to a few little pockets in the country."

Mr. Kibaki opposes the poll tax. Also he believes that taxes proper should be paid in money. "Combined with this you can have your community programs where everybody, including professors in the universities, including Cabinet Ministers, go digging the roads, go building a school. It has a wider dimension than merely a form of tax. It is concerned with creating the will to develop, of creating the social cohesion which somebody talked about the other day, so that the whole society feels involved. That is why we have community development, and not precisely as a payment for tax."

Hon. J. M. Paturau, of Mauritius, said that family planning takes a long time, and "even if you have a family planning campaign operating successfully, you will have to take care of those who were already born before the demographic rate of increase could be controlled."

He recommended the creation of advisory boards to bring about better cooperation, through linking know-how and managerial abilities in the private sector with the needs of the government sector for efficient development.

Mr. Paturau supported the capital/output ratio, with all its shortcomings, as an instrument for fixing priorities easily understandable by the politicians. Private investors can choose from the list of projects, "but the conditions given by the development bank for loans, the tax exemptions, the customs rebates and all that will vary according to the priority of the industry chosen."

Mr. S. B. Nicol-Cole, of Sierra Leone, was convinced that development need not take five generations. "If Dr. Enke is familiar with the development that has taken place in countries that became independent only five or ten years ago, and if he was acquainted with the circumstances in those countries prior to independence, he will certainly see the marked and substantial development that has taken place. And we are not satisfied with the way things are moving in some of our countries, not because we are not satisfied that think are moving at all, but perhaps most Africans realize that the alternative to development is a return to backwardness.

"This question of soaking the rich. Well, if you don't tax the rich, whom do you expect to tax? To tax the poor for the betterment of the rich, that is what we are trying to avoid. The whole idea of economic development and economic aid carries the concept of taxing those who are able to make the extra provisions for those who are not able to help themselves."

Senator A. Arca-Parro, of Peru, said that a problem in achieving the social basis for economic development is that many of the LDCs have two or more cultures which are trying to blend. Population control has succeeded in the industrialized countries so far. It is a question of mentality, and not just a matter of prescription.

Industrial societies offer attractive ways of living that make urban dwellers think differently about family planning. "But within the primitive society, within the agricultural society when there are not mechanical means developed, every new child is a labor saver, a future unit of work. With the onset of mechanization in agriculture, when people see that a country can be worked with less labor force, then automatically they may stop to think that it is a misery to have so many children."

He added that "there are still countries where the mortality indices are high, so if we reduce the rate of birth, and the mortality index is still high, that practically means there would be a diminishing population. We have to think very carefully about these propositions."

A Plea for Private Enterprise

There is a bias against allowing public funds to go to the private sector. People who have become rich in business are likely to be adept at selecting investments that will yield a good return.

Dr. Abba Lerner, of the U.S., defended the need for population control. "A speaker said that population control can take time, which is just the reason why it is important for those countries that are not now suffering from extreme over-population to make a start. I think there is no getting away from it, birth control is one of the central problems of a future viable world."

Dr. Lerner went on: "Since in many underdeveloped countries there is more prejudice against private enterprise than against public enterprise, I can understand Dr. Enke emphasizing the usefulness of having governments lending money to private enterprise, wherever they can do a better job. This is a fundamental principle of what I like to call free enterprise—a phrase which sounds more positive than mixed economy."

Dr. Lerner does not believe in letting private banks create money. But if one believes "and with some justification, that there is a prejudice against supplying the private sector from public funds, then there is a case for advocating that funds be created by private banks, that have a preference for lending to private enterprise—which will offset the preference of the government for not lending to private enterprise."

The phrase "soaking the rich" should be put differently. What is meant is that "you must be careful not to let your concern for removing inequalities go to the point where you do more damage, by removing functional payments which are necessary to bring about production, when the result of doing this will be to have less for everybody including, very likely, less for the poor as well as less for the rich, because you have interfered with the normal mechanisms of society."

In the question of consumption versus investment, there is "a kind of cross-classification. You want to go from consumption for the rich to investment for raising the standards of the poor. The problems involved would be easier to deal with if these two aspects were separated. It is important to have more investment for the poor to raise their standards, but if this is going to come out of consumption by the poor, the question then arises whether the cost is really worth it or not. Then we have the problem which seems not to have been discussed in this conference, of the difference between the extreme forms of current deprivation in the Communist histories of Russia and China, and the less extreme forms elsewhere."

The issues are between high priorities and low priorities (both in consumption and investment), and between consumption now and consumption in the future. "If we can separate that from the rich and the poor, we can then come more seriously to a question we can deal with."

Dr. Lerner said that "the emphasis on investment seems to be a case, which is very common in economic discussion, of a means becoming an end. Through wanting investment for some particular purpose, namely to raise the standard of living of the poor, we come to think of investment itself as a good thing. It leads to a stress on the development of financial intermediaries, these being considered as ways by which you can shift resources from consumption to investment." But investment is not automatically a good thing. It is necessary first to be sure what the money is going to be used for.

*   *   *

Dr. Enke answered a number of points raised in the discussion. On the poll tax, "my idea is that it should be a monetary poll tax, but that a person can pay it by offering his own labor if he wants. An individual whose time is very valuable will pay in cash, and a person whose time is not very valuable will presumably work. But the main point is that the tax does not discourage production and may even encourage it."

The proposal to issue private bank-notes is intended for a certain early stage of development only. "The point here is that there are certain investments, maybe small investments, maybe investments in agriculture, where local knowledge such as a bank manager in a small town would have, is useful. I am not suggesting that these private banks take over the whole investment operation from the central bank. I am suggesting that they both operate, and that if necessary the State can put a maximum limit on the size of these loans that the small private banks make."

Dr. Enke took up Dr. Lerner's observations about the purpose of investment. "I think there is a tendency among many of us to feel that saving automatically leads to useful investment. Saving may lead to investments, but many investments are not useful, they turn out to be bad investments and a waste of resources. Investing is an art, a real art which many of us don't have. I do not think that government officials, because they are government officials, are necessarily good at this job of investing. I think we have to try and use all the talents we can, both private and public. The advantage of having private investment, is that the kind of people who have private wealth are very often those that have invested successfully in the past. It may be that they were just lucky, but I would rather bet on wise investment decisions by a man that has been proved right in the past in his investments, than by someone who has never invested before."

Dr. J. Saenz, of Mexico, speaking as Chairman, added after the summing-up that Dr. Enke had presented to the committee a provocative and genuine viewpoint which has to be taken into account. "There is a tendency to forget that one of the aspects of development is getting the cooperation of those nations which are already developed, and who may have somewhat different ideas, ideologies and different social attitudes toward the problems. It is always interesting to receive from the advanced sector of the world a viewpoint which, although different and perhaps even disagreeable for some of the developing countries, is none the less indicative of a problem that does exist.

"Although we have travelled far on the road to common interests between the developed and underdeveloped countries, there are still many psychological obstacles to getting a true communion in this particular field. I think that Dr. Enke's paper has been most valuable in voicing clearly and honestly a different point of view from those that have been expressed by the majority."

16

SAVING AND INVESTMENT THROUGH GOVERNMENT BUDGETS

By P.N.C. OKIGBO

Economic Adviser, Nigerian Government Ambassador to the European Economic Community

Recent discussions of the problems of growth in developing nations have begun to focus attention not merely on the absolute level of investment but also on the forms in which available saving is transformed into investment. Further, it has now become generally accepted that investment cannot explain all the growth in output and that some of this must be attributed not only to capital and labor but also to technical progress—a catch-all phrase for all the residual rate of growth that cannot be explained by conventional factors of production. Nevertheless, in their attempt to mobilize their resources for growth, developing nations themselves place greater and greater emphasis on investment plans in the public sector. Consequently, an examination of the role of government as an engine of capital formation is an important contribution to an understanding of the process of change in new nations.

Public investment can be financed through the following sources: current saving by governments and state enterprises, past saving and reserves, current internal borrowing and borrowing from abroad. To secure the growth of investment in the private sector many new nations have adopted measures calculated to attract foreign private capital—tax holidays for a period of years, reliefs from customs duties for certain raw materials, liberal foreign exchange policies for repatriation of capital and profits and guarantees of the security of investment from nationalization or expropriation. In the public sector, many new nations have had to rely on their reserves and past saving to finance investment and have supplemented them through current saving. Internal borrowing has been relatively small because of the underdeveloped nature of the capital and money markets and the central banking institutions. With investment plans growing bigger, reserves have declined to levels sometimes inadequate even to support the monetary system, and the public authorities are being driven to rely more and more on their current saving for the financing of development. So it is necessary to examine the possibility of increasing saving and investment through government budgets.

273

Method of Analysis

We divide aggregate saving into two components: saving by government (including state enterprises) and saving by the private sector (companies and households). If the Nigerian experience can serve as a guide, the distribution of investment between the two components stood as follows in the decade 1951–1961.

TABLE 1

Gross Domestic Fixed Investment by Type of Sponsor
(per cent)

	1951	1952	1953	1954	1955	1956	1957	1960	1961
Public sector	30.4	33.7	33.9	36.1	34.9	33.1	33.1	38.8	40.9
Private sector:									
Companies	29.6	28.9	31.5	26.2	28.4	28.6	27.8	13.8	11.6
Households	40.0	37.4	34.6	37.7	36.7	38.3	39.1	47.4	48.5
Total	100	100	100	100	100	100	100	100	100

It is noteworthy that in many developing nations in Asia and Africa, government contribution to gross investment is generally of the order of about 30 per cent. In Nigeria, investment by government (including statutory corporations) represented some 30 per cent in 1951 rising to nearly 41 per cent in 1961. It is also noteworthy from Table 1 that the share of private companies has declined from 29.6 per cent in 1951 to 11.6 per cent in 1961; this decline was offset by a corresponding increase of 10.5 percentage points in the share of the public sector and of 8.5 percentage points in the share of households. If the public investment programs for 1962–1968 are fulfilled, the share of government in gross investment will be expected to rise to over 50 per cent by 1968.

The distribution of saving between the public and private sectors may have important consequences on the rate of aggregate saving. The channels available for transfer of savings from the private to the public sector may weaken private incentives to save and invest. Aggregate saving will rise only if the measures adopted by the public authorities merely bring into the exchequer resources additional to the saving that would have been made by the private sector. But it is possible that through the effects on the distribution of income, measures for such transfer may dampen the motivations for saving and thereby reduce private saving to such a low level that aggregate saving declines. Consequently, public saving will raise the rate of

TABLE 2

Government Revenues as Per Cent of Gross Domestic Product[1]

	1950	1951	1952	1953	1954	1955	1956	1957	1958	1960	1961
Government revenues (£ m)	34.8	47.4	57.7	62.3	74.6	78.1	85.0	91.5	103.8	136.8	147.5
GDP (£ m)	512.1	573.2	614.5	665.0	774.2	827.5	870.6	910.0	952.8	1,026.8	1,046.8
Government revenues/GDP (%)	6.8	8.3	9.4	9.4	9.6	9.4	9.8	10.1	10.9	13.3	14.1

[1] There is some asymmetry in the gross domestic product series. For 1950–1957 there exists a constant series at current prices; for 1958–1961 the figures are at constant prices. In 1958 and 1959 prices were somewhat lower than in 1957 but they rose in 1960 to the 1957 level. Consequently the series for 1958–1961 would tend to be higher in 1958 and 1959 than they should be at current prices and would appear about right for 1960 and 1961.

saving in the economy only if private saving is not correspondingly reduced thereby.

Current saving by government arises from two sources: through budget surpluses (excess of current revenues over current expenditures) and through the transfer of retained earnings by government corporations or state enterprises. At the early stage of development, many state enterprises tend to incur losses often because they tend to undertake activities that private enterprise would not find profitable at that particular time or in a particular location. In the interest of even development the locational pattern for industries may be distorted to the point where a potentially profitable industry is turned into a subsidized industry. There are, of course, cases where strategic or other considerations are paramount—for example, armaments industries—where state enterprises are established with only scant regard to efficiency criteria. In addition to these factors, the price of the product, e.g., in energy and power production, may be determined not by economic considerations of demand and supply or market structure (i.e., extent of competition), but by social policy. This situation is often associated with state monopolies in telecommunications, transport, power and utilities where social policy may be directed to establishing "fair" prices without regard to what the market can bear. As is often the case too, pricing in the private sector may be influenced by state action through the erection of tariff walls (ostensibly for the protection of infant industries) which buttress inefficient firms. In such cases, state enterprises may make profits in spite of their inherent deficiencies. However, it is difficult to expect the state enterprises in new nations to contribute significantly to the government exchequer through transfers of retained earnings. Consequently, greater importance must attach to budgetary surpluses if governments are to raise the rate of aggregate saving.

Budgetary Saving

In Nigeria, government revenues have risen faster than the national income. In 1950, government revenues (central, regional and local) represented 6.8 per cent of the gross domestic product (the only national income aggregate for which there exist consistent figures); by 1960, this proportion had risen to 13.3 per cent. Table 2 shows the relationship.

This increase may appear remarkable in the absolute sense. Nigerian fiscal policy can be said to have been relatively successful in its objective of channelling proportionately greater increases in the

TABLE 3

Budget Surplus as per cent of Government Revenues, 1950–1961

(£ million)

	1950	1951	1952	1953	1954	1955	1956	1957	1958	1959	1960	1961
Government revenues	34.8	47.4	57.7	62.3	74.6	78.1	85.0	91.0	103.8	114.7	136.9	147.5
Federal	28.2	38.8	43.8	47.8	44.7	34.6	34.5	36.3	42.9	45.1	62.3	60.9
Regional	10.7	12.8	17.2	18.5	37.4	32.4	39.4	40.5	44.4	52.2	55.0	66.3
Local	5.7	6.0	7.3	8.7	8.7	14.2	18.4	21.3	22.4	21.4	24.8	25.2
Budget surplus	13.8	24.1	28.9	28.9	37.9	21.2	18.4	21.1	30.6	22.7	31.7	32.8
Federal	9.0	18.7	22.1	23.6	15.2	11.7	11.1	10.4	13.9	8.9	22.5	17.5
Regional	3.6	4.9	5.4	3.3	21.4	8.4	5.4	7.1	10.6	10.9	3.8	12.1
Local	1.2	0.5	1.4	2.0	1.3	1.1	1.9	3.6	6.6	4.0	5.8	3.8
Surplus Revenues (per cent)	39.6	50.8	50.1	46.4	50.8	27.1	21.6	23.2	29.5	19.8	23.1	22.2

national income into the government exchequer. However, the proportion is low compared to the relative levels in other countries. In Burma, for example, the proportion was 27.7 per cent in 1960, in China (Taiwan) 23.5 per cent and in Japan 27 per cent; but the experience of India and Pakistan shows a relatively poorer picture with the proportion at 11.7 per cent and 10.2 per cent respectively.

Alongside this notable development, government saving as a per cent of government revenue declined between 1950 and 1961. From Table 3 it will be seen that in 1950, 39.6 per cent of government revenues was saved in the form of budget surpluses (at the central, regional and local levels), whereas by 1959 only 19.8 per cent was so saved. No doubt, we cannot expect budget surpluses to increase proportionately each year since they are an instrument of contracyclical policy. The principle should be that over a long haul, the proportion of revenues saved should be increased. On the average, between 1950 and 1961, about 35 per cent of the revenues of the central and regional governments has been saved. This proportion compares favorably with the experience of some of the best countries in Asia-China (Mainland) with 35 per cent and Japan with 32.5 per cent during the same period. It is also significantly better than the performance in countries like India (12.6 per cent) or Malaya (16.7 per cent) and Pakistan (12.6 per cent).

In the recent years 1958–1961, the proportion of government revenues saved by the Nigerian governments declined to an average of 23 per cent, bringing Nigeria in line with countries like Ceylon and Singapore. This decline is due in part to the growth in public current expenditures stemming from the expansion of the responsibilities of the regional and central governments. In addition, the capital program of the governments in the decade 1945–1955 generated an increase in the current expenditures in the subsequent decade. For it must be recalled that the ten-year development program concentrated on social overhead development—education, health, transportation and water supplies. The impact of the expansion of these facilities on recurrent budgets was not felt until the late 1950s. By 1964, the burden of the recurrent budgets had become so heavy that surpluses had practically disappeared in the Federal Government's budget. Whereas in 1958 the Central Government saved 37.9 per cent of its revenues, by 1964 this proportion had declined to 1.8 per cent.

It is appropriate to examine what possibilities there are for the Nigerian public authorities to maintain a conscious policy of high budget surpluses in the next decade. Government revenues are now roughly 15 per cent of the national income; in order to maintain the 1950 ratio of public saving to the national income it would be necessary for the governments to aim at a budget surplus of at least 19 per cent. To ensure that the rate of aggregate saving is raised by the contribution from the public sector, budgetary surpluses must average between 20 and 25 per cent of government revenues in the next decade. The dilemma of the 1960s is that to raise the rate of public saving from the low ebb of 1964 to a target rate of 20–25 per cent will undoubtedly affect the incentives to save and invest in the private sector. This dilemma underscores the importance of a well planned fiscal policy.

Fiscal Policy for Higher Budgetary Saving

The search for this policy must cover the following fields: increasing the yields from existing sources of revenue (and possibly introducing new ones), curtailing or containing the bulge in expenditures through a more prudent current expenditure policy and a more rigorous investment policy, increasing the opportunities for efficiency of the state enterprises thus faciliting the transfer of retained earnings and curtailing the need for subsidies. To this problem we shall now turn.

One of the features of the fiscal system in developing countries is the low tax base, the relatively regressive tax structure, the enormity of tax evasion and consequential low per cent of tax revenues relative to other sources of revenue. In Nigeria, for example, direct taxes on personal incomes represented only 6 per cent of total revenues (central and regional) in 1961. The sources of government revenue are shown in Table 4 below.

This may appear to be of the same order of magnitude as that in many countries of Asia and the Far East. For example, it is of the same order as in Cambodia, Ceylon, Taiwan, Thailand and South Vietnam. But in countries like Pakistan the proportion rose from 6 per cent in 1950 to 10 per cent in 1960 while in India it fell from 17 per cent in 1950 to 11 per cent in 1960. There are favorable chances that Nigeria can raise the proportion from 6 per cent in 1961 to near to 10 per cent by 1970; but this can be achieved only through very good reorganization of the fiscal administration.

Similarly, in 1961, taxation on companies accounted for roughly 5 per cent of total government revenues. This is roughly the same order as in India (6 per cent), higher than in Pakistan (3 per

TABLE 4

Revenue of Public Authorities, 1961

(£ million)

Source of Revenue	North	West	East	Lagos	Total
Tax Revenue					
Individual direct taxes	8,373	3,430	4,690	2,244	18,737
Company taxes	—	—	—	5,951	5,951
Jangali and cattle tax	1,342	—	44	—	1,386
Import duties	7,932	7,110	7,688	34,295	57,025
Export duties	5,451	5,760	1,970	67	13,114
Produce Sales/Purchase Tax	780	1,109	1,590	—	3,479
Excise and others	2,665	4,823	1,391	3,739	12,618
Total	26,543	22,232	17,373	46,162	112,310
Income from property					
Interests	395	590	373	3,893	5,251
Royalties	219	243	592	2,504	3,558
Premium on mineral oil licences and leases	—	1,177	2,614	1,866	5,657
Rents and profits	631	494	824	2,555	4,504
Total	1,245	2,504	4,403	10,818	18,970
Transfers					
Payments and grants from Marketing Boards and Development Corporations	1,021	1,932	38	735	3,726
Grants from Overseas	27	—	—	—	27
Payments and grants from others	68	81	214	218	581
Total	1,116	2,013	252	953	4,334
Other receipts					
Fines, fees and licences	1,337	2,436	2,109	1,462	7,344
Earnings and sales	771	274	393	1,759	3,197
Other receipts NES	684	183	63	381	1,311
Total	2,792	2,893	2,565	3,602	11,852
Total—Current Revenue	31,696	29,642	24,593	61,535	147,466

cent) and Thailand (3 per cent) but considerably lower than in Ceylon (11 per cent), Indonesia (11 per cent), Philippines (17 per cent) not to mention oil rich countries like North Borneo (10 per cent) or Burma (46 per cent). Again, it seems that more than in the area of personal income taxation, there exist opportunities of doubling this proportion in less than half a decade through improved and more stringent application of existing laws and regulations.

There are two main areas for reform in the tax system of developing states like Nigeria—the system of assessment that allows gross undervaluation of incomes and the system of collection that permits gross evasion of tax payment. The one can be rectified by a more vigorous system of inspection of the business of self-employed persons and by bringing the task of assessment down to as local a level as possible. Only people with intimate local knowledge can properly estimate the level of a neighbor's business in a community where no accounts are kept and maintained. There is no substitute for local knowledge in illiterate societies. Consequently, tax areas have to be divided into wards with local representatives on the committee for assessment. But these assessors have to be instructed in their duties and in the methods of differentiating capital from income. The task of the assessor can be made easier by breaking down urban and rural wealth—trucks, shops, houses, farms—into different categories with different levels of income imputed to such categories. In this exercise, local knowledge of climatic, agricultural and business conditions can be of great help.

This practice is adopted in many parts of Nigeria but it has not been an unqualified success. In some cases, the local assessors have yielded too readily to the temptation to reduce the tax liability for the taxpayer and split the difference with him; in some, the assessors have used their power as an instrument of political vendetta against their opponents. In Lagos, the system of local assessment committees was disbanded for no very good reason and the responsibility was transferred to the Board of Inland Revenue, understaffed, under-equipped and undertrained for the task. It is therefore not surprising that the tax collection has fallen short of expectations.

With respect to collection, the problem often arises that at very low incomes where poll rates apply, the taxpayer finds it difficult to pay his tax all at one time. The burden would be lighter for him if the could pay by instalments through the use of revenue stamps. This practice was quite successful in Kenya but was discontinued in 1961. It is being considered in Nigeria.

In the field of company taxation the weaknesses exist in the assessment and evaluation of taxable income. Because of the dearth of qualified personnel, close scrutiny of the returns by the companies is infrequent; the verification of the deductions allowed under the law and the examination of the qualifying expenses are left to a government staff that are too few in number to cope with the number of returns, too ill-equipped professionally to detect anomalies except the most glaring ones, and not sufficiently well paid to resist the temptations easily placed in their way by unscrupulous company directors. At the level of assessment of the taxable income of companies, the fiscal authorities are therefore working under a severe handicap. Much of the weakness in this area can be rectified by training and close supervision and by inculcating in the officials a higher sense of public responsibility and integrity.

In addition to this shortcoming there is a more important defect. The company profits taxation laws allow very generous deductions from income for the purpose of determining taxable income. For instance, initial allowances of the order of 40 per cent are given for plant and machinery, 20 per cent for other industrial building expenditure and 25 per cent for mining and plantation expenditure. In addition, annual allowances of 15 per cent are given for mining and 10 per cent for other buildings. Even the businesses operating in West Africa agree that these rates of deductions and allowances are too generous and that a reduction in the rates now current should not affect the incentive to invest. There are additional benefits offered to private businesses through remission of customs duties for imports of raw materials, through tax holidays for companies engaged in "pioneer" industries and through tax exemptions granted by the Finance Minister at his discretion. The reduction in the rate of initial allowances to the order of 20 per cent for machinery and plant and annual allowances to 5 per cent on industrial buildings (narrowly defined) will add some £3 million to £4 million a year to the public revenues; the revision of pioneer reliefs so as to relate them not to the capital invested but to the level of profit earned will save another £2 million to £3 million annually. These two measures can raise the ratio of revenues from company profits taxation to gross revenues from the current level of 5 per cent to about 10 per cent. The aim is to reduce the losses in revenue without unduly restricting the inducements for private foreign investment in Nigeria.

Control of government expenditures is a difficult problem in countries that have only just become independent. Police, army, internal security and representation abroad are new areas that demand increasing attention. And it is difficult for the new states, jealous of their newly won independence, to agree to curtail their efforts toward maintaining internal security at home and enhancing their prestige and image abroad. Further, most of these states emerge into independent status with an administration hardly up to its task. They soon find, therefore, the need to expand their services and consequently the cost of government to cope with the enhanced responsibilities that stem from independence.

It is perhaps in the field of investment expenditure that there is room for considerable improvement. It is common knowledge that many new nations have embarked on prestige projects—manufacturing activities with little or no feasibility studies beforehand, office and residential buildings far more luxurious than the economies could support. In many cases, the lack of adequate feasibility studies and proper accounting procedures has led to an exaggeration of the cost of the projects. Other inefficiencies and bottlenecks lead to additonal waste of resources.

In state enterprises in new nations, inefficiencies arise from many sources. First, at the control level, the Boards are made up mostly of people who have shown no special talent for the activity into whose Board they are injected. Second, the managers may be professional men but because of the composition of the Boards they are subjected to pressures that they can resist only at the risk of losing their position. Influence—political and social—interferes with deployment of personnel with the result that appointments, promotions and transfers are not often related to efficiency or need. The management often begins with a large indebtedness because the enterprise is overcapitalized. The break-even point is delayed beyond the normal level in similar private enterprises. Third, the government appears always too willing to rescue the enterprise from collapse.

Consequently, the urge to run the business efficiently is dampened by diseconomies inherited at the inception, by ineptitude of the management and the gullibility of the government. Improvements can come about only through a radical orientation of the government to state enterprises and a firm determination to get rid of subsidies. More often than not the government is not fully aware of the extent of subsidies that it pays to state enterprises.

In Nigeria, the need for a more rational investment policy is underscored by the fact that whereas in the period 1950–1954 government saving exceeded government investment, the position has been reversed in the period 1955–1961. Table 5 below illustrates the relation between saving and investment in the government sector. By the end of the period, government saving accounted for only 13 per cent of investment. In the earlier part of the period (1950–1954), there were sufficient surpluses and reserves to draw from and the absolute level of investment expenditure was relatively low. The picture had changed by 1955 and the two sides of the scissors were coming closer: investment expenditures were growing rapidly (in 1962 they were six times the level in 1951), while surpluses were drying up (in 1962 they were a little more than a third of the 1951 level). In the face of the picture depicted by Table 5 below, the public authorities have not only to attempt greater public saving but also to promote those conditions that would foster private saving and investment.

TABLE 5

Saving and Investment in the Public Sector, 1951–1962

	1951	1952	1953	1954	1955	1956	1957	1960	1961	1962
Investment (£m)	11.5	18.2	19.9	25.8	29.9	33.5	37.4	60.1	70.5	67.0
Saving (£m)	23.6	27.5	26.9	36.6	20.1	16.5	17.5	17.3	14.6	8.7
Saving/Investment (%)	205	151	135	142	67	49	47	29	21	13

Budgetary Policy

We now conclude this analysis with an examination of what should constitute appropriate budgetary policies. First, the governments must seek an increase in revenues from direct and indirect taxation concentrating on the development of those sources that are income-elastic. Second, they should seek to contain the bulge in non-developmental expenditures by restraining such increases to a minimum adjuged necessary for carrying on the administration. Third, a cardinal objective of policy should be to provide for surpluses in the current account. Such surpluses should not come purely as a residual after all desired expenditure has been met; rather they should be consciously determined as a target, and policy should be directed toward achieving that objective. We have recommended that in Nigeria a surplus of between 20 and 25 per cent of revenues is the minimum necessary to guarantee an increase in public saving and raise the proportion of national income saved in the economy. This target should serve as a benchmark for a period of years—five years preferably—so that taking the good years with the bad, the governments can aim at attaining it in the long haul.

Consideration can be given by the governments to the proposal to earmark the increase from certain income-elastic revenues to the development fund. In the Nigerian experience, contributions to the development fund are made from surpluses, such surpluses being determined as a residual. In the new suggestion such payments to the development fund are part of the current expenditure estimates and become additional to the surpluses that would be recorded in the traditional system of government accounting. There is much to commend this view; governments may thus denote a proportion of certain receipts for contribution to the development fund and this becomes a fixed charge on revenue in good as well as bad years. If a reduction in expenditure is necessitated by low revenues, the cut in expenditures is not confined only to the payment to the development fund. It may also be expected that the public might accept more readily their burdens in respect of additional taxation if they knew that the whole of it was to be devoted to investment. But this must be supplemented with greater prudence in investment planning and in costing, accounting and management of investment allocation.

DISCUSSION

The papers of Dr. Koichi Emi and Dr. Okigbo
were discussed at the same session.

Economic Sputnik

Deficit financing works if the output effect is greater than the price effect. After achieving economic take-off, efforts must be made to restore budgetary stability, with the aid of increased taxes on growing incomes.

The transfer of resources to the public authority is of no avail unless a rational investment policy makes sure the money is used constructively. Plans must be accompanied by long-term forecasts.

Dr. Koichi Emi said that in the Meiji period there was no full-scale banking system to mobilize savings, nor was there a fully operating tax system. The only alternatives were to borrow and/or issue paper money. The paper money went not just to public works, but to loans for private industry as well. According to Mr. Emi, the loans to industry are more important from the fiscal point of view because they increase incomes.

What is the impact of such an inflationary policy? "If the output effect is larger than the price effect, we would say that such a policy was successful in increasing the national income." The accompanying inflationary influence must be considered as temporary and inevitable. In due course, as incomes grow, tax rates can be increased.

In the second stage, these taxes replace inflationary financing. "Multiplier effects are created, and the foundations are established for regular government revenue." In the third stage, the government issues long-term bonds in the domestic market.

Case II, after the last war, also showed three stages. The first was again paper money; the second was taxes combined with U.S. aid; and the third was Treasury loans and private savings.

Dr. Emi went on: "The most important point is that enormous motivating power is required to establish the foundations of economic development. It is just like the enormous energy needed to put a sputnik into orbit. In the Japanese experience it was the huge amount of paper money issues and the borrowings from abroad which played an important role. The next important point is that investment should be ahead of saving. Without investment, income is not generated and then savings are not created. Furthermore we greatly appreciated the stimulating effect of Treasury loans to private industry."

In conclusion Dr. Emi expressed the opinion that, for LDCs today, "foreign aid is more effective than an inflationary policy in the domestic economy."

Dr. P. N. C. Okigbo said, "It might very well be desirable to inculcate a deliberate policy to budget for a surplus rather than to arrive at this surplus purely as a residual factor after all desirable and, in many cases, unjustifiable expenditures of the public authorities have been met."

The difficulties of taxing the self-employed might make it desirable "to introduce a system whereby the assessment is by reference to the wealth held by this class of taxpayer.

"At the company tax level, the experience we have had shows that we tend to be over-generous in the granting of tax reductions, tax incentives and tax exemptions, presumably, as was pointed out in the discussions yesterday, in the hope of attracting foreign investments. I find particularly attractive the suggestion that was made yesterday that there might be some need here for the developing countries to swap ideas and exchange information, because it appears that the tax incentives that have been offered by each individual country have done relatively little to pomote the level of investment by foreign enterprises; and what is even more remarkable is that a lot of these foreign enterprises do not themselves really want these tax exemptions. They themselves have said that some of the concessions are over-generous, and that they could do with much less.

"If a justification for increasing public savings can be made on the grounds that this would bring forth additional savings in the aggregate and that it would improve the quality of investments through the transfer of resources to the public authorities for investment, it becomes all the more necessary to establish a rational investment policy—otherwise the transfer of resources to the public authorities could be wasteful."

Mr. Edmond A. Lisle discussed the three case studies, two given by Dr. Emi and one by Dr. Okigbo.

During the coming years, he stated, the Nigerian government will control, according to Dr. Okigbo, 50 per cent of the country's gross fixed capital formation. Mr. Lisle contends that "he who controls investment controls growth"—and there is the rub, because government saving in Nigeria (i.e., the budget surplus) has dropped from 40 per cent to a little over 20 per cent of Government revenues in a decade, i.e., to 3 per cent of the gross domestic product.

Dr. Okigbo advanced as one reason for this decline that past development plans involve recurring current expenditures which weigh heavily on the government's resources. Governments commonly undertake new capital investments without making provision for running costs, that must extend far into the future. Secondly, public savings are treated as a residual item—what is left after the fixed budget commitments have been met. These two facts "themselves rest upon a third reason which I think is more fundamental, namely that governments tend to take too short-term a view in forming economic policy. They tend to think a little too much in terms of the current or next fiscal year, and not enough in terms of five or ten years hence."

They should "begin to draw up long-term financial schedules accompanying their long-term development projects." This makes it possible to estimate how much money can be provided from public sources over the next ten or fifteen years. If not enough is available, the government must determine "whether it can borrow and to what extent it can run the risk of going into inflationary financial procedures.

"In fact, I think one of the main conclusions which we could draw from the Nigerian experience is a very strong case for long-term forecasting and planning by the government, and the need for setting up institutions which can draw up these plans."

Dr. Emi's paper showed the role of the government in "fostering economic take-off or initial thrust process through a combination of physical and financial programs," leading in the Meiji era to "a very rapid monetization of the economy which in turn led to the setting up of financial intermediaries."

Hon. Mwai Kibaki, of Kenya, took issue with Dr. Okigbo's criticism of inefficiency in public corporations, and attributed the shortcomings mainly to a lack of clear political direction. In Kenya, the confusion has been between two objectives, that of having State ownership, as part of socialist program which is seen as good in itself; and that of using public corporations as a vehicle for channelling savings into productive investment.

The budget surplus is "a worthwhile objective, but I believe that, looking to the near future, it is a near impossible objective . . . We have to expand education, health services, all the minimum basic things that people expect the government to bring about."

What Kenya has in surplus is human labor, particularly during the lax period while waiting for the crops to grow. "Therefore we are going to take taxes in a direct form, through having people contribute their labor to development projects."

This can be described as "a self-help program, where the villagers form into a committee, and build their own schools and build their own dispensaries. It has helped in that we have been able to save the initial costs of construction, and equally we have been able to generate among the people a sense of the necessity of *their* making a contribution to the public fund, so that the man who used to think that taxation is a method of being oppressed by a foreign government will at last accept that taxation is a necessity.

"This underscores the point that Mr. Lisle emphasized—the need for governments to plan long-term. When we started that program, we hadn't really planned long-term, so we landed ourselves in the position where some villages have built more schools or more dispensaries than we can find the recurrent expenditure for, in terms of qualified personnel or in terms of finance, and therefore we have landed ourselves into embarrassing difficulties."

As regards restraining government expenditure, Mr. Kibaki asked whether it is possible to define which expenses are non-developmental and therefore subject to restraint, since education, health, etc., all seem to be concerned with fostering the capacity to be productive.

It is not practical to expect Finance Ministers to plan for the long term, so Dr. Kibaki suggests creating within the Budget Bureau a special department dealing with long-term planning.

More Pre-Investment Studies

"Blanket concessions" should be superseded by aid given to individual undertakings on their merits. Each project should be approved only after it has been thoroughly studied, and graded by government planners in their list of priorities.

Mr. Christopher Musoke, of Uganda, supported Mr. Kibaki's denial that State enterprises are always inefficient. On the contrary, many in Uganda have shown particular success. It depends on the instructions they receive. If they are tools for the social distribution of goods and services, then you must be prepared that they have got to be subsidized.

Mr. Musoke agreed on the need for tax concessions to stimulate foreign enterprise, "but I disagree with the method so far employed, namely of giving a blanket concession, without knowing what is being offered to each project. I agree entirely with Dr. Okigbo that some private enterprises do not require the concessions at all. I wonder whether it would not be more practical if these tax benefits were given through the budget, instead of issuing what amount to blank checks.

"The reason why I am saying this is that governments do not actually know the costs of these concessions. If they were made as payments through the budget, it would be known that Company A, which established a paper mill, is saving so much. Then I am sure there would be an opportunity for annual reviews of the appropriations for these subsidies."

Conceding that the choice of investments is not always judicious, Mr. Musoke spoke up for a more objective selection process. "Here is a way we could copy from the developed countries, and employ modern sophisticated tools for allocating limited resources in a manner which is more objective and less subjective."

Mr. Robert Nkamgang, of Cameroun, listed four objections to the technique of pump-priming adopted by the Japanese in 1868. Many of the LDCs lack powers in the monetary field; have limited borrowing powers both internally and externally; lack people with enterprise and technical knowledge; and the people have no collaterals against which to raise credit.

The limited powers enjoyed by governments in the African monetary zone may be salutary in the first phase to maintain equilibrium,
but the needs change as countries enter the second, development
phase.

Mr. Nkamgang asked into which of his three models Professor
Galbraith would grade the Japan of 1868.

Dr. J. B. Kelegama, of Ceylon, said that exports account for one-
third of Ceylon's GNP and provide half the revenue. During the last
ten years (1955 to 1964) the terms of trade have worsened by 23
per cent of which 18 per cent was due to a fall in export prices
and 5 per cent to a rise in import prices. In the circumstances it is
hard to follow Dr. Okigbo's advice that revenue should be increased.
The economies that can be made in expenditure are limited. Inflationary methods of promoting growth and employment opportunities are hard to apply in a country that lives by foreign trade. Last
year the government had to counter the import boom by drastic
import and exchange controls.

Hon. Unia Gostel Mwila, of Zambia, thought that the government
should tax more than it spends, putting the money aside as a form of
community saving. "I would say that in times of inflation, governments may deliberately budget the revenue surplus, not with the intention of spending the money immediately, but to remove the purchasing power from the public. The money can be held idle by the
government until the danger of deflation develops."

Government enterprise is essential owing to the lack of private
enterprise. The Zambia government is setting up a second cement
factory and invests in many other industries jointly with private
companies.

Mr. Shimon Shapira, of Israel, warned about having too great a
bias against public corporations, since private enterprise can be just
as bad—when the concessions given to induce private firms to go
into business include a system of cost plus. He recommends emulating
Italy's example, where large holding companies have been set up
to act as a "political umbrella," guarding public corporations against
outside intervention and political pressure. Another system is to introduce "analytical control system," as in France, making it possible to
know what is going on in a public company. "Then the question whether they make a profit or not is not so important, because it is
possible to pin down *why* they lost money."

Mr. Alex Eshiabor, of Ghana, said that in order to achieve maximum output from investment, most LDCs have a development plan—

but no scale of priorities. This gives leeway to the politicians to exercise pressure, because they want to show results. "Along comes a bright financier and he wants to sell you some factory. Now the officials have not had the time to study the feasibility of the thing, the location and whether we really need it. But then the Minister of Industry or the Minister of Agriculture or some other political leader wants to do something, so he says: 'Well, we've got this. We say we want foreign loans, and now you're delaying it. Why?'

"I think it is not enough to have magnificent seven-year plans or five-year plans, but to have a concrete list of priorities."

To promote domestic savings you need monetary stability. Otherwise people will invest in flats, "particularly when interest rates are kept low, to assist the Accountant-General to get his ways and means at cheap rates."

Dr. Yehuda Don, of Israel, gave as another example of an economic take-off prompted by capital inflow the rapid growth that overtook Germany in 1871, thanks to French reparations. "The German experience of the 1870s and 1880s showed that subsidizing a public utility, where the price elasticity of demand is high, speeded up to a very great extent the use of that public utility. I am referring to railway transport especially, which was among the most important accessories to fast economic growth in Germany. So it might be that, in cases where such conditions exist, covering the full average cost of the public utilities might not be the optimum policy."

Dr. Don went on to ask, "Is the Japanese experience in the Meiji period really desirable for the LDCs?" Between 1868 and 1875, the Japanese distributed nearly 40 per cent of their total budgetary expenditure to the *samurai*, for turning this feudal clan into capitalists. "Would it be desirable, according to modern concepts of income distribution, to put such a huge amount of your budget into the hands of, let us say, a prospective capitalist class?

"Further, about 30 per cent of the budget in the 1870s went to the payment of interest on the national debt. Again it was indicated by Dr. Emi that the debt was created partly by taking loans from rich merchants. It involved taking money through the land tax from low income-bracket people with a rather low propensity to consume, and placing it at the disposal of high income-bracket people with a rather high propensity to save."

So the question is not only how to save money and how to invest, but also what are the social and economic implications of the various alternative methods.

Dr. Emi underlined that deficit budgeting in the Meiji period was only applicable at the starting point of the economic take-off, but afterwards the government had to return to balanced budgets on the basis of the increased taxable income.

He mentioned two factors that facilitated Japanese development. There was an accumulation of gold and silver in the feudal society which helped in the Meiji period to solve balance of payment deficits. These precious ornaments were converted, as it were, into cotton textile machinery.

Secondly, after World War II, the annual increase of 10 per cent in output was made possible by a sharp reduction in military expenditure—from 60 per cent of government revenue in 1940 to 8 per cent today. This has released considerable resources for use in economic development.

Dr. Okigbo assented that some State enterprises in the LDCs do extremely well. If the accounts of public corporations are brought out into the open and governments become aware of the magnitude of the direct or indirect subsidies they enjoy, then it becomes feasible to require that clearer directives be given or that political intervention be diminished.

The use of self-help schemes has been tried in Nigeria. As in Kenya, the building of hospitals, schools, etc., "generated enormous requirements for public support through the provision of teachers, equipment, drugs, materials. The tendency now is to channel community effort into other forms of endeavor, for building bridges and roads instead."

Speaking about the budget surplus, Dr. Okigbo said, "What is often observed is that invariably, as soon as the budgetary authorities declare that there is likely to be a surplus, a whole welter of new claims appear. And that is why I have proposed that the surplus be hypothecated to development projects."

PART IV FOREIGN EXCHANGE

A major obstacle to continuous growth is the depletion of foreign currency reserves. Heavy and comprehensive industrialization is successful in countries that have a big internal market, like Brazil. Smaller countries have done best by fostering their existing exports of agricultural products and raw materials. If a small country builds facilities for producing intermediate goods like steel, without achieving full economies of scale, it is apt to be saddled with heavy tariff protection, inflation and stagnation of exports.

Bottlenecks threaten when LDCs terminate the phase of creating import substitutes. Further industrialization after that raises the question how to pay for imported fuel, materials and parts. Industrial workers also demand food, which the local agriculture is laggard in supplying. Present trends suggest that certain LDCs may in due course become importers of food and exporters of manufactures, which will shift the terms of trade in favor of agriculture and against industry.

The inflow of loans from the Western countries is meanwhile saddling the LDCs with a growing foreign currency debt, which has risen from nil at the end of World War II to $30,000 million in 1963, creating a "foreign exchange constraint" that will hamper the developing countries increasingly as their need for imports grows.

One suggestion for easing this constraint is to supplement the gold exchange standard with a "commodities currency." An international institution could stockpile non-perishable raw materials and foodstuffs in times of boom, for sale when times are slack. The institution can pay for the goods it buys by issuing its own currency. This would create a new source of liquidity in international trade, benefiting in the first place the LDCs that need it most.

293

17

PROBLEMS THAT FACE DEVELOPING COUNTRIES

By Giuseppe Ugo Papi

Rector, University of Rome
President, International Economic
Association, Italy

After some years of experience in Singapore and other British administered parts of Borneo, Sir Sidney Caine, Director of the London School of Economics and Political Science, pointed out some characteristics of the less developed countries: income per head less than the average of advanced countries in Europe and North America; not a great deal of saving and investment, that is, of domestic capital formation; little industrial development; rather primitive "subsistence agriculture"; highly organized and directed production for export; and less organized production for domestic market.

The role of monetary policy in countries like these is rather modest. The government has to provide some kind of physical money. As a basis of money was adopted some variety of British coin or, as in many countries, old Spanish or Mexican silver dollars.

The Banks are organized either as offshoots of banks operating in the United Kingdom, or with their head offices in London and very close association with the British banking system.

The creation of a Central Bank can be considered a sign of independence, just as the acquisition of a flag and a national anthem. A Central Bank has as its main function the maintenance of monetary stability—as well as other functions: banker of bankers, banker and adviser of the government. But in less developed countries Central Banks are also thought of as being active promoters of development, giving positive stimulus to investment and somehow offsetting fluctuations in income.

Now there is a very obvious difference in the position facing a Central Bank in a less developed country and a Central Bank in the major European countries. The former has nothing like the same facilities open for the use of the traditional techniques of monetary management.

Frequently in the developing countries there is no money market; no habitual dealing in short-term government securities, bills and so on. There is no short-term rate of interest and no one highly publicized activity of the Central Bank. In an economy of which a large part consists of subsistence agriculture—the influence of monetary measures is comparatively small.

The industries most highly organized and more susceptible to monetary influences are those producing for exports; but they depend on international demand. In other terms, the amount of credit the banking system can provide is determined not by local conditions, but by conditions in a metropolitan country. So an attempt, for instance, by a local monetary authority to tighten credit would almost certainly be defeated.

In what concerns the fluctuations of export income arising from fluctuations in prices, there are some other national and international mechanisms more effective than monetary measures. There are, for instance, Marketing Boards for the major products considered. There is little evidence that purely monetary influence can start people up on a process of growth in countries which need new attitude of mind, skill, increase in education and provision—either from inside or outside—of capital for the creation of infrastructure.

Initially in less developed countries the role of a monetary policy is very modest. It becomes of growing importance only as the economy matures.

Trade Policy

In the developing countries, the main characteristics of international trade still remain the export of raw material and agricultural products to the industrialized countries, and the import of manufactured goods from these countries. There is, however, more intense trade with other developing countries, as is shown by the creation of the Latin American Free Trade Area; and the studies for similar agreements in the countries of Asia and Africa. Moreover, besides raw materials and food products, the developing states also export certain manufactured goods in exchange for others and they import to an increasing extent raw materials and food products, in addition to manufactured goods.

The larger part of the trade flow, however, remains traditional: raw materials and agricultural products in exchange for manufactured goods. But the expansion of exports is slower than the development of world production and income and the expansion of imports of capital goods faster than the development of exports.

The slower rate of the development of exports is due to various factors. A first factor is the lack of elasticity of the demand for agricultural products of the developing countries—food products, textiles fibers—with the growth of the income in the industrialized countries.

The second factor contributing to the slower rate of exports of the developing countries is the technological progress, which in the industrialized countries directs the preference of consumers toward more complex products, or gives rise to substitutes: for instance, synthetic products.

The third factor—not less important that the other two—is the agricultural protectionism of the industrialized countries which accompanies the increase in the home production of goods, formerly imported from the developing countries. Despite the regulations of the General Agreement on Trade and Tariffs (GATT), the industrialized countries often encourage the home production of food products by import quotas, custom duties, or by subsidies and guaranteed purchases, which imply restrictions on imports from the developing countries.

There are, of course, substantial reasons for this protectionism: shortage of agricultural products during the war; balance of payments difficulties and the necessity of ensuring a minimum income to agricultural producers.

"Quotas" and other forms of "quantitative restrictions" on imports are capable of cancelling the eventual tariff concessions, which the developing countries might have obtained from the industrialized countries following laborious negotiations.

There are, however, some misunderstandings, which have to be eliminated. It is not always realized that no less than one half of the total value of exports of primary products—excluding petroleum and the exports of the central planned economies—both originates in and is absorbed by the developed countries of North America, Western Europe, Oceania and Japan. The pattern of trade in this group of commodities is largely influenced by the domestic "agricultural stabilization" and "support policies" of all the importing countries and of the United States—which is, of course, a large exporter.

With regard to the other half of the world commodity trade which originates from the developing countries, the nature of problems once again is quite different. This trade consists primarily of tropical agricultural products—though it also includes some temperate-zone agricultural exports from semi-developed countries of Latin-America—and to a lesser extent of minerals.

In the case of these tropical export products and minerals the problem of the narrowing of markets due to protectionist measures by the importing countries exists only in a few cases: notably sugar. For this reason the primary exporting countries have relatively little to gain from the usual kind of multilateral negotiations for the reciprocal reduction of tariffs and quantitative restrictions.[1]

There are also supply factors that slow down export expansion. Technical inefficiency prevents reduction of costs. Better methods and organization could have increased productivity, reduced the price of the various products and prevented the industrialized countries from making recourse to substitutes.

Added to this is a growing evidence of a structural overproduction of a large number of tropical products. Available projections of the main tropical products for the period up to 1970[2] indicate a growing excess of world production over world consumption, even on the most optimistic assumptions concerning the growth of demand in the high-income countries.

Often the developing countries depend upon the production of one or two products only; and such a limited diversification exposes them more easily to risks of losses, without possibility of compensation.

Finally there is an almost total lack of consultations among the countries, the development of which is dependent upon exports: so it is not possible to specify the extent both of the total demand and of the total supply, with a view to a better coordination of the national policies.

Under these conditions the basic tendencies of trade between developing and industrialized countries very clearly set the problem—in the developing countries—of the basic imbalance of their economies and—in the advanced countries—of the most efficient aid to be given to the former.

Only nine-tenths of the imports of developing countries are covered by the income from exports. The trade deficit—including freight and insurance items—as well as payments under the heading "interest and dividends" on loans obtained, have been covered by a considerable movement of capital.[3]

During the period 1953–1958, the growing deficits of the coun-

---

[1] G. Blau, *International Commodity Agreements* (Vienna: Congress of International Economic Association, 1962).

[2] *Agricultural Commodities Projections for 1970* (Special Supplement to the *FAO Commodity Review*) (Rome: 1962).

[3] International Monetary Fund, *Balance of Payments Yearbook* (Washington, D.C.: International Monetary Fund, 1959).

tries in the course of development were compensated by capital flows of almost $ 4.5 billion, of which more than $ 2.5 billion consisted of official grants.

During the same period, North America and Western Europe—thanks to a modification in their favor of the terms of trade—benefited from an increase in real national income of $ 2.8 billion. At the same time these modifications had the effect of reducing the import capacity of the non-industrialized countries by $ 1.7 billion. That is to say, the modification of the terms of trade resulted in a gain of a billion dollars for the industrialized countries. Official grants and long-term capital, which amounted to $ 2.5 billion, benefited in the first place the developing countries, but also the industrialized countries, on whose markets the capital was spent.

Table 1 summarizes the various items of aid:

TABLE 1
Aid Contributions (DAC Members)

	Millions of dollars			
	1960	1961	1962	1963
A. *Aid supplied by DAC member countries*				
Bilateral contribution of the public sector	4,207	5,214	5,334	5,679
Contributions of the public sector to multilateral organisms*	655	811	602	396
Private contribution to multilateral organisms	77	75	214	−12
Bilateral contributions of the private sector**	2,446	2,532	1,885	2,083
Total	7,384	8,632	8,035	8,146
B. *Aid Received by Less Developed Countries*				
Bilateral contribution of the public sector	4,207	5,214	5,334	5,679
Contributions furnished by multilateral organisms**	307	342	446	618
Bilateral contributions of the private sector***	2,446	2,532	1,885	2,083
Total	6,960	8,088	7,685	8,380
Memorandum				
One to five years public loans (net)	81	62	36	−27
Export credit guaranteed from one to five years (net)	289	225	227	248

* IMF excluded.
** Excluding credits guaranteed for less than five years and contribution by private non-profit organizations.
*** The figure represents an estimate made by the DAC Countries. It corresponds to 80% of total net payment.

In order to evaluate the total amount of resources received by the less developed countries from all the different aid distribution organizations, it is necessary to add to the global net bilateral contributions (both public and private) of DAC member countries, the total contribution supplied by multilateral organisms, as well as public and private contributions of all the other industrialized countries, including China and the U.S.S.R. Although some signs lead to believe that the Sino-Soviet contributions have been slightly reduced, it may be supposed, in the absence of more accurate information, that the bilateral contributions of all these countries were maintained at the level estimated for 1962. In this case the total resources received in 1963 by the less developed countries can be estimated at about $ 9,035 million; i.e., $ 710 million above the sum calculated for 1952.

This imbalance between imports and exports in developing countries has produced the argument that international trade between industrialized countries and those in the course of development is always a disadvantage to the latter.

At the root of this contention, there are three arguments: (a) that the prices of raw materials tend to decrease as compared with the prices of other goods entering into international trade; (b) that the proportion of income spent on the consumption of primary goods decreases with the increase of income; (c) that in developing countries, there is always a disguised unemployment of productive factors.

As regards the first argument, it is necessary to go into the reasons for which agricultural prices decrease.

If the prices fall as a result of increased productivity in agriculture, the benefit will go to all consumers and the deterioration of the terms of trade will not have dangerous repercussions for the developing countries.

If, on the other hand, agricultural products are obtained at high costs, which are not remunerated by prices on the international market, because the products are supplied in excessive quantity compared with home and international demand, it is a problem of setting up a policy of "structure improvements"—of improving the quality of labor, of assuring mobility of labor and of promoting hygiene and public health. Only with the solution of all these problems can the agricultural income of developing countries start to rise.

The second argument is that the tendency of the poor countries to become poorer results from the decreasing expenditure on consumer goods as income increases. But technical progress, the progressive industrialization of the developing countries and increase in population always oblige a considerable part of income to be spent on primary consumer goods.

As regards the third argument—the existence of a mass of unused production factors in the developing countries—the fact simply indicates that the transfer of agricultural population towards other productive activities has not yet been sufficiently developed.

Summing up, experience and logic do not agree with the opinion that the progress of the developed countries damages the developing countries. The progress of the industrialized countries has always represented a net benefit for all the developing countries. It is true that, sometimes, this benefit has been neutralized or hidden by an increase in population. But it is no less certain that if there were not the more advanced countries, to whom could the developing countries sell their products?

The necessity of speeding up the rate of economic expansion of the non-industrialized countries in order to improve their living conditions implies an availability of capital far in excess of the present possibilities of low-income countries. The production and export capacity of the low-income countries is dependent upon the demand of the industrialized countries. It is, therefore, very normal to inquire: what are the present prospects for this demand?

It is true that the demand for primary products on the part of the industrialized countries does not tend to increase in proportion to the economic growth of such countries. However, it must be recognized that the imports of the industrialized countries tend to increase with the progress of their regional integration.

Official documents show that, during the 1950s, the value of Western European trade—inter-regional trade as well as trade with other countries—did increase more rapidly than that of world trade as a whole. In 1959, trade between Western European countries exceeded the 1950s' figures by 127 per cent, while in the same period world trade increased by only 86 per cent.

In order to import widely, the developing countries have to export even more widely. To make possible an expansion of industrial export in the developing countries the old industrial countries should not refuse to reduce the obstacles to the introduction of such products into their respective markets and should give up a part of the production of light industries in favor of the newly formed industries in the developing countries. Industrialized countries have to concentrate their respective factors of production on the more specialized and more dynamic sectors of industrial production: upon which depends, whatever the circumstances, the economic growth of the advanced countries, and in which these countries will find the necessary compensation.[4]

In Geneva, in March 1964, in the framework of the United Nations, a Conference was convened for the discussion of the problems concerning trade and development of low-income countries.

The debates, however, centered much more on trade problems than on development. Both in the Geneva Conference and in the General Assembly of the United Nations at the end of 1964, the Latin American delegations put forward a "theory of equitable remuneration" for basic products. They have maintained

(a) that the selling prices of basic products coming from the less developed countries were too low, assuring therefore either a large rent to the consumers, or large profit to the entrepreneurs utilizing these raw materials in the production of finished goods, sold at high prices;

(b) that a remuneration—a selling price—can be considered equitable, only if it covers the cost of production in such a measure as to allow economic development of the exporting country.

This peculiar presentation of the so-called "equitable" theory neglects the following facts:

(a) that every economic activity is based on a positive difference between costs and profits;

(b) that this positive difference between cost and profit is distributed among other factors, applied to the production of final goods in the importing country.

In any case, no more than the elimination of obstacles to trade could be asked for. But we have seen how limited is the importance of this measure for the less developed countries. So the theory was rapidly abandoned in favor of other requests: long-term loans— for the creation in less developed countries of new industrial activities; engagements by the industrialized countries to buy the industrial products of favored developing countries; and reinvestment by industrialized countries of every gain obtained by their loans, which in practice implies that the loans are transformed into gifts.

Concerning the possibility of lowering by the industrialized countries of Western Europe and North America the customs duties and

---

[4] H. Wyndham White, "Conference Given Under the Auspices of the Italian Study Center for International Reconciliation," Rome, June 1960.

quotas on agricultural products, raw materials—and manufactured goods—one cannot disregard the danger of a profound disorganization of the market, unless the richer countries proceed with great caution.

It is a matter of transformation, which cannot take place rapidly. When an industrialized country gives up at least in part the production of certain goods to import them from developing countries, it is necessary for the government to assist the industries, which are gradually eliminated. It is necessary to assist the workers, by means of subsidies and by offering to them wide possibilities of professional requalification.

Structure Policy

Behind the balance of payments deficit of a developing country there is the more fundamental food "deficit" or "gap."

Two-thirds of the world's people live in countries with nutritionally inadequate national diets. The diet-deficient areas include all of Asia except Japan and Israel, all but the southern tip of Africa, the northern part of South America, and almost all of Central America and the Caribbean.

The distribution of the deficit among the subregions with inadequate diets and the deficits *per capita* are as follows:

Subregion	Share of deficit %	Deficit per capita Dol.
Central America and Caribbean	1.3	2.10
South America (excl. Brazil, Argentina and Uruguay)	1.0	1.05
North Africa	1.0	0.64
West, Central Africa	2.1	1.07
East Africa	0.3	0.27
West Asia	1.7	1.17
India	13.2	1.69
Other South Asia	5,0	2.07
East Asia (excl. Japan)	12.0	2.61
Communist Asia	62.4	5.04

Food deficiencies merely reflect the low standard of living in general. About 93 per cent of the deficit is accounted for by countries in the Far East. Communist Asia is responsible for 62 per cent.

Some progress is expected in the diet-deficient area during the rest of this decade. The calories level by 1970 is expected to be 8 per cent above the base period (1959/61). However, a food deficit will still exist in 1970.

The basic problem of the diet-deficient countries is one of productivity. The people cannot produce enough food to feed themselves or produce enough other products to afford to buy the food they require.

Solving this problem is a formidable task. In the densely populated diet-deficient countries, new lands are no longer available at a reasonable cost, so agricultural development requires improvement in yields per acre. This is difficult to accomplish when the labor force is largely illiterate, lacking in technical and managerial skills necessary for adopting cultivation methods, lacking capital not only for agriculture but also for a rapidly growing non-agricultural sector and urban population.

We have to face and solve structure problems. In low income countries structure policy implies all the efforts toward the creation of most of the "external and internal economies," which could mitigate heavier costs of production and prepare the new environment in which greater productive efficiency can be reached.

The Government can be expected to contribute to:

(a)   the production of general public services: defense, administration of justice, education and public health;

(b)   the production of special public services, such as transport and communications;

(c)   the carrying out of public works: roads, ports, land reclamation and electric power stations.

The use, on the part of the State, of all these means results in a reduction of the risks to be faced by individual producers and a reduction of the cost of production that will bring about an increase in the income of the entrepreneurs.

The second important approach to a "structure policy" concerns the necessity of encouraging the evolution of the different sectors of production, starting with the improvement of the human element and of the agricultural activity.

The low income in agriculture is due to many other reasons besides demographic pressure. For example, to the difficulty of introducing modern production and planning methods.

The low income is also due to the fact that there is a large number of small holdings, the limited dimensions of which do not permit the use of modern means of production. Thus in a large part of the Italian territory, the agricultural economy cannot be considered a "market economy." A large part of the Italian population consumes directly an increasing part of the agricultural produce.

All these factors are reflected in the disparity of the development of the income in agriculture and in other sectors of production and in the disparity in development between regions.

We are now in a position to underline a certain sequence of a "structure policy." The first stage is marked by a large-scale public general services production and public works program, in order to make more receptive the human element and the environment destined to receive private investment. The second stage is marked by the rationalization, industrialization and commercialization of agricultural production. The industrial activity is to be based on:

(a) production of instrumental goods for agricultural improvements;

(b) transformation and processing of agricultural produce.

Toward such newly created industries the excess of agricultural manpower can pertinently flow.

Stabilization Policy

In the trade of primary products between developing and industrialized countries—against the background of long-term trends —violent fluctuations are found in the prices of export goods and, as a result, in the earnings from such exports. Numerous stabilization measures have been proposed, following careful study and experience acquired.

Quite apart from the stabilizing measures, which concern the entire economy of a country and are adopted by the various governments, it seems appropriate to concentrate attention on certain measures of stabilization, which concern:

(a) the entire economy of a country—for example, those which aim at stabilizing the earnings from total exports, but are adopted as a result of internal initiative; and

(b) the international market for individual products which are also adopted on international initiative.

Among the stabilization measures concerning the entire economy of a developing country and adopted on international initiative, there emerges the Development Insurance Fund (DIF).

On the basis of the project of the UNO experts, the industrialized countries would contribute, in the form of a loan, to a far greater extent than that to which they could expect compensation for an eventual fall in their own exports; whereas the developing countries would obtain benefits far greater than the contributions paid.

According to the scheme, the industrialized countries are invited to participate, not on the basis of a more or less measurable risk, which it is desired to avoid, but as donors only. It is far from preparing a solid basis for the assertion that, in the end, by participating in this scheme, all countries stand to gain and must, therefore, contribute to establishing it.

The project so far examined tends to place the burden of financing the compensation on the industrialized countries. On the other hand, the project of the Organization of American States (OAS) for the stabilization of export earnings in countries producing raw materials calls upon these to participate to a wide extent in the financing of the compensation which they can expect to receive, in harmony with the concept of "God helps those who help themselves."

The intention is that of lending—for periods of three to five years —convertible currencies to the developing countries. In order that it may have a certain efficacy in the country which adopts it, the American project—like any other measure of stabilization—requires that at the same time the problem of structure of the country in question be dealt with.

We now pass to examine the main points of some measures proposed for the stabilization of earnings from exports of individual products—always on international initiative. The main difficulty appears in the fact that, for a country, the exports of individual products are more exposed to vicissitudes than total exports.

In addition, a compensatory system for individual products implies the transfer of funds from importing countries to exporting countries. The funds may be distributed between the exporting countries in relation to fortuitous circumstances, concerning the percentage of coverage and the operations of the scheme not in harmony with the actual requirements of each country.

It follows from the above that:

(a)   in facing problems of compensation of short-term fluctuations, preference is to be given to a system which concerns total exports, rather than exports of individual products;

(b)   it is necessary to ascertain and thoroughly examine, in the developing countries, also the long-term problems, in order to reach satisfactory solutions within the framework of an organic program of development and stability for the country taken into consideration.

Passing, lastly, to examine measures for the stabilization of the market and prices of "individual" products, arising from national initiative, it seems appropriate to affirm that the most efficient contribution to the stabilization of markets is offered by Stocks and Stabilization funds for the products.

The advantages of the Marketing Boards are:

(a) the protection of producers; prices fixed in advance remain stable through the season;
(b) by means of a suitable distribution of the sales, avoiding bottlenecks and price depressions at harvest time;
(c) the possibility of eliminating fluctuations, by storing surpluses.

Emergency Policy

Following a Resolution of November 24, 1961, adopted by the FAO Conference, there was instituted the World Food Program. The Administration of the World Food Program must meet the urgent needs of populations which still have insufficient nutrition. The projects will be drawn up only on the basis of a request from beneficiary countries.

The advantages of a system of aid in the form of food products are quite specific. The flow of such aid drives away the danger of inflationary pressures and permits a higher level of investment. Aid in the form of foodstuffs can facilitate the payment of wages in kind. They can create counterpart funds in local currency, which, in turn, are employed in the retribution of labor, as well as in the purchase on the home market of goods and services necessary for the execution of development projects.

Obviously aid in the form of foodstuffs can never substitute forms of aid which, more or less directly, contribute to the development of a country. It must integrate itself with these in proportions which vary according to the economies of the donor country and of the beneficiary country.

Since the beginning of its operation, the World Food Program has provided emergency relief to the victims of natural disasters in nine countries and to refugees in three others, at a total cost of over $9 million, including transport and insurance.

As of July 31, 1964, a total of eighty projects have been approved, for which over $ 36 million of WFP commodities has been committed. In addition, over fifty requests from member governments were, at that date, under active consideration.

Coordination Policy

Only an "organic conception" of the various problems to be faced in the developing countries and of the most adequate solutions can lead the so intricate subject of an efficient aid toward lasting and satisfactory achievements.

The conviction is growing that technical assistance and financial aid of whatever kind and to whatever country it may be supplied should be brought to the attention of a single international organization which, by mutual consent, would be empowered to promote and implement a diligent coordination of the many-sided activities, even if only in a given field such as, for example, food and agriculture, of such widespread importance in all developing countries.

Coordination does not imply suppression of existing activities, or absorption of them by one single organization, however meritorious it might be. Coordination simply implies elimination of overlapping, duplications and loss of time, energy and money.

Coordination starts from an assiduous confrontation of policies in the framework of an international organization for:

(a)　ascertaining the situation of developing countries desiring to obtain aid from industrialized countries;

(b)　promoting a "progressive integration" of the economies of such developing countries in order to compensate disequilibria due to obsolete methods of production, etc.

(c)　favoring a confrontation of agricultural structure policies and stabilization policies:

    (i)　between industrialized countries;

    (ii)　between developing countries;

    (iii) between industrialized and developing countries.

Coordination has to realize the practical necessity of preparing country by country in the framework of an International Organization and with the collaboration of interested national representative programs of economic development, as did FAO in elaborating the Mediterranean Project.

Appropriate estimates of the financial consequences implied by each program will permit the calculation of the orders of magnitude of the total expenditure to be faced. According to some criteria selected by consent, industrialized and less developed countries can allocate a huge financial effort in the coming decades.

18

IMPORTANCE OF SIZE FOR THE ORIENTATION OF ECONOMIC POLICY [1]

By Barend A. de Vries
Deputy Director, Economics Department
International Bank for
Reconstruction and Development

Fluctuations in international commodity markets and their impact on developing economies have greatly influenced economists advising governments on their growth policies. There have been persistent calls for policies designed to isolate these countries from disruptive external influences, and especially for diversification through industrialization. Frequently, these policies have entailed departures from the more classical prescriptions of monetary stability, fiscal balance, free trade and unitary exchange rates.

The experience of countries in the past ten to fifteen years gives us some insight into the crucial factors which govern the orientation of national policy, and also into the influence different orientations have had on the pace and pattern of growth. Since the weakening of commodity prices in the mid-1950s—in the wake of the post-Korean boom—countries most adversely affected have, in practice, followed widely diverging policies and, consequently, experienced wide differences in monetary stability, foreign trade and internal growth patterns. This chapter discusses for a group of countries their response to weakness in export demand and the implications of different responses for the pace and pattern of growth and for monetary stability. The discussion is focused on the experience of countries in the middle income range (say, $ 200–$ 600 per annum *per capita*). Our findings also have relevance to policy decisions in countries below this income range, which have similar monetary policy problems and still face basic choices concerning the pace and orientation of their industrialization.

A key element in my definition of a country's policy orientation is whether it undertakes the construction of heavy, integrated industry, designed to produce primarily for the domestic market, and whether there is a simultaneous tendency to neglect exports. This is inward

---

[1] In the preparation of this chapter I was assisted by Mr. Eugenio Lari of the IBRD Economics Department. The views expressed in this chapter are not necessarily those of the IBRD.

orientation. A review of the experience of different countries suggests that a crucial factor underlying the choice of policy orientation is the size of the external market share (i.e., the country's share in world markets for its leading primary commodity exports) while the success of the policy is governed primarily by the domestic market size. To facilitate the study, I have used a country classification which is discussed in the first section below. It leads to a tentative finding that the size of external market shares (or the elasticity of foreign demand for an individual country's exports) tends to be a decisive factor in the choice of policy orientation. The second section discusses the similarities and differences in growth experience associated with contrasting policy orientation. It draws special attention to the type of country which appears to have the most difficult problem of monetary management in the development process—that of a small or medium-sized country which, because of its large external market share, has chosen an inward policy orientation. The third section reviews the monetary consequences of different growth policy orientations with special emphasis on the impact of inflation on resource allocation and on savings in the development process.

It will be clear that this chapter focuses on the problems arising from the establishment of heavy and complex industry—e.g., steel, engineering, capital goods and chemical industries—rather than light and consumer goods industries. The size of the capital outlays for heavy industry and its consequences for public finance, as well as the length of the gestation period and the economies of scale, pose problems in formulating financial, commercial and exchange policies which are quite different from those associated with the establishment of light industry.

Difference in Market Size and Orientation of Growth Policy

To provide a simplified framework for the discussion, I have classified countries according to the orientation of their growth policy, the size of their internal market and their share in the markets for their leading exports. The classification is simplified by limiting to two the possibilities for size and trade (labelled as either large or small in each case) and for policy orientation (either inward or outward).

First, as to the orientation of growth policy. Inward orientation can best be characterized by diversification through heavy industrialization aimed at production for the domestic market and by neglect

—at least in the initial stage—of primary and agricultural production for export markets. (This is, of course, a narrower definition than "import substitution policy," which also extends to light and processing industries which may be more competitive in smaller markets than heavy and intermediate goods industries.) The country attempts to maintain domestic demand in the face of reduced resources caused by lower exports and to diversify internal production by building up heavy industry, i.e., producing steel and other intermediate goods and eventually capital goods. Investment in capital-intensive industry comes in big spurts of very substantial amounts which, with supporting infrastructure investment, is bound to expand public outlays at a rate faster than public savings. In real terms, domestic supply lags behind demand during a transitional diversification phase in which basic industry is established and new manufacturing plants come into production. Unless external resources supplement domestic resources, inflation will ensue during the transitional phase (the gestation period of new basic industry) which, taking the diversification effort as a whole, may easily last ten years, even in the more successful cases. Inflationary pressures on the domestic price level tend to overvalue the exchange rate, but corrective action will be slow during the transitional phase when policy emphasis is on diversification of industrial production for domestic markets rather than on export expansion.

Outward policy orientation calls for cautious domestic expenditure policies and maintenance of prices at internationally competitive levels. Expenditures for power, transport, education, etc., may be as high (relative to total public outlays or GDP) as in the former case, but there is no costly drive toward industrialization. Instead, public expenditures may be directed to stimulate agricultural export production. Following a decline in export earnings (relatively more important in the small economy) there will be pressures on total resources, but they are kept to a minimum—some countries have even cut public investment in these circumstances. Moreover, when pressures on domestic prices are reflected in exchange rate overvaluation, corrective action is usually taken expeditiously. Trade and exchange policies, which are always easier to pursue when financial conditions are stable, are relatively free from controls and multiple rates.

The choice of a benchmark for domestic market size is governed by our definition of policy orientation. In view of the importance of heavy industrialization under inward policy orientation, I have measured domestic markets by the size of the market for steel, and used as a benchmark in defining "large" and "small" markets the volume at which steel production becomes economic. This procedure emphasizes the strategic role of the steel industry. I have selected one million tons (ingot equivalent) as the cut-off point, but realize that the cost of raw materials and domestic transport, especially where the former is unusually low and the latter abnormally high, would change the cut-off point.[2] Basic in the selection of this cut-off point is the realization that at a certain phase in the industrialization process industry will consume steel in amounts that make integrated domestic production economic. Parallel with steel—but sometimes later—may be the development of other intermediate industries, especially chemical, which we have not tried to use as a determinant in measuring domestic market size. Moreover, when steel consumption has reached the million ton mark, the consuming industries employ labor, technical and managerial skills, and require infrastructure support at levels marking a considerable advance in the development process. The size of GDP will, of course, also have exceeded a certain minimum.

The third characteristic in the classification is the country's commodity trade position: its share in the markets of its leading export commodities. This share is often an important factor in determining the country's reaction to external market weakness and its strategy of export expansion. The smaller its market share, the better its chance of improving it without upsetting world prices. The market share is, of course, only a rough approximation of the price elasticity for the country's product which (with the income elasticity) is a more essential parameter.[3] Somewhat arbitrarily, I have used a 10 per cent share in the market of one or more of its commodity markets as the cut-off point in defining what is a "large" or "small" trade position.[4]

---

[2] One can argue for a cut-off point of 0.5 million tons, often the capacity of the first stage in a steel plant program. Chile is the only country in our sample with consumption between 0.5 and one million tons.

[3] Assuming other producing countries keep their supplies constant, the price elasticity of demand for an individual country's output equals that of the demand for world output times the inverse of the country's market share.

[4] A more precise measurement would be M. Michaely's commodity-weighted export share [see his *Concentration in International Trade* (Amsterdam: North-Holland Publishing Company, 1962)].

Our classification may be summarized in the following table:

Category Number	1	2	3	4	5	6	7	8
Policy Orientation	I	O	I	O	I	O	I	O
Economic Size	L	L	L	L	S	S	S	S
Foreign Trade Position	L	L	S	S	L	L	S	S

(L = large; S = small; I = inward; O = outward)

An essential feature of the classification is the recognition that economic size cannot be changed quickly so that, for example, in the process of development, a country cannot move easily from Category 8 to 1.[5]

Below are illustrations of the more important categories. (Categories 2, 3 and 7 are less likely to occur in practice.)

Category 1: Brazil (coffee); India (tea, jute); Argentina (meat).

Category 4: Mexico (coffee, cotton).[6]

Category 5: Chile (copper); Colombia (coffee); Ceylon (tea).

Category 6: (with large external market share): Thailand (rice); Ecuador (bananas).

Category 8: Peru, Central American Countries.

Mexico has an extensive industrialization program but, in contrast with Brazil, it has encouraged exports through competitive price policies and the direction of public investment (e.g., irrigation). Peru is an almost classical case of free and flexible trade and exchange policies even though it is building a steel plant and has an industrialization program centered in its capital city. In both of these cases, as in others, we have to weigh the various aspects of a country's policy, using the dominant characteristics in determining whether its orientation is inward or outward. The reader will note that we have characterized Ceylon's policy as having inward orientation even though it is not engaged in heavy industrialization.

It appears that countries with a large trade position tend to follow policies with inward orientation. (See Categories 1 and 5.) This throws light on the motivation behind the choice of policy orientation. World demand being inelastic, the pursuit of realistic pricing

---

[5] Dudley Seers describes some key categories in our classification as phases in the development process. (*The Stages of Economic Development of a Primary Producer in the Middle of the Twentieth Century,* The Economic Bulletin of Ghana, Volume VII, No. 4, 1963).

[6] Mexico's lead exports are relatively small in its total, but large in the "world market." The latter is rather narrow since the United States and the U.S.S.R. are both leading producers and consumers.

policies, it is felt, does not benefit the countries with a large world market share. Instead, they oriented themselves inward with a tendency toward neglect of the export sector. On the other hand, those countries which have a relatively small share of the markets for their leading export commodities have had a more outward orientation, maintaining competitive prices and encouraging their export sectors. They felt that their market shares were small enough so that price and other export incentives would pay off even if total world demand might be inelastic.[7] Exceptions worth noting are Thailand and Ecuador which have persisted in outward orientation despite their relatively large market shares. For these countries the small internal market size apparently determined the policy choice in favor of outward orientation. Perhaps if all, including the large producers, had an outward orientation, the competitive price pressures would have been even larger on some of the already weak international commodity markets.

Growth Experience and Policy Orientation

A study of the impact of policy orientation on economic growth must allow for several aspects of a country's growth experience. In addition to the pace of growth we need to take into account, *inter alia,* levels of efficiency achieved, the pattern of growth especially in the export sector, the provision of alternative employment opportunities for the rural poor, the extent of external financing and the country's ability to manage external indebtedness without impairing the growth process. As to the first of these—the pace of growth— it is well known that available aggregate GDP data are very crude indicators at best. The high statistical rates achieved in the initial phases of import substitution may look less impressive after allowance is made for the levels of efficiency in the growing economy. Some countries may have financed a much larger share of their expansion with external savings than others, and among the former, debt repayment capacity will vary considerably depending on the efficiency of the new productive facilities for which the debt was incurred and on the growth of the export sector.

---

[7] The essential condition inducing a certain policy direction is whether or not the external demand for its products is elastic or inelastic. When total world demand is elastic, the country may opt for outward orientation even if its market share is large.

Experience in the Categories at the Two Extremes

Categories No. 1 and 8 are extreme opposites in that all three characteristics—policy orientation, size and trade position—are different. It is striking that in these two categories we find countries—e.g., Brazil in No. 1 and certain Central American countries in No. 8, which over the past ten to fifteen years have enjoyed fairly vigorous growth rates (5 per cent per annum, sometimes higher) despite contrasting policy orientations.

The phasing of growth over the period has perhaps been different for these countries: in Category 1, under the impetus of the industrialization drive, the growth rate was higher in the early part and lower later on (in part because of the financial consequence of the policies, as is illustrated by the Brazilian experience). In Category 8, the growth rate suffered from the initial export decline but recovered later in the period as exports improved through the strengthening of external prices and diversification.

While the growth rate has been similar in these two cases, they have experienced contrasting growth *patterns*. In Brazil, for example, industrial production for the domestic market has been the dynamic factor, with manufacturing output growing often twice as fast as total output. The growth of basic and capital goods industries was accompanied by rapid urbanization (and development of social, health and educational facilities): the rural poor gained opportunities of improved employment and living conditions. The foreign trade sector tended to stagnate: there was no export growth or diversification and imports declined as a percentage of GDP, suggesting success in import substitution.

In the countries of Category 8, the growth and diversification of exports tended to be the dynamic factor in total growth. One might say that with export growing faster than total output these countries became even more dependent on world markets. On the other hand, in some highly successful cases—e.g., Guatemala and El Salvador—exports were diversified considerably. On the other hand, these countries experienced less spectacular urban development and the rural population was left without sufficient alternatives for employment and education, despite the often rapid growth of commercial agriculture in the export sector.

While countries in the categories at the two extremes have enjoyed similar growth rates, they have had contrasting financial and monetary experience. This is discussed in the section beginning on p. 317.

Inward Policy Orientation and the Domestic Market Size

Not all countries giving an inward orientation to their policy have had favorable growth experience. The size of the internal market would seem to be a crucial factor in deciding whether a policy with inward orientation can succeed. For example, the size of the Brazilian market, among the largest in the developing world, makes possible production at competitive cost levels, if only after the initial diversification phase. Despite the costly financial legacy (inflation, heavy external debt, etc.) of inward policy orientation, Brazilian industry is beginning to compete with imports and to export, and will thereby contribute to the strengthening of the country's financial position, both short- and long-term. This would suggest that the return on industrial investments was high, not only in a financial but also in an economic sense, and that consequently the resource allocation fostered by directing investment into heavy industry was, at least from a longer-run viewpoint, an economic one. Such a sound resource allocation should provide a base for the successful execution of the more cautious financial policies needed to combine long-term growth with external financial strength.

Similar policy orientation may be less successful in countries with small domestic markets. This leads us to Category 5, perhaps the most difficult one from the viewpoint of monetary management in a developing country. In this category fall the countries which, despite their small domestic market size, are driven by external market problems toward an inward policy orientation. In these cases the resulting resource allocation may have been less economic than in the larger countries and consequently the solutions to their current problems may be more difficult to achieve. For example, in Colombia, with an internal market about one-fifth of Brazil's, import substitution policies appear to have encouraged a high cost and monopolistic industrial structure which has made use of financial policy tools less effective than Brazil's in improving the financial balance and the allocation of resources. The relatively high manufacturing cost levels make industry dependent on protection and throw doubt on their export capacity over the longer term. Unfortunately, continuation of protectionist policies might well form an obstacle to Colombia's growth and threatens to result in poor export performance by the new industries and a continuation or an increase of the country's dependence on external resources. The economic cost of protection and the associated misdirection of investment will weigh heavily on further development. It will tend to reduce resources available for development as well as the economic returns on investment which is being encouraged to enter lines of relatively high-cost production.

In the Brazilian case the transitional period—characterized by industrialization with heavy protection, export stagnation and inflation—seems about to end with the emergence of increasingly competitive industry providing the real resource basis for improvement in the financial position. Not so in the countries with smaller domestic markets. For example, in Colombia the manufacturing industry is, with a few exceptions, not yet competitive. It may take much longer to achieve competitive cost levels than will industries in countries with larger domestic markets. In the smaller countries a basic reorientation of policy and investment direction may well be called for lest the cost of protection turns out to be a continuing burden on the economy. Mexico, Peru, Thailand and Taiwan, among others, have demonstrated that it should be possible to develop a more diversified export package by maintaining competitive price conditions and orienting investment policy toward exports. In the smaller countries this policy orientation will involve less emphasis on heavy industry for some time to come—a lesson of particular importance to those still below the middle income range in the developing world.

The restrictions imposed by internal market size on the country's freedom of action may be removed by economic integration. However, so far very limited progress has been made in this direction among developing countries. Of special importance are the synchronization of the financial policies of trade partners and the provision of cheap transportation.[8] These two conditions are not easy to bring about. In the Central American region, where integration has made progress, the regional market is still relatively small.

Monetary Experience

Inward policy orientation has a strongly inflationary bias. The drive toward expansion of heavy industry, through direction of public investment, credit policy and foreign exchange measures, widens for some years rather than narrows the gap between domestic resources and the demand upon them. On the other hand, countries oriented toward export expansion rather than diversification through heavy industrialization do not need to increase investment as rapidly and

[8] Cf. Tibor Scitovsky, "International Trade and Economic Integration as a Means of Overcoming the Disadvantages of a Small Nation," *Economic Consequences of the Size of Nations,* ed. E. A. G. Robinson (London: 1960).

can be more cautious in their expenditure policies: consequently, they have experienced more monetary stability.

This is not to say that countries orienting their policy toward export expansion do not experience inflationary pressures. They will need to respond to a weakening in export markets with a cutback in public and private expenditures, something not easily accomplished in an ongoing development program. Even the maintenance of public investment at the earlier level may be inflationary when, as often occurs, public revenue is correlated with export earnings. Moreover, when these countries succeed in increasing exports, they experience, as is well known, an expansion of domestic demand similar to that resulting from the increase in investment which is a crucial tool of the policy with inward orientation. As far as inflationary pressure is concerned, the two crucial differences between the two policy orientations are as follows. First, inward orientation calls for substantial increases in public investment, especially in industry; while outward orientation makes possible more cautious expenditure policies. Secondly, the expenditure policy with outward orientation has a faster payoff in terms of new production and foreign exchange earnings, providing means to satisfy the increase in import demand, which is bound to occur under either orientation when it leads to expansion in domestic demand.

In either situation external capital may supplement domestic resources, thereby counteracting domestic monetary expansion and mitigating price instability. Reviewing again the experience of the past ten years, it does not seem that the orientation of policy as such has been decisive in determining over the longer run the net contribution of external resources. In both situations long-term external capital has usually been available for the "hard" infrastructure projects (e.g., transport and power). Focusing on the differences in the role of capital inflows, we note that the countries emphasizing heavy industrial investment received substantial external financing of industrial equipment, mostly provided by foreign manufacturers on short- and medium-term. In the countries with outward orientation much of the capital inflow took the form of commercial credit financing of the expanded foreign trade volume under conditions of relative stability and freedom from controls.

Inflation and Resource Allocation

In general, we are concerned with the effects of inflation on the allocation of resources and especially on the direction of investment.

This assumes—as is widely accepted—that it is the utilization of available resources which is a decisive factor in determining the rate of economic growth. This raises two questions about the effect of inflation on which there is a great scarcity of systematic observation and analysis. They are: (i) does inflation encourage investment with lower returns than would otherwise have taken place? and (ii) does inflation discourage savings?

Where other factors collaborate—especially levels of skills and available infrastructure—policies encouraging heavy industrialization may foster an investment pattern with higher returns than would otherwise prevail. Where—as we have seen is likely—such policies are accompanied by inflationary pressures, the crucial questions are (a) whether the inflationary process diverts investment into sectors with lower yields and thus retards the growth process; and (b) whether inflation generated by the development policy begins to play an independent role in the process of transferring resources into sectors where investment yields are higher. Any exploration of these questions must allow for the possibility that the very policies which intensify inflation may, in the first instance, have concentrated investment on higher yielding projects.

The impact of inflation on investment yields is determined in part by the behavior of relative prices and of wages. Do high priority activities benefit from shifts in the domestic price structure engendered by inflation? Do money wages lag behind prices, and real wages behind productivity in high priority industries? The answer to both questions appears to have been affirmative in Brazil for some years—say, during 1955–59—before inflation accelerated above 25 per cent per annum.[9] Internal price movements in favor of industry were induced by trade and exchange policies, as well as by the maintenance of effective demand for industrial goods, while the lags in wages were related to internal migration and the weakness of trade unions. But once inflation began to accelerate above 25 per cent per annum, wages seem to have caught up with prices (and productivity), and balance of payments pressures became so strong that policies were forced in the direction of exchange rate unification (which reduced the disparity between prices in agriculture and industry). Brazil became caught in a vicious cycle in which inflation

[9] See also Werner Baer and Isaac Kerstenetzy, "Some Observations on the Brazilian Inflation," *Inflation and Growth in Latin America,* a publication of the Economic Growth Center, Yale University (Homewood, Ill.: Richard D. Irwin, Inc., 1964).

was no longer effective as a transfer agent. Moreover, the behavior of prices in the Brazilian inflation was one of great divergence within the industrial sector and it certainly cannot be argued that within the manufacturing sector there was a clear trend toward relatively higher prices for industries with high priority.

Questions concerning the impact of inflation on the direction of investment or, more precisely, investment returns, are much harder to answer since so little is known about the relation between sectoral allocation and investment returns even under stable price conditions. It is the scarcity of empirical work which has made discussions of the impact of inflation on development so inclusive.

Given the state of empirical work and techniques, the calculated returns on alternative investment patterns have to be quite far apart to warrant a clear-cut policy recommendation. This may be the case when there is a widely felt shortage of a particular public service, such as was caused by the lack of inter-city road transportation in Colombia in 1950.[10] There was no doubt that the recommended road construction program would have high returns in terms of additional potential national production, and that an alternative pattern postponing construction would have had a high cost in potential production foregone.[11] Fortunately, the question of inflationary financing did not arise since most of the needed resources in the initial years of the program were, in effect, provided by increased export earnings; after 1956, when export earnings had declined abruptly, the backbone of a national road system was in place and further road construction had lower returns and relatively less priority.

Another situation exists today in many middle-income countries which are beginning to derive the benefits of extensive infrastructure investment programs. Since many of these countries now enjoy fairly adequate provision of social overhead services (power, transport, etc.), commodity production can expand without substantial increases in infrastructure investment. From the point of view of the whole economy (as against the individual project) the return on investment in commodity production may substantially exceed that in infrastructure. Monetary and fiscal policy should make special allowance for the potential returns in the commodity producing sectors.

---

[10] Cf. IBRD, *The Basis of a Development Program for Colombia* (Washington, D.C.: International Bank for Reconstruction and Development, 1950).

[11] Manufacturing industry in one city could not sell its products to other cities. The country's economic geography is characterized by four major cities separated by stiff natural barriers—mountains and swamps.

Inflation and Savings

Over a relatively short period—say, five to ten years—the impact of inflation on resource allocation is more important than the impact on savings: resource allocation and utilization is the primary determinant of income growth which, in turn, provides the basis for a country's savings effort. This would certainly also apply to what we have called the initial diversification phase in which industry is integrated and diversified. Since—as we have already suggested—inward orientation typically neglects export expansion, the chances are that external savings play a substantially larger role than domestic savings in financing the increase in investment. This is a consequence of the policy orientation, and not an effect of inflation, although—as before—these movements in investment and savings will be accompanied by inflation.

Over a longer period, the behavior of savings determines the country's ability to finance additional investment with its own resources and eventually repays its accumulated external debt. Parallel with an improvement in saving, there would need to be a gradual reduction in the current account balance of payments deficit, which will require a resumption in growth of exports from the country with inward orientation.

Observing developments in countries which have had inflation for, say, ten years or more, it seems clear that annual price increases of 20–25 per cent, or more, are detrimental to the formation of institutions essential to the mobilization of savings in the commodity-producing sectors, as well as the formation of personal savings habits. Beyond this rather general observation there is need for more systematic empirical work on savings behavior before we can draw conclusions about the impact on inflation in the process of development. Cross-section studies covering groups of countries with varying degrees of price stability have not produced results showing that total domestic savings suffer from price instability. During the 1950s an increasing trend in gross domestic savings can be observed both in certain inflationary countries (e.g., Brazil and Chile) and in some stable countries (e.g., Costa Rica, Honduras).[12]

---

[12] The same conclusion can be derived from the divergent trends in domestic savings presented in the *U.N. World Economic Survey 1960;* see especially Tables 2–3. Our analysis suggests that in Mexico there was a sharply rising trend in domestic savings from the early fifties to the mid-fifties (apparently associated with the impact of the 1954 devaluation) but, again, a gradual erosion in the late fifties (although to a level well above that prevailing at

The behavior of public savings is a significant indicator of total savings. It may be a leading factor in changing the trend of total savings.[13] An increase in public savings—if achieved through higher taxation rather than reduced current expenditures—may depress private savings which, if offset by expansion of credit to the private sector, may in itself exert an inflationary pressure. From available data, there is no clear indication that public savings declined in inflationary countries and improved in stable countries.[14]

From these admittedly incomplete analyses one gets the impression that—at least over a period of not much more than ten years—the behavior of total and public savings did not greatly depend on the degree of price stability. A factor which, at least in the short-term, may have had a more direct influence is the growth—or lack of growth—in export earnings.[15] This emphasizes the greater importance of resource allocation, in determining not only growth rates but perhaps also savings rates.

Concluding Remarks

The interrelationship between domestic market size and the fruits of an inward policy orientation seems to me a crucial consideration in judging the impact of inflationary policies on the growth process. Where the market is large enough to support competitive heavy industry, the country should have the basis to overcome the financial problems bound to arise during the initial diversification phase. The acid test of success of the industrial diversification drive is the country's ability to resume increasing its exports by selling abroad the products of its new industries. To make this come true, however, a reorientation of policies may be required, giving more encourage-

---

the start of the decade). In Colombia, savings increased substantially from the early to the mid-fifties when the government undertook an austerity program creating a budget and balance of payments surplus to repay accumulated external debt.

[13] U.N., *op. cit.*

[14] In Brazil, despite the more than 25 per cent per annum inflation from the mid-fifties to the early sixties, there was a gradual improvement in gross revenue of the government sector (relative to GDP) and, parallel with this, a slight improvement in government sector savings. The government sector is defined as the public sector excluding autonomous state enterprises). On the other hand, in certain more stable countries, public savings remained constant or deteriorated. Examples: Mexico, public savings virtually constant between 1951–53 and 1960–62; Honduras, deterioration; and Ecuador, gradual improvement from 1951–53 to 1957–59.

[15] This also followed from the data presented in the U.N. study, *op. cit.*

ment to exports. Even countries with relatively large domestic markets may continue to be plagued by a shortfall of domestic savings and, consequently, by inflationary problems: for them the maintenance of competitives prices may require a flexible attitude toward exchange rate adjustments, something which is never easily implemented.

Export orientation and industrial diversification are not necessarily incompatible, as is demontrated by the example of Mexico. Mexico has diversified its exports of foodstuffs and primary commodities and has managed to increase its manufactured exports.

For those countries which are still in the early phase of development—battling with public service shortages and not having decided on the nature of their industrialization—two lessons emerge from the foregoing. First, a drastic shift in investment patterns usually involves an increase in investment which cannot be accomplished without a shortfall in non-inflationary financial resources and its attendant problems. Our present techniques of computing returns on investment are such that we cannot foretell with sufficient certainty the growth implications for major changes in the composition of a national investment program. Unless the case is quite convincingly on the side of major shifts in investment, an incremental approach of changes in smaller steps executed within foreseeable means would seem to give greater assurance that resources are put to their most economic use. Secondly, the great majority of emerging countries have domestic markets of relatively small size. They should be careful not to embark on industrial schemes whose cost would be beyond their present resources and whose pay-off in terms of competitive production would be highly uncertain.

DISCUSSION

Only Large Countries Should Build Heavy Industry

Small countries ought to lower the costs and extend the output of their conventional export products. Big countries may risk inflation by undertaking massive investments in heavy industry, because their internal market is sizable enough to yield a profitable return.

In explaining his paper, Dr. de Vries talked about the debate that exists between the advocates of a *laissez-faire* approach and those of full-scale planning, or between the monetary and the structural policy schools. The orthodox monetary policies are applied by small territories that concentrate on export. The larger countries plan the development of heavy industry to the neglect of exports, particularly if they face an elastic foreign demand, as Brazil does for its coffee.

Large countries apply inward-facing policies, and consequently meet up with problems of inflation, because returns on investment in producer goods industries take time to eventuate. This inflationary "diversification phase" should last about ten years, judging by Brazil's experience. The inward-policy countries face balance of payment difficulties because their export lag—though ultimately the success of their industrialization—will be measured by whether they achieve a renewed spurt in their export trade, this time in a more diversified form. Brazil, for example, is now exporting steel at competitive prices.

But a difficulty occurs. By manufacturing import substitutes and capital goods, the inward-facing countries are imposing structural limits on the extent to which they can absorb foreign capital. For instance, the Brazilian government "simply is not able to purchase abroad goods and services up to the amounts that it has available in foreign exchange resources, given the amount of capital inflow that is available." This is a new and more meaningful definition of the phrase "absorptive capacity."

Outward-oriented countries suffer much less from inflation. Both groups show a satisfactory growth trend, e.g., India and Brazil among the big industrializing countries, and El Salvador and Nicaragua among the smaller, export-promoting countries.

The medium-sized territory that takes an inward-policy orientation possesses an insufficient internal market and ends up with a high industrial costs structure, which reflects low returns from the type of investment that the authorities have induced. An example is Colombia.

Dr. de Vries stressed that generalizations condemning inflation outright have an inadequate empirical base, because there is no evidence so far that inflation—unless on a "galloping" scale—impedes investment, the allocation of resources, or even savings.

Small countries should leave heavy industry alone and follow orthodox policies, to keep their exports growing at competitive prices. Gluts can ensue if *all* small countries follow this counsel, as has happened with coffee. The solution is that the large countries, as their economies become diversified, cease exporting the commodities in question. "The large country has the economic alternative of entering into other branches of production, because it has a basis for an efficient industry."

Dr. Zvi Ophir, of Israel, said that among the smaller countries, some have exports for which demand is inelastic. They fall between two stools. Dr. Ophir suggests developing light industries, which are less capital-intensive and have a smaller optimal size.

Dr. Germanico Salgado, of the Organization of American States, said that policy decisions are often forced on a country by external circumstances. Many Latin American States found themselves immobilized by balance of payment problems. Mexico and Peru were able to elaborate outward-oriented policies because they did not suffer from this pressure.

Countries facing a low demand elasticity for their products abroad had no option but to create new internal demand if they wanted to keep development going—hence the industrialization effort in Latin America during the 1950s.

If small countries are advised not to industrialize, this puts a stop to their development. They need the assistance of the advanced nations to get over this hump—capital transfers to weather their foreign payment difficulties, and the opportunity of taking over traditional industries from the Western countries, as suggested by Mr. Horowitz. Regional economic integration should also not be neglected.

Dr. Ephraim Kleiman, of Israel, drew attention to the fact that it is not known yet whether economies of scale do apply to most manufacturing industries. "If there are no economies of scale, then part of the arguments against industrialization in small countries are no longer valid." Public savings do not have to be at the expense of private savings but can and should be taken from consumption. "I think this is important, because public savings offer one of the few alternatives, if not the only one, to inflationary financing of development."

The speaker recalled Dr. de Vries' suggestion that the smaller countries should not accelerate their industrialization too fast. "Now this is the sort of conclusion which makes economists very unpopular. It raises the claim that instead of development with a certain misallocation of resources, they suggest no misallocation of resources at the price of no development.

"The truth is—and it is a very bitter truth—that the economic profession loves marginal changes, for the simple reason that we know what happens when changes are small. We don't know what happens when changes are large."

Dr. John Mars, of the U.N.'s Economic Commission for Africa, queried Dr. de Vries' determination of what are small and large countries, and argued that "the whole of Africa is an example that you can pursue both policies, the inward-looking and outward-looking policies, at the same time, and I can see no contradiction in that."

Import-substitution need not reduce capital imports. With the aid of foreign loans, Africa is undergoing an increase in total imports, but with a change in its composition, the accent being now on complicated, sophisticated types of capital goods. There is no intention of decreasing imports. The object is rather to keep them constant, with a shift in their composition.

Liberia has rich iron ore deposits, and could make 700,000 tons of steel more cheaply than imports from abroad, to meet the demand in West Africa that totals 1,100 m. tons. But it cannot be done. All the countries of West Africa want counter-benefits if they are to open their frontiers to Liberian steel. "In other words you would have to present all the fourteen countries of West Africa with a package deal. For instance, Ghana produces aluminium, so the other West African States must promise to take that. The land-locked countries rear cattle, so they would produce the boots and shoes ... Unless you can forget those ludicrous frontiers that are the historic heritage of colonialism, you cannot make any headway at all."

Apart from the profitability of industrial development, there is the social return to consider—the fact that there will be income earners who before had nothing—and infusion of technical knowledge which is then spread.

Dr. John Sackah Addo, of Ghana, said that Africa wants to increase the imports of capital goods, but the ultimate objective is to cut the need for imports. To reduce imports during the development phase, however, would be to become static.

Mr. Christopher Musoke, of Uganda, said that if neighboring countries integrate to afford a large market for their industries, what benefit does member country A get from industries located in member country B?

Mrs. Suparb Yossundara, of Thailand, spoke of her country's policies and problems. Growth has been assisted by orthodox monetary policies. Exports face difficult conditions. Most rice consumers are the poorer people of Asia. Yet Burma has long-term export agreements, and the U.S. competes in Europe with the payment-in-kind system, and mainland China exports without consideration of costs. In the case of rubber, Malaysia has lowered her production costs. "So we still have to pay a lot of attention to our export of agricultural products, which are our main lifeline." Meanwhile the government is encouraging industrial growth, chiefly through private enterprise, which has proved more efficient.

* * *

Dr. de Vries answered the debate by emphasizing that his recommendation for small countries was against heavy industry, like steel and chemicals, which involve big capital outlays and long gestation periods. He does not ban light industries. A country that cannot consume 1,000,000 tons of steel, which is the kind of output necessary for economies of scale, is a small country for this purpose. Thus "Pakistan is a big country, but as far as steel is concerned, it is a small country."

Most small countries in the underdeveloped world, though not all, do enjoy an elastic demand for their export products, according to Dr. de Vries. Referring to a criticism that governments tend to go for public works and urbanization, he said that the heavy industrialization effort in the big countries goes together with urbanization.

But if small countries devote their efforts to export branches, this can lead to a slow-down of urbanization. Thus in Guatemala Indians are missing out on progress, as are the Indians in the highlands of Peru.

Countries must base the construction of a steel plant on an internal market, because technical and managerial know-how is insufficient in the early stages for undertaking export commitments. It is risky to base the plant on a regional common market in the LDCs, because no transport network and insufficient ideological synchronization exist to unite the member countries. The African States are fortunate that they have not yet established a steel or chemical industry, so they still have time to decide where to locate any heavy industry efficiently. Latin Americans have largely passed this stage, with Peru and Venezuela having steel mills that are clearly uneconomic.

Concerning economies of scale, Dr. de Vries is sure that a steel plant of less than 500,000 tons (and such exist) must lose money and require protective tariffs.

19

INFLUENCE OF DEBT BURDEN AND THE PROBLEM OF FLEXIBILITY

By Dragoslav Avramovic

Director, Special Economic Studies,
International Bank of
Reconstruction and Development

The large expansion of international capital flows which took place over the last fifteen years was accompanied by a substantial increase in international indebtedness, especially on public account. The developing countries were virtually free of debt as the Second World War ended. At the end of 1963, their aggregate public and publicly-guaranteed indebtedness, including short-term obligations on which payments were delayed and the obligations to the International Monetary Fund, was of the order of $30 billion.[1]

Growth in outstanding indebtedness and in debt service payments was particularly fast since the mid-1950s. A sample of 37 developing countries, including the most important debtors and accounting for almost three-fourths of the population of all developing countries[2] owed about $7 billion on public account at the end of 1955 (debts with an original maturity of one year and over, i.e., exclusive of short-term obligations as well as of obligations to the IMF). By the end of 1963, their aggregate public and publicly-guaranteed debt of this type reached $21.5 billion—a yearly growth exceeding 15 per cent. Debt service obligations of the same group of countries and with respect to the same category of debt rose from $0.7 billion in 1956 to $2.8 billion in 1964, a four-fold increase in eight years.

The rise in the volume of financial transactions and the increase in indebtedness of developing countries have been striking features of the post-war economic scene; and it is virtually certain that these features will continue to characterize the world economy for a long time to come.

Factors Underlying Growth in External Debt

This expectation is based on the hypothesis that most of the developing countries will need foreign capital for a substantial period

---

[1] International Bank for Reconstruction and Development, *Economic Growth and External Debt*, Vol. II (Baltimore, Maryland: The Johns Hopkins Press, 1964).

[2] Excluding the centrally planned economies.

in the future. International indebtedness, its level and its growth, reflect the cumulative resource gap, changes in it over time and the terms on which external funds needed to fill the gap are made available. The larger the initial resource gap, the longer the period needed to close the gap, and the higher the rate of interest on borrowed funds, the higher the level of indebtedness and the level of the associated debt service.

The Debt Cycle

The length of the borrowing period, the behavior of capital inflow and the size of indebtedness and of debt service can be illustrated by what may be called a debt cycle. Three stages can be distinguished in such a debt cycle; and they are closely linked with the course of economic development.

In the first stage, as investment increases, savings, starting from a low level, are inadequate to finance domestic investment requirements. A country has to borrow not only to finance part of the investment, but also to meet amortization charges and to pay interest on the debt that is accumulated in the process. In this way, it obtains a net addition to its domestically generated resources available for investment. During this stage the burden of servicing foreign capital is continuously postponed. Debt increases very rapidly; since interest on debt incurred previously is paid out of new borrowing which also carries interest, the familiar law of compound interest operates in all its force. However, if an adequate proportion of the newly generated income can be saved, the country would, over time, meet an increasing share of its investment requirements from its own domestic resources.

The second stage begins when the savings have grown sufficiently to provide for all domestic investment requirements. In this stage, savings would not, however, be sufficient to meet the entire additional burden of interest and amortization payments on accumulated debt. At the beginning of this stage, debt would continue to grow, but at a slower pace than in the first stage. Toward the end of the second stage, debt has reached its peak and ceased to grow, as savings cover not only the domestic investment requirements but also the entire interest burden on external debt.

The third stage is one of declining indebtedness. The savings generated in the economy are sufficient to finance not only all domestic investment and interest payments on external debt but also to provide a surplus to retire the debt. Gross borrowing continues for some time, but at a decreasing pace. As gross borrowing approaches zero, the external debt declines rapidly.

Figure 1 shows the three stages of the debt cycle. A growth model, showing the inter-relationship of the target income growth rate, the investment rate, the productivity of capital, the savings rate and the volume and terms of capital inflow, has been used for purposes of illustration. Income growth target is set at 5 per cent p.a.; the initial average gross domestic savings rate is postulated at 10 per cent and the marginal gross savings rate at 20 per cent, i.e., double the average. The gross incremental capital-output ratio is assumed at 3:1 and the gross investment rate at 15 per cent. Foreign capital inflow initially finances one-third of gross investment. It is borrowed at an average interest rate of 6 per cent per annum and average maturity of fifteen years, terms fairly representative of conventional lending.

With these values for the variables and starting from zero debt, the debt cycle lasts thirty-six years. The phase in which indebtedness rises lasts about twenty-five years. This period of rising indebtedness has two stages. During the first fifteen years, the country obtains net addition to domestic resources, on top of repayment and interest; in the subsequent decade, borrowing takes place to meet service requirements.

The Problems of Productivity and Savings

Whether the model variant is representative of reality crucially depends on whether the values for the return on capital (measured here in macro-economic terms by the numerical relationship between capital investment and output generated, i.e., by the incremental capital-output ratio) and for savings rates are properly selected. The debt cycle would last considerably longer if the return on capital is lower than implied in the incremental capital-output ratio of 3:1 and if the initial savings rate is below 10 per cent and the marginal savings rate below 20 per cent. And conversely, the period of external borrowing would be shorter and the indebtedness level lower if the productivity of capital is higher and if the income plough-back rate is raised above 20 per cent.

The relationship between capital investment and output generated is determined by a number of factors: the availability of human skills, the capacity to combine and organize the factors of production in an optimal fashion, natural resources endowment, the sectoral distribution of investment, the rate of capacity utilization, the

FIGURE 1

*Relative Movement of Resource Gap, Net Capital Inflow and Gross
Capital Inflow—The "Model" Case*

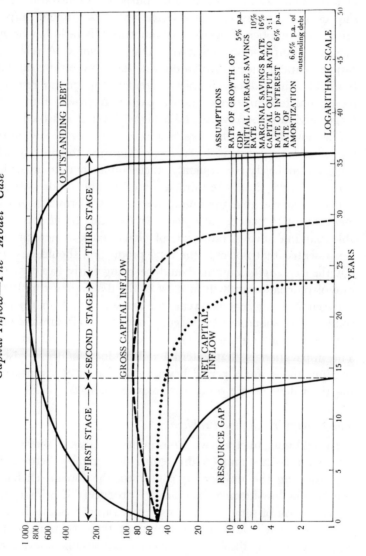

durability of assets created by investment. A number of these factors are structural in nature and require considerable time and effort to change; and the very fact of underdevelopment may put a country in a disadvantageous position with respect to one or more of these factors. While we have assumed for purposes of illustration a relationship of 3:1 between capital invested and gross annual output generated, in a number of developing countries this ratio has been higher (i.e., the return on capital lower) than this value. A relatively high ratio of capital investment to output—i.e., low returns to capital in terms of value added—implies a greater demand on resources, domestic and foreign, to maintain a particular growth rate and thus a longer period of borrowing and a higher level of indebtedness.

The low level of *per capita* income implies a low initial savings rate. In a number of very poor countries, this rate is below the 10 per cent level; consequently, their initial investment-savings gap may be larger than one-third assumed in the model variant, provided, of course, that the absorptive capacity permits a gross investment rate of 15 per cent or higher. On the other hand, for an appreciable marginal savings rate (rate of plough-back of new production), it is essential that not only the total production should be increasing, but the *per capita* output should be rising fairly rapidly. Since the rate of population growth in most of the developing countries ranges between 2–3 per cent per year, the rate of growth in *per capita* income is correspondingly reduced. Under these circumstances, it may take some time to attain a marginal savings rate of 20 per cent or so. The implication is that external indebtedness in these cases would continue to rise for a period beyond the quarter of a century, assuming the values of the other variables unchanged.

The Foreign Exchange Problem

In addition to the two constraints discussed above—the constraint on savings and on the return on capital—there is the third one affecting the developing countries: the foreign exchange constraint. The low-income countries are producers of primary products. Consumption of some of these rises very rapidly. Some, however, are victims of Engel's Law of Consumption: their use may be declining, relatively or even absolutely, as income of consumers increases. Some are being displaced by technologically superior and cheaper substitutes. As a result, international demand for the majority of primary products increases at a slower rate than imports of materials and equipment needed to sustain a satisfactory growth in real income.

Lagging exports limit the rate of growth of income, since they limit the capacity to import the investment goods needed to expand the capacity to produce; and the limit to the rate of growth of income makes it difficult to raise the rate of savings, particularly when the initial level of *per capita* income is low. Consequently, these countries have to develop exports of manufactured products and of service activities for which international demand rises relatively rapidly; alternatively, they have to embark upon a program of accelerated import substitution.

The problems of adjusting to the country's own growth requirements as reflected in growing demand for imported goods, as well as the problems of adjusting to structural changes in the world economy, are not confined to less developed countries. The difference between the dilemma of primary producers and that of industrialized countries is in respect of the required period of adjustment. Factors are much more mobile, institutions much more adaptable and skills are much more widespread in advanced, diversified and industrialized countries than they are in the underdeveloped world. The more severe the foreign exchange constraint and the more stringent the limits to which the rate of savings can be pushed in a low-income country over a certain period, the greater the required capital inflow and the longer the period of external borrowing for a given income growth target.

The possible impact of the limitations to obtaining a high productivity of capital and rate of plough-back is illustrated in Figure 2. It depicts a stylized "long-haul" case in economic development: it is assumed that the low level of *per capita* income, the high rate of population growth, the obstacles to productivity of capital and the constraint on export growth tend to prevent a sharp increase in the marginal savings rate. Even in this case, the latter is substantially above the average; but instead of being postulated at double the average, it has been assumed at 60 per cent above the average. A comparison of the projections in the "model" case and in the "long-haul" case shows that the variation of the marginal savings rate from 20 per cent (Figure 1) to 16 per cent (Figure 2) more than doubles the period required to close the domestic resource gap. Further, in the "long-haul" case, the build-up of interest payments and external debt is so rapid that gross capital inflow is a continuing phenomenon and never ceases. The country has become self-sustaining in the thirty-seventh year, in terms of the basic relationship between its domestically generated savings and domestic investment requirements; but it has remained a dependent economy in terms of continuously rising debt to infinity, as long as the conditions defined in Figure 2 prevail. In cases of this sort, financing of economic development cannot take place on conventional terms if the breakdown of the growth-cum-debt mechanism is to be avoided.

At the opposite end are countries where conditions are very favorable; output grows fast, the plough-back is large and increasing, the rate of return on investment is high, the composition of output responds quickly to external demand conditions and to the country's growth requirements. In such a country the conditions are such that the debt cycle would be completed faster than indicated in Figure 1. Paradoxically, it may so happen that the stage sequence of the cycle does not take place because the borrower has been too successful. Foreign investors are eager to employ their funds in this country because returns are large and secure. A country which has fully succeeded in the growth process may not reduce its indebtedness for a long time, i.e., the third stage of the cycle may be postponed for a long time. Its position is analogous to that of a successful corporation whose debt grows with its own growth.

The Liquidity Aspect of the Debt Servicing Burden

On balance, it can be argued that the majority of developing countries are facing a fairly long period in which they will need large external resources to fill their savings and foreign exchange gaps. If this is accepted, it follows that their debt service liabilities will also tend to increase over a long period. Furthermore, if most of the capital inflow is contracted on a fixed servicing schedule, i.e., as loan capital, most of the debt service obligations become contractually fixed.

The debt servicing problem is essentially the problem of reconciling competing claims on resources. The payment of debt service implies that the borrowing country has to forgo a certain amount of purchasing power, which could otherwise be used for consumption or investment. This is the cost of foreign capital to the national economy: against this cost there is the benefit which was derived from foreign resource inflow in the past in terms of an increase in the rate of capital formation, and also the benefit which may be expected in the future from further capital inflow.

The problem of reconciling competing claims on resources has a different complexion, depending on the time horizon under consideration. At a point of time, or over a short period, debt servicing difficulties take the form of a liquidity crisis in the balance of payments. Fixed debt service liabilities, if they are of a large magnitude, introduce a serious element of rigidity into the debtor's economy. Since the economic system, and particularly the foreign exchange receipts, continue to fluctuate, while debt servicing obligations remain contractually fixed, the entire impact of downward fluctuations must be borne by imports or the country must run a deficit in the current balance of payments. How successfully a debtor will cope with such a liquidity crisis depends on the relative strength of the elements of rigidity (i.e., the contractually fixed external obligations, minimum tolerable level of imports) and countervailing elements of flexibility (i.e., availability of compensatory finance, inessential imports). It also depends on the skill of the authorities of the debtor country in managing the balance of payments.

Difficulties in transferring debt service payments at a point of time may result from cyclical or accidental fluctuations in exports, capital inflow and imports, or from capital flight or a bunching of repayment maturities. Alternatively, the liquidity crisis may be a symptom of structural weakness of the economy. Frequently, it is a combination of transitory disturbances and long-term factors.

From the long-run viewpoint, the crucial factor in the debt servicing problem is the rate of growth of domestic output; reconciliation of competing claims on resources is much easier when total resources are growing than in a stationary economy. As long as the incidence of debt service falls on a part of the increment in *per capita* income, it is possible for consumption and nationally financed investment to rise *pari passu* with debt service payments. And if the rate of increase in real income and savings, remaining available after the claims of foreign capital have been met, is reasonably high; if growth occurs in a continuous fashion; if the country has succeeded in removing or at least alleviating the foreign exchange constraint; and if the benefits of growth are widespread, it can plausibly be argued that the opportunity cost of fulfilling external obligations is less burdensome than in a situation in which service payments impinge on existing living standards and employment levels.

However, even in a successful long-run growth-cum-debt case, liquidity difficulties may occur and they may be very serious. If the debt structure is unfavorable (i.e., if a large proportion of the total debt is repayable in a short period), if compensatory facilities are insufficient and if export declines, even temporarily, are violent—

FIGURE 2

*Relative Movement of Resource Gap, Net Capital Inflow and Gross
Capital Inflow—The "Long-Haul" Case*

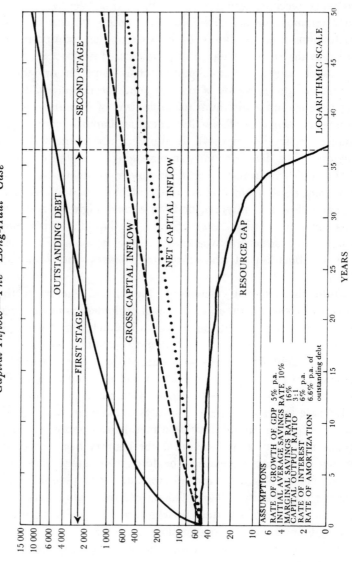

the debt servicing problem may be formidable although the long-term trends of savings, investment and exports may be perfectly consistent with self-sustained growth and may indicate a successful completion of the debt cycle. The balance of payments pressure occurs here just as much as it occurs in the "long-haul" case. The difference between the two cases is that in the pure "cash-squeeze" case the liquidity difficulties are temporary and they may be remedied through an extension of grace and maturity periods on new loans and through rescheduling of maturities on the existing debt. In contrast, in "long-haul" cases, these measures may not be sufficient, since the source of debt servicing difficulties goes deeper. The cash squeeze here is primarily a function of continuously rising interest payments on a continuously rising debt, rather than of bunching of maturities in a short period or of a temporary export decline.

The Problem of Rigidity

Inflexible obligations are potentially dangerous under any circumstances. This danger was present even in the classical system of foreign investment in earlier periods of economic history. The unmitigated violence of the international business cycle, at that time, frequently created havoc in international investment. There were, however, two redeeming features. Foreign private direct investment which accounted for a considerable share of total flow, was concentrated heavily in activities producing primary products for exports; and as export sales fluctuated, so did profits in export industries. The other redeeming feature was the complex inter-relationship of interest rates, risk premia and the anticipated behavior of debtors in periods of crisis. It was expected that borrowing governments would default occasionally on their fixed-term loans, when a depression or other causes reduced exports and budgetary income; but to offset this, debtors were charged an interest rate which included a risk premium high enough for the lenders to feel that foreign investment was a worth-while proposition.

The present situation is different from that described above. A major part of private direct investment still flows to export industries in less developed countries. The return flow of profits from these "enclave" investments fluctuates *pari passu* with export sales. But another part of foreign direct investment in the developing countries now goes into industries that produce goods to replace imports. Domestic demand for these products is increasing rapidly and without much fluctuation. Consequently, profits also tend to increase as the volume of domestic sales expands; and the less fluctuations there are in this rising domestic market, the smaller will be the fluctuations in the profits earned by foreign-owned companies.[3]

The above is one illustration of a much wider problem. Most developing countries now consider the acceleration of economic growth a major task facing the present generation. The responsibilities of governments in promoting investment and faster growth are greater today than they were, on the average, in earlier periods. Therefore, there is demand for massive capital inflow from abroad, and the major channels through which this inflow is transferred are governments in developing countries, which either borrow on their own account or guarantee loans to private parties. The return flow on this capital is fixed: it is loan capital that is borrowed. And as capital inflow proceeds, these contractually fixed obligations also increase. True, debtors are now in a better position than they were in earlier periods, because the rates of interest in international lending are now kept at a relatively low level. The lenders, or more accurately, their governments have assumed the risk of default. But precisely because most of capital flows are under governmental control and sponsorship and because interest rates are relatively low, debtors are not expected to default. The net result is a continuing increase of indebtedness and of debt service charges predominantly of a fixed nature.

Disturbance Variables

The size and the gravity of the payments problem which debt countries facing a fixed servicing schedule may encounter at a point of time, depend on the value and inter-relationships of a number of variables. Three of these variables may be called disturbance (fluctuating) variables: exports, capital flows and emergency and inflation-induced imports.

A major element of balance of payments vulnerability of most developing debtor countries arises from instability of export earnings. Short-term declines in these earnings have in the past originated largely in cyclical declines in international demand. In addition, there have been falls in export receipts caused by occasional natural failures in supply. Further, a number of developing countries

[3] See IBRD, *Economic Growth and External Debt,* Vol. III: S. Shahid Husain, *Relationship Between the Fluctuations in Export Earnings and Direct Investment Income Payments—A Statistical Test* (Washington, D.C.: International Bank for Reconstruction and Development, 1964).

have experienced reduced earnings over the medium term, originating in excess production of primary products in relation to demand.[4] Finally, export declines have been caused by domestic policies which have adversely affected the incentives to produce for exports or to sell on the international market.[5]

How far does the experience of the recent past provide a guidance to the future? Falls in exports caused by breakdowns of supply are likely to continue. The problem of medium-term supply-induced fluctuations still exists in all its intensity, and it can be solved only if an advance is made in systematic diversification of the production and export structures of countries heavily dependent on products experiencing medium-term production cycles and if these countries undertake some measure of international coordination of their investment programs and achieve further progress in their joint export sales strategies. Export declines resulting from domestic measures having a restrictive effect on export sales are likely to be less frequent than in the past: in a number of developing countries there is an increasing realization of the need to adopt policies stimulating export growth within the constraint given by the absorptive capacity of the international market. With respect to demand, it would seem that violent business fluctuations, so significant in the pre-war period, are not likely to recur: since the Second World War, the industrialized countries have successfully controlled the forces underlying the normal business cycle. This does not mean that the problem has been solved, however. Cyclical variations in demand and in business activity in the major world industrial centers still exist, although their amplitude has been dampened; and these cyclical swings lead to alternating upward and downward multi-year price movements which affect all or most commodities simultaneously.[6]

The second source of instability is to be found in the capital account. Until the Second World War, capital flows were by far the most sensitive element in the total payments picture, reacting violently to the ups and downs of the business cycle. During a depression, the liquidy problem, frequently originating in the cur-

---

[4] The best example is the coffee crisis after the mid-1950s.

[5] For a detailed appraisal of factors causing export declines and export instability generally, see IBRD, *The Commodity Problem*, 1964, a paper submitted to the U.N. Conference on Trade and Development.

[6] In the post-war period, a commodity price cycle can clearly be established. The Commodity Boom lasted from the end of the war through the mid-1950s. It was followed by the Commodity Slump in the years 1956–1962. The Price Recovery started in late 1962.

rent account under the impact of an export decline, was most seriously aggravated by cessation or even the reversal of capital flows.

International capital flows to developing countries as a group
have displayed a great degree of stability in the post-war period. The
largest component of these flows consists of funds provided by national and international lending agencies; and these funds have not
been sensitive to cyclical fluctuations. Frequently, they have tended
to compensate for the declines in export receipts.

This stability in the over-all flow, however, has not always
meant stability for individual recipients. Government-to-government
flows are sensitive to non-economic factors affecting bilateral relations. Private direct investment has continued to fluctuate in response to changing conditions in both the capital-importing and ca-
pital-exporting countries. Suppliers' credits are sensitive to the short-
term balance of payments position of the borrowing country: the
terms may become progressively disadvantageous as the liquidity crisis
approaches, and the flow is likely to cease when payment difficulties
become severe. Thus, despite the stability in the aggregate flow and
even in the flows to individual countries recorded thus far, for the
majority of countries it is not in present circumstances possible to
forecast with precision and for a longer period the prospective level
and fluctuations of capital imports and the terms on which they
will be available.

Swings in the flow of foreign capital are not the only disturbance in the capital account of developing countries. Another disturbance which can be of great importance in some countries in particular periods is flight of domestic capital. It is frequently caused by
political factors; but it can also be caused by monetary developments.
Countries which have experienced bursts of inflation and successive
devaluations would be particularly exposed to capital flight.

Domestic inflationary pressures affect not only the capital account but they cause disturbances in the current account as well.
Import increases are a natural consequence of inflationary finance
if the exchange rate is pegged. There has been an increasing aware-
ness in the developing countries of the consequences of inflationary
finance in the recent past; however, it would probably be too optimistic to expect that inflationary pressures will not recur. The impact of this source of instability can be reduced if the balance of
payments management is flexible; but even so, a high and continuing
degree of inflation will make the external financial position increasingly difficult over time, particularly if capital flight ensues.

Some of the disturbance variables discussed above are beyond the control of the debtor country; this refers in particular to export fluctuations that are induced by swings in international demand and to autonomous changes in foreign capital inflow. And conversely, domestic authorities can exercise substantial influence on some of the variables; this refers to inflation-induced increases in imports and reductions in exports and to capital flight. Only a combination of domestic policies geared to a minimization of internally generated disturbances and of international policies aimed at stabilization of receipts from commodity exports and from capital inflow can assure that the development process proceeds without interruption and that debt servicing obligations are discharged smoothly.

Offsetting Variables

As an alternative to stabilization of receipts from exports and from capital inflow, there are three ways in which the impact of export declines and of swings in capital inflow can be offset. The debtor country may build up its foreign exchange reserves in periods of export upswings and use them in periods of decline. Secondly, compensatory finance from abroad can be provided on a loan or grant basis to offset the effects of declines. Thirdly, the debtor country may find it possible to curtail its imports of non-essential goods in periods of decline and thus continue its growth process, although personal consumption, or its growth, may have to be curtailed.

In countries where export receipts fluctuate over a relatively short period, if the government of a country conducts an anti-cyclical policy and has perfect foresight, it may take advantage of a period of above-trend exports to accumulate international reserves and pay off short-time debts, and would thus be prepared to face a period of below-trend exports. Such compensatory policy has been in evidence in some developing countries since World War II. But this has not been a general rule. With emphasis on economic development and growing need for investible resources, the opportunity cost of maintaining foreign currency and gold reserves has risen, and a number of countries have partly run down such reserves for financing domestic capital formation. In others, reserves have been used to finance excessive import increases: periods of above-trend exports have also been periods of high consumption and investment expenditures, and optimistic expectations regarding the duration of high prices, coupled with imperfections of the monetary mechanism and monetary policies, have occasionally led to excessive spending and thus to excessive imports. Finally, in another group of countries, the very fact that export declines have lasted a long period, has made it impossible to carry out a systematic reserve policy: reserves have been spent in the initial period of the decline and it has proved impossible to rebuild them while the decline has continued. Whatever forces have been at work, the fact is that reserves of developing countries are now substantially smaller, in relation to imports, than they were fifteen years ago; consequently, their own ability to weather a crisis without cutting consumption and investment has been reduced.

Table 1

Reserves[a] as Percentage of Imports[b]

	All developing countries	Latin America	Asia
1948	70.0	44.0	86.9
1953	56.6	46.1	53.7
1958	42.7	33.2	34.2
1963	39.2	28.1	32.0

[a] Gold, Fund Gold Tranche Position, Foreign Exchange.
[b] Commodity Imports.

Countries' own reserves are not the only offsetting variables. Compensatory borrowing abroad is an effective supplement of reserves; and the operations of the International Monetary Fund have to a certain extent reduced the need to maintain large reserves of gold and convertible foreign currency. The lack of flexibility introduced by the reduction of reserves has thus been partly compensated by the establishment and activity of the international machinery specifically designed to supplement the nationally owned supply of liquidity facilities. Recently, the Fund introduced a new compensatory facility to offset fluctuations in export earnings: this facility is directly aimed at primary producing countries suffering from temporary shortfalls in export earnings.

The Fund is not the only source of compensatory finance: national lending agencies in some developed countries engage in these operations and also there is a flow of private funds, of limited magnitude, available to a few developing countries.

It is natural that compensatory financing is not available without limitation: these limitations operate with respect to both the amounts that can be drawn and the conditions under which drawings can be made. Furthermore, it is in the nature of conventional compensatory financing that it is repayable over a relatively short period. This raises serious questions concerning the position of countries whose export declines may last a long time. More generally, repayments by countries which will be net importers of capital for a long time will inevitably have to be financed out of new gross capital inflow.

Rigid Variables

It has already been emphasized that the fluctuating nature of external receipts of debtor countries stands in sharp contrast to the fixed nature of their debt servicing obligations. Interest on external debt is the most rigid element in the balance of payments. It is contractually fixed and is a recurring charge on the economy regardless of borrower's fortunes. Fixed interest debt in most developing countries consists today largely of public and publicly-guaranteed debt. Consequently, any failure to pay this recurring charge adversely reflects on a government's ability to save and to transfer savings, and thus inevitably undermines its credit standing.

From the viewpoint of the balance of payments, service on loan capital borrowed by private parties is equally rigid. On the other hand, it is usually assumed that returns on equity capital fluctuate with export earnings. As indicated above, this assumption is only partially valid: it applies to profits and dividends originating in export industries, but it does not apply to earnings of foreign investment employed in activities catering to the domestic market. In the post-war period, such foreign investment has been of significance: it has been flowing not only into consumer goods industries but also into industries producing capital goods and intermediate products in a number of industrializing developing countries.

The implication of this development is that a change in the economic structure, which will have favorable long-term effects, has been accompanied by an increase in the short-run rigidities in the balance of payments of the countries concerned. Their exports still consist of primary products which continue to fluctuate, while returns on foreign capital originate in a rising and barely fluctuating market. Furthermore, the proportion of interest and dividend payments in total export earnings is bound to increase during the initial stages of economic development of most countries if this development is financed by capital inflow to any considerable extent: given the constraint on international demand for primary products, export earnings are unlikely to increase faster than 4 per cent per annum, while debt service liabilities tend to build up at a much more rapid rate if lending takes place at conventional or even half-conventional terms.[7] And the higher the proportion of loan capital in total capital flow, the greater the proportion of domestically oriented industries in the total equity stock held by foreign investors; the greater the constraints on international demand for primary products and the greater the fluctuations in the prices of these products—the more significant will be the element of rigidity.

The other component of debt service payments—amortization—is also a rigid element in the balance of payments, although it could be argued that there is a substantive difference between this element and interest. It is the exception rather than the rule that the less developed countries are expected to reduce the absolute level of their debt in the near future, which would happen in the case of net repayment. However, there is no certainty, under present conditions, that new loans will be extended and thus offset or more than offset payments due on the loans of the past. The contractual obligation to pay amortization exists irrespective of what happens to other elements of the balance of payments. The irony of the situation is that precisely when a country is facing liquidity difficulties, creditors, faced by unpaid or delayed bills, may feel compelled to refrain from rolling over old debts and extending new credits.

The most severe liquidity crises are caused by the concentration of maturities in a short period—the so-called "cash squeeze" cases. If the debtor country has to repay a large proportion of its debt within a few years; if no foreign exchange reserves have

---

[7] If net transfer of resources of 1,000 units takes place every year (net of amortization and interest), debt service payments will show the following values in the 20th year of borrowing:

Interest Rate %	Repayment over (number of years)	Debt Service		
		Interest	Amortization	Total
6	15	2,026	3,480	5,505
6	40	2,026	1,019	3,045
3	15	754	2,674	3,428
3	40	754	774	1,528
0.75	50 (of which 10 years of grace)	153	93	245

been accumulated to enable the retirement of the debt; and if the creditors are not willing to undertake the refinancing of the debt —liquidity difficulties will be acute. Creditors may be reluctant to reschedule the debt over a longer period because of their past experience: rescheduling would not help much if the debtor were to pile up new short-term debts as soon as the existing ones have been funded. On the other hand, the debtor country, if it is unable to space over time the maturities, is almost compelled to resort to more short-term borrowing, frequently at prohibitive interest rates. Its debt structure worsens further. Breakdown is avoided if the debtor country drastically curtails its imports and thus releases resources for the liquidation of short-term debts: this helps restore its credit abroad, but in the meantime the process of economic growth is arrested. Alternatively, creditors may agree to postpone collections, and this provides a breathing spell. But if the postponement is only for a few years, a new liquidity crisis occurs in short order. This succession of crises inevitably affects the flow of long-term capital needed for development. The solution of the "cash-squeeze" problem is unlikely to prove lasting unless an advance is made in coping with the basic factors responsible for the financial crises that have been experienced.

An unfavorable debt structure does not necessarily lead to a liquidity problem: whether such a problem will in fact arise depends on the size of service payments in relation to the major macro-economic variables, particularly export earnings, and on the possibilities of contracting new capital inflow. The latter cannot be statistically measured; they will depend on the circumstances in particular cases. The former can be expressed in the form of the debt service ratio.

Debt Service Ratios

A convenient indicator of rigidity and of the actual and potential pressure on the balance of payments is the ratio of debt service—interest and amortization—to exports. Foreign exchange is one of the scarcest, if not the most scarce, inputs for the developing countries. The debt service is a continuing charge against this scarce resource. The proportion of exports absorbed by debt service reflects the pressure to which a debtor country would be exposed and the· effort it would have to make if capital inflow were to cease. Furthermore, since current account receipts also fluctuate, debt service ratio indicates the potential strain which a debtor country would experience when its exports contract: the proportion of export earnings absorbed

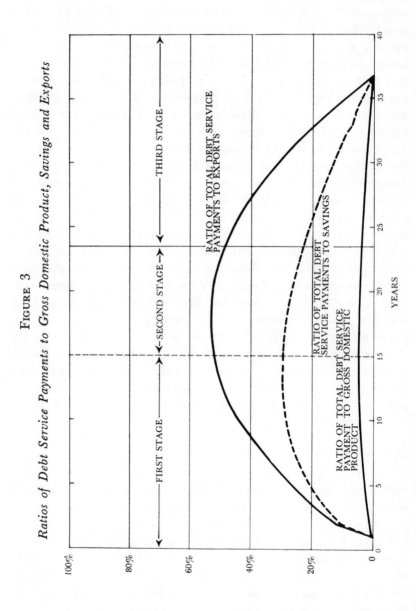

FIGURE 3

Ratios of Debt Service Payments to Gross Domestic Product, Savings and Exports

by debt service would go up when exports decline and there would occur a proportionate reduction in the amount of foreign exchange available to the country for financing imports needed for domestic consumption and investment.

The rigidity in the balance of payments on account of public debt service has increased for almost all countries included in the sample. The increase in rigidity—and its general level—would be even greater if the ratios included the service on private loan transactions, investment income payments generated in foreign owned industries catering to the domestic market and obligations on account of commercial arrears.

The debt service ratios can attain very high values in the course of the debt cycle. If foreign capital is lent on conventional terms, if the domestic growth variables have the values as described in the growth-cum-debt model, if the initial ratio of exports to income is 10 per cent and if exports grow at the post-war historical rate of 4 per cent per annum, the debt service ratio would reach 50 per cent at the peak of the debt cycle, i.e., one-half of exchange earnings would be absorbed by debt service (see Figure 3). This is a high degree of rigidity. It should be emphasized, however, that if the proportion of exports to total income is higher than 10 per cent—i.e., the economy is more "open"—the level of the ratio would be lower than indicated in Figure 3. Further, to the extent that lending takes place at a rate of interest below 6 per cent, the ratio would be correspondingly reduced. Finally, in the context of short-run analysis, the impact of a high level of the ratio in the period of crisis may be offset by a high level of exchange reserved.

Debt service is not the only element of rigidity in the balance of payments of a developing country. As its industrialization process proceeds, the composition of its imports undergoes significant changes. Expansion of the industrial base requires expanded imports of fuels, raw materials, spare parts and capital goods. Reduced imports of these goods may cause unemployment and affect the momentum of growth. Furthermore, the post-war period has been characterized by a rapid expansion of the import of foodstuffs into developing countries: domestic food supplies have lagged behind increasing demand. Reduced imports of staple foods are rendered extremely difficult: imported food, in most cases, serves to supplement local supplies to urban centers whose population has grown rapidly since the war. Experience suggests that there are severe limitation to the possibilities of reducing food supplies to these centers.

TABLE 2

Proportion of Exports Absorbed by Public Debt Service[a]
(Debt Service Ratios), 1956 and 1963

	1956	1963		1956	1963
Argentina	1.9	18.3	Iran	1.2	6.4
Bolivia	4.1	23.0	Israel	51.4	33.8
Brazil	12.2	23.8	Pakistan	6.2	13.9
Chile	9.2	19.1	Burma	n.a.	3.7
Colombia	6.5	23.1	Ceylon	0.7	2.3
Costa Rica	4.3	12.7	Malaya	0.6	1.2
Ecuador	5.5	13.6	Philippines	1.9	8.8
El Salvador	1.3	3.5	Thailand	1.5	4.2
Guatemala	0.2	7.7			
Honduras	—	3.0	East Africa[b]	4.4	7.6
Mexico	11.3	30.0	Ethiopia	1.1	7.7
Nicaragua	7.6	5.9	Federation of		
Panama	2.9	7.4	Rhodesia and		
Paraguay	14.5	8.8	Nyasaland (former)	3.8	8.3
Peru	9.6	10.8	Nigeria	0.6	5.7
Uruguay	5.4	7.8	Sudan	0.2	7.8
Venezuela	0.3	4.3	Turkey	n.a.	42.1
India	0.9	14.5	Yugoslavia	17.3	17.2

[a] Service on public and publicly-guaranteed indebtedness with original maturity
of one year or more.
[b] Kenya, Tanzania and Uganda.

Some Implications

The rigidity phase in the development of debtor economies is
a temporary phase if the growth-cum-debt process is successful.
The critical questions concern the length of the period of rigidity
and the policies which the debtor countries pursue. While there is a
tendency for imports to be concentrated on the most essential items
and the demand for imports is strong as a result of income growth
targets, this can be further intensified by inflationary domestic fiscal
and monetary policies which are frequently pursued irrespective of
the phase of the price cycle and the state of external accounts. Inflationary policies, of course, interfere with a smooth reconciliation
of domestic and foreign claims on aggregate domestic output; and
this can be translated into debt servicing difficulties.

We do not know how long it takes a developing country to
overcome the worst phase of the strains on its balance of payments.
In particular, we do not know at what speed an industry which has

been built initially to supply the domestic needs can be made sufficiently competitive to penetrate the international market. Sooner or later, if economic growth is a success, the structural change of the economy will inevitably lead to a structural change in external accounts with a consequent rapid rise in exports and a relaxation of rigidities. There are industrializing countries which have accomplished the transition from domestic to export orientation swiftly, in about a decade or so. Their experience should be carefully studied.

The problem of rigidities arising from debt servicing burden can be handled in a number of ways. An acceleration in the rate of growth and structural change of the borrowing countries, accompanied by maximum inducement to export development, will tend to increase the flexibility of their economies. Flexible balance of payments management will make it possible to accommodate more smoothly the competing claims on resources and thus to maintain the debt service flow. Elimination of barriers facing the exports of developing countries, both of primary products and of manufacturers, will enable these countries to raise their rate of export growth and thus to reduce the adverse impact of the foreign exchange constraint. Reduction in the amplitude of fluctuations of primary product prices will alleviate the difficulties arising from the varying nature of external earnings of developing countries against which they face fixed repayment obligations. Softening of the terms of capital inflow would reduce the rate of growth in external indebtedness and in debt service payments and thus reduce the debt servicing burden and the accompanying rigidities to which it gives rise.

20

INTERNATIONAL TRADE AND ECONOMIC GROWTH

By W. Arthur Lewis

School of Public and Internal Affairs, Princeton University, U.S.A.

A country cannot begin development from a subsistence level by producing for the home market only. An increase in *per capita* income increases the demand for nearly everything, but no country can produce nearly everything, since no country has every kind of mineral, climate and soil. Hence an increase in *per capita* income causes imports to increase. Income which has been generated in producing goods for the home market only is spent instead on buying imports. Some of the goods are unsold; producers are bankrupted, and development stops. Self-sustaining progress can continue only if the increase in imports is matched by an increase in exports.

This is why historically the beginnings of economic development in every country are associated with increased foreign trade. Exports are the engine of the first stage of economic growth. This can be a very prosperous stage. Production for exports raises the incomes of all those who are directly involved—small farmers, wage-earners, middlemen and investors, since nobody need be involved (outside a slave society) unless involvement raises his income. These incomes also provide a base from which to move forward to other stages of development, both by increasing productive capacity, and also by creating a challenging home market.

Productive capacity is increased because these incomes support considerable improvement of infrastructure and of skills, whose benefits are not confined to the products which pay for them. Capital is invested in transportation (harbors, roads, railways, telecommunications), in electric power, in banking and commercial institutions, and in public services (schools, hospitals, water supplies and general administration). The community acquires a new set of resources and skills which would serve it to produce new commodities even if the original exports disappeared. (This is why it pays to mine and export ores, even though this disposes of a wasting asset.)

The proceeds of exports are used to buy imports. Thus import substitution becomes a challenge to domestic producers. The export industry buys many commodities to use up in production (fuels, chemicals, timber, machines, ores, fibers, etc.). It is thus linked, on

350

the production side, to many other industries whose output is thereby stimulated. The industry also pays out incomes to farmers, wage-earners and others, whose expenditure is also a challenge to consumer goods industries. At first, much of this income goes in importing consumer goods, but as productive capacity increases, import substitution takes place.

Thus the second stage of economic development is import substitution, producing for the home market. A country cannot start its development by producing for the home market, but given export production, can generate further progress by substituting home production for imports. (Not for exports, but for imports.) The range of possibilities is wide. Import substitution is not confined to manufacturing consumer goods and industrial equipment. Production of raw materials can also be stimulated. Also, increasing income changes the pattern of food consumption (from roots to cereals, meat, milk, vegetables and fruits) and the failure of farmers to keep up with these changes is reflected in increased imports of food.

Now developing countries differ immensely in the extent to which they seize the opportunities created by expanded exports, and move into the import substitution stage. For this there are both technical and political reasons.

It is technically easier to produce some commodities rather than others. Generally speaking, it is easier at low levels of development to start growing agricultural crops for export than to start manufacturing industrial commodities for export. Agriculture requires special soils and climates, but industry requires only skills and equipment, which can be duplicated anywhere; hence it is easier to be superior in agriculture than to be superior in manufacturing, at low levels of development. So at the beginning, the engine of growth is always not only exports, but exports of agricultural or mineral raw materials in which the country has some geographical advantage. In drawing up a Development Plan for a subsistence economy, the first task is to discover, by surveying its natural resources, what geographical advantages it may have.

Once having started with some favorable commodity it is very easy to overspecialize; this is why so many countries pass through a stage of monoculture. Specialization pays; it is the secret of economic success. So all the resources associated with the new export tend to specialize in its requirements. Transport is designed to serve it, geographically. Banks, commodity exchanges, legal contracts, research institutes, training facilities, universities and practically everything else, specialize in the problems of this one export commodity, to the neglect of most other opportunities. The community maximizes its gain from this commodity, at the expense not merely of other potential gain, but also of becoming dependent on a market which may easily disappear for reasons beyond its control.

A sensible community should fight against over-specialization. This requires a deliberate and expensive effort. Money must be spent on research, training and investment in commodities which are not now as profitable, or do not now seem as promising as the dominant export. Such money would have to be raised by taxing the dominant export. But those associated with this export—not only the capitalists but also the farmers and wage-earners—tend to be powerful politically, and therefore to prevent efforts to develop other forms of production. They demand that these others "stand on their own feet," while forgetting how much effort, governmental and otherwise, had to be put into the now dominant export before it learned how to stand on its own feet. Failures in this respect can be especially damaging to incipient industrial production for all the reasons enshrined in the infant industries' argument for protection (economies of scale, investment in skills, external economies) as well as in those cases where manufacturing costs are high because firms are required to pay wages in excess of what their workers could produce in alternative occupations.

The institutional structure of foreign trade can also be important. Where exports come to be handled by a few big foreign wholesalers who also bring in most of the imports, perhaps even using their own ships, there is small chance that the challenge of import substitution will be met. For the interest of these traders in imports and shipping will make them hostile to measures aimed at reducing imports.

Failure to pursue import substitution is associated with imperialism, but is not confined to that political system. Imperialism virtually ensures that measures will not be taken to pursue import substitution, but political independence does not ensure that the challenge will be taken up, since those associated with the dominant export are not necessarily foreigners, and can be just as powerful in a sovereign state as in a colony.

The Great Depression of the 1930s, followed by the Second World War, did more to promote import substitution than any political change, since both these events emphasized the dangers of over-specialization and destroyed the ideological scheme (misuse of a static Law of Comparative Costs) on which the defense of over-specialization was based. Since the Second World War most countries have progressed rapidly along the path of import substitution, confining themselves, unfortunately, mainly to manufactures, while tending to ignore raw materials and food. Annual rates of increase of industrial production of 8 to 10 per cent have become quite common, in countries where agricultural output increases only by 3 per cent or less. Thus, in several the possibilities of import substitution of manufactures are already exhausted, or about to be exhausted, and development must move into a new stage, or decelerate.

II

In an underveloped economy the possibilities for manufacturing are limited on the one hand by technical factors, and on the other hand by the size of the market. Technical factors include absence of the heavy raw materials needed by some industries, absence of specialized skills needed by others, and the large scale of output of still others. Thus, it will always pay to specialize: the biggest importers of manufactures are the countries which themselves export manufactures.

Apart from these technical factors, which determine which manufactures to make at home and which to import, the market for manufactures as a whole (domestic and imported) is limited by the standard of living. In a country where half the people are subsistence farmers, with no surplus to spend on manufactures, the scope for industrial production is inevitably limited.

Agriculture and industry depend on each other. This is clearest in the closed economy. An increase in industrial production raises the demand for food and raw materials from the farmers. If farm output is stagnant, this raises agricultural prices. This in turn raises wages, reducing the profitability of industrial production, even perhaps to the point of bringing industrial growth to a standstill. In an open economy the required food and raw materials can be imported, without prices rising; but they must then be paid for by exporting industrial products. Industrialization thus demands either a balanced growth of industry and agriculture, or increased exports, or some combination of both.

Industrialization for import substitution is viable until the economy is substituting for all the manufactures it can produce economically. In this stage the increased imports generated by increased income are paid for with the foreign exchange released by import substitution. But this is only a temporary stage. When import substitution is exhausted the economy may bog down in stage three, where exports are again the engine of growth, but living standards remain low, because most of the people are subsistence farmers. Or it may move forward into stage four, the bottleneck-breaking state, where rapid progress in food production (or in eliminating whatever else may be the bottleneck in supply) makes possible balanced (or nearly balanced) growth. When this stage is completed, elasticities of supply will be fairly high, but the country will still not be able to produce everything it consumes; in this final stage of development, the limiting factor on growth will be again the rate at which exports can be expanded. Stages four and five are related. The rate of growth of national income, the propensity to import and the propensity to export must be consistent with each other. Given the propensity to export, the growth rate can be raised by reducing the propensity to import (stage four); or given the propensity to import (stage five) the growth rate can be raised by increasing the propensity to export. Which of these is the more appropriate remedy at any given time may be uncertain, as currently in the case of Great Britain.

Most developed economies are in stages four or five, maintaining high growth rates either by keeping the propensity to import low (and therefore having nearly balanced growth) or by keeping the propensity to export high (since very few countries have all the minerals, climates and soils which balanced growth requires). At this level of development a high proportion of exports does not menace economic dependence, since the high level of resources and skills makes possible a diversified pattern of exports, such that there is small dependence on any one market. What distinguishes the underdeveloped economy in stage one is not the fact that its export ratio is high, but rather the fact that its exports are so highly specialized that a change in a single market can plunge it into poverty. With maturity a country does not necessarily reduce its export ratio (though it may do so); what it mainly does is to spread its risks over many different baskets.

Latin America furnishes examples of economies in the first four stages. Venezuela is in stage one: an economy growing at over 6 per cent per annum, with exports (oil) as the engine of growth. Brazil was in stage two through the 1950s: a high growth rate based on import substitution of manufactures. Chile is in stage three: the limits of import substitution of manufactures have been reached; further growth requires either an agricultural breakthrough, or an export breakthrough (possibly more copper). Mexico has achieved the agricultural breakthrough, and is in stage four, balanced growth.

Countries in stage three (import substitution exhausted, no breakthrough in agriculture or exports) are ripe for what is now called "structural inflation". Further investment in manufacturing raises real income and therefore the imports of food (and other commodities). This causes both a balance of payments deficit and also deflation in the home market (income generated in producing manufactures being used instead to purchase imports). The action taken to eliminate the balance of payments deficit (devaluation or tariffs) raises the cost of living, and thus starts an inflationary spiral, in which wages and prices chase each other. Alternative action directed in the first instance at eliminating the home deflation (increased monetary circulation, budgetary deficit) has the same effect. Persistence along these paths, to maintain continued growth of industrial production, must produce persistent spiralling inflation. Growth without inflation requires either balanced development of industry and agriculture, or a breakthrough in export trade.

For most underdeveloped countries the hardest problem seems to be to achieve a breakthrough in agriculture; few achieve a growth rate of 3 per cent, whereas an industrial growth rate of 8 per cent needs an agricultural growth rate of at least 5 per cent to support it (once import substitution is exhausted, and in the absence of increased mineral or industrial exports).

The failure in agriculture is due mainly to political rather than to technical factors. The bases for agricultural progress are well known. The terms on which small farmers hold their lands must be such as to give incentives to effort. Large landowners must not be allowed to hold fertile lands empty while small farmers scrape a living on infertile soils. Money must be spent on research and agricultural extension, to bring knowledge of new seeds, fertilizers and pest and disease control to the farmers. Investment is needed in roads, water supplies, and processing facilities. And so on. Such methods have achieved results in the few countries which have tried them on an adequate scale. Failure to solve the agricultural problem is due rather to failure to make the necessary effort.

It is desirable to increase agricultural productivity irrespective of whether a country will be a net importer or net exporter of agricultural products. The pattern of trade in agriculture depends to a considerable extent on the ratio of population to cultivable area. Some underdeveloped countries, such as India, are already too heavily populated to have a net agricultural surplus for export. A rapid increase in their *per capita* output (say, a doubling in thirty years) is almost certain to increase the demand for agricultural products faster than the domestic supply. Such countries (Egypt is another example) will have to live by exporting manufactures and importing agricultural products. However, since it is not easy to export manufactures, their need for maximum agricultural effort is all the greater. In other countries (e.g., much of West Africa) cultivatable land is abundant, and it should be possible in all in the foreseeable future for agricultural supply to keep pace with demand.

In any case, any country is liable to want to export some manufactures, whether it becomes a net exporter of manufactures, or remains a net importer. For as its skills improve, and its resources increase, there will be some manufactures in which it has a relative advantage. Rapid industrialization since the Second World War has brought this situation into focus, and caused some shift of emphasis in the discussion between developed and underdeveloped countries of the barriers to international trade. When it was assumed that the underdeveloped world must concentrate on primary products, remaining forever in stage one, this discussion centered on methods by which the developed protect their agriculture, and on measures to stabilize the prices of primary commodities. But the United Nations World Trade Conference of 1964 found underdeveloped countries concentrating as well, for the first time, on the developed countries' tariffs against manufactured goods. This problem will grow in importance.

Taking the underdeveloped world as a whole, exporters of primary products have not since the Second World War played quite the dominating role as engine of growth as they did before the First World War. This is due partly to concentration during the last fifteen years on exploiting the opportunities for import substitution in manufacturing. But it is also due partly to having higher growth targets than exports of primary products can sustain (taking the group as a whole). During the 1950s the exports of underdeveloped countries increased at an average annual rate of 3.6 per cent. This is probably as high as at any time in the past, but it is not high enough to sustain the growth rates which underdeveloped countries would now like to achieve.

The underdeveloped countries have so far exported mainly to the developed, and mainly primary products—minerals, fuels and tropical agricultural commodities. The demand for these is limited in the developed world; and there is in any case no reason why the growth rate of the underdeveloped countries should be tied to the growth of demand for their products in developed countries. If the underdeveloped can achieve among themselves balanced growth of their manufactures, minerals and agriculture, their rate of growth will not be tied to exports to the developed world.

Such balance is not now in sight because of failure on the agricultural front. The underdeveloped world has been increasing its industrial production at a rate of about 8 per cent per annum, while its agricultural rate is less than 3 per cent per annum. Balance requires a ratio of about 8 to 5. In the absence of balance, the underdeveloped countries will come to depend increasingly on the developed for their food supplies, and will in due course be net importers of food, paid for by net exports of manufactures. Given the persistence of current trends, the turning point is calculable. The underdeveloped countries now import manufactures equal (including the value of raw materials) to about 30 per cent of their national incomes. If industrial production grows by 8 per cent per annum, agriculture by 3 per cent, national income by 5 per cent, and use of manufactures by 6 per cent, net import of manufactures will fall to zero in 22 years. Persistence of current trends would therefore swing the terms of trade sharply against manufactures in favor of agriculture, making it increasingly difficult for the underdeveloped countries to continue the pace of their industrialization. When we remember that population growth is also accelerating in the underdeveloped countries, from 2 per cent to almost 3 per cent per annum, such an outcome is not at all implausible. Some writers assert that the terms of trade must always move against agriculture in favor of industry, but there is no support for this in the historical record— which merely shows that the terms of trade for agriculture improve when industrialization is rapid, and decline when industrialization slows down. Continuance of current trends in the underdeveloped countries must turn the terms of trade in favor of agriculture; this will favor those countries which make an agricultural breakthrough, but damage those whose agricultural stagnation forces them to rely on importing food and agricultural raw materials.

The underdeveloped countries have ceased to be "on the periphery" of the developed, in the sense that the demand of the developed countries is no longer their only engine of growth. Most of them have passed out of stage one, into stage two. Import subsitution will take them some way, but already a number have passed through this stage, and bogged down in stage three, where agricultural stagnation restrains the whole economy. If home demand is to be the engine of growth—and this is one definition of economic independence—they must succeed in reaching stages four (breaking bottlenecks in the way of balanced growth, especially agriculture) and five (achieving and maintaining a growth rate of exports high enough to satisfy the irreducible propensity to import). In the mature economy exports are no longer the engine of growth, but if neglected they become the brake.

21 INTERNATIONAL MONETARY REFORM AND THE DEVELOPING STATES

By PIERRE MENDÈS-FRANCE
Former Prime Minister, France

This chapter is different from those appearing in the present volume from other sources. It does not claim to make an original contribution to the discussion of technical problems relating to underdevelopment, but only wishes to draw attention to a situation which should facilitate improvements which have already been studied elsewhere on earlier occasions and which now arise under new conditions which might be usefully exploited.

A range of important issues have so far been the subject of separate negotiations: reform of the international monetary system, stabilization (and revaluation) of the prices of raw materials and agricultural products, aid to developing countries, the fight against depressions and booms, etc. These issues are now meeting at the political level, thanks to circumstances which will be noted here.

As the Rehovoth Conference meets, the governments of the States which have the largest monetary responsibilities are consulting (bilateral talks, Committee of Ten, preparations for the annual meeting of the International Monetary Fund, etc.). Whatever their differences may be, they are engaged in a joint search for a basis on which the Gold Exchange Standard is to be reformed; for while no one is wholly satisfied with the present monetary system, no one, notwithstanding certain resounding declarations, seriously thinks of replacing it by the straightforward gold standard as described by some theoreticians.

In a general way one may say that:

On the one hand, everyone is aware of the inadequacies or imperfections of the prevailing system, in which the extent of international liquidity depends on the payment deficit of a country whose currency grows weaker in the very same measure as it extends the services expected from it;

On the other hand, as far as the future is concerned, all (or nearly all) monetary authorities agree:

(a) to retain a central function for gold;

(b) to maintain, concurrently with the gold base, the aid which the International Monetary Fund provides for its members;

(c) likewise to maintain, if necessary with adjustments, the facilities resulting from certain arrangements which have made available additional international credits, notably the Paris Agreements of 1961.

These different monetary factors, which today supply the bulk of international liquidity, will probably be confirmed tomorrow without major changes. But beyond that point, differences emerge. For the Gold Exchange Standard procedure presently provides an excess of credits which, while heavily criticized from certain sides, seem quite indispensable. At any rate, one will hardly take the risk of abolishing these possibilities without replacing them by something which is yet to be determined—failing which, a general deflation would be certain to result. There is need for additional monetary means (which essentially is why recourse is had to the Gold Exchange Standard in the manner in which it is being applied), but as soon as one seeks ways and means, objections arise which cannot easily be reconciled.

In some views, the solution should be found through a change in the price of gold or, if one wishes, by the concurrent devaluation of the gold rate of all currencies. Apart from the fact that the United States, the principal interested party, has declared itself utterly opposed to this procedure, it should be noted that it would, if adopted, result in a very uneven and very unfair division between the countries benefiting from the measure and those harmed by it; in any case it would not regulate the sterling problem (and sterling finances 40 per cent of international trade) or in any way help the poorest countries: the developing ones. Moreover, across-the-board devaluation of all currencies, even if it would provide certain countries with the advantage of momentary book profits, would make no difference to the state of the exchange: a year or two later we would be back at the same point, and the countries which suffer from a payments deficit now would do so still or again. Nothing would be settled.

Certain economists who for these reasons oppose a change of the gold price, propose the establishment of a new fiduciary currency which would be called Collective Reserve Unit and which, one way or another, would be guaranteed by the financially strongest States. This currency would benefit the different countries in proportion to their gold holdings; it would mean the creation of a greater volume of rights, but again on a given gold basis; which would make the richest countries the principal beneficiaries and aggravate inequalities which are already generally considered excessive.

That is why other specialists, more daringly abandoning all reference to gold, propose that an international authority be charged with opening the necessary credits in the world exchanges; as to how and on the basis of what criteria, opinions vary widely. Some of these suggestions are certainly most attractive, but it must be admitted that they often involve the risk of inflation, since the increase of international liquid means would swell the assets of the central banks and permit a monetary expansion which would no longer be counteracted either by the present brakes and limitations, or by the far more brutal ones which would result from the functioning of the gold standard. Thus the structural imbalances of national economies found at present would tend to become permanent, and industrial orientation would take a progressively more misdirected course. Finally, a world bank with considerable monetary powers is hardly thinkable without a political organization capable both of maintaining and controlling it; failing a world government (the creation of which does not seem to be a matter of the near future), one wonders whether this solution is a realistic one.

What we need, therefore, is a self-sufficient solution with a built-in regulatory device. It should offer the advantages of automatic operation which some theoreticians ascribe to the gold standard, but without the disadvantage of its too narrow base, caused by its consisting of one single commodity which is available in limited quantity, whose production is irregular, and which is the object of unpredictable speculation. These disadvantages result in a serious disproportion between the growth in volume of the monetary base provided by gold, and the development of the world economy. In order to establish a better correlation, it would according to the supporters of the "commodities currency" doctrine, in principle be sufficient:

> that the base of the currency should no longer consist of gold alone, but of as large as possible a number of as diverse as possible commodities; and
>
> that the volume of currency be modified as necessary, taking into account the prevailing market forces, viz., the tendency to build up commodity stocks or the propensity to increase money holdings.

Actually, it is not very likely that the governments responsible will adopt this theory at present. But one may ask oneself whether proposals inspired by the same principles would not stand a better chance of being accepted if the question was not one of upsetting the whole present system but merely, while maintaining the backing of currencies by gold, by the International Monetary Fund and by different credit agreements, of adding a new element which would establish at least a partial correlation between general economic needs and the sum of international liquid assets.

Obviously, there can be no question of backing even part of the liquid assets with the total production, if only because of the multitude and variety of goods, raw materials and manufactured products, the changes they undergo in the course of time, the difficulty of storing them and measuring their value, etc. Rather, one would content oneself with a judiciously selected sample of homogeneous, storable and non-perishable basic products.[1] In other words, in addition to gold reserves, one would have complementary reserves in the form of primary products[2] according to a list compiled so as to supply a sample of which the price movements would be representative of the development and fluctuations of the world economy. Experience shows (and it is easy to explain) that the world market prices of the principal commodities and agricultural products tend to increase when world trade, as well as industrial output, is expanding, and tend to soften when industrial activity slows and an economic crisis is in the offing. Subject to caution and necessary corrections, it may be said that the price indices of basic products are a fairly good indicator of world-wide monetary pressures, an indicator which can be used as a yardstick when it comes to the question of whether the creation of additional liquidity ought to be stepped up or slowed down, according to circumstances, so as to sustain economic growth without inflation. Since the new countries are the chief sellers of these primary products and most clearly derive their export revenue from them, a close link would thus be established between the international monetary problem, that of the prices of primary materials and that of aid to the developing world.

How would this system operate in practice?

An international institution would be charged with opening credits and, if necessary, issuing currency against goods from the selected list supplied to it, which would act as a counterpart in the market and have a restraining effect on excessive slumps. (The

---

[1] As a matter of fact, the supporters of the commodities currency doctrine are known to have adopted such an approximation. For an up-to-date exposition of these ideas, cf. paper by Nicholas Kaldor, Jan Tinbergen and Albert Hart (United Nations Conference on Trade and Development, February, 1964).

[2] About 25 of them, according to the above (see note 1).

opening of the credits established in this way would directly benefit the developing countries.) The international institution would stockpile the goods bought by it just as any bank stocks its cover, and reissue them against currency of its own issue repaid to it. Primary materials needed by the world economy could at any given moment be purchased from the institution at prices approximating those in effect when the stocks were established (with the addition of a charge for overhead).[3]

The aim of the scheme should by no means be understood to be the rigid price maintenance of any given raw material or any single one of the commodities concerned. It is their price level *as a whole* which must be kept on an even keel. To act otherwise could be uneconomic, because it would be contrary to basic forces such as the market demand for individual commodities. Conceivably, it could even lead to the price support of raw materials which no longer satisfy wants; such would be the case, for instance, with natural products which are being replaced by synthetic materials. It will be necessary, therefore, to agree on a price index of selected commodities. Such an index will have to be weighted according to the relative share of its components in international trade. Intervention with a view to regulating and stabilizing the index will not prevent price fluctuations peculiar to specific products.

This would result in the price stabilizing effect which has so often been called for, notably at the International Trade and Development Conference (Geneva, 1964). For the developing countries, it would provide the security which they lack. But the industrialized countries would also derive great advantage from it, for they are also often victimized by instability, though in another way. In times of expansion, price rises always threaten to be accompanied by dangerous exaggerations; in times of stagnation, governments hesitate to resort to pump priming since, failing a braking of regulatory device, they fear to set off an uncontrollable inflation.[4] The stabilizing effect of stockpiles and the conjunctural control which they permit would

---

[3] This outline, needless to say, is a simplified version of the proposal, intended to bring out its salient features. The system lends itself to a good many variations. For example, the organization charged with its implementation on the national level need not actually buy goods in kind; it may also be permitted to buy storage certificates or warrants for future delivery, issued by authorized national or international dealers or agencies and guaranteed, or not, by the central bank concerned.

[4] This has been the case with France in 1964 and 1965.

eliminate the so rightly feared danger of disproportionate price rises involved in full employment policies. Governments and international institutions could in the future take measures aiming at the stimulation of expansion with less concern than in the past, if a safety valve of sorts for the international economy would be created by linking the money circulation to the establishment of regulatory stockpiles.

We have already referred to the enormous advantage which the developing countries would derive from such a situation. This is the more worth noting as we are reaching the point where the whole system of direct international aid seems to require revision. In recent years this aid has already been sufficient; and according to all information available, it will be reduced even more if its present forms and structures are retained.

Moreover, aid to developing countries has so far been distributed in an unsystematic and arbitrary manner. Stabilization—and as far as possible under conditions yet to be determined, revaluation—of raw material prices by the means proposed above would render future development aid more objective, less political, more multilateral. It would increase the volume of aid depending on efforts and progress in improving production rather than on political considerations and pressures. It would eliminate the too frequent political and military deals between suppliers of aid and its recipients. And it would, moreover, spare the governments of the donor countries certain campaigns aimed at restricting the cost of international solidarity, and render foreign aid more palatable to public opinion, since everyone understands the legitimacy of a fair and normal consideration for the work supplied by the produce of goods and commodities needed by the whole world.

When the Trade and Development Conference called for the establishment of regulatory stockpiles, one difficulty it ran into was that of financing them. The monetary reform which we envisage allows this obstacle to be overcome, since it consists precisely in the establishment of stockpiles of raw materials as currency cover.

Moreover, if everyone admits that it is necessary to supply the international exchanges with adequate liquid assets, it is legitimate that their issue should in the first place benefit not the richest countries (as would be the case if certain of the proposals mentioned above were entertained), but those whose development must be supported at all costs.

At the moment when major decisions of a monetary nature are

being prepared, it is important to realize that the political, monetary and financial situation now makes it possible to accept formulas which may, at one and the same time, assure the better operation of the monetary system, reduce excess economic fluctuation, and provide the developing countries with aid which is at once more effective and more exactly tailored to their true needs.

An international arrangement based on the coordination of these related problems has become an urgent necessity, because the monetary situation has deteriorated markedly of late. In fact, the efforts by the United States and Great Britain to improve their balance-of-payments situation have had severe repercussions on the volume of international liquidity and its distribution. To the extent that these two countries enabled the rest of the world to increase its monetary reserves, the reduction of their balance of payments deficit has perforce entailed a reduction of the reserves hitherto at the disposal of all other countries. The effect was strongly felt in the "Third World,"[5] while Europe did not escape it either. Hence the setback with regard to the liberalization of the international capital movements in the industrial and the underdeveloped countries; hence, too, the undesirable increase in gold hoarding.

It would be risky to let this development go on unchecked and to stand by idly until increased and grave difficulties create more trouble and complicate the international economic situation further.

DISCUSSION

Currency Needs Collateral

Credit should indeed be expanded, according to Professor Johnson—but not by storing a variety of commodities. The trouble is that all other proposals run up against the impossibility of endowing an international body with powers of creating credit arbitrarily.

Professor H. G. Johnson, of the U.S., disapproved of Mr. Mendès-France's proposal, for two reasons. First, it constitutes a request for

---

[5] Industrial countries are slower to feel the impact of a slowing down in the formation of international liquidity than the underdeveloped countries, whose situation, moreover, tends to be more dangerously affected by an actual reduction of international liquidity.

additional aid, which should be addressed to the developed States "who have the decisive power as to whether or not to accede to these recommendations." The subject is therefore irrelevant to the present dialogue which, according to Professor Johnson, is concerned with technical problems connected with fiscal and monetary affairs.

Secondly, Dr. Johnson considers the scheme impractical. He allowed that "the developing States do have an important interest in the reform of the monetary system, because its malfunctioning at present operates in many ways to impede and conflict with the advancement of the developing countries."

One example is the cost of tied aid, which in the case of Pakistan works out on the average at 20 per cent above world market prices, though loans have to be paid back in full; so "you are paying far more than you think you are for the aid you are actually getting."

In Europe, the tying of aid results from protectionist policies and is designed to keep inefficient industries running. "In that case, of course, the aid ought to be given as a grant or an export subsidy, and not forced onto the shoulders of the less developed countries" as a tied loan. In the case of Britain and the U.S., aid is both tied and limited in quantity for fear that it may contribute to balance of payment difficulties, which themselves are connected with the inefficiencies of the present international monetary system.

These inefficiencies result from the fact that "we have a dollar exchange standard in which the dollar substitutes for gold, and that standard involves rigid exchange rates, and contains no really effctive adjustment mechanism. There is no way by which adjustment of balance of payment difficulties is brought about, other than through a prolonged and bitter process of mutual recrimination among the developed countries, while they wait for each other's currencies to inflate or levels of employment to fall."

There are three likely solutions, which all involve ending or at least reducing the link of the world's monetary system with gold. One is to make the dollar the basis of the world's monetary reserves; the second is to replace the dollar by a composite reserve unit (CRU), which gives other currencies as well a role in international finance; and the third is to turn the International Monetary Fund into a world central bank.

"If we had a more effective international monetary system, which would generate more demand and permit the developed countries to be more expansive, this would accelerate the shift of inefficient activities—inefficient, that is, at high wage levels—to the developing countries. It would then be unnecessary for the developed countries to place barriers in the way of exports from the developing countries, because it would be obviously inefficient to do so. This would tend to stimulate the growth of the developing countries through an expanding world market."

The process involves dislocations in the advanced countries. It is a problem that concerns the European countries and the U.S.— how to share the burden of adjustment, and whether it is to be borne by the surplus countries through inflation or by the deficit countries through unemployment. "My preference obviously would be to design it so that inflation and not unemployment be the basic adjustment mechanism, because that would contribute most to cutting the developing countries in on the growth of world demand."

The scheme proposed by Mr. Mendès-France prefers a monetary arrangement which involves a direct gift to the LDCs. If so, it would be better to let the IMF buy securities issued by the developing countries or World Bank securities. "There are all sorts of ways by which you could steer the savings involved in an expanding international money supply towards the less developed countries, without obliging them to do anything in particular to earn it."

Dr. Johnson listed his particular objections to the Mendès-France proposals. The benefits would be shared unequally, because some countries produce more and others less of the basic primary products suggested for a "commodities currency." Secondly, credit can be created more cheaply than by digging the ground for commodities to stockpile.

Thirdly, there is no particular virtue in stabilizing the money price of commodities. The troubles of the LDCs do not derive in the main from price fluctuations, but from fluctuations in export earnings. Even if prices remain unchanged, supplier countries can get progressively poorer if their productivity does not increase as fast as other peoples'. The proper way to stabilize earning would be to arrange compensatory finance based on the total earnings and the debt service capacity of individual countries.

Professor Nicholas Kaldor, of Britain, took up Professor Johnson's assertion that monetary reform is a field which should be left to the rich countries. "It is perfectly possible to have monetary reforms which reserve the benefits of that reform largely to the rich countries, and which benefit the rest of the world only indirectly and incidentally."

It is true that within each country credit and paper money replace commodities. However "the management of any kind of credit money involves an exercise of power which, in my opinion, rules it out of consideration in any reasonable future as an international possibility." The schemes suggested by Professor Johnson "wreck on one insuperable obstacle, that they give to an international authority discretionary powers which no powerful government is ready to surrender, no matter how the voting system in the authority is composed."

Leaders of the French government have been attacking what Professor Johnson describes as the "dollar exchange standard." Far from agreeing that gold is on its way out, President de Gaulle advocates returning to the gold standard. The reason is that with gold reserves countries feel secure, for whatever atavistic reasons. "With money, there is always a danger that a political disagreement will lead to its sudden elimination or destruction." The Chinese government has kept its reserves in sterling, because it does not like holding dollars, and recently it has converted these reserves into gold. The French government is reducing its dollar holdings and is not willing to accept any further dollars in international settlements. The French CRU proposal amounts to a re-establishment of the pure gold standard for the rich, by raising the price of gold in general and increasing the supply of gold to the rich countries.

There are great advantages in a commodity standard such as the gold standard. "The gold standard does not work properly because the supply of gold is too small for the needs of the world. But there is nothing in the nature of the metal which makes a gold standard possible and monetary commodity standard impossible."

The world as a whole should be seen as a vast underdeveloped economy, dotted with prosperous metropolitan zones. The chief hold-up to economic growth is the supply of food and raw materials, since manufacturing consists of processing basic materials. If raw material production grows at the rate of 5 per cent yearly, that probably sets a limit of somewhere round 10 per cent to the growth rate of industry.

So the real limiting factor on the rate of growth in the world economy ought to be the growth of productivity on the land. This is not the case in practice, seeing that food and raw materials are already in surplus. Such an "unnecessarily bad state of affairs is due to our monetary system, our credit system—our political system, if you like." Professor Kaldor blames the rich countries for their reluctance to give the world's raw material producers the same protection and price stabilization they offer their own farmers.

An acceleration of industrial production "due to little things like World War I and World War II" does cause a lift in raw material prices, and causes thereby extended investment in the raw materials sector and thereby accelerates the growth of raw material output. "Yet when the prices of raw materials fall, this exerts no marked influence at all in accelerating the growth of industrialization— though that is what it ought to do in a rational world. Well, with a commodity reserves currency, the requisite growth acceleration would automatically happen."

Killing Two Birds with One Stone

The commodities currency scheme would promote the output of primary goods for which demand is sagging. Yet a market will always exist for food and raw materials, even though the choice of individual items within the basket keeps changing. Mr. Mendès-France argues for stabilizing a general index—and using the scheme as a basis for creating new credits to the benefit of the LDCs.

Dr. Josue Saenz, of Mexico, observed that Mr. Mendès-France's analysis hits at the heart of the problem. Investment generates income before it generates production, which inevitably spills over into excess demand, causing a balance of payments problem which is one of the most serious obstacles to development today. Had the Bretton Woods decisions accorded more closely with Keyne's position, we might have had a "super-national bank, computer controlled and completely goldless, supplying the necessary amount of liquidity to the right parties at the right time."

The basic problem is that the gold supply increases by 2 per cent annually, whereas the volume of world trade goes up by 5 and 6 per cent each year. Furthermore there is a global maldistribution of purchasing power derived from the weakening terms of trade for the LDCs—which has wiped out practically all the international aid given over the last ten or fifteen years.

Mr. Mendès-France has done an invaluable job in throwing out this idea for discussion. But it requires elaboration in statistical terms, and this encounters difficulties. The stockpiling of raw materials is expensive. Secondly, it comports dangers, because it promotes the cultivation of primary products "which is precisely the type of production we are trying to get away from.

"In the short run, there is no doubt that each and every under-developed country would be delighted to have its own particular export products monetized to provide means of payment for the essential imports which it requires. But the question is, can this continue? Is the demand for raw materials, primary products of this type, sufficiently elastic to absorb indefinitely all that we are now turning out? I think the answer to this is quite clearly negative."

Thirdly, the political problem of deciding which commodities are to be stockpiled, at what prices and from whom, is practically insoluble at this stage.

Dr. Saenz criticized the U.S. Congress for protesting against a 5 cents a pound rise in coffee prices, though when the price of an automobile goes up by 5 to 10 or 15 cents a pound, there are no objections. Primary product prices have been going down, however, not up, and any stabilization program is bound to involve a subsidy from the developed to the underdeveloped countries. The question is whether Mr. Mendès-France's procedure is the best way of making this subsidy available.

Mr. Christopher Musoke, of Uganda, said, "At the risk of repeating the point made by the delegate from Mexico, the questions which came to my mind are: which primary products would be monetized, and who would select them? Should it be the FAO, should it be the U.N., should it be the consumer countries— who should actually be the authority to decide on the commodities to be selected as the reserve currency standard?

"The other point is whether the monetizing of primary products would stabilize their prices. At the moment, the price of primary commodities is determined by the law of supply and demand. We know that because of advances in technology, the petrochemical industry has made it possible for certain synthetic materials to replace natural fibers. Thanks to technology also, fewer and fewer raw materials are required to go into the manufactured product.

"Going on to food commodities, such as coffee and cocoa, we know that with each increment in the income of the developed countries, very little if any is spent on extra food. Therefore while the supply of coffee, cocoa and other food crops is increasing, the market is very limited indeed. Unless the food crops are going to be sold in developing countries, I fail to see how the scheme could stabilize prices at all. In fact the stockpiles that are going to be made possible because of these proposals may depress the prices of primary commodities further.

"It could be done this way. Because of the need to diversify the economies of developing countries, a lot of them will go and try to produce the reserve currency crops, if I may use that as an expression. This will lead to over-production of the crops for which there is a limited demand."

In conclusion, Mr. Musoke said, "The present failure of the existing monetary system is due not to anything done by the developing countries, but to the lack of cooperation and agreement between the developed countries... What I actually think is that more reflection should be given by the developed countries to proposing a better and more realistic proposal."

Mrs. Gerda Blau, of the FAO, disagreed with Professor Johnson's antagonism to discussing with LDCs matters which only the developed countries can handle. "One of the first kinds of self-help I can think of is to know what to ask for in the way of help from others."

Mrs. Blau was in accord with Professor Kaldor that credit is something which must be shared and not kept in the hands of the few; also that food and raw materials are basic factors in output. But she does not agree with Dr. Kaldor's conclusions, because 50 per cent of all international trade in primary products is among the developed countries themselves, and the proportion is higher still if you include internal trade within the advanced countries. So some of the aid in financing international stocks would go to the Western powers and not the LDCs. This growing raw material base inside the developed countries in the last decade is one of the causes of the serious structural fault that has overtaken the economy of the LDCs, for which buffer stocks cannot be a fundamental remedy.

The problem of fluctuating prices is still with us, but it also works against the commodity reserve system. "If you want to stabilize a bundle of commodities while allowing individual prices within that bundle to fluctuate against each other so as to allow some flexibility to changing market conditions, then instability in one set of commodities would cause an opposite instability of the prices which have to be charged for others in the bundle—otherwise the bundle would no longer add up to the same total as before."

Mrs. Blau stressed that trade has unquestionably been adverse for primary commodities, yet the effort of the LDCs at industrialization during this Development Decade depends on adequate primary export earnings. All that can be done is to adopt the constructive approach—to tackle the problem in a non-spectacular manner from all sides, focusing energies on practical measures like the

Horowitz Proposal, Unilateral Free Trade, and "all the things we can do to help us get over the hump."

Mr. Pierre Uri, of France, drew attention to the fact that Johnson and Kaldor are on the same side in favoring expansion rather than contraction, and in proposing revolutionary methods rather than the old type of gold standard.

Mr. Uri submitted two objections. One is that there is no absolute consistency in the short run between the increase of trade in primary commodities and the increase of trade in general. Likewise, when choosing commodities for the bundle, there is not likely to be any absolute consistency between the trend of a group of commodities—chosen on such technical grounds as whether they are storable, and whether they can be stockpiled cheaply—and the need for over-all stabilization.

It is possible to retain one or two features out of the Mendès-France scheme. In the creation of international liquidity, the trend of prices for primary commodities should be considered as the most important criterion. Secondly, additional liquidity ought in the main to go directly to the LDCs that need it most, which is the opposite of what would happen with the composite reserve unit.

* * *

Mr. Mendès-France answered criticisms made during the debate by clarifying the objectives of his scheme. The intention is not to stock any commodity at any price, but to stabilize a sort of general index of raw materials and basic agricultural commodities. The price of each item would vary according to its own supply and demand situation. If the market for a particular product sags, its price would fall until it eventually disappears from international trade, while other products replace it in the stockpile.

So the selection would be of products constituting the bulk of international trade. A study has shown that twenty or thirty items cover between 85 and 90 per cent of commerce in primary products. It does not matter that a part is supplied by the developed countries. They derive only a small proportion of their earnings from trade in primary materials, whereas the LDCs depend on it for most of their living.

The cost of stockpiling is not great if the list is confined to non-perishable, homogeneous, easily classified goods. Anyway the central authority would include its expenses in the selling price. As it is, stocks are being kept in the world, but in a disorganized and sometimes speculative manner, which makes the operation more costly than its needs.

Mr. Mendès-France noted that Mrs. Blau comes from the FAO, an institution which has been preoccupied for a long time with the problem of creating stocks, to aid famine areas or ward off price recessions. The task has continuously been obstructed by lack of finance. The only solution is to monetize these stocks. When the economic cycle takes an upward turn, threatening over-heated boom conditions, the holding institution would start selling its accumulated supplies, against payment in the currency it has been issuing.

Mr. Uri drew attention to technical difficulties—but they exist in order to be overcome. Concerning the references made to Bretton Woods, Mr. Mendès-France observed: "As one of the few survivors of that conference, I recall that we had a great number of technical difficulties in creating the International Monetary Fund." They were not less difficult than the problems facing the present issue, "yet a solution was found—not perfect, but which has rendered service."

In answer to Professor Johnson's objections of principle, Mr. Mendès-France asked him how else the modern world is going to handle the problems in this field, on which no real progress has been made in the last twenty years. "Some of the issues are more pressing today than they were five or ten years ago. The gap separating the rich and poor countries has widened. In the monetary field we are on the verge of major difficulties for which the necessary decisions have not been taken in good time." Unless something drastic is done, the LDCs face the risk that aid may become smaller than in the past. The monetary reforms at present under discussion may well turn out to be more disadvantageous than in the past to the poor countries and more favorable to the rich. This means that existing inequalities will be supplemented by further inequalities still.

Professor Johnson advocates the creation of credit—but a credit based on what? Measured by what? Shall an international institution be granted an arbitrary right to take whatever decision it deems proper? Mr. Mendès-France does not believe that, under the existing condition of internation relations, "it is possible or even desirable to give an institution composed of technicians, bankers, economists and even professors, the extraordinary responsibility of taking sovereign decisions in the monetary field, without any criterion other than their conviction and good faith and—let us add—the political pressures to which they would be subjected."

These pressures would probably be exercised in the direction of inflation, whipping up international economic activity to a pace beyond what can be considered wholesome. As Professor Kaldor has insisted, we must work out a system having the advantages of automatic control possessed by the gold standard, but not dependent on such a narrow and partial regulator.

Governor Horowitz has made a comparison with what happened in the industrialized countries a century ago. It came to be understood in those days that the submerged classes have to be granted a larger portion of the collective wealth and a larger share of rights and powers in the State. This was not done by increasing the budget of the social welfare bureaus or amplifying the means devoted to charity. Wages were raised, social laws enacted and more employment given, so that working folk could make a greater contribution to global production.

"Today exactly the same has to be done for the underprivileged countries. We must raise their salaries, i.e., augment what they receive in exchange for their work and output," Mr. Mendès-France said.

PART **V** SUMMARY

Reports recapitulating the deliberations of the two conference committees, on monetary and fiscal problems respectively, were delivered by Dr. Raymond Goldsmith and Dr. Jacob Mosak. Professor Don Patinkin gave a concluding address summarizing the conference.

22

CENTRAL BANKS AND FINANCIAL INSTITUTIONS
By Raymond Goldsmith
Vice-President,
Development Center, OECD

I shall start with a few comments on what I regard as one of the most fruitful ideas brought to the attention of Committee B, both from the point of view of economic theory and, I am inclined to believe, also in the long run from that of financial practice. This is Professor Gurley's treatment of finance—in the sense of the creation, change-of-hands and extinction of financial instruments—as one of the alternative methods of making possible the additions to a nation's stock of durable assets, whether that stock is defined narrowly as limited to so-called productive reproducible tangible objects or is interpreted more broadly, as the tendency now is, to include such expenditures on human capital and organization as have enduring effects on output.

Professor Gurley's basic idea that finance (including inflation) and its alternatives—self-financing, central planning and taxation—have specific costs and benefits; that these vary in different stages of development and in different political, administrative and economic situations, and that there exists an optimum combination of these alternatives, I regard as extremely promising. To show its power this basic idea, however, will have to be expressed in a form which lends itself to quantitative measurement and to empirical test.

When this is done I am sure it will be found that it is not the real costs of running the financial system—the labor of the bank clerks or the office buildings and equipment of banks and insurance companies—which are the critical magnitudes. I doubt whether the financial system absorbs in any country more than a very few per cent of total real resources. Since the alternatives are not costless, the difference is much too small to provide a basis for choosing between finance and its alternatives. That choice will have to be made primarily on the basis of allocative efficiency. After a generation of sometimes heroic efforts we know how far we still are from measuring and comparing allocative efficiency in concrete situations. Professor Gurley's paper contains interesting presumptions for some situations (particularly in the third section), but the essential task of making them applicable to concrete situations remains to be done.

377

It requires calculation of the costs and benefits of finance in its different forms, and of its alternatives. This will help determine the optimum combination of alternative approaches, as applicable to the several types of underdeveloped country which we find in the world today. Conclusions should take into account the experience of the now developed countries—the planned as well as market economies —together with the results of theoretical analysis.

How Countries Became Developed

If we want the LDCs to benefit from the experience in the field of finance and its alternatives achieved by the now more developed countries, we must be clear about what the essential features of that experience have been. They may be condensed into less than a dozen statements, greatly simplifying but, I trust, not falsifying the experience of the developed market economies, and stressing those features that seem to have relevance for now less developed countries.

1. The ratio of the superstructure of financial assets to the real infrastructure of national wealth and product has increased considerably during the period of development, first rapidly, then more slowly, and in some countries now seems to be approaching the horizontal.

2. The financial inter-relation ratios of developed countries (financial assets/national wealth) show a tendency to cluster around unity when the temporary distorting effects of open or repressed inflations or of heavy dead-weight (war) debts have worn off. By contrast no underdeveloped country shows a ratio of much above one half, and the ratio is more often in the neighborhood of one third.

3. In the course of development, indirect financing through financial institutions has gained continuously at the expense of direct financing, in which savers hold claims against, or equity securities of those units that make capital expenditures. As a result of this tendency, financial institutions now appear as either holders or issuers of between one half and three-quarters of all financial instruments.

4. Among financial institutions the banking system predominates during the early phases of development. Later, first specialized saving and then insurance and pension organizations gain in importance, and they finally come to surpass the banking system in terms of assets. Paralleling this development, the share of money (currency and check deposits) in total financial instruments declines.

5. Within the banking system, the deposit banks grow more rapidly than the central bank, except in time of war or inflation.

6. The growth and specialization of the financial system have been accompanied, through not without exceptions, by a reduction in the differences in availability and cost of funds among sections and regions.

7. Very little is known unfortunately about trends in self-financing in different countries and sectors. It would appear, however, that the proportion of capital expenditures paid for by the investor without recourse to external financing was first decreasing—roughly until World War II—and then increased, particularly as a result of the rising share of total capital expenditures paid for out of current surpluses in the government's budget.

8. Economic development in the last hundred to 150 years has taken place against the background of a generally rising price level (the two main exceptions were 1875–95 and the 1930s). However, protracted substantial inflations—say, annual price rises of more than 5 per cent for a decade or more—have been very rare in developed countries.

9. Monetary policy over the last century has extended its scope. To a considerable extent it has changed its aims and its methods, and has become integrated –even if slowly and as yet incompletely—with fiscal policy. These changes are visible in the shift of function among the central banks. At the beginning, they acted only or predominantly as a lender of last resort. In due course, they came to be concerned with the liquidity position of the entire economy and the stability of the price level. On the technical side the once dominating instrument of the rediscount rate has been relegated to a secondary position compared to open-market operations, reserve requirements, credit ceilings and specific controls of certain sectors of the money and capital market, primarily the security loan, consumer credit, home mortgage and foreign trade credit markets.

Prospect for the LDCs

Let us now turn to the basic question: What can underdeveloped countries learn from the financial experience of now developed countries? Which features of the financial technology of developed countries—financial institutions, financial instruments, financial techniques—can and should underdeveloped countries take over? Which of the monetary policies that have been followed in developed countries should LDCs adopt—or maintain; and which ones should they reject, or accept in modified form only? Can underdeveloped countries speed up the process of financial growth which has taken between fifty and 150 years in the advanced countries? Can they omit certain phases of financial development? Are there important differences in this respect between LDCs of different types, such as the three types distinguished by Professor Galbraith?

You obviously do not expect me to answer a host of questions of this difficulty in a few minutes. All I can do is to make a few comments and suggestions on some of them.

1. I shall start with possibly the most controversial subject, and one which in one form or another came up continuously in the discussion of committee B: the role of price level stability as the main objective and ultimate test of monetary policy. On this problem, I am afraid, converts are rare. I do not therefore claim to represent the consensus of opinion—because there was none—when I conclude that LDCs should not be unduly influenced in their monetary policy by the fear of a moderate upward trend in the price level.

This conclusion would be accepted, I believe, by the majority of participants, if accompanied by three qualifications. First, "moderate" means an average price rise of not over 5 per cent, and perhaps less per year, and no annual price rise of more than, say, 10 per cent. There is general agreement that galloping inflation involving price rises of more than, say, 20 per cent a year for a protracted period serves no economic purpose. It is to be avoided wherever that can be done without bringing on a deep economic depression or protracted stagnation. Secondly, even this moderate upward drift in the price level should occur because the authorities yielded to pressures inherent in the economic and social structure under a situation of full employment and high-level demand. Inflation should not be a policy consciously fostered and planned by the authorities. It is by using the term "planned," when he probably did not mean anything else but what I have just been stating, that Professor Johnson invited the opposition of many participants. Thirdly, the willingness to yield to this moderate extent should not be an "announced" policy, but should be kept as secret as possible, according to the Biblical saying (II Samuel, Chapter 1), "Tell it not in Gath and publish it not in the streets of Ashkelon lest the daughters of the Philistines rejoice," which I would translate into: "Tell it not in Quito and and publish it not in the streets of Nairobi, lest the bankers in Zurich and Washington object."

If underdeveloped countries follow these policies, they need not be too much concerned about the problem of "linking" discussed in Dr. Morag's paper. A somewhat higher rate of interest will compensate sufficiently for the small upward drift in prices. Although this subject occupied one of the five sessions of Committee B, it seems primarily an Israeli phenomenon, depending on a combination of two factors: an upward trend in the price level well in excess of 5 per cent, and a population very sophisticated in financial matters, being also personally acquainted with rapid inflations in their countries of origin.

2. My second conclusion, again personal rather than the expression of a non-existing consensus, may sound even more heretical to some of you. It is that underdeveloped countries should not be overly impressed by the supposed need of a sharp separation between short- and long-term assets and liabilities. Financial institutions after all are primarily means of "transforming" what are formally short-term liabilities, often having in fact a slow turnover, into longer-term financial assets. Mexico has during the past decade provided what probably is the outstanding example, where the distinction of short- and long-term institutional liabilities has practically disappeared without bringing about the supposed terrible retribution, indeed to the accompaniment of or resulting in vigorous economic growth and rapid financial development. If this arrangement fosters economic growth, as I feel it does, there is no reason to oppose the trend, which, by the way, is also evident in developed countries. If most savers enjoy the feeling of liquidity, by all means give it to them, but do so at the price of the least possible restriction of economic growth.

There has been in Committee B some discussion of hoarding, again rather inconclusive. It seems to me that hoarding, in the sense of the accumulation by households and business enterprises of bank-notes and demand deposits of low activity, is to be welcomed rather than deplored or opposed. It is an interest-free loan, actually of long-term duration, to central or commercial banks, in a form which the population seems to want and which is entirely compatible with sound economic growth. In underdeveloped countries there is considerable scope for this type of hoarding as monetization progress and real income rise, without having to fear that sudden dishoarding in the future may force the monetary authorities to take sudden offsetting action.

3. The third aspect of monetary policy to which I would like to draw attention was hardly touched upon in the papers or discussions —the role of central banks in LDCs compared to their position in the financial system of the developed countries. We know from statistics that central banks bulk much larger among financial insti-

tutions in the LDCs than in developed countries. Thus, in the LDCs the assets of the central bank in general amount to at least half of those of the commercial banks or, indeed, of all financial institutions, and in many cases they actually exceed them. Compare this with the situation in developed countries where assets of central banks come to about one-third of those of commercial banks and less than one-sixth of the assets of all financial institutions. The difference is even more striking if we compare assets with gross national product. We then find that the ratio of central bank assets to national product is about the same in underdeveloped as in developed countries, namely about one-sixth; but that the assets of commercial banks typically amount to only about one-fifth of national product in underdeveloped compared to more than two-fifths in developed countries, while the assets of all financial institutions represent not much over one-third of a year's national product in LDCs compared to nearly a full year's product in developed countries. Obviously then the function of central banks is different in underdeveloped countries. Here they are the primordial, all-purpose financial institution. They cannot just be a copy of the central banks in developed countries. We should have learned this from the reorganization and reorientation of many of the Latin American central banks set up in the 1920s in the image of the Federal Reserve System. Central banks in the LDCs must pioneer many financial activities, even in the field of long-term credit, which are handled by separate institutions in developed countries, and which may be taken over by such institutions in the now underdeveloped countries in the course of their financial growth. I do not have the time to elaborate, but recommend to you similar reasoning in an interesting book by Professor Nevin.[1]

4. Considerable attention was paid in the papers and in the discussions to the possibilities of increasing the saving ratio in under-developed countries, particularly in Dr. Mars' paper. As with mother-hood, charity and peace, everybody is in favor of saving. Ten to fifteen years ago increased saving was regarded as the crucial problem in the take-off and the transition from underdeveloped to developed status. You certainly remember Arthur Lewis' assertion that the basic problem of development was to lift an economy from a 5 per cent to a 12 per cent saving ratio. Since then we have come to put less emphasis on the aggregate saving ratio, but more on the origins, distribution and uses of saving. Serious discussion of this

[1] *Capital Funds in Underdeveloped Countries* (New York: Macmillan, 1961).

problem, however, is hampered if not practically prevented by our lack of quantitative knowledge about the saving process in under-developed countries, and by the fact that a large part of that saving does not go through the capital market.

I must admit that I could not find in the papers or the discussions much that would help to formulate a saving policy for the private sector, even in Dr. Mars' paper which abounds in suggestions but fails to indicate priorities. There seems to be agreement that in underdeveloped countries the government will have to provide a much larger proportion of the national savings than is now the case in many, though not all developed countries; and more than was the case in developed countries at an earlier stage of their development. There is also a feeling that the saving potentialities may be larger than we imagine even for poor countries (at least Dr. Mars thinks so); but here it seems to me that our ignorance of the facts is just too great to say anything meaningful. Professor Kuznets' call for more factual knowledge seems to me appropriate in this field more than in any other.

5. Fifthly and finally, I turn to a problem which was hardly raised in the papers or in the discussions, but seems to me to be of great importance for the formulation of monetary and financial policies in underdeveloped countries. It is the question whether LDCs as they develop will follow the same path that the developed countries have trod. This means in the field of financial institutions the development first of commercial banks, particularly as short-term lenders, then the rise of specialized savings organizations, and finally insurance and pension organizations. It means in the field of financial instruments the prevalence for an extended period of purchases by households of government securities, industrial debentures, mortgages and corporate stock. The problem then is whether underdeveloped countries will have to go through this period of direct external financing of government and business by households, or whether they can short-circuit all this and proceed immediately to the phase in which indirect financing through financial intermediaries predominates—a phase which one developed country after another has been reaching or approaching since World War II. Under that system, as you know, households buy relatively few government securities, corporate bonds, mortgages or stocks in operating corporations, but instead acquire claims against financial institutions (commercial and savings banks, saving and loan associations, credit cooperatives, insurance companies and pension funds), or buy shares in investment companies. It is the

financial institutions that acquire most of short- and long-term debt issues, and a good part of the stock by which government and business finance capital expenditures which they cannot cover by their own saving. This system has the great attraction for underdeveloped countries that it requires much less psychological reorientation of the population than direct financing does. It also has technical advantages, and what is more important, it probably is less likely to lead to speculative excesses. In that connection I would like to question the urgency expressed in at least one paper of setting up stock exchanges in underdeveloped countries. There is, however, one problem which may be more difficult to solve under indirect financing, although it is important only for one of the three types of underdeveloped countries distinguished by Professor Galbraith, the Latin American type. This is the distribution of the stock of corporations now closely held by a family or a small group of business associates. The development of investment companies and the growth of insurance organizations, which can invest part of their funds in equity securities, may provide a solution.

Theses to Shoot At

When one realizes how far the monetary and fiscal authorities of the developed countries, after the experience and experiments of one or two centuries, still are from assuring a reasonably steady rate of growth at close-to-full employment, from securing a fair distribution of income and wealth with political stability, and from eliminating the economic causes of poverty in their own countries; when one thinks of their inability to establish a stable and equitable order in international economic relations—*vide* the difficulties of improving the obvious shortcomings in the present international monetary system; if one is aware of how far we economists still are from understanding the process of economic growth and the causes of economic backwardness; and if one finally remembers the continuous reiteration during our discussions of the diversity of underdeveloped countries, one should be chary of offering advice for action to the authorities in the LDCs. But discussion of these problems there must be, and such discussion may well be helped by providing hypotheses or theses to shoot at. That is all I have tried to do, possibly making less use of what has been specifically written for or said at this conference than I ought to.

I do not apologize, however, for having indulged in generalizations. The insistence that every country and every concrete situation is a case *sui generis,* which I am afraid has been quite popular in our discussion, is scientific nihilism, not sophisticated realism. I am the last one to deny the specific elements in every problem—I am *"au fond un historien manqué"*—and I believe in Benjamin Constant's assertion, *"il n'y a de la verité que dans les nuances."* But these specific elements are epiphenomena, and what we are after are the regularities behind them. This, I believe, may be even more true in the field of money and finance than in many other parts of the economic world. The role of rational behavior and rational policies, the possibility of experimenting with alternative solutions, and the scope for testing hypotheses are, it seems to me, greater in finance than in most fields of economics. Possibly more important for this conference, financial experience and financial technology seem to be more easily and more rapidly transferable among countries than industrial or agricultural technology, not to speak of social structure and personality characteristics. The Tokugawa banking system disappeared much more rapidly than the belief in the divinity of the Emperor; and the Hundee bankers will have disappeared well before reverence of the cow. If these assumptions are false, then the Third Rehovoth Conference will have been a most enjoyable social and tourist event and no more. But I believe that these assumptions are reasonably true. That is why I hope and trust that all the participants in the conference, and particularly those from Africa, Asia and Latin America, will take home something beyond an understanding of the remarkable achievements of Israel, viz., the idea that it may pay to look at the hard-won experience of the other part of the world in order not to copy it, but to adapt it creatively to the needs, potentialities and limitations of their own countries.

23

PRIORITIES IN THE USE OF FUNDS

By Jacob Mosak

*Director, U.N. Bureau of
Economic Research and Policies*

Since no resolutions were adopted in Committee C of the Conference, my report on its deliberations and findings must inevitably be a subjective one.

The discussions yielded a considerable measure of agreement on many important fiscal problems in LDCs, but they also brought to light very sharp differences in position on some of the issues; and to this audience I am sure that it will come as no great surprise that the differences among the economists themselves were frequently far sharper than the differences between them and the government officials.

The discussions were quite closely related to those held at the plenary session in Jerusalem on the problems of economic growth and economic policy in developing countries. Since the papers and the two sets of meetings were all prepared independently of one another, this close correspondence suggests how central a position fiscal policy must occupy in economic policy for growth.

The basic setting of the discussion, I think, was well set out in Professor Goode's paper, particularly his discussion on the role of fiscal policy in promoting stable economic growth. This role differs in several important respects from that which it has in the developed countries. Its function in promoting short-term stability is inevitably more limited because of a fundamental difference in the source of instability.

In the developed countries the major sources of instability are fluctuations in aggregate effective demand, which lead to changes in the level of employment and economic activity. These can be adequately compensated by offsetting fluctuations in the government budget, so as to stabilize aggregate demand.

In the LDCs on the other hand, short-term instability is largely the outcome of fluctuations in harvests or in terms of trade with the rest of the world, both of which cause variations in real income, even with unchanging levels of employment. Such changes in real income cannot be easily or readily offset by compensatory changes in fiscal policy. The best that can be hoped for in fiscal policy in this instance

386

is to spread the costs of benefits of the fluctuations throughout the economy as a whole, instead of permitting its effect to remain concentrated in the sector of primary impact.

With respect to promoting long-term economic growth, the differences in the role of fiscal policy between developed and developing countries are perhaps somewhat narrower, but they nevertheless remain very significant. In a developed country, where resources are mobile, and social forces cohesive, fiscal policy for the promotion of growth may concentrate largely on the problem of matching aggregate effective demand with the continuing growth in productive capacity stemming from increases in the labor force and improvements in productive technology.

In a LDC, however, where resources are much less mobile, and social forces much less cohesive, fiscal policy must concentrate much more actively on the problem of allocating an ever-increasing proportion of the country's resources for high-priority development purposes. Such high-priority development expenditure includes investment in the productive sectors of the economy, but not in luxury building, nor in the establishment of inefficient industries behind permanent shelters of protective tariffs.

On the other hand, though useful development would exclude nonessential consumption, it does include expenditure on education, research and health which, while commonly treated as consumption, represent investment in human resources.

In this context attention should also be called to the emphasis placed by Mr. Enke on the great comparative advantage of government expenditure on family planning in the scale of government investments designed to raise *per capita* income. Other criteria besides *per capita* income are surely relevant in determining family size. Also the problem of population growth can hardly be of equal importance in all developing countries. It remains that birth control has certainly come to the forefront as a key problem in the densely populated countries of Asia.

How to Allocate Funds

Traditionally fiscal policy discussion tends to focus on problems of financing the necessary volume of development expenditure. Questions of how the necessary volume of expenditure is to be determined and how it is to be allocated as between different industrial sectors, or as between the government and the private sector, have frequently been ignored in such discussions. This may be due to the fact that the traditional attitude was developed primarily in the developed countries, where these problems perhaps did not loom quite so large, since presumably they were to be determined largely by market forces.

It has been a striking feature of this conference, that it has explicitly focused attention not only on the problem of financing an already determined level of development expenditure, but also on problems relating to the determination and allocation of expenditure.

The conference has dealt with the role of government in planning the level and allocation of expenditure for accelerating economic growth. Since this question was discussed at length in the plenary session, I need not dwell on it much here. I should like to call attention, however, to a striking point made in Dr. Arnon's report, that the danger in planning is not only that too little will be done but also that too much may be attempted. He called attention to the fact that many developing countries have suffered because they were too optimistic in estimating the resources at their disposal.

The conference may be interested in this context in examining Part I of the recent United Nations World Economic Survey, which has just appeared in print. This survey is devoted to an appraisal of targets and progress in the plans of the developing countries.

I might also mention in this context the criticism made in Dr. Enke's report against much of the literature on development planning, according to which resources are to be allocated among different branches of economic activity on the basis of so-called incremental capital/output ratios. While this subject has been intensively debated in economic literature, I shall permit myself only to note that our examination of many of the plans of developing countries in the survey to which I have just referred casts considerable doubt on whether these ratios are, in fact, widely used as an important criterion in the allocation of resources as between the major economic branches.

The conference has also dealt in Committee C with the specific role of public investment in a developing economy. The role of public investment in what has come to be known as the infrastructure of the economy—mainly investment in roads, railways, ports, postal services, and in the context of Israel, we should also mention water resources—is now quite generally understood. But the role of public investment in commodity-producing industries, as distinct from service-producing industries, is still a highly controversial subject.

On the other hand, the dispassionate and highly pragmatic treatment of the subject in Dr. Arnon's report was, in my opinion, one of the outstanding contributions to this conference. Dr. Arnon's approach was entirely free of ideological considerations. Where private capital is available in adequate volume, he suggests that it be encouraged to undertake the activity. But where political or economic risks appear too high for the private investor—whether it be the foreign or the domestic investor—the government itself should proceed to act as entrepreneur. This is also the case where the investment yields returns only after a very long gestation period, while being essential to the acceleration of economic activity.

A very wide, though not complete consensus emerged, that in such cases the government-formed company should act in the same way as a company in a capitalist economy, and should seek a reasonable return on its investment, instead of socializing its losses. In such a mixed economy Dr. Arnon suggested that the government would find it useful, at later stages of development when the company has become profitable, to transfer its shareholdings to private interests, provided, of course, that it does so at a fair market value, and thereby obtains funds which it could invest again in other branches of the economy where government entrepreneurship was still essential.

Propensity to Invest

There was general agreement that the main task of fiscal policy in a developing state is to finance the large and growing government expenditure in an orderly, efficient and fair manner. There was also wide but perhaps somewhat less general agreement on the very limited role which expansion of money and credit could be expected to play in the financing of development expenditure.

Dr. Goldsmith has already pointed out a little while ago that money stocks can be expected to grow somewhat faster than the gross national product in a developing country, particularly as production becomes more and more monetized. This increase in demand for cash holdings can therefore make possible some limited increase in development expenditure, without generating inflationary pressure.

The study on saving and investment through the government budget in Japan, presented by Dr. Emi, also presented a very striking case study on the use of a large-scale expansion of money supply over a short period of time as the major propulsive force, to supply the initial thrust for the development of Japan in the 19th century. This was, however, limited to a very short period of time, after which output and government revenue rose sufficiently to permit the cessation of such monetary expansion.

In general it was agreed that while inflation and development are not necessarily incompatible, inflation is inefficient and unfair, and it loses its effectiveness if prolonged or accelerated. I quote here from Dr. Goode's report. The main reliance for the financing of economic development must therefore be on government revenue, except to the extent that foreign capital may be available. Here Mr. Horowitz' proposal about the need to increase foreign aid found a considerable echo in the deliberations of Committee C.

One of the most interesting suggestions in this context, in fact, emerged from Dr. Okigbo's report on saving and investment via the government budget in Nigeria. Dr. Okigbo proposed that it should be a cardinal objective of fiscal policy to provide not merely for a balanced budget in global terms, but in fact for a surplus on current account, and that such a surplus should come not merely as a residual after all the desired expenditure had been met, but rather that it should be consciously determined as a target, and government policy should be consciously directed toward achieving the target. Otherwise, as Dr. Okigbo pointed out, there is a great danger that increases in revenue may be eaten up by increases in less essential current expenditure.

A more extreme comment in this context was to the effect that governments, in fact, have a lower propensity to invest than the high-income earners. This suggestion, instead of posing the need for a more careful planning of government expenditure, questions the wisdom of enlarging the role of government budgets in promoting the growth of developing countries, a suggestion which found little support among either economists or government officials.

All speakers stressed the need for modernizing the tax system. Emphasis was placed on the need for improving tax administration and collection, for keeping the tax system as simple as possible in developing countries, and for increasing the weight of income-elastic taxes in the total tax base. Many speakers, however, pointed out that these criteria are not always mutually consistent, since taxes with more elastic yields tend to be more complex than the traditional taxes in developing countries and, if the rates are made too steep, may in fact adversely affect production incentives.

Controversial proposals were those relating to the introduction of new taxes, including progressive annual land taxes based on "potential" rather than actual output, taxes on wealth to be administered conjointly with income taxes, and universal comprehensive value added taxes. Dr. Kaldor defended his proposals on several grounds. First, they could tap major sources of taxable capacity in developing countries. This capacity, he pointed out, is much higher than is commonly assumed for countries with low levels of income, because taxable capacity is a function not merely of the average income level, but also of the degree of inequality, which is very great in developing countries. Second, such taxes would reduce the steady growth in inequality occasioned by spontaneous economic forces. Third, value added taxes would improve the allocative efficiency of the economy. Finally, progressive land taxes would provide a positive incentive for added production in agriculture, owing to the backward sloping supply curve at present characteristic of agriculture in developing countries.

Dr. Kaldor further emphasized that the most important aspect of the progressive land tax might be the powerful leverage they would provide, in the Model II Countries presented by Dr. Galbraith, to transform the economy from a feudal society, based on land ownership, to a modern industrial society.

The principles on which the above proposals were based found support among a number of speakers, particularly from the developed countries. Other speakers, however, especially from LDCs, believed that the taxes are far too complex to administer in a developing economy, or that they would involve too severe disincentives on production in the agricultural sector. It was also noted that these measures have yielded little result in several countries where they were recently tried. Dr. Kaldor conceded the point made by a number of speakers, that his land tax proposals are not relevant to the circumstances prevailing in most African territories. Also advocated was an agreement between the LDCs on uniform policies in allocating top concessions to foreign capital.

24

PATHS TO ECONOMIC PROGRESS

By DON PATINKIN

*Eliezer Kaplan School of Economics
and Social Sciences
The Hebrew University of Jerusalem, Israel*

The opening lectures by Kuznets made it clear that we cannot hope to find a single, monolithic, invariant law of growth, and that different countries in different periods have found different ways to achieve economic progress. Correspondingly, even though the developing countries can learn from the experience of the already developed ones, they must take care to select as an example those patterns which are most appropriate to their own experience.

The heterogeneous nature of developing economies was also the theme of Galbraith's paper, though from the viewpoint of cross-section studies, as contrasted with the historical viewpoint emphasized by Kuznets. And though there were many of us who challenged the rigorous categories of Galbraith—and objected even more violently to being classified in one or another of them—I am sure there are none among us who will deny the variety of growth experiences.

This variety has expressed itself in the working of the two committees of the conference. Surely it is no accident that the number of delegates attending the meetings of the Fiscal Committee was much larger than that of the Monetary Committee. Again, it is no accident that the African countries supplied twice as many discussants of papers in the Fiscal Committee than in the Monetary one. It seems to me that this is a clear manifestation of the fact that, for new countries in their earliest stages of development, it is the fiscal problems which are most concrete and most pressing for solutions, and that problems of monetary policy are a relative luxury, to be enjoyed only by countries who have already moved somewhat along the path of development. More specifically, we have spoken much during our conference of the social innovations which are a necessary part of the growth process. I submit that the relative levels of activity in our two committees, as well as the intensity of discussion on the fiscal papers of, say, Kaldor and Enke, as compared with the much more academic atmosphere that prevailed in the discussion of the monetary papers of, say, Gurley and Morag—I submit that these differences reflect the simple point that, long before the invention of money as a means of exchange, the historical empires of Babylonia, Assyria and Egypt already had their fiscal agents. Similarly, though the tax collector is a well-known figure in the Bible, the central banker is barely mentioned.

This leads to the thought—which was indeed made explicit by one or two of the discussants—that it would be useful in the future to arrange a conference from a more homogeneous cross-section of developing countries, from countries at roughly the same level of *per capita* income, and, accordingly, from a group of countries confronted with a more nearly similar set of problems.

In somewhat more concrete terms, monetary policy in the usual sense of the term deals with central banks, security markets and financial intermediaries of all kinds. As has been emphasized by several speakers, these play a minor role in most of the developing countries represented at the conference. As has become evident from the papers, the main "monetary" problem of many of these countries is to extend the geographical extent of money transactions. But this is simply the monetary aspect of the real problem of developing economies, which is to bring the agricultural, self-subsistent hinterland (that in the early stages of development constitutes the vast majority of the population) into contact with a market economy. This, then, is the obverse side of the structural changes a developing economy must undergo; it is not monetary policy proper.

There is, however, one aspect of monetary policy which is fundamental for developing economies even in the early stages of development—and this is the problem of inflation, which has received so much attention during our conference. The consensus that arose from the discussion of Johnson's paper would seem to be that inflation at the rate of 4 to 5 per cent does not constitute a serious danger—though even here it was emphasized that this inflation must come as the result of certain processes, and not be deliberately planned. The example of Japan described by Emi, whose initial "thrust" in the nineteenth century was financed mainly by printing money, has been most edifying. I must add that this has also characterized Israel's experience—whose first Development Budget in 1949 was by far the most inflationary in its history. Nevertheless, some degree of stability in the value of money must be a necessary precondition for increasing the extent of the market economy, in the way so essential for developing economies.

In this context, I would like to comment briefly on the problem of linkage discussed by Morag and Attyeh. Linkage is not an alternative to a proper anti-inflationary policy, but it is a most useful palliative for a government that cannot resist the temptation. As Johnson has emphasized, the main damage caused by inflation to an economy stems from the fact that there are certain sectors whose prices are rigid—and whose relative prices are thus thrown out of line as inflation proceeds. Linkage (and linkage of debt in particular) is accordingly designed to prevent the distortion of one of the most important prices in a developing economy—the price of capital. Linkage of debt assures us that the prospective investor, be it a private or governmental body, bases its decision on the true, real rate of interest, and not a fictitious nominal one. And with respect to the claim that the linked debt is too sophisticated an instrument to be understood by the people of a developing economy—I can only say that only a professional economist who has to convince himself that he has derived value from his prolonged education can delude himself about this. The man in the street, be it in Africa, Asia or Europe, has no illusions about the fact that the purchasing power of money declines as prices move upwards, and makes his plans accordingly.

A recurring theme of the papers, particularly those on fiscal problems, is the necessity of creating an administrative organization of people with integrity. This has once again brought home to me the desirablity of carrying out a study, if it is at all possible, of the economic value of honesty. There can be no doubt that corruption, and particularly corruption in high places, can be a most serious impediment to rapid growth. Honest government and the sanctity of contracts were among the fundamental components of the infrastructure for economic growth stressed long ago by Adam Smith—though, of course, he did not use this term. And that truth remains equally vital for the developing countries today.

A second point relates to planning. As I listened to the discussion of Lisle's paper I was struck by the fact that nobody had a clear idea of what was meant by "planning"; that everybody emphasized that the data necessary for planning were not available in developing countries; and that everybody was in favor of planning. I believe that there are some semantic difficulties here. Most of the time all we really mean by "planning" is a rational approach to economic problems. From this viewpoint, an essential part of planning is to estimate the costs and benefits of any proposed investment project. None of us here would disagree with this proposition. At the same time we all know that one of the most valuable contributions of an economist in government is to drive home this simple truth. As Marshall said long ago, an economist who is popular should be greatly concerned.

For his true function is to go among the policitians with a coarse, brutal and, some would say, even visionless question: "What does it cost?"

It is also misleading to contrast the activities of government in developing countries today with the alleged purely *laissez-faire* governments in England and the United States in the 18th and 19th centuries. For historical studies have shown that the governments in those times also undertook activities and decisions which had a vital impact on the growth of their countries. There is more of a difference in degree here than in kind.

In one respect, however, governments today carry on their activities under much more favorable conditions than those of two centuries ago, and that is the relative wealth of data with which these governments—and their populations—can discuss problems. I cannot forget the fact that thirty-three years ago a President of the United States had to appoint a special commission to estimate the number of unemployed in the country—this at a time when there were 11 million men unemployed. Even more vivid are my memories of only fifteen years ago in Israel, when we had no idea of our national income, balance of payments, or any of the other main macro-economic magnitudes which are the major raw material for rational economic decisions. This should be compared with our detailed information today. I am sure the same experience has been shared by many other countries represented at this conference. More generally, if we speak of the technological innovations which have stimulated economic growth, we must surely include the development of economic statistical estimates. If I ask myself what is the major difference between economics today and twenty-five years ago, it surely lies in the extent of our knowledge of national-income magnitudes and related economic data, and much less in the realm of theory.

The foregoing point has already been emphasized in our conference, that one of the major stimuli to healthy economic development is the widespread knowledge among citizens of the facts which confront them, and the widespread and intelligent discussion of the implication of these facts for economic policy. This is another fundamental aspect of the crucial role played by research and education in economic development.

Our conference has not concluded with any fixed or specific set of resolutions. Though some have complained of this fact, it should be emphasized that it was not and could not be our purpose. We wished to create a dialogue. I hope we have done so. And if in two, three or four years from now, some of us here will as a result of this dialogue approach a practical or theoretical problem in a somewhat different way than we would otherwise have done; if we will approach it with a new insight generated by the dialogue carried on in these halls—then our purpose will have been accomplished.

APPENDIX—CONFERENCE MEMBERSHIP

HONORARY PRESIDENTS

ABBA EBAN
Minister for Foreign Affairs, Israel
Chairman, Continuation Committee of
the Rehovoth Conferences

GOLDA MEIR
Former Minister for Foreign Affairs,
Israel

PINHAS SAPIR
Minister of Finance, Israel

DAVID HOROWITZ
Governor, Bank of Israel

ELIAHU ELATH
President, Hebrew University of
Jerusalem

MEYER W. WEISGAL
President, Weizmann Institute of
Science

LIST OF PARTICIPANTS

AFRICA

BURUNDI
Mr. Eric MANIRAKIZA
Deputy Governor,
National Bank of Burundi, Kitega

CAMEROUN
Mr. Robert NKAMGANG
Inspector of Taxes,
Ministry of Finance, Yaounde

CHAD
H.E. Adoum Maurice HEL BONGO
Minister of Public Health, Fort Lamy

Mr. Paul RARIKINGAR
Vice-President
of the National Assembly, Fort Lamy

CONGO (Leopoldville)
Dr. Bernard RYELANDT
Institute of Economic and Social
Research, Lovanium University,
Leopoldville

Mr. Jean NSELE
Governor, Socobank, Leopoldville

DAHOMEY
Mr. Emmanuel AMAH
Director of Cabinet of Minister of

Finance, National Economy and
Planning, Cotonou

Mr. Cosme HOUNKPONOU
Director, Budget Bureau, Ministry of
Finance, Cotonou

ETHIOPIA
Mr. Ato Wubishet DILNESSAHU
Vice-President of Business, Haile
Selassie I. University, Addis Ababa

GAMBIA
The Hon. Sheriff S. SISAY
Minister of Finance, Bathurst

Mr. H. R. MONDAY, Jr.
Deputy Financial Secretary, Bathurst

GHANA
Mr. John Sackah ADDO
Executive Director, Bank of Ghana,
Accra

Mr. Alex Eril ASHIABOR
Principal Assistant Secretary,
Ministry of Finance, Accra

Mr. Emmanuel Wright ASUMANG
Economist, Bank of Ghana, Accra

397

KENYA

The Hon. Mwai KIBAKI, M.P.
Assistant Minister, Ministry of
Economic Planning and Development,
Nairobi

Mr. Joseph GATUIRIA
Assistant Secretary, Ministry of
Finance, Nairobi

LIBERIA

Mr. D. Franklin NEAL
Director, Bureau of Projects Preparation and Evaluation, Office of National Planning, Monrovia

MALAGASY REPUBLIC

Mr. RALISON-RAKOTOVAO
Controller-General, Currency Emmis-
sion Institute, Tananarive

Mr. Leon RAJAOBELINA
Bureau of Studies, Ministry of Finance,
Tananarive

MAURITIUS

The Hon. Joseph M. PATURAU
Minister of Industry, Commerce and
External Communications, Port Louis

NIGER

Mr. Ouramou SIDIKOU
Director of Taxes, Niamey

Mr. Izhak CARMEL
Economic Adviser, Niamey

NIGERIA

Dr. P.N.C. OKIGBO
Economic Adviser, Nigerian Govern-
ment, Ambassador, European Economic
Community, Lagos

RWANDA

Mr. Jean Baptiste BIRARA
Deputy Governor, National Bank of
Rwanda, Kigali

Mr. Ignace HAKIZMANA
Paymaster-Treasurer,
Ministry of Finance, Kigali

SIERRA LEONE

The Hon. R.G.O. KING
Minister of Finance, Freetown

Mr. E. L. COKER
Acting Permanent Secretary,
Ministry of Finance, Freetown.

Mr. S. B. NICOL-COLE
Deputy Governor, Bank of Sierra
Leone, Freetown

TOGO

H.E. Antoine MEATCHI
Vice-President; Minister of Finance,
Economy and Planning, Lomé

H.E. Jean AGBEMEGNAN
Minister of Commerce, Industry and
Tourism, Lomé

Mr. Bawa Sandani MANKOUBI
Administrator, Planning Office, Lomé

UGANDA

Mr. Christopher MUSOKE
Under-Secretary of the Budget Bureau,
Ministry of Finance, Entebbe

UPPER VOLTA

H.E. E. YAMEOGO
Minister of National Economy,
Ouagadougou

Mr. Guy R. MATON
Adviser to Minister of National Economy, Ouagadougou

Mr. Emmanuel OUDRAOGO
Technical Adviser, Ministry of
Finance, Ouagadougou

ZAMBIA

The Hon. Unia Gostel MWILA
Parliamentary Secretary,
Ministry of Finance, Lusaka

ASIA

CAMBODIA

Mr. Phan THUL
Director-General of Taxes, Ministry of Finance, Phnom Penh

Mr. Hak Hem SAY
Director of Credit, National Bank of Cambodia, Phnom Penh

Mr. Chan SUN
Director of Planning, Ministry of Planning, Phnom Penh

CEYLON

Dr. J. B. KELEGAMA
Economic Adviser, General Secretariat, Ministry of Finance, Colombo

IRAN

Mr. Nasser AMERI
Vice-Governor, Central Bank of Iran, Teheran

JAPAN

Dr. Koichi EMI
Institute of Economic Research Hitotsubashi University, Kunitachi, Tokyo

KOREA

Mr. Se-Ryun KIM
Governor, Bank of Korea, Seoul

Mr. Young Nam KANG
Secretary to the Governor, Bank of Korea, Seoul

LAOS

H.E. Oudong SOUVANNAVONG
Governor, National Bank of Laos, Vientiane

Mr. Sisafath SOUVANLASY
Director-General, Ministry of Finance, Vientiane

NEPAL

Dr. Yadav Prasad PANT
Secretary, Ministry of Finance, Katmandu

PHILIPPINES

Dr. Placido MAPA, Jr.
Deputy Director-General, Program Implementation Agency, Manila

Mr. Conrado PASCUAL, Jr.
Technical Chairman, Office of Monetary Board, Central Bank of the Philippines, Manila

Mr. Roman A. CRUZ, Jr.
Philippine Bankers' Association, Manila

THAILAND

Mrs. Suparb YOSSUNDARA
Director, Department of Economic Research, Bank of Thailand, Bangkok

Dr. Snoh UNAKUL
Chief Economist, Financial Policy and Over-all Planning Branch, National Economic Development Board, Bangkok

Mr. Chanchai LEETAVORN
Senior Economist, Ministry of Finance, Bangkok

CENTRAL AND SOUTH AMERICA

DOMINICAN REPUBLIC

Mr. Moises M. de Herrera BAEZ
Chargé d'Affaires, Embassy of the Dominican Republic, Israel

EL SALVADOR

Mr. Francisco AQUINO h.
President, Reserve Bank of El Salvador, San Salvador

GUATEMALA

H.E. Miss Francisca FERNANDEZ-HALL Ambassador, Embassy of Guatemala, Israel

MEXICO

Dr. Josue SAENZ
Professor of Economics, University of Mexico, Mexico City, D.F.

PERU

Senator Alberto ARCA-PARRO
Lima

VENEZUELA

Mr. Hernando ARNAL
Coordinator, General Planning
Department, CORDIPLAN, Caracas

NORTH AMERICA

UNITED STATES OF AMERICA

Dr. Mortimer ANDRON
Presiding Officer of Academic Senate
University of California, Santa Barbara

Dr. Stephen ENKE
Institute for Defense Analyses
Washington, D.C.

Dr. John Kenneth GALBRAITH
School of Economics, Harvard University, Cambridge, Massachusetts

Dr. John G. GURLEY
Department of Economics, Stanford
University, California

Dr. Harry G. JOHNSON
Department of Economics, University
of Chicago, Illinois

Dr. Simon KUZNETS
School of Economics, Harvard University, Cambridge, Massachusetts

Dr. Abba LERNER
Department of Economics,
Michigan State University

Dr. Max G. MUELLER
Department of Economics, University
of California, Los Angeles

EUROPE

GREAT BRITAIN

Prof. Nicholas KALDOR
King's College, Cambridge

FRANCE

Mr. Edmond A. LISLE
Deputy Director, CREDOC, Paris

Mr. Pierre MENDÈS-FRANCE
Former Prime Minister, Paris

Mr. Pierre URI
Consultant, The Atlantic Institute,
Paris

RUMANIA

Mrs. Maria STANESCU
Economist, Institute of Economic
Research of Rumanian Academy,
Bucharest

MEDITERRANEAN

CYPRUS

Mr. Afxentois AFXENTIOU
Senior Economic Officer, Head of
Economic Section, Ministry of Finance,
Nicosia

ISRAEL

Dr. Ya'akov ARNON
Director-General, Ministry of Finance,
Jerusalem

Dr. J. ATTYEH
Eliezer Kaplan School of Economics

and Social Sciences, Hebrew University
of Jerusalem

Mr. David HOROWITZ
Governor, Bank of Israel, Jerusalem

Dr. Amotz MORAG
Eliezer Kaplan School of Economics
and Social Sciences
Hebrew University of Jerusalem

Dr. Don PATINKIN
Dean, Eliezer Kaplan School of
Economics and Social Sciences
Hebrew University of Jerusalem

INTERNATIONAL ORGANIZATIONS

E.C.A.

Dr. John MARS
Special Adviser, Economic Policy and Integration, United Nations Economic Commission of Africa, Addis Ababa

F.A.O.

Mrs. Gerda BLAU
Director for Special Studies, United Nations Food and Agriculture Organization, Rome

I.B.R.D.

Dr. Barend A. DE VRIES
Deputy Director, Economic Department, International Bank for Reconstruction and Development, Washington, D.C.

I.M.F.

Dr. Richard GOODE
Director, Fiscal Affairs Department International Monetary Fund, Washington, D.C.

Dr. U TUN WAI
African Department,
International Monetary Fund
Washington, D.C.

O.E.C.D.

Dr. Raymond W. GOLDSMITH
Vice-President, Development Center

Organization for Economic Cooperation and Development, Paris

ORGANIZATION OF AMERICAN STATES

Dr. Germanico SALGADO
Director, Economic Affairs Department Washington, D.C.

UNITED NATIONS

Dr. Jacob L. MOSAK,
Director, Bureau of General Economic Research and Policies, New York

SCIENTIFIC SECRETARIES

Coordinator: Mr. Meir HETH
Senior Economist, Research Department, Bank of Israel, Jerusalem

Mrs. Miriam BEEHAM
Falk Institute for Economic Research in Israel, Hebrew University of Jerusalem

Mr. Aharon GILSHON
Senior Economist, Resarch Department, Bank of Israel, Jerusalem

Dr. David OTTENSOOSER
Senior Economist, Research Department, Bank of Israel, Jerusalem

Mr. Eliezer RONEN
Economist, Research Department
Bank of Israel, Jerusalem

COUNTRY REPORTS

The following countries' reports were submitted to the conference:

BRAZIL	'The Politics of Fighting Inflation,' by Robert de Oliveira Campos, Minister of Planning and Coordination (not represented at the Conference)
CENTRAL AMERICA	'Tax Reform and Regional Integration: The Case of Central America,' by the Dept. of Economic Affairs, Pan-American Union, Organization of American States
CONGO	Presented by Dr. B. Ryelandt
EL SALVADOR	By Francisco Aquino
GABON	(not represented at the conference)
GAMBIA	
KENYA	Presented by Mr. M. Kibaki
KOREA	
LIBERIA	By D. Franklin Neal
MAURITIUS	
NEPAL	By Dr. Y. P. Pant
NIGER	By E.H. Courmo Barcougne, Minister of Finance of Economic Affairs, presented by Mr. O. Sidikou
PERU	By Alberto Arca-Parro
PHILIPPINES	By Hilarion M. Henares Jr.
SIERRA LEONE	By R. G. O. King, presented by Mr. E. L. Coker
RWANDA	
THAILAND	Presented by Mr. C. Leetavorn
UGANDA	By Christopher Musoke
UNITED NATIONS	'Some Considerations Relating to the Establishment of the Asian Development Bank,' by U.N. Economic Commission for Asia and the Far East

CONTINUATION COMMITTEE
of
THE INTERNATIONAL CONFERENCE
ON SCIENCE IN THE ADVANCEMENT OF NEW STATES

CHAIRMAN: Mr. Abba Eban, Minister for Foreign Affairs, Israel

SECRETARY: Dr. Amos Manor

AFRICA

Dr. C. A. ACKAH	**Ghana.** Principal, University College of Cape Coast.
Monsignor M. BAKOLE	Vice-Rector, University of Lovanium, **Congo** (Leopoldville)
Chief AKIN DEKO, F.A.O.	Regional Representative for Africa, Accra, **Ghana.**
Mr. H. R. BINNS	Director, East African Veterinary Research Organization (CSA/CCTA)

Dr. S. E. IMOKE	Minister of Education, Eastern Region of **Nigeria**
Mr. D. K. JAWARA	Prime Minister of **Gambia**
Mr. S. JUSU-SHERIFF	Minister of Trade and Industry, **Sierra Leone**
M. A. KACOU	Minister of Transport and Communication, **Ivory Coast**
Dr. A. KARIM-GAYE	Minister of Rural Economics, **Senegal**
Dr. J. G. KIANO	Minister of Commerce and Industry, **Kenya**
Mr. Y. K. LULE	Vice-Chancellor, Makerere College, Kampala, **Uganda**
M. A. MEATCHI	Vice-President of **Togo,** Minister of Finance, Economy and Planning
Mr. M. M. NGOBI	Minister of Agriculture and Cooperatives, **Uganda**
Dr. D. NICOL	Principal, Fourah Bay University College of **Sierra Leone**
Mr. D. J. NJAU	Acting Deputy Principal, College of Agriculture, Morogoro, **Tanzania**
Mr. A. NWACHUKU	Former Minister of State, the Treasury, **Nigeria**
Chief J. A. O. ODEBIYI	Former Minister of Finance, Western Region of **Nigeria**
Prof. H. A. OLU-WASANMI	Dean, Faculty of Agriculture, University of Ibadan, **Nigeria**
M. R. RASIDY	Minister of Agriculture, **Malagasy Republic**
Dr. R. RATSIMA-MANGA	High Commissioner of **Malagasy Republic** in Paris
M. A. M. SACCAS	Director, Center of Agricultural Research, **Central African Republic**
Dr. S. C. SAR	Director, Veterinary Service, **Senegal**
Mr. S. TOLBERT	Former Secretary of Agriculture of **Liberia**
Prof. R. L. WEEKS	President, University of **Liberia**

ASIA

Prof. C. C. DE SILVA	Past General President, **Ceylon** Association for the Advancement of Science
Prof. D. R. GADGIL	Director, Gokhale Institute of Politics and Economics, **India**
Mr. M. LIM	Former Secretary for Commerce, **The Philippines**
Senator M. P. MANA-HAN	Chairman, Committee of Scientific Advancement, Manila, **The Philippines**
Dr. Y. PANT	Secretary, Ministry of Finance, **Nepal**
Lt. Gen. PHYA SALVID-HANNIDES	Chairman, National Research Council of **Thailand**
Dr. R. WEITZ	Head, Rural and Urban Settlement Study Center, Rehovoth, **Israel**
Mr. YONG NYUK LIN	Minister of Education, **Singapore**

E U R O P E

Prof. G. AUBERT	Institute of Tropical Research, **France** (CSA/CCTA)
Prof. M. CEPEDE	President of the Interministerial Committe on Food and Agriculture in **France**
Prof. J. H. DE BOER	Scientific Adviser to the Netherlands Government
Prof. P. R. CALDER	Professor of International Relations, University of Edinburgh, **United Kingdom**
Prof. W. Gentner	University of Heidelberg, **Western Germany**
Ir. S. HERWEIJER	Director, Government Service for Land and Water Use, Utrecht, **the Netherlands**
Prof. G. MYRDAL	Institute for International Economic Studies, **Sweden**
Prof. J. PAGOT	Director-General, Institute of Veterinary Medicine in Tropical Countries, **France**
Prof. E. H. J. S. PERRIN	Head of the French Atomic Energy Commission
Prof. M. PIHL	University of Copenhagen, **Denmark**
M. P. MENDÈS-FRANCE	Former Premier, **France**

A M E R I C A

Dr. J. AHUMADA	Director, CENDES, Caracas, **Venezuela**
Prof. L. V. BERKER	President, Gratuate Research Center, Dallas, **Texas**
Dr. G. BROCK-CHISOLM	Formerly Director of WHO, **Canada**
Dr. M. CLAWSON	Director, Land Use and Management Program, Resources for the Future, **Washington, D.C.**
Prof. J. DE CASTRO	**Brazil**
Dr. R. V. GARCIA	Dean of Faculty of Science, University of Buenos Aires, **Argentina**
Prof. Sir W. A. LEWIS	Professor of Public and International Affairs, **Princeton**
Prof. W. C. LOWDER-MILK	Formerly Associate Chief, Soil Conservation Service, U.S. Department of Agriculture
Prof. J. R. ZACHARIAS	Massachusetts Institute of Technology